Racing & Football Outlook

JUMPS

GUIDE 2006-2007

Statistics • Results
Previews • Training centre reports

D1823277

Contributors: Geoffrey Adby, Neil Clark, Nick Deacon, Steffan Edwards, Dylan Hill, Mark Howard, Tony Jakobson, Kel Mansfield, Steve Mellish, Mark Nelson, Dave Nevison, Ben Osborne, Nick Watts, Richard Williams.

Grateful thanks due to Jim and Carol – it's about time – and to Louise – always an inspiration!

Feedback!

If you have any comments or criticism about this book, or suggestions for future editions, please tell us.

Write: Nick Watts, 2006-2007 Jumps Annual,
Racing & Football Outlook,
Floor 23, 1 Canada Square,
London E14 5AP.

email rfo@mgn.co.uk or **Fax** 0207 510 6457

Designed and edited by Nick Watts & Dylan Hill

Published in 2006 by Outlook Press
Raceform, Compton, Newbury, Berkshire RG20 6NL
Outlook Press is an imprint of Raceform Ltd, a
wholly owned subsidiary of MGN Ltd

A catalogue record for this book is available from the British Library.

ISBN 1-905153-21-X

Printed and bound in Great Britain by William Clowes Ltd, Beccles, Suffolk

Sponsored by Stan James

racing & football outlook

Est. 1909

Contents

Introduction		5
Irish profiles	Philip Rothwell	7
	Noel Meade	11
Irish 15 to follow		17
British profiles	Ben Pollock	21
	John Spearing	27
British 15 to follow		32

2006–2007 Preview

Ante-post tips	36
Jerry M (Ireland)	48
Downsman (Lambourn)	52
Hastings (West Country)	56
Borderer (North)	60
Southerner (South)	64
John Bull (Midlands)	67
Aborigine (Newmarket)	70
Hunter chasers	73
Dave Nevison	76
Morning Mole	79
Time Test	82

2005–2006 Review

News diary	86
Big-race review	96
Novice review	113

Statistics, Races and Racecourses

Trainer statistics	123
Trainer and jockey tables	144
Fixture list	149
Big-race dates	155
Big-race records	158
Track-by-track guide	177
Record and standard times	222

Final furlong

Evan Williams	232
Competition	235
Horse index	238

Sponsored by Stan James

Editor's introduction

Welcome to a new era in National Hunt racing. Ever since he won the 1981 Triumph Hurdle with Baron Blakeney, the figure of Martin Pipe has dominated the sport to such a degree that he won 15 out of 17 champion trainer's titles between 1989 and 2005, with only a brief wrestling of power by the late David Nicholson denying him a clean sweep throughout that period. While never the most universally popular character, Pipe undeniably revolutionised the way horses are trained in terms of fitness and meticulous preparation, as well as being the ultimate punters' pal and one of the most instantly recognisable figures in the sport.

At the end of last season, though, Pipe made the shock announcement that he was to hand over the reins at his Nicholashayne yard to his son David, having just endured his most disappointing season in years as fierce rival Paul Nicholls strolled to the trainer's title. A National Hunt scene without Pipe will be a strange place indeed, particularly when Cheltenham's Open meeting in November, a three-day affair dominated by Pipe to an astonishing degree since the turn of the century, comes around.

Having said that, David Pipe will be hoping the transition is seamless as he still has a strong team at his disposal, backed by owner David Johnson. The brilliant Well Chief, second in the 2005 Champion Chase before missing all of last season, returns to throw down the gauntlet to a couple of new two-mile superstars in Kauto Star and Newmill, while Pipe could also have a live Gold Cup contender on his hands in Celestial Gold. How ironic it would be if, in his first season at the helm, David Pipe lands the race that eluded his father for so long!

Pipe's team is assessed by Hastings as part of our tour round the training centres, in which you are advised to pay particularly close attention to Jerry M's Irish preview given their remarkable dominance of the jumping scene in recent years, claiming the Gold Cup, Grand National, Champion Hurdle, Champion Chase and King George for each of the last two seasons. Will Macs Joy continue to get closer to Brave Inca, or will Harchibald return to top them both? Will Kicking King and War Of Attrition finally get it on when both are at their peak?

In addition, the RFO is justifiably proud of its Irish coverage, both in this guide and from week to week, given we have an enthralling tour of the powerful Noel Meade yard, featuting Harchibald and potential new star Iktitaf, in the pages to follow, and pulled off one of the ante-post coups of all-time last year when Newmill was tipped at 100-1 to win the Champion Chase.

Other invaluable trainer interviews are provided by Philip Rothwell in Ireland and Ben Pollock and John Spearing in England. These should hopefully provide winners at all sorts of levels.

Other than that, the guide is everything you have come to expect from the RFO down the years. We've got a brilliant ante-post Cheltenham preview from Steffan Edwards, looking at the four major prizes at the Festival; our top 15 horses to follow from either side of the Irish Sea; the views of professional punter Dave Nevison and the insightful Steve Mellish; plus Mark Nelson analysing the evidence of the clock.

Then we get into the reams of stats which should help all the number crunchers work out where your money is best invested this season.

The rest is up to you! Don't forget to get your copy of the RFO every week for all the latest news and views, and together we can hopefully enjoy another hugely profitable campaign!

IRELAND

LAST year was the first time in the RFO Jumps Annual that we included a hugely expanded Irish section.

The reason behind it was simple enough – most of the big races in recent years have gone into Irish hands, so it made perfect sense not only to include more Irish-based features, but also to go over and speak to some of the trainers whose horses have been making off with some of the best pots.

To that end, interviews were undertaken with Paul Nolan and Martin Brassil, and both of them more than justified their inclusion in the book.

Nolan had a great season back home right through to this summer when he scooped the prestigious Galway Hurdle with Cuan Na Grai (pictured below), who was highlighted in his *Trainer File* as one to follow.

Accordion Etoile again showed how much he liked Cheltenham when winning there for the second time last November, and, after a mid-season lull, came back with a bang when winning the Swordlestown Cup at the Punchestown Festival.

And as for Martin Brassil! Only a small stable numerically, he really rose to prominence last season, mainly through the exploits of Numbersixvalverde, who of course won the Grand National.

However, the contribution of Nickname should also be recognised as he won on his chasing debut at Leopardstown in scintillating style. He was also highlighted in the *Trainer File* section.

In the Irish 15 to follow, the claims of Whyso Mayo (pictured below) were put forward as a hunter chaser to watch during the season.

He proceeded to win the Foxhunter at Cheltenham at 20-1 before following up at Punchestown.

Winners like that proved the decision to give the annual a more Irish feel was completely warranted, and with no sign of the status quo being restored in National Hunt racing just yet, it seemed sensible to do it again. Let's hope we have many more winners waiting on the following pages.

CUAN NA GRAI: on the up

WHYSO MAYO: star hunter

Profiles for punters
Philip Rothwell

PHILIP ROTHWELL: hoping for more of the same after a season to remember

Profile by Nick Watts

TWENTY-SEVEN years of age seems to be scarily young to be training big-race winners, but that is how old Philip Rothwell was when Black Apalachi won the Paddy Power Chase at Leopardstown in December 2005.

The horse in question, having only his fourth run over fences, made light of his inexperience to defeat 25 other rivals and really put Rothwell on the map in only his fifth season as a trainer.

That feat alone would be enough for most people to feel happy come the end of the season, but add a Cheltenham Festival winner and the birth of your first baby into the mix and you've got all the ingredients of a fairytale. This is precisely what happened though.

In a heady week last March, Philip Rothwell found himself in the rather unique position of having a live Festival contender in Native Jack as well as a heavily pregnant wife due to give birth at any moment.

Native Jack was an old-timer who had been rejuvenated since moving to Rothwell's County Wicklow-based operation to become one of the favourites for the Sporting Index Cross Country Chase. He had rather late in life taken a shine to racing over banks courses, and came into the event on the back of a facile success in a similar event at Punchestown.

This time it was much harder, as perennial challenger Spot Thedifference put down a stern challenge, but in keeping with the mood of Rothwell's week, Native Jack summoned up extra reserves on the run-in to provide a double first.

Approximately 48 hours earlier Rothwell's partner, Niamh, kept to her side of the bargain by providing a healthy baby daughter, Cara. As weeks go, they don't come more action-packed or memorable than that.

Native Jack subsequently went on to try to secure a £50,000 bonus for the stable by winning the La Touche Cup at the Punchestown Festival, but unfortunately the luck went against him on this occasion as he got brought to a standstill in a pile-up six fences from home.

No matter, his job for the season had well and truly been done, with his victory making sure that anybody previously unfamiliar with the Rothwell name now knew what he was about.

It's not a great surprise that he has been such a fast learner.

When your apprenticeship of working in yards includes the names of Jessica Harrington, Willie Mullins and Aidan O'Brien you'd have to think you'd learn a few tricks from that collective brains trust.

Those experiences enabled him to set up his yard on the family farm at Tinahely at the tender age of 21, and it has been a case of onwards and upwards ever since.

The yard's facilities have improved year-on-year, with a recently installed All-Weather gallop helping to keep the equine population fit and healthy.

The drive of the man is impressive. You get the distinct feeling that although he achieved a long-held ambition to have a Festival winner, it did come in one of the lesser races at the meeting (if there is such a thing).

The ultimate, according to Rothwell, would be to win a proper championship race – a Queen Mother or a Gold Cup would probably do.

In order to meet that aim, Rothwell isn't a numbers man when it comes to horses. He has no ambitions to become champion trainer, but would prefer a streamlined stable packed with promising animals, one of whom may grant him his wish and make it through to the top.

It may take a year or two to achieve, but when you're still in your twenties, time is still very much with you and it may simply be a question of 'when' rather than 'if'.

The horses

Amorini
7yo chestnut gelding
Shernazar – Leallen (Le Bavard)
Has done well for us, winning a beginners chase at Down Royal, and then a valuable Listed handicap chase at Wexford last November very easily. He's not the soundest, but we've brought him back in early, and we hope to go for the Paddy Power Chase at Christmas which we won last year. He wants yielding to soft ground.

Arturius
4yo bay gelding
Anabaa – Steeple (Selkirk)
Did really well during the winter on the All-Weather, picking up races at Lingfield and Wolverhampton. Disappointed in the Winter Derby afterwards, but has now been gelded and we're going to go over hurdles with him. Hopefully he should do well.

Black Apalachi
7yo bay gelding
Old Vic – Hattons Dream (Be My Native)
Did us proud last season – his first over fences. He won the Paddy Power Chase at Christmas last year under John Cullen and that was only his fourth race over fences. He went on to run well at Cheltenham in the Kim Muir too, but he was still immature and weak last season, so we hope he can go on to better things still this season. His main target is the Irish National, and he will probably have a spin over hurdles before then. He's had a good long summer holiday and is definitely one to look forward to.

Cool Blues
6yo grey mare
Terimon – Romany Blues (Oats)
A nice mare who could be really well handicapped over hurdles. She hasn't run for a

good while, but has shown us some decent ability.

Dark Bolero
4yo bay gelding
Alderbrook – Bobsyourdad (Bob's Return)
This is a good one. He finished second at Gowran in the summer in a maiden hurdle to a horse of Michael O'Brien's called Barati. We then put him back in a bumper at Down Royal at the beginning of September where he could finish only sixth. We might persevere with him in bumpers and wait a little before going over hurdles again, but he does have ability.

Four Chimneys
5yo bay gelding
Denel – Treat A Lady (Lord America)
A lovely bumper horse. He showed up well on his debut at Clonmel in March when fifth of 11 on soft. He's had one run since then at Tramore where he finished in mid-division and he should be able to win a race this season.

Gotcha Covered
5yo bay gelding
Silver Patriarch – Seastream (Alleged)
Had a good bumper season last term, finishing fifth in a decent race at Fairyhouse, before winning at Down Royal in February – beating one of Noel Meade's. He stayed on really well to get up that day on yielding ground and he should make a good novice hurdler this time.

Grangehill Dancer
5yo chestnut mare
Danehill Dancer – Bella Galiana (Don Roberto)
She'll be a lovely type for mares' novice chases this season. She's already won three races for us, the latest of which came at Clonmel in October 2005. She ran some great races in defeat last season over fences, finishing second twice, and she always tries her heart out.

Jak Dream
5yo chestnut gedling
Dreams End – Jaki's Roulette (Rolfe)
Only lightly raced, but showed some ability for us last season, notably when third last February at Fairyhouse. The ground was atrocious that day, and the field were strung out like washing, but he finished third, and Cuan Na Grai, the Galway Hurdle winner, was in

second place that day. He could win a handicap hurdle before going chasing, possibly next year.

Loughanelteen
8yo bay gelding
Satco – Ruths Rhapsody (Creative Plan)
A very nice horse who is on a nice mark for chases and will be out around Christmas. He was smart over hurdles, winning twice, and he should be able to win some chases over two miles on good or good to soft ground.

Mission Possible
5yo bay gelding
Benefecial – Coolavanny Queen (Furry Glen)
Won a maiden hurdle at Bellewstown in the summer in good style, but then wasn't quite so good in two runs afterwards at Galway and Tralee. The latter was a good race won by Maxxium however, and he was bang there until the third-last. He'll go handicapping and can win again when he gets a bit of decent ground.

Mollies Dolly
8yo chestnut mare
Over The River – Spring Trix (Buckskin)
Won a maiden hurdle at Kilbeggan for us in September last year, and is gradually getting her act together over fences. She wasn't disgraced at Kilbeggan last time behind a horse of Noel Meade's and ought to be able to win a novice over a good trip.

Monoceros
6yo bay gelding
Over The River – Spring Trix (Buckskin)
Definitely worth keeping an eye on. He won his bumper at Thurles in January 2005, and then came back last November in a novice hurdle at Fairyhouse where he was second to Michael Hourigan's smart horse Mossbank. He wasn't right on his last start where he pulled up so we gave him a break, and he will come back novice hurdling. Three miles is his trip, and all his family stayed very well.

Mr Blacktie
6yo bay gelding
Saddlers' Hall – Dorrha Daisy (Buckskin)
A half-brother to Native Jack, he won for us at Bellewstown in July over three miles,

but then injured himself when he was brought down at Galway on his chasing debut last time. He will make a lovely summer chaser.

Native Jack
12yo brown gelding
Saddlers' Hall – Dorrha Daisy (Buckskin)
Won at the Cheltenham Festival last season over the cross-country fences – what an incredible day that was! Although he's now a veteran, he has no miles on the clock at all and we'd be hopeful of another good year with him. His first major target will be the Becher Chase at Aintree, and that will help us make up our minds as to whether to go for the National itself or go back to the banks. He's still got enough pace to win over 2m4f if he had to.

Shearbolt
5yo bay gelding
Presenting – Daring Dream (Phardante)
Weak last season when he had two runs in bumpers, but is definitely good enough to win one as he strengthens up.

Silver Adonis
5yo grey gelding
Portrait Gallery – Fair Fontaine (Lafontaine)
He could be very good. He just couldn't handle the heavy ground at Limerick on his sec-

ond start, but then on a good to firm surface at Bellewstown on his next start he won by 6l. He then won again at Roscommon in August, and although he didn't jump that well on his hurdling debut at Tipperary recently, he will be absolutely fine once that has been remedied.

The Black Mouse
5yo bay mare
Presenting – Catch The Mouse (Stalker)
Her form stood up well last season, where she finshed second at Tramore and then won a competitive handicap at Fairyhouse next time over 2m4f on softish ground. To get her placed in a Listed event would be the aim for her.

Useyourimagination
5yo bay gelding
Accordion – Miss Florida (Florida Son)
I made a mistake of running this horse at four, as he's a big, raw horse and came home with leg trouble. He then got a bout of colic, so he's had his problems, but he could be very good if they all came right. Touch wood, he's ok at the moment, and he will be out in high-class company this side of Christmas. He's had two bumper runs to date, and was third in the second of them at Tipperary, and while he's not easy to train, he is exciting.

NATIVE JACK (left): jumps the last on his way to success at Cheltenham

Profiles for punters
Noel Meade

PAUL CARBERRY AND NOEL MEADE: a devastating combination at their best

Profile by Nick Watts

WHENEVER you visit a training establishment every one of them seems more idyllic and tranquil than the last, and Tu Va Stables in Castletown, County Meath is no different.

A row of schooling fences in a small entrance just on the other side of this impeccably-kept village ten miles north of Navan is the only hint that a training maestro resides here.

On reaching the house, however, you are left in no doubt as to where you are, as every window sill seems to house one trophy or another that has been won during the previous 35 years in the game.

This has been the home of leading Irish jumps trainer Noel Meade ever since he commenced training back in 1971, and has seen him land an impressive four National Hunt trainer's titles as well as a stack of big-race successes.

Although a more than capable trainer on the Flat, as evidenced this year by Arch Rebel's Listed success at Leopardstown and Rockall Blizzard's recent win at Galway, it is without doubt his exploits in the jumping game for which Meade is best known.

Most, if not all, major Irish jumps races have found their way back to Castletown over the years, including over fences the Irish National via the superbly-named The Bunny Boiler, the Lexus Chase with Johnny Setaside and the Paddy Power Chase with Coq Hardi Diamond.

Hurdle successes have included the AIG Champion Hurdle with Cockney Lad, the Morgiana Hurdle at least three times, as well as the most recent renewals of the two championship novice events at the Punchestown Festival via Iktitaf and Nicanor. And that barely scratches the surface.

More recently, it is his relationship with Paul Carberry, which began some seven years ago, that has sealed Meade's place at the top table of the jumps game, marrying together two extremely gifted minds.

The sight of Carberry stalking on a Meade-trained animal bedecked with its usual sheepskin noseband is one that will be familiar with National Hunt enthusiasts.

More often than not, when Carberry lets them down they go on to win, although in the case of Harchibald in the Champion Hurdle of 2005, they didn't – quite.

That race, possibly more than any other in the recent history of jumping, has attracted furious debate on both sides of the argument.

Certainly the sight of a horse coming to the last in a championship race hard on the steel is an unusual one, and the sight of a jockey delaying his challenge in a championship race until 50 yards from the line took the breath away.

John McCririck led the defence, John Francome the attack, but, importantly, the three people who mattered – Carberry, Meade and owner Des Sharkey were all satisfied.

The criticism got to Carberry, who was moved to say: "It's absolute rubbish to say the horse had no heart. He was sick ten days before the race and was only just coming back to himself."

Unfortunately, the horse didn't win over his critics on his next start at Punchestown where an almost exact replica of Cheltenham took place again.

Carberry did start the challenge a little earlier this time, but an inspired Tony McCoy and Brave Inca did what Hardy Eustace had done at Prestbury.

Having missed Cheltenham last season through injury, Harchibald is back in training now, and Meade is confident that all is going according to plan. Indeed, according to his trainer, the horse has "got bigger" during his enforced absence.

There's little doubt either that a 2007 Harchibald victory at Cheltenham would give Meade huge satisfaction, and it's encouraging to note that the horse did allay fears of a Cheltenham hoodoo when winning the Bula there last season.

Meade must have been quietly satisfied with his own Cheltenham haul of last season too, as the Bula win was one of three wins at the venue last season.

Sir Oj won the Robin Cook Memorial Chase, and perhaps more importantly, Nicanor provided the Irishman with his second success at the Cheltenham Festival when comfortably beating hotpot Denman in the Royal & SunAlliance Novices Hurdle.

Sausalito Bay provided the first back in 2000, but despite having plenty of close shaves and fancied horses, there was a six-year hiatus until the next.

Meade himself confessed after the Nicanor success (and the Sweet Wake reverse the previous day) that "if we didn't have a winner today I wouldn't be coming back".

Plenty of top-class trainers have struggled to get winners at the Holy Grail of jumps racing – on this side of the water David Nicholson and Josh Gifford both had monumental struggles to achieve their first, but then went on to enjoy many, many more. You get the same feeling with Meade.

Now the second success has been achieved, it would not be in the least bit surprising if, like buses, several more successes came along in quick succession.

As you walk around the 100-strong set of boxes, you are constantly reminded of the extraordinary strength in depth of the Noel Meade yard.

Another recent addition which has merely served to hone even further the younger, up-and-coming brigade of horses is Nina Carberry.

As stable amateur, she gets to ride most of the small army of bumper horses Meade possesses, and last season they combined to win a healthy amount of National Hunt Flat races, giving such types as Leading Run, Cleni Boy, Casey Jones, Lord Lumey, Major Stampi and Azalea a perfect early education before they graduate to the bigger league. It's a fair bet that a few of the names above make it through the ranks.

So there you have it – a top-class set-up from all angles that will only lead to success, and more successful forays to Britain. The Meade/Carberry combination is still firing on all cylinders.

Afistfullofdollars
8yo bay gelding
Be My Native – Myra Gaye (Buckskin)
Had only one run last season, winning a novice chase at Down Royal in great style. Has had his injury problems, but is potentially top class if we can keep him sound. Stays well, and ideally wants three miles and soft ground.

Aitmatov
5yo bay horse
Lomitas – Atoka (Kaiseradler)
He was useful on the Flat in France. Had only two runs for us, at Fairyhouse last January when seventh and more recently when third at Galway. He could be worth keeping an eye on in novice hurdles this season.

Azalea
4yo brown filly
Marju – A-To-Z (Ahonoora)
Won very well first time up in a bumper at Kilbeggan for Nina (Carberry), but then we took her to Galway and she really disappointed. However, she came back lame from that and I wouldn't read too much into it. She's a half-sister to Royal Alphabet of Willie Mullins' and could be anything, but I do like her.

Back To Bid
6yo bay gelding
Mujadil – Cut It Fine (Big Spruce)
Had a good season last time, winning his bumper and a maiden hurdle before finishing fourth behind Black Jack Ketchum in the Brit Insurance at Cheltenham. He will be going chasing this season, and he stays very well.

Ballyagran
6yo bay gelding
Pierre – Promalady (Homo Sapien)
Always works like a good horse, but hasn't yet done it on the track. Finished second at Kilbeggan in the summer, and if we can find the key to him there might be a good race in him.

Billy Bonnie
9yo chestnut gelding
Anshan – Sinology (Rainbow Quest)
Won well at Tralee recently over 2m4f, but he stays well and would be effective over three. The ground is important to him though, and he wouldn't want it too soft.

Casey Jones
5yo bay gelding
Oscar – Arborfield Brook (Over The River)
Won his bumper well at Gowran in April on yielding to soft ground (his only start to date). He is a nice horse who should make a good novice hurdler over 2m4f.

Cleni Boy
4yo bay gelding
Panoramic – Kailasa (Rb Chesne)
Disappointed us first time out when only fifth. He then bumped into a good one of Willie Mullins' next time, but made no mistake on his final start of last season, winning at the Punchestown Festival. Won his hurdling debut at Galway convincingly in September. He wouldn't want it soft as he's not over big.

Corrigeenroe
6yo bay gelding
Revoque – Amenity (Luthier)
A very big horse who has needed a bit of time and who suffered a cracked hip too. Ran well in maiden hurdles last season over 2m-2m4f without getting his head in front but he should win his races this time.

Failte Arais
5yo bay gelding
Bob Back – Foreign Estates (Be My Native)
His name means 'welcome home' in Gaelic. He won his bumper first time last season at Leopardstown and then went on to be third in a good race at Fairyhouse. Only

BACK TO BID (nearside)

small, but stays well and is a nice jumper who will win his hurdles.

Freddie Foster
7yo chestnut gelding
Be My Native – Myra Gaye (Buckskin)
Has never quite got it together as yet, but he's coming down in the weights and we haven't given up on him winning a decent handicap this season. His best run last season came when second to Studmaster at Leopardstown over two miles on yielding ground.

Harchibald
7yo bay gelding
Perugino – Dame D'Havard (Quest For Fame)
You know, it's amazing to think it because he will be eight next year, but he seems to have grown and got a lot stronger since he's been back in. He missed the second half of last season through injury, but seems to be fine now. After going for the Tipperary race he won last season, he'll probably go for the Morgiana before ending up at Cheltenham again. I think he's genuine, he just finds things so easy and jumps so well during a race. He's a very good horse and God willing the engine is still intact.

Hotel Hilamar
7yo chestnut gelding
Be My Native – Myra Gaye (Buckskin)
A nice horse who was fourth in a good bumper at the Punchestown Festival last April on his only start for us. He will go jumping this season, and should win his share.

Iktitaf
5yo bay gelding
Alhaarth – Istibshar (Mr Prospector)
He's strengthened up well over the summer, having had a great novice campaign last term. He came from John Gosden's yard, and then won the Royal Bond for us at Fairyhouse last December. An injury ruled him out of Cheltenham, but we got him back for Punchestown and he put up a great show to beat Straw Bear easily (although Straw Bear is still rated higher than us!). A very good horse who should do well this season, and hopefully will be good enough for a crack at the Champion Hurdle.

Jazz Messenger
6yo bay gelding
Acatenango – In The Saltmine (Damister)
He never jumped that well last season and that held him back a little. He still won two

at Navan though, and finished seventh behind Noland in the Supreme Novices. He hopefully should jump much better this season. Has loads of speed, and we wouldn't be scared of running him on the Flat.

Khetaam
8yo bay gelding
Machiavellian – Ghassak (Persian Bold)
Surprised us to win on his return in a two-mile handicap hurdle last season after an long absence. Ran well at Cheltenham in the County Hurdle and will now go chasing over two miles. Has plenty of speed.

Leading Run
7yo bay gelding
Supreme Leader – Arctic Run (Deep Run)
Won all his bumpers last season, culminating in a Grade One event at Punchestown where he beat Hairy Molly, who won the Cheltenham bumper. He's very laid-back, but is also tough, and should do well in novice hurdles this season over 2m4f. He goes on any ground.

Lord Lumey
5yo bay gelding
Lord Americo – Kissantell (Broken Hearted)
Second in both bumper starts last season, including when behind Equus Maximus, a good one of Willie Mullins', at Leopardstown in January. Has loads of gears and jumps well, so one to watch in two-mile novice hurdles.

Major Stampi
5yo bay gelding
Visto Si Stampi – Rugged Sand (Sandalay)
Finished runner-up in three bumpers last season. Has ability and jumps like a rocket, so he should win his novice hurdles this season over two miles.

Mattock Ranger
6yo bay gelding
Oscar – Siberiansdaughter (Strong Gale)
Very tough horse who won at Thurles (twice) and Navan on his final start over 2m7f. He's grown a lot over the summer and will go chasing this term. Three miles on soft ground would be ideal for him.

Mr Nosie
5yo bay gelding
Alphabatim – Cromogue Lady (Golden Love)
Unbeaten last season, including in a Grade One and a Grade Two, until he went to Cheltenham for the Royal & SunAlliance Hurdle. Finished fourth then, putting up a great ef-

SO MUCH TALENT: but can Harchibald win the Champion Hurdle in 2007?

fort. Has had a slight knock since then, but will go for three-mile novice chases when he's back, and having won a point-to-point already, he should do well over fences.

Nicanor
5yo bay gelding
Garde Royale – Uthane (Baby Rockette)
He jumped moderately early on, otherwise it's possible he could have gone through the season unbeaten. Great second half to the campaign, winning at Cheltenham and then following up at Punchestown. He's going over fences, and the Drinmore at Fairyhouse in December would be a likely target in the early part of the season.

No Half Session
9yo chestnut gelding
Be My Native – Weekly Sessions (Buckskin)
Disappointed us at Cheltenham in the William Hill Chase where he never really had a cut at his fences. Did well prior to that in decent handicaps and that will be the plan again this winter.

Power Elite
6yo grey gelding
Linamix – Hawas (Mujtahid)
Plenty of ability but has disappointed us re-

cently and made no show on the Flat recently at Leopardstown. We might give him a try over fences and see how he goes. He's still young enough to come back.

Rosaker
9yo bay gelding
Pleasnat Tap – Rose Crescent (Nijinsky)
Won a Grade Two event at Leopardstown last Christmas over three miles, and has plenty of ability. He does panic a bit, and has disappointed on his two trips to Cheltenham, but he's very consistent over here.

Sigma Digital
4yo grey gelding
Kayf Tara – Silver Fan (Lear Fan)
A nice horse, very laid-back. He won his only start at Kilbeggan in a bumper last May by 6l and should do well novice hurdling this season.

Sir Oj
9yo brown gelding
Be My Native – Fox Glen (Furry Glen)
We thought he would take to Aintree last season, but he never took a cut at the fences and eventually fell at Becher's second time. Had previously won the Robin Cook at Cheltenham and he will be going for similar races.

Snow Tern
5yo bay/brown gelding
Glacial Storm – Cool Eile (King's Ride)
Won a maiden hurdle at Navan last January but will be going straight over fences this season. He stays very well and could be anything.

Sweet Wake
5yo chestnut horse
Waky Nao – Sweet Royale (Garde Royale)
He disappointed us when the big tests came in the spring at Cheltenham and Punchestown, but we've not given up on him by any means. He might benefit from the break he had during the summer, as he'd been on the go for a while, and he won a Group Two on the Flat in Germany. We don't think he's lost any of that ability and he's still right up there.

Toofarback
6yo bay gelding
Mister Lord – Lady Pharina (Phardante)
Came back lame from Cheltenham when behind Black Jack Ketchum but had previously won consecutive races at Punchestown and Naas over 2m4f on soft ground. He will be a nice staying chaser in the making and has plenty of scope.

Watson Lake
8yo bay gelding
Be My Native – Magneeto (Brush Aside)
We never had a proper run with him in the second half of last season with various little niggles. Still won a Grade Three at Navan in the spring, and finished fourth at Punchestown over 3m1f behind War Of Attrition. Ruby got off him that day and is convinced he will stay, so we might try him in the Lexus over Christmas to find out.

Wild Passion
6yo bay gelding
Acatenango – White On Red (Konigsstuhl)
Disappointing in novice chases last season and had a bad fall on his last start in the Powers Gold Cup. We might therefore put him back over hurdles this season to get his confidence back. Don't forget he was second in the Supreme Novices a couple of years back and is a serious horse.

Zum See
7yo chestnut gelding
Be My Native – Weekly Sessions (Buckskin)
Won two chases last season and is very good on his day. Needs a fast-run two miles to show his best and will always pop up somewhere during the season.

TOOFARBACK: could be a top staying chaser for the Meade/Carberry combo

Nick Watts' 15 Irish Horses to Follow

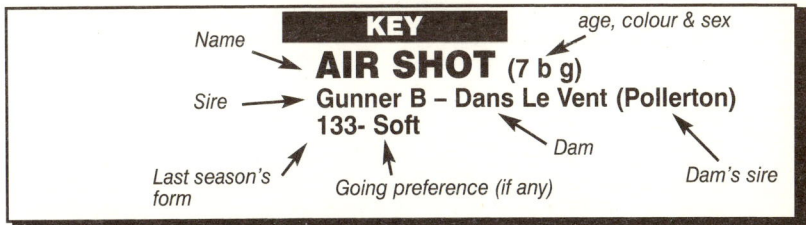

BALLYTRIM (5 b g)
Luso - Helynsar (Fidel)
109-

Caused quite a stir when winning his bumper at Thurles last February by 25l. Making all at a decent pace, he quickened impressively in the closing stages to win as he liked. Subsequently ran in the Festival bumpers at Cheltenham and Punchestown, and while not living up to the promise of that debut effort he shouldn't be written off. Has already won his point-to-point, so expect him to make a big impression novice chasing this season.

Willie Mullins

CONNA CASTLE (7 b g)
Germany – Mrs Hegarty (Decent Fellow)
63112-1

Multiple point-to-point winner who had a great first season hurdling last term, showing surprising pace in the process. Wins over two miles at Punchestown and Naas last winter earned him a trip to Aintree for a Grade 2 event in which he beat all bar the smart Straw Bear. Acts well on heavy ground and should stay much further, so is one to watch if, as expected, he tries chasing this season. His trainer doesn't have many horses, but did win the National with Monty's Pass in 2003.

Jimmy Mangan

FIRTH OF FORTH (6 b g)
Flemensfirth - Penny Star (Al Hareb)
22113-

Won both of his bumper starts two seasons ago, and made a decent impression when sent hurdling last term. Runner-up behind smart types in Alexander Taipan and Merdeka on his first two outings, he made handsome amends by then winning his next two, including over three miles at Fairyhouse on the latter occasion. Seems to stay very well and goes on soft ground, and if he showed an aptitude for chasin, it wouldn't be a surprise to see him contest a decent handicap before the season is out.

Joe Crowley

GLENCOVE MARINA (4 b g)
Spectrum - Specifiedrisk (Turtle Island)
11-

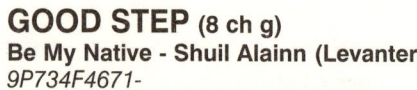

Pulled very hard when making a winning debut in a bumper at Thurles last February (yielding to soft). The race didn't look great at the time, and the winner bypassed Cheltenham, but with good reason. He reappeared in the Goffs Land Rover Bumper at Punchestown and absolutely routed the 22-strong field under Katie Walsh, making all and careering away in the straight to win easily. Looks to have plenty of toe and should make his mark in the top two-mile novice hurdles this season, if his tendency to pull in the early part of his races can be curbed.

Willie Mullins

GOOD STEP (8 ch g)
Be My Native - Shuil Alainn (Levanter)
9P734F4671-

The latest in the Bolger production line of cross-country specialists, he could take over the mantle held by Spot Thedifference for so long. Has won the La Touche Cup now for the past two seasons, on the second occasion under an inspired ride from Nina Carberry. A cautionary note – he has yet to win in three tries at Cheltenham's cross-country track, but he did finish third there in December 2005 and it might be unwise to read too much into his course record. Stays well and jumps soundly.

Enda Bolger

JAGOES MILLS (4 b g)
Dr Massini – Thistle Chat (Le Bavard)
15-

Not a horse many will be familiar with yet, but remember the name. He made a winning bumper debut at Naas last March (heavy), beating a subsequent winner from the Colm Murphy yard, and was then thrown in at the deep end for his hurdling debut in a Grade 1 event at the Punchestown Festival. He ran well to finish fifth behind Willie Mullins' Quatre Heures when he hurdled well and wasn't knocked about, and is definitely one to keep an eye on in the novice hurdling division this season over 2m-2m4f.

Thomas Gerard O'Leary

KERRYHEAD WINDFARM (8 br g)
Bob Back – Kerryhead Girl (Be My Native)
21325462F42-0

Despite winning a novice chase at Fairyhouse early last season, his jumping got worse as the season progressed, culminating in a fall at Aintree last April. He subsequently returned to hurdles for the stayers' event at the Punchestown Festival, finishing a four-and-a-half length second to Asian Maze. That was a great effort (at odds of 100-1) and showed the engine is there, so don't be surprised if he pops up at a big price this term, as he is generally underestimated over hurdles at the highest level but is a very good horse.

Michael Hourigan

MOSSBANK (6 b g)
Kadeed – Miromaid (Simply Great)
11235F5-

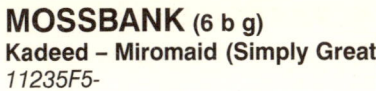

Has been described as the new 'Beef Or Salmon' by his trainer and it's easy to see why. A fine, big, strapping type, anything he did over hurdles was always going to be a bonus – and he didn't do badly
over them. He won novice events at Limerick and Fairyhouse, as well as finishing
third in a Grade 1 at Navan shortly afterwards. Finished the season on a bit of a low,
but given three miles and soft ground, he will win his novice chases this season,
and the Royal & SunAlliance Chase at Cheltenham in March would be an obvious
target if things go well.

Michael Hourigan

O'MUIRCHEARTAIGH (6 b g)
Accordion – Brian's Delight (Celio Rufo)
112028-

It was a tale of two halves last season. The first half of the
season went smoothly, as he picked up a Cork bumper and
a Grade 3 at Navan last November. He then went for the Grade 1 Royal Bond at
Fairyhouse when he was beaten 5l by Iktitaf (no disgrace). The wheels came off
subsequently, however, and he wasn't sighted at either Cheltenham or Punchestown.
Nonetheless, if he goes chasing this season over two miles, he should still be able
to take high rank and he could be an Arkle contender.

Eddie O'Grady

OULART (7 ch g)
Sabrehill – Gaye Fame (Ardross)
47P6022823-

A former winner of the Pertemps Hurdle Final at Cheltenham,
this horse has plenty of class and should have a decent long-
distance chase in him this season. His first season chasing was generally disappointing, but the one bright spot was his performance in the Irish National. On better
ground (which seems to suit him well), he beat all bar Point Barrow, jumping well
and running on strongly in the closing stages. Extreme trips could be the making
of him on that evidence, and don't be surprised if he can win a few during the winter
to see him take his place in the Grand National field next April.

Dessie Hughes

ROYALDOU (6 b g)
Cadoudal – Royale Sea (Garde Royale)
224-

Still a maiden after three starts, so shouldn't be hard to place
in novice hurdles this season. He started off life at Leopardstown last Christmas, finishing second behind Sweet Wake, and then occupied the
same position behind Mr Nosie in a Grade 1 on the same track a couple of months
later. Heavy ground may have been his undoing when beaten at 2-5 on his last start
at Navan and not too much should be read into that. High-class hurdling prospect.

Arthur Moore

SLIM PICKINGS (7 b g)
Scribano – Adapan (Pitpan)
21F4123-

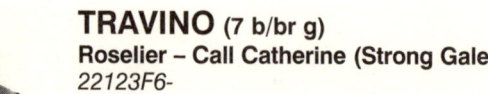

Progressive form in novice chases last season over three miles. Wins at Punchestown and Cork proved his ability, but his best effort probably came in a Grade 2 at Punchestown last April when runner-up to the high-class Missed That over a 2m5f trip. It was only after jumping the last that he gave best to the winner, and when he is moved back up to three miles a good handicap should come his way this winter. Seems to act on any ground.

Robert Tyner

TRAVINO (7 b/br g)
Roselier – Call Catherine (Strong Gale)
22123F6-

It will be disappointing if this huge horse can't make a major impact over fences this season. He showed a consistently high level of form over hurdles last season, which included a Grade 1 win over Royal & SunAlliance winner Nicanor at Navan last December, and a third behind Black Jack Ketchum at the Cheltenham Festival in March. Three miles on good to soft or soft ground would be ideal for him, as would races like the Drinmore and the PJ Moriarty.

Margaret Mullins

WHITEHILLS (5 b g)
Oscar – Carrigpreme (Supreme Leader)
60143-

His useful bumper form of last season suggests he should make the grade over hurdles this season. He won a good bumper at Leopardstown on Boxing Day, beating the well-touted Lord Lumey from the Noel Meade yard. Then, on his final start of the campaign at Punchestown, he finished third of 21, not beaten far by Nesserian in a good-looking contest. Two miles on good or softer ground will be ideal and he should win his races throughout the winter.

Francis Flood

WOLF CREEK (6 b g)
Anshan – Sleeven Lady (Crash Course)
37035142-

Appeared to improve dramatically once sent over fences in the latter half of last season. Finished third on his chasing debut at Thurles last February, and got off the mark two starts later over 2m4f at Clonmel in a beginners chase. A crack at the four-miler at the Cheltenham Festival followed, and he looked a likely winner under Nina Carberry, but having pulled during the race he had nothing left at the business end and settled for fourth. A second place at the Punchestown Festival in a novices' handicap on his final start confirmed him at least as being useful, and he ought to improve again this season. He is well worth another crack at an extreme trip.

Eddie O'Grady

Sponsored by Stan James

BRITAIN

Profiles for punters
Ben Pollock

BEN POLLOCK: former amateur jockey now forging a fine career as a trainer

Profile by Neil Clark

THE road sign tells us you are entering 'Leicestershire – Heart of the English Country' and it certainly feels that way as you gaze out over the rolling hills and woods. This is prime hunting country: the vista of fields, hedgerows and woodland punctuated by church spires and beautiful villages with names such as Great Bowden, Weston by Welland and Neville Holt.

This delightful, unspoilt corner of England is also home to one of National Hunt racing's brightest young training talents.

Back in January, Ben Pollock, in only his third season, saddled his first Grade One winner, when A Glass in Thyne impressively won the Skybet Chase at Southwell.

That high-profile win brought Pollock's name to the attention of many for the first time, but even before that red letter day, the likeable Midlander could already boast an impressive CV.

Although not born into a racing family, Pollock has always been passionate about horses, beginning his riding career on a pony when he was not yet three. Show-jumping was his main interest as a teenager, but by the age of 15 he was already becoming more and more interested in racing.

"I got a Saturday job working for John McConnochie, who had taken over from Mercy Rimell," he says. "John was based at Alscot Park, about half an hour from my mum and dad's in Stratford-upon-Avon.

"His stable jockey was John Short who recommended I went to ride out at Dick Saunders' yard in Northamptonshire. John McConnochie very kindly got me in there.

"I always wanted to train horses, but never really gave much thought to being a jockey, but I thought I'd give it a go."

Saunders, who had memorably ridden Grittar to victory in the 1982 Grand National at the age of 48, was a source of great encouragement and gave Pollock his first point-to-point ride and first winner. "He was a great man. You wouldn't meet a nicer bloke."

Pollock's racing education also included spells with two other legends of the game. While studying at Cirencester Agricultural College, Ben rode out every day before lectures for the late David Nicholson, and then spent a year working for three-times Grand National-winning trainer Captain Tim Forster.

"Both were great men but were hard taskmasters. I remember one morning at the Captain's when one of the work riders had been carried off by a horse: 'There are 60 million people in this country. Twenty million are idiots. And every single one of them has had a job with me!'" he said.

"Once I came back into work having ridden Brown Windsor to victory in a point-to-point the day before. 'The horse won a Whitbread and you won a point-to-point on him' was the captain's reaction. 'Great!'"

Pollock enjoyed a highly successful time as jockey for Dick Saunders and his daughter Caroline, riding 75 point-to-point winners and 51 under Rules.

"It was Caroline's golden period," he recalls, and Pollock rode many great horses, including Castle Mane, whom he piloted to victory in the 1999 Cheltenham Foxhunter's and the 2000 Horse and Hound Cup, and Teeton Mill, who later won a Hennessy and King George for Venetia Williams.

"I'd say Castle Mane was the better horse of the two over 3m2f, but Teeton Mill was the best at 2m4f. But as good as they both were, I'd say the best horse I ever rode was Teaplanter. At the age of 13, he gave 4lb to Cool Dawn at Kempton and was only beaten 6l. A couple of years later Cool Dawn won the Gold Cup!"

Pollock, who is also a fully qualified farrier, started training point-to-pointers with his wife Ninga in 2000, while he was still riding.

Their first winner was a certain grey horse called Ice Saint, who later, when trained by Matt Gingell, became famous as the horse involved in the Sean Fox 'unseated rider' controversy at Fakenham.

Having originally started three pointers in his father-in-law's back garden, Ben moved with Ninga to their present base in the small village of Neville Holt in 2001.

They haven't looked back since. Ben took out his public licence in April 2003, leaving Ninga to take care of the pointers, and trained his first winner (Beau Torero at Taunton) in November of that year.

Five winners followed in the 2004/05 season (including his first winner on the Flat) and then last season the total rose to seven. Pollock now has 28 horses, and with the facilities he has at his disposal, is confident of being able to continue his progress.

"We've got a four-and-a-half-furlong All-Weather gallop, a grass gallop, schooling fences and hurdles, a horse walker and 45/25 metre outdoor school. There are 20 acres of post and rail turn out paddocks. We've got all the toys!

"We could take up to 35 horses but I wouldn't like any more than that. I'm not a number cruncher, I never was when I rode, it's just my mentality. I'm more interested in raising the quality rather than the quantity of what we've got here.

"If we can go up to about ten winners a year and winning a Grade One every year, and then build up to having 20 winners a year and go to Cheltenham with three or four with chances, that would be great."

Location-wise, Pollock's present base is hard to beat. "We can go north, south or stick to the Midlands tracks. Three hours from here you can get to an awful lot of racecourses.

"As for favourite courses, I like Towcester, it suits a certain type of horse; from a purist's point of view I think Newbury is the loveliest track in the country, but you've got to have a good horse to go there. For atmosphere you can't beat Fakenham, you get a very loyal crowd and if anyone wants a great day out you'll always get it there.

"One of the greatest thing about jump racing, in particular, is that you can have success without spending a fortune. You can come into National Hunt and within a very short period of time you could be competing against the very best in a relatively short period of time. You can become very high profile, very quickly.

"Good owners are very hard to find and I've been very lucky. A Glass In Thyne, for example, is a horse you've got to be very patient with and fortunately he's got exactly the right owners.

"The best quote I've ever heard about racing is from Sir Mark Prescott, who said that he'd rather train a bad horse for a good owner than a good horse for a bad owner. Because when the bad horse is gone, you've still got the owner."

For punters keen to follow this up-and-coming stable on a regular basis, Pollock has some words of advice. "From a punting point of view you just want to forget my bumper horses and my hurdlers: this yard's all about chasing. When they go chasing, that's when you want to watch them.

"Also, for me, the season runs from November until the end of March. I'm not a huge fan of summer racing."

The figures back up Pollock's words: last year anyone backing the yard's chasers on a level-stakes basis would have been rewarded with a £25 profit to a £1 stake.

Regarding jockey bookings, watch out for when Pollock books the services of Andrew Thornton. The talented English rider has a 21% strike rate overall when riding for the yard and an even more impressive 32% when piloting Pollock's chasers.

Racing is renowned for its 'glorious uncertainty'. But, if the way Ben Pollock has started his training career is anything to go by, we can be sure we're going to hear a lot more about this bright and talented young man in the years ahead.

YOUNGER DAYS: Ben wins the 2000 Horse and Hound Cup on Castle Mane

The horses

A Glass In Thyne
8yo brown gelding
Glacial Storm – River Thyne (Good Thyne)

He's a beautifully proportioned horse with the heart of a lion and he always gives everything. Unfortunately he is fragile, which is why we've had to be very patient with him. He needs plenty of time between his races. He finished last year on a mark of 137 and I'd like to think there could be a further 8lb improvement in him. He'll start off at Ascot in the old United House Chase at the end of October and we'll see how he goes from there. If, please God, he's in one piece, he'll probably be entered for the Grand National as he was last year, but I wouldn't want to build his whole year around it. He's been a wonderful servant and doesn't owe us anything.

Beau Torero
8yo grey gelding
True Brave – Brave Lola (Dom Pasquini)

Won twice for us last year, a conditional jockeys' handicap hurdle at 14-1 at Fakenham on his first start for over 500 days, and then a selling hurdle at Catterick. He's a grand horse, but has terrible legs which is why he's so lightly raced. He's rated 94 over hurdles, 92 over fences – he's definitely capable of winning off his current chase mark. It's just a question of whether the suspension holds up when he goes chasing. He will be very fit first time out as I can't waste runs with him.

Crownfield
7yo bay gelding
Blushing Flame – Chief Island (Be My Chief)

Ran at Southwell in a terrible selling hurdle, I thought he'd definitely make the first three, but he ran an absolute shocker. I don't know why – he shows enough at home to win a selling hurdle or a little handicap chase. He needs good to firm ground and I'm sure he can win a race for us.

Dino's Dandy
7yo chestnut gelding
Midnight Legend – Edina (The Parson)

No world-beater. Twice ran desperately over hurdles last year and crippled his sore shins. He'll now have one more run over hurdles to get him handicapped and then he'll go chasing off that mark. He wouldn't be quick enough to win over hurdles, but I think he

A GLASS IN THYNE: will be entered for the Grand National at Aintree in April

Sponsored by Stan James

could be the item in low grade handicaps in soft ground over fences.

Game On
10yo bay gelding
Terimon – None So Brave (The Parson)
There's a saying in racing that a horse that wins one race one season will win another one the next, but the horse that wins three will win none! This fellow proved it last year. He went up to a mark of 111 after winning at Market Rasen in February 2005, his third win over course and distance that season, but couldn't get his head in front last year. Age is catching up with him, but he is slowly being reassessed and I think he'll be able to win a handicap off a mark in the low 90s (he's now rated 98). He never runs well first time out.

Honest Abe
5yo bay gelding
Houmayoun – Blasgan (Yashgan)
Is out of a half-sister to the mare of Panto Prince. Had three runs over hurdles last year, he's got a rating of 92 and will go straight to chasing off that mark. He's a nice horse and I like him a lot.

Launde
7yo bay gelding
Norwich – Carbia's Last (Palm Track)
Won his maiden really well at Leicester in February. In fact his form was good all year. He was seventh on his racecourse/chasing debut at Sandown, then fifth at Leicester, before finishing second at 50-1 at Chepstow over Christmas. After he won his maiden, he was only beaten a length by Nyctoos on his handicap debut at Chepstow. I stepped him up to 2m6f at Haydock as I was really convinced he would stay, but I got it completely wrong. He wants two miles – he's a typical Norwich. He's rated 120 and there's a handicap chase at Wetherby at the end of October which we'll kick off in. He wants a big galloping track and doesn't want extremes of ground. He doesn't mind it soft, but not good to firm or heavy.

Moscow Leader
8yo chestnut gelding
Moscow Society – Catrionas Castle (Orchestra)
Came from Richard Guest's and was bought for a syndicate. He will run plenty and should be able to win a handicap chase in the course

of the year. He's on 95 at the moment, is very stuffy and will probably need a couple of runs to get fully fit, but on the third or fourth time on soft ground, over three miles and at a big galloping track, he should give you a bit of value.

Never Awol
9yo chestnut gelding
John French – Lark Lass (Le Bavard)
He's a real law unto himself! Whenever I think he's going to win he runs out or pulls himself up; whenever I don't, he goes and wins! He needs a track where they don't quicken up three out (he loves Towcester and Carlisle) and he likes to front-run but he doesn't like being in front. He has gone up a fair way in the handicap – he's up to 90 now and actually ran the best race of his life when he finished second to Heartache at Towcester. The handicapper's probably got hold of him, but if the mood takes hold of him he'll win another race. Don't ask me when he's going to do it as I have absolutely no idea – he's the sort of horse you're better off level-staking as when he pops up it will be at a decent price. I've only had him two years and he's won three handicaps, but God, it's seems to have been a long journey in between!

Orinocovsky
7yo chestnut gelding
Grand Lodge – Brilliantina (Crystal Glitters)
Used to belong to Nigel Shields, and has won on the All-Weather and over fences. He's just come into work, and we haven't decided what to do with him yet. He could run in anything, he'll be out around Christmas and we'll see where he takes us. He's got a bit of ability.

Rebel Raider
7yo bay gelding
Mujadil – Emily's Pride (Shirley Heights)
He's run 11 times over hurdles, has finished second six times and never runs a bad race. He always runs well first time out and will be as fit as you like when he reappears – I haven't decided whether that'll be on the Flat or over jumps. Unfortunately has very fragile legs. Whenever he's running over hurdles you can always have a few quid on him each-way as he'll always do his best for you and give you a run for your money. I'm very determined to win a hurdle with him. He's

been incredibly unlucky not to win up to now – at Fakenham he was 15 lengths clear of the third, beaten by a horse called Alph who went on to finish second behind Royal Shakespeare in a Listed race at Sandown. What was he doing running at Fakenham!

Samakin
8yo bay/brown gelding
Topanoora – Samika (Bikala)
Had three runs as a novice hurdler. The first time he got beaten 9l by Turpin Green, then he finshed fourth at Market Rasen when he should have won without a doubt - he didn't get the greatest of rides. Then he was clear at Wetherby before breaking down. He's had 18 months off and has been fired and will go straight to novice chasing. If the wheels hold up, he could do well and although he's yet to do it, he's showing me all the right things.

unraced horses

Bouncing Back
4yo gelding
Bob's Return – King's Dream
A big raw horse. He's done everything very nicely at home and is a real big staying chaser in the making.

Little Shilling
4yo gelding
Bob's Return – Minouette
Related to Mini Sensation, he's only little but tough as teak, a nice little horse who will start off in hurdles at Christmas time and then go chasing.

No Telling
4yo gelding
Supreme Leader – Kissantell
He's a really nice horse, but not one to be punting this year. Watch him in his novice hurdles and then get excited in about two years when he goes chasing.

Unnamed
4yo gelding
Norwich – Bit Of A Diva
Has shown me all the right signs. Will run in a bumper around Christmas, he's one of the better youngsters.

Unnamed
4yo gelding
Overbury – Edina
A half-brother to Dino's Dandy. More of a racey type who will be out in bumpers around Christmas.

NEVER AWOL (nearside): quirky, but will pop up somewhere in the winter

John Spearing

JOHN SPEARING: still going strong and producing some fine horses

Profile by Neil Clark

WHEN John Spearing first took out his licence in 1971, Ted Heath was at Number 10, a pint of beer cost 12p and Ernie was driving the fastest milk cart in the West.

Thirty-five years on, Ted Heath and Benny Hill are no longer with us, but John Spearing thankfully is, and the veteran Worcestershire handler is enjoying a real renaissance.

Born in the same week that Sir Winston Churchill became Prime Minister for the first time in 1940, a liking for cigars is not the only thing that Spearing and Britain's wartime leader have in common.

Like Churchill, Spearing is a natural-born winner – whether as an amateur rider or a trainer of point-to-pointers, Flat horses or jumpers. His CV is mightily impressive, with victories in the Welsh National, Listed races at Phoenix Park and Sandown, and top handicaps on the Flat and over jumps. The names of some of Spearing's best-known horses bear witness to his extraordinary versatility: Run N' Skip, Lucedeo, Rapid Lad, Thihn, Tom's Prize, Eskimo Nell, Vax Lady, Cashel Mead and Hakim, who never touched a twig when landing the Grand Sefton Chase over the Grand National obstacles at Aintree.

Last year, Spearing trained 14 winners over jumps, five up on the previous year and four up on the year before. Anyone backing the yard's runners blindly, would have made a profit of £5.50 to a £1 stake, but those focusing solely on Spearing's chasers would have seen their profits rise to a whopping

£63.75. In fact, punters level-staking Spearing's chasers would have made a profit in three of the last five years, with an overall profit of £51.73 to a £1 stake.

What, then, is the secret of John Spearing's enduring success?

His partner Kate, who modestly describes her role in the operation as a 'general dogsbody', believes a lot is down to Spearing's "instinct" about horses.

"John's father was a stockman, and I think he's inherited that skill from him," she says. "He can tell just by looking at a horse what's wrong with them. He knows all his horses really well as he is very hands-on and rides out every morning.

"He also tries to give all the horses as natural an existence as possible. The horses are turned out to graze every day after work, and that's important. They are very happy and none of them are ever highly-strung."

I can certainly vouch for that. Even at a recent owners' day I attended, all the horses, despite the extra commotion, seemed relaxed and on good terms with themselves.

Spearing is not one to rush his younger horses into unrealistic assignments.

"I am a great believer in giving horses plenty of time and not overfacing them in the early stages of their careers," he says.

"I try and win as many races as possible with them and that means starting them at the bottom and letting them climb the ladder – not the other way around. If you pitch them in good races too early, the handicapper will get hold of them and you won't win as many races."

The campaigning of young chasers Jack's Craic and Simon last season was a good example of Spearing's modus operandi, both winning three races each as they gradually climbed the handicap ladder to land races worth £70,000 and £16,000 respectively.

Spearing's patience is also shown by his extraordinary record with horses returning after long layoffs. Hakim was off the track for nearly two years with leg trouble before reappearing over hurdles at Hereford last

RUN N' SKIP (back, jumping fence): one of the best trained by John Spearing

Sponsored by Stan James

June and, though well down the field that day, he powered to an emphatic 25l victory in a handicap chase at Stratford next time.

"Given the context of the race, the overall form is not going to mean very much for the future," was the verdict of the Racing Post's race analyst, but he couldn't have been more wrong as the New Zealand-bred chestnut went on to win his next three starts, including that pillar-to-post win in the Grand Sefton.

Hakim finished his campaign with three highly creditable second places, including a narrow defeat in the Topham Trophy back at Aintree, to finish the campaign on a mark of 125, a whopping 37lb higher than when he returned over fences in June. Not bad at all for a horse that had previously been off the track for close on 700 days.

Similarly, Curraheen Chief had an amazing five-year absence to overcome prior to a novice hurdle at Chepstow in April, yet had soon chased home Penzance over fences at Hereford and was travelling well at Towcester before taking a fall. He looks sure to open his account over fences this term and his trainer's assessment can be read below.

Spearing moved to his present base in the picturesque village of Kinnersley, in the shadow of the Malvern Hills, in 1998.

"We've got a 6f All-Weather gallop, grass gallops, an All-Weather manege, starting stalls, schooling fences, a horse walker and lots of lovely hills where we can hack up and down. Routine is the key, but we can also give the horses a bit of variety too."

Kate also pays tribute to the staff at the Kinnersley operation. "There are six-full time staff and many others who come in on an occasional basis. Everybody in the team is crucial – they are a really nice bunch who muck in together. Our head girl, Marie, and the grooms, Becky and Nan, have been here a long time, Denise goes out to work at Tesco after she's mucked out the horses and Ray comes in and drives the tractor."

The yard's geographical location, close to Junctions 7 and 8 of the M5, is ideal for reaching many of Britain's racetracks within two or three hours.

Spearing's strike rates at northern tracks such as Catterick (50% in five years), Wetherby (50%) and Aintree (40%) are very impressive, but over the same period a healthy level-stakes profit could have been made at Fontwell (29%), Folkestone (25%), Wincanton (27%), Taunton (20%), Newbury (18%), Uttoxeter (17%), Stratford (16%), Leicester and Bangor (both 14%).

Indeed, over the last five years, Spearing showed a level-stakes profit at 13 of the 22 jumps venues he has had runners at – a testament both to his remarkable consistency and the fact that, despite its success, the stable is still underrated by many punters.

Kinnersley Racing Stables has a proud history. From the 1950s to the 1980s the yard was famous as the base for Fred and Mercy Rimell, who sent out four winners of the Grand National (ESB, Nicolaus Silver, Gay Trip and Rag Trade), two Gold Cup winners (Woodland Venture and Royal Frolic) and two Champion Hurdle winners (dual hero Comedy Of Errors and Gaye Brief).

A link with that illustrious past is provided by Mercy Rimell, who is still involved in the yard as an owner of the exciting chaser Simon, who is from the family of Gaye Brief and Gaye Chance.

The Rimell's won four Welsh Nationals during their time at Kinnersley and, in Simon, the yard looks to have another ideal candidate for the Chepstow marathon.

"John is a very good trainer and that's why I have a horse with him," she says. There are very few people in racing who would disagree with her assessment.

MERCY RIMELL: Kinnersley resident

The horses

Blue Sovereign
6yo grey gelding
Sovereign Water – Slack Alice (Derring Rose)
Blotted his copybook when running out at Newton Abbot in August. He doesn't want it too soft and I'm hopeful he can win a race for us.

Curraheen Chief
11yo bay gelding
Little Bighorn – Sprightly's Last (Random Shot)
Finished second behind Penzance at Chepstow in May on his second start back having been off the racecourse with leg problems since 2001. He was travelling well when he fell seven out at Towcester on his next run. He'll win a novice chase. He likes it soft/heavy and won lots of points in Ireland.

Dickensbury Lad
6yo bay gelding
Luchiroverte – Voltige De Cotte (Saumon)
He progressed really well last year, finishing second three times and then winning a novice chase at Stratford by 7l on his final start. He's a big horse, and prefers good ground, so will be out earlier rather than later, in October. At the age of six, I think there'll be plenty more to come from him.

Hakim
12yo chestnut gelding
Half Iced – Topitup (Little Brown Jug)
Did really well last season, winning four times and finishing second in his other four runs. He won the Grand Sefton at Aintree in November and finished second in the Topham there in April. He'll have Liverpool as his target again and the plan is to give him one run before the Grand Sefton and then another run before going back to Liverpool in April. I don't see any reason why he can't run well there again. For a 12-year-old he's very lightly raced – he's had only 21 starts because he's had two long lay-offs with injury. The key to him is to give him plenty of recovery time between his races – he ideally needs five or six weeks – and so we won't be overracing him. He acts on the soft, but goes on anything really as he had some good form as a hurdler on firm.

Hop Fair
7yo chestnut mare
Gildoran – Haraka Sasa (Town And Country)
Won a bumper at Ludlow on her first start,

HAKIM: the 12-year-old measures another Aintree fence with superb precision

Sponsored by Stan James

and although she hasn't won yet over hurdles she is improving. Forget her last run at Market Rasen, where the ground was too soft for her – the official description was good but they had over-watered. She likes fast ground.

Jacks Craic
7yo bay gelding
Lord Americo – Boleree (Mandalus)
He's the highest-rated horse in the yard, finishing the season on a mark of 143. He won three races last year, none of which were just confined to novices but open handicaps. I will carry on the handicap route with him for the time being. His last run at Ayr was probably one run too many, the thing is that he is no good travelling up overnight. He didn't eat up properly and became very nervous and jittery. If that race had been locally, say at Stratford, I think he might have won. He may start off in a two-mile race at Ascot at the end of October.

Jamaaron
4yo chestnut gelding
Bachir – Kentmere (Galetto)
Has done really well over the summer, running seven times and winning once, but will have a break over the winter before coming out again next year. We'll keep him for the summer racing as he must have quick ground.

Kayf Aramis
4yo bay gelding
Kayf Tara – Ara (Birthright)
Has done well for us in staying handicaps on the Flat this summer and may go hurdling. We tried schooling him before over hurdles and he didn't seem to like it much, but we'll give it another go and will send him away to a loose school. If he still doesn't like it, we'll keep him for the Flat, but if he does, he would be a useful addition to the winter team. He likes a good bit of juice in the ground.

Simon
7yo bay gelding
Overbury – Gaye Memory (Buckskin)
A nice young chaser who progressed really well last season. He needs a long trip and likes soft ground. He won over three miles at Bangor on his last run but will get further.

The Welsh National would certainly be one option as he'd be very likely to get the ground he likes there and be able to get in off a decent weight.

Sashenka
4yo bay filly
Silver Patriarch – Annie Kelly (Oats)
Won a bumper by 12l on her second start at Market Rasen, but then was a bit light next time and could finish only third. We've given her a nice break and she'll come back in and go straight over hurdles.

Soulard
3yo bay colt
Arch – Bourbon Blues (Seeking The Gold)
A newcomer to the yard who was trained on the Flat by Jeremy Noseda. He won his maiden well at Catterick in July over 1m6f (he made all) and I think he might develop into a nice hurdler.

Westmere
6yo bay gelding
Alderbrook – Midnight Air (Bold Owl)
Ran well at Market Rasen on his last run, staying on strongly up the run-in after making a mistake three out to finish third. He didn't jump too well, but that was only his second run over hurdles and he will improve. He'll have one more run in novices to get him handicapped. He needs three miles and likes good ground.

SIMON: a Welsh National type

Richard Williams
Best of British

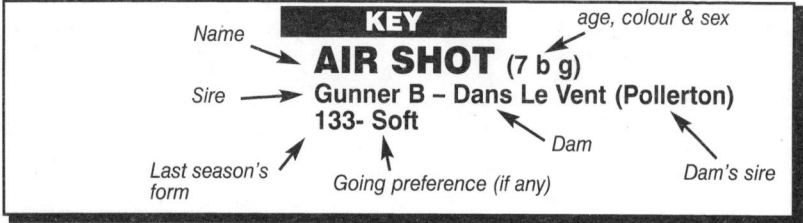

KEY

Name → **AIR SHOT** (7 b g) ← age, colour & sex

Sire → **Gunner B – Dans Le Vent (Pollerton)**
133- Soft

Last season's form ↗   Going preference (if any) ↑   Dam ↙   Dam's sire ↖

AUX LE BAHNN (5 b g)
Benefecial - Helvick Lass (Mandalus)
1-

This one turned some heads when dotting up in a Warwick bumper in December. The Irish point-to-point winner had the proverbial ton in hand. Although he will make a chaser one day, Noel Chance intends a hurdling campaign this season. His reappearance should be around Christmas and long-term targets include the SunAlliance Hurdle and the long-distance hurdle races at Aintree and Punchestown. He likes some cut in the ground.

Noel Chance, Lambourn

BLUE SHARK (4 b/br g)
Cadoudal - Sweet Beauty (Tip Moss)
2311-

There's one vital thing about this potentially top-class horse – he must have soft ground. That was what he got when making his British debut at Chepstow in the Grade 1 Finale Juvenile Hurdle which he won by 8l. He hasn't raced since because of a leg injury in February which, unluckily, put paid to his chance in the Triumph Hurdle, for which he was 12-1. His trainer reports him to have made a fantastic recovery and will bring him back around December when the ground should be deep enough.

Nicky Henderson, Lambourn

CLOUDY LANE (6 b g)
Cloudings - Celtic Cygnet (Celtic Cone)
1F21121-

Cloudy Lane did nothing but make progress last season, starting off in a bumper, rising up through the ranks of novice hurdlers and finishing with a win in a novices' handicap hurdle off a mark of 124. All three of his hurdle victories were over Haydock's fixed brush variety which are good practice for would-be chasers. Donald McCain intends sending Cloudy Lane over fences this season and he should prove adept over them. He must have some cut in the ground.

Donald McCain, Cholmondeley

Sponsored by Stan James

GOLD MEDALLIST (6 ch g)
Zilzal - Spot Prize (Seattle Dancer)
1115P/-

Missed the whole of last season with injury but has recovered and will go chasing. A smart stayer on the Flat who won the Group 2 Prix Kergorlay for David Elsworth, he took to hurdling immediately when joining Philip Hobbs and rattled up a hat-trick. He was sent off 9-2 joint-favourite for the Royal & SunAlliance Hurdle but could manage only fifth behind No Refuge. Already proven over three miles-plus on ground ranging from soft to good (firm on the Flat), the chances are that he will mix it at the highest level as a chaser, with the Royal & SunAlliance a distinct possibility.

Philip Hobbs, Minehead

GRANIT JACK (4 gr g)
Glaieul - Line Grey (Le Nain Jaune)
71111-

Was purchased out of Jacques Ortet's yard in March with a view to going hurdling. This might seem a surprising strategy by Paul Nicholls considering Granit Jack rattled up a four-timer over fences in France, but he took the same route with another French chaser, Neptune Collonges, last season and that one won four times over hurdles. Granit Jack will run in the colours of John Hales, the owner of stablemate Noland. All his French wins came on ground with cut in it.

Paul Nicholls, Ditcheat

HALCON GENELARDAIS (6 ch g)
Halcon – Francetphile (Farabi)
F41115-

Here's a young staying chaser who should be fun, and more importantly, profitable to follow. He thoroughly impressed on his winning debut over fences which came at Warwick in January. Thrown in at the deep end against Iris's Gift, he stalked that one until Iris's Gift fell four out. Two more wins followed before he was upped in class and trip to the 4m1f Scottish Grand National in which he finished fifth. Races such as the Hennessy and Welsh National beckon.

Alan King, Wroughton

L'ANTARTIQUE (6 b g)
Cyborg – Moomaw (Akarad)
2201214-

A decent novice hurdler with very easy wins at Haydock and Doncaster before disappointing at Wetherby in February when upped to Grade 2. It transpired that he sustained a fracture at Wetherby and he has had a good long rest since then. Built like a chaser, he has grown over the summer according to Ferdy Murphy and will start off in a beginners chase. Murphy describes him as a "high-class chaser in the making" and, if he is as good as hoped, he could go for races like the One Man Chase or the SunAlliance. He must have soft ground.

Ferdy Murphy, West Witton

LE VOLFONI (5 b g)
Sicyos – Brume (Courtroom)
643211121F632-

The ground is the key to this fellow and he will be campaigned only in testing conditions which may mean that he misses the spring festivals. But he can mop up plenty of prizes in the depths of winter, especially at the West Country tracks. The French-bred begins the season on a reasonable mark and is young enough to progress and stay a step ahead of the handicapper. His last run was in the usually informative Future Champions Novice Chase at Ayr over 2m4f when he was beaten 4l by Monet's Garden. Admirably consistent throughout a long season, he should pay his way.

Paul Nicholls, Ditcheat

MY WAY DE SOLZEN (6 b g)
Assessor – Agathe De Solzen (Chamberlin)
21112-

Won the World Hurdle (formerly the Stayers' Hurdle) over three miles at the Cheltenham Festival, just seeing off Golden Cross after a titanic struggle, and is due to go chasing this season. There seems no reason why he shouldn't succeed. The Royal & SunAlliance Chase is the target at the moment but such is this horse's potential that he might even go for the Gold Cup. Alan King was extremely worried about the fast ground in the days leading up to Cheltenham but My Way de Solzen made a nonsense of the theory that he is just a soft-ground horse. Although beaten by Mighty Man at Aintree afterwards, he lost nothing in defeat.

Alan King, Wroughton

NOLAND (5 b g)
Exit To Nowhere – Molakai (Nureyev)
631111-

In which Cheltenham Festival hurdle race did the last three winners of the Gold Cup finish first or second? The answer is the Supreme Novice Hurdle, won this year by Noland. Arguably he was a bit lucky to beat Straw Bear a neck because the runner-up lost his footing at the last. Noland was being niggled along four flights from home but produced a great run up the hill. Built like a chaser, he should stay at least 2m4f and possibly much further. Ideally the ground should be neither too quick nor too soft.

Paul Nicholls, Ditcheat

OUMEYADE (4 b g)
Smadoun – Debandade (Le Pontet)
3-

This French import will run in the colours of Jim Lewis, made famous by Best Mate. A useful hurdler in France, he is a half-brother to Ladalko, the horse who was touched off in last season's Scottish Grand National. He qualifies for novice hurdling until the end of October, after which he could tackle conditions events. His trainer Henrietta Knight told us that he was one of the brightest prospects in her yard.

Henrietta Knight, Wantage

OVER THE CREEK (7 br g)
Over The River – Solo Girl (Le Bavard)
/-

Halfway through last season Over The Creek, who had been 6-1 favourite for the Royal & SunAlliance Chase, met with a training setback. He was last seen running second to Moulin Riche in the three-mile Brit Insurance Novice Hurdle at the Cheltenham Festival of 2005 for which he was sent off 5-1 on the back of some excellent handicap form. The French horse was too good for him that day but he was far from disgraced. He's built like a chaser and can make up for lost time.

David Pipe, Nicholashayne

STRAW BEAR (5 ch g)
Diesis – Highland Ceilidh (Scottish Reel)
11212-

Here's the best chance England have got of retaking the Champion Hurdle, albeit he is owned by Irishman JP McManus and is likely to be ridden by Irishman Tony McCoy. Straw Bear was an unlucky second in the Supreme Novice Hurdle, a race which Brave Inca won in 2004. He was bought out of Sir Mark Prescott's Flat stable from which so many good jumpers emerge. After Cheltenham he went to Aintree and won by 13l before being beaten at Punchestown when feeling the strain of three top-class races in quick succession.

Nick Gifford, Findon

THE PIOUS PRINCE (5 ch g)
Shahrastani – Ara Blend (Persian Mews)
1-

This horse, who won his only start at Ayr, has a fascinating pedigree combining the best of Flat and jumps racing. His sire is a Derby winner, bred by the Aga Khan. His dam is a half-sister to the Whitbread winner Topsham Bay. He absolutely hacked up in a bumper at Ayr on soft ground, hardly turning a hair to come home 13l clear. Len Lungo will give him another run or two in bumpers before sending him hurdling. He looks the sort to run up a sequence.

Len Lungo, Carrutherstown

TIDAL BAY (5 b g)
Flemensfirth – June's Bride (Le Moss)
22-

Graham Wylie bought him out of Alistair Charlton's yard at Doncaster's spring sale for 300,000 guineas. No doubt Wylie was impressed by Tidal Bay's second to Pangbourne in the Aintree bumper, in which he produced a storming late run after looking green in the early stages. It was a big step up on his previous Wetherby run and the sky is the limit for him. Charlton reported that the phone started ringing with offers for Tidal Bay right after the race which explains why Wylie had to pay so much and Howard Johnson will now send Tidal Bay hurdling. Charlton has had several useful bumper horses in the past, such as Bold Bishop – let's hope this one can prove just as good.

Howard Johnson, Crook

Outlook

Ante-Post Preview

with Steffan Edwards

At the 2006 Festival the Irish topped their nine-race haul from 2005 with ten wins, including victory again in the Champion Hurdle, Champion Chase and Gold Cup. They also secured five of the six places in those races, and were only narrowly denied in the World Hurdle. They won the Grand National for the fifth time in the last eight years, and restricted the visiting British to just one winner at the Punchestown Festival. They currently have great strength in depth at the top level and, ante-post wise, I think in general it's probably wise to favour their candidates over ours.

Perhaps another thing to bear in mind is that, while we have grown accustomed to seeing the ground ride on the fast side at Cheltenham in March, that could be about to change. One of the key recommendations of the Horseracing Regulatory Authority's report into the deaths of nine horses at last season's Festival was that the course management should "consider aiming for ground officially easier than the regulatory requirement of good." As a result mudlarks may not be as disadvantaged this time around as in the past.

Champion Hurdle

Unsurprisingly the betting is headed by **Brave Inca**, who showed all his customary tenacity to see off Macs Joy and record his second career success at the Festival in last year's Champion Hurdle.

His improvement last season coincided with the employment of Tony McCoy in the saddle, though, and it would be something of a concern were he not available to ride him this time around. His retainer with owner JP McManus means that he would have ridden Lingo in last season's Champion had he not suffered a fatal injury in the weeks leading up to the Festival, and this time Straw Bear has the potential to develop into a candidate.

That would result in a new jockey having to be found for Brave Inca. Of course, things may well work out differently and McCoy may be free to ride him, but the champion will also be nine in March, and that's a touch on the old side. In the last 13 runnings of the race, only Rooster Booster proved himself fast enough to win at that sort of age.

Macs Joy got the better of Brave Inca only once in five meetings last season, at the end of a long campaign at Punchestown, a track that suits him better than his big rival. While clearly a high-class hurdler, Cheltenham would not be his ideal venue as he is a speedier type more suited to sharp tracks, and it's difficult to see how he can reverse the form.

The most talented hurdler around is probably **HARCHIBALD**, but since finishing runner-up, one place in front of Brave Inca, in the 2005 Champion Hurdle, he has failed to beat him in three subsequent meetings.

Those defeats came on soft ground in Ireland, though, and his turn of foot is undoubtedly more of a weapon on quicker ground. Off the track since getting injured when beaten at Leopardstown towards the end of last year, he has since had surgery

ASIAN MAZE: a contender, but for which race? The Champion or World Hurdle?

to remove some birch from his off-hind pastern but is said to have recovered well, and while his attitude under pressure remains a slight concern, a fast pace at Cheltenham will play into his hands.

In addition, from a trading point of view, it's easy to imagine him arriving at the Festival as a leading contender, with a string of easy wins in the trials under his belt, so double-figure prices look big at this stage.

Colm Murphy is in the fortunate position of having not only the reigning champ Brave Inca in his stable but also a serious pretender to that crown in the shape of the mare **Feathard Lady**.

Unbeaten in seven starts to date, including five over hurdles, she came from nowhere last season to dispute favouritism for the Champion Hurdle after her demolition of a useful bunch in the Christmas Hurdle at Sandown.

Unfortunately, a sprained hind fetlock joint prevented her making it to Cheltenham, but the fact that she is comparatively lightly-raced and remains progressive means she should be a leading contender this time around.

She's won on ground ranging from firm to heavy, although a bit of cut probably suits her best, and loves a strongly-run two miles, as we saw at Sandown. Prior to 2004 mares would get a 5lb allowance in the race, but that has since been raised to 7lb, which can only help her chance.

Reports that she has suffered another injury in the off-season and won't be seen out until 2007 tempers enthusiasm from an antepost perspective, though.

Asian Maze is the only mare to have competed in the race since the allowance was increased, but her challenge ended early last season when she fell at halfway.

While clearly a high-class performer over 2m4f and further, her inability to lead over the shorter trip of two miles may have been largely responsible for that mishap, and she looks likely to be a stronger candidate for the World Hurdle crown this time around.

The previous season's Triumph Hurdle winner almost always features prominently in the betting for this race, and this year is no exception, with **Detroit City** the shortest-priced of the British challenge.

There are a number of worries about him, though, not least the suspicion that he will want further than two miles this season and the lamentable record of five-year-olds in the Champion. In my opinion, he would be of more interest for the World Hurdle, though the record of five-year-olds in that race is even worse.

Straw Bear is a potential improver this season. Mugged close to the line in the Supreme on only his third start over hurdles, he bolted up at Aintree next time out before getting turned over by Iktitaf on his final start in Ireland, when the race wasn't run to suit. He needs some cut in the ground to be at his best and coming off a strong pace in a big field will suit him, but there's a possibility he will also need further than two miles.

While **Iktitaf** beat Straw Bear comfortably at Punchestown, he had the advantage of arriving there fresh having been off the track for two and a half months with an injury. The race was also run to suit him, the steady gallop allowing him to use his turn of foot to best effect. In a more strongly-run the positions may well be reversed.

Some bookmakers quote **Black Jack Ketchum** for this race despite reports that he will be campaigned with the World Hurdle in mind. He has a smart turn of foot for a horse that stays three miles and it wouldn't be the biggest surprise in the world if he demonstrated his ability to compete over the minimum trip and caused connections to have a change of heart. He can hardly be recommended at this stage, though.

The 2004 and 2005 champion **Hardy Eustace** ran a fine race in defeat last season despite arriving on the back of a far from ideal preparation. He won't be getting any quicker this time around, though, and it's very difficult to envision him regaining his title at the age of ten.

Paul Nolan, who sent out Accordion Etoile to finish fourth in 2005, may well have a contender this time around in the shape of Galway Hurdle winner **Cuan Na Grai**.

A front-runner who likes fast ground and jumps well, he's improving all the time, and his trainer has already nominated the Greatwood Hurdle as his autumn target.

Accordion Etoile won that race en route to the Festival and in recent years the race has proved a decent trial for the big one.

However, it's worth remembering that Cuan Na Grai didn't win his first hurdles race until May of this year, which means he will still be a novice in March, and only five years ago Westender took the Greatwood before going on to finish second to Like-A-Butter-fly in the Supreme Hurdle at the Festival.

Arcalis was the British No. 1 this time last year, but after a promising win in the Fighting Fifth his season went downhill.

Pulled up in atrocious ground at Haydock on his next start and a well-held fifth in the Champion, he finished the season off with a couple of poor efforts at Ayr and Sandown. His stable was out of form for most of last season and hopefully he can bounce back, but even his best form leaves him with a lot to find with the principals.

Noble Request might develop into a stronger candidate from this side of the Irish Sea. He progressed through the handicapping ranks last term, rounding things off with success over the increasingly frustrating Faasel in both the Scottish Champion and Betfred Million Hurdles, and has a preference for a sound surface.

In the spring he had to settle for second behind **Desert Quest** at Cheltenham and **Wellbeing** at Aintree.

The former, trained by Paul Nicholls, was impressive in winning the County Hurdle – albeit off just 131 – but before flopping behind Straw Bear at Aintree. He needs to improve a lot to come into consideration for the Champion, but it wouldn't be the biggest surprise to see him make the leap.

Wellbeing was getting plenty of weight from Noble Request at Aintree, but he came off a strong gallop to run out a nine-length winner. The major doubt is that he'll be ten come March and may well be sent chasing.

Champion Hurdle

Cheltenham, 13 March 2007

	Bet365	Coral	Hills	Lads	S James	Tote	VC	Betfair
Brave Inca	5	9-2	4	5	4	7-2	5	6.4
Harchibald	10	8	7	8	10	8	8	11.5
Macs Joy	10	8	8	8	10	8	7	11.5
Feathard Lady	10	7	9	10	10	8	10	21
Asian Maze	10	12	10	12	12	8	10	16
Detroit City	12	14	12	14	10	12	14	14.5
Straw Bear	14	14	16	14	14	14	12	22
Iktitaf	16	16	12	14	16	12	14	21
Hardy Eustace	25	16	14	25	14	16	20	46
Noble Request	25	20	20	25	20	20	20	34
Cuan Na Grai	25	25	25	25	16	25	33	44
Arcalis	33	33	33	33	20	33	33	34
Desert Quest	33	33	33	33	25	33	40	34
Faasel	40	33	33	-	25	33	40	80

each-way 1/4 odds, 1-2-3 (except Betfair)
Others on request, prices correct at time of going to press

Sponsored by Stan James

Champion Chase

The bookmakers currently go 7-1 the field in what at first glance looks an open race, but I think a number of the main contenders can be taken on.

Newmill had everything fall his way on the big day last season. The ground was perfect for him (on the fast side), Kauto Star crashed out early and hampered Moscow Flyer, and he enjoyed what was more or less an uncontested lead throughout.

However, the way he stormed up the hill to come 9l clear of Fota Island suggested there was no fluke about the result, and he confirmed the impression by giving that rival another pasting at Punchestown on his next start, where again he made all.

Newmill is certainly the one they have to beat, but he may not be given the easy lead he seems to need to produce his best with **Ashley Brook**, forced to miss last term's big spring meetings after picking up a knee injury in the Tingle Creek in December, now reported to be back on track. Kevin Bishop's stable star, at his best on good ground, won't

be easy to dominate.

Ashley Brook's conqueror in the Tingle Creek, **Kauto Star**, was sent off just 2-1 for the Champion Chase but got no further than the third fence. That was only his fifth start over fences, though, and he clearly remains open to further improvement.

His win at Sandown suggested he was set for the top, but there are plenty of doubts about him. All his form to date has come with cut in the ground, and when he won on his chasing debut at Newbury back in December 2004 his connections spoke of him as a potential Gold Cup horse in the making. Talk of him being entered for the King George this season suggests they still believe three miles will pose few problems for him, and it's also possible that a flat track will see him at his best.

Last season's Arkle had the look of a quality renewal on paper and the race itself justified that view.

The time of the race compared very favourably indeed with the following day's

NEWMILL: leading Central House in the early stages of the Champion Chase

Champion Chase and, given that the ground was getting quicker as the meeting went on, that was no mean feat.

The race went to **VOY POR USTEDES**, who jumped brilliantly throughout before staying on strongly up the hill to beat **Monet's Garden**, the pair clear of the rest.

The runner-up looks likely to make a staying chaser but Alan King's charge is a two-miler through and through, and will be campaigned as such.

Arkle winners have a good record in the following year's Champion Chase, and while some will oppose him on the basis that only one six-year-old has ever won the race, that would be foolish in my opinion.

Very few six-year-olds have actually competed, and those that have run have tended to perform with great credit. In the last 20 renewals six six-year-olds have tried their hand, two of them finishing runner-up, one finishing third and the other three finishing unplaced. I would argue that that is actually a very good record.

FOREMAN did best of those who were held up in the Arkle, finishing strongly up the hill to claim third place.

A former Irish Champion Hurdle winner, he's also finished fourth in the SunAlliance and Champion Hurdles in the past, earning himself a good bank of Festival form.

He enjoyed the easier ground and being ridden closer to the pace when getting his revenge on Voy Por Ustedes at Aintree and, granted a strong pace, he will have every chance of confirming that form in the Champion Chase this season.

The Arkle fourth **Wild Passion** has plenty of size about him and looks the type to progress again this season. His form to date suggests he's at his best on soft ground and, if the rain arrived in March, he could not be discounted.

When it comes to horses returning from lengthy injury lay-offs it usually pays to follow the maxim that 'they never come back', and that will be put to the test by **Well Chief**.

Last seen when clashing with Azertyuiop in the Celebration Chase at Sandown in April 2005, Well Chief never made it to the track last season despite initial indications that his injury wasn't that serious.

Plenty of faith is required to believe that David Pipe's stable star will return as good as ever, but if he does – and let's not forget he's still only seven – he will have a major say in the Champion Chase. After all, at this stage last year he looked destined to take over from Moscow Flyer as the top dog, and was a best-priced 2-1 for the race.

Champion Chase

Cheltenham, 14 March 2007

	Bet365	Coral	Hills	Lads	S James	Tote	VC	Betfair
Kauto Star	5	5	6	5	5	7	6	7
Newmill	5	6	7	7	6	5	6	7.8
Well Chief	5	6	8	8	7	7	7	8.6
Voy Por Ustedes	6	6	8	8	15-2	8	8	9
Foreman	12	12	10	12	16	12	12	17
Ashley Brook	16	12	16	16	16	16	16	32
Monet's Garden	16	-	12	-	16	-	-	48
Accordion Etoile	14	16	16	16	20	20	14	18
Watson Lake	25	-	-	-	20	-	-	75
Contraband	-	20	25	-	20	-	-	95
Central House	20	20	33	-	25	33	25	55
River City	-	-	25	25	33	-	-	42
Fota Island	20	20	20	40	16	20	20	75
Dempsey	25	25	-	-	33	33	40	60

each-way 1/4 odds, 1-2-3 (except Betfair)
Others on request, prices correct at time of going to press

Last season Steffan Edwards recommended War Of Attrition to win the Gold Cup at 33-1

Sponsored by Stan James

Accordion Etoile was let down by his jumping at Cheltenham and Aintree, but he bounced back to beat Justified at Punchestown. That form still leaves him with a bit to find, though, and he really needs fast ground to have any chance at the top level.

Justified, on the other hand, has a preference for some cut in the ground and is likely to be campaigned over furthe.

Andreas remains open to improvement but is another who needs fast ground to be seen at his best, and his last experience of Cheltenham wasn't a pleasant one.

Contraband lost the plot last season, **River City** isn't good enough, **Dempsey** needs to go right-handed and **Watson Lake** needs both soft ground and a longer trip.

Rathgar Beau, **Fota Island** and **Cloone River** will all be 11-year-olds in March, and past their best. Moscow Flyer was still good enough to win the Champion Chase at that age, but they are not.

World Hurdle

There are doubts about many of the leading contenders for the World Hurdle this season, despite their apparent suitability for the race, and from an ante-post point of view very few make any appeal.

The clear favourite is **Black Jack Ketchum**, who is unbeaten in seven starts and won at both Cheltenham and Aintree in highly impressive fashion last term.

On the ratings he doesn't even have to improve on his novice form to compete with the very best in the staying division, but the chances are that he will, and that he'll therefore take plenty of beating wherever he turns up during the upcoming campaign.

Described by Jonjo O'Neill, who sent out Iris's Gift to win this race in 2004, as the best horse he has ever trained, there can be little doubt about the seven-year-old's talent, but whether he's worth backing at just 5-2 for this race is another question.

While his trainer has said that the gelding will compete in races around 2m4f to three miles en route to the World Hurdle, he has never looked short of pace, and there will surely be a temptation to try him out over shorter. Winning a recognised trial for the Champion Hurdle, which might not be too difficult given the shortage of genuine contenders on this side of the Irish Sea, may well result in Black Jack Ketchum being switched to tackle the more presitigious race.

In addition, his owner has a super-sub for the race in the shape of **FIRE DRAGON**, who won the Cleeve Hurdle last season before finishing fourth in the World Hurdle.

Last off the bridle in that race, he might not have got the trip as well as some, but the stats say he faced an impossible task trying to win the race at the age of five, and he should be a far more formidable proposition this time around.

Those who supported **Asian Maze** down to 7-1 for the World Hurdle last season must have been less than happy when her connections decided to re-route her to the Champion Hurdle instead, a race in which the market suggested she was nothing more than a lively outsider.

In the event, she fell at the fourth and couldn't take up her engagement in the World Hurdle two days later.

Impressive in handing out a 17l drubbing to Hardy Eustace at Aintree on her next start, she is clearly a very smart hurdler indeed, but she strikes me as similar to Limestone

FIRE DRAGON (nearside)

Lad – a front-runner who had the pace to be effective over two miles and the stamina for three, but was at his very best over 2m4f. My guess is that the lure of the Champion Hurdle will be too great again and the World Hurdle will only be a back-up option.

Hardy Eustace is a much better horse at Cheltenham than at Aintree and his Festival form reads 1113. While he may have lost the speed to win another Champion Hurdle, this former SunAlliance winner should still be capable of smart form over further, and it wouldn't be a surprise to see him line up for the World Hurdle this time around. Age stats will still be against him, though.

The reigning champion **My Way De Solzen** has been earmarked by his trainer for a novice chasing campaign this season, so he cannot be considered ante-post for this race. Of course, were he not to take to jumping fences for some reason, then he would have to re-enter calculations.

However, even if My Way De Solzen did run, it's open to question whether he could confirm form with **GOLDEN CROSS**, whom he beat only narrowly last season.

Michael Halford's gelding was perhaps a little unlucky as the winner hung right and took his ground on the run-in just as he was in the process of staying on strongly. Both finished nicely clear of Mighty Man in third and the form looks pretty solid.

Golden Cross suffered a cut to his near-fore leg in the race which meant that he was unable to race again last season, but the injury wasn't thought to be serious.

Earlier in his career he won a Grade 1 over two miles, but he always shaped as though he would do better when stepped up in trip, and his performance at Cheltenham – only his second over a staying trip – proved that stamina is his forte.

I like the way he's building up a nice portfolio of Festival form, having now finished in the frame in both the Triumph Hurdle and World Hurdle, and run a creditable seventh in the Champion two seasons back. His best form has come with some cut so hopefully he'll get easier ground as well.

One associates Henry Daly with chasers rather than hurdlers and, while **Mighty Man** isn't the biggest, it wouldn't surprise me at all if the six-year-old went novice chasing this season.

He did well to reverse Cheltenham form with My Way De Solzen at Aintree, albeit in receipt of 4lb, and is young enough to still be improving, but perhaps a flat track like Liverpool suits him better than Cheltenham. After all, he won there as a novice, too.

No five-year-old has ever won this crown and that's enough to put me off **Detroit City**, who would otherwise be interesting. I can see the stiffer test of the World Hurdle suiting him better than the Champion Hurdle, in which he will surely get outpaced, but his owner is keen to go the two-mile route.

Another who is currently seen as more of a Champion Hurdle contender is **Straw Bear**, but as the season develops it wouldn't be a shock to see him develop into a World Hurdle horse. He saw his races out strongly as a novice and it was a case of being beaten for speed when he got turned over at odds-on at Punchestown.

At his best **Inglis Drever**, the 2005 winner, would be decent value at 10-1. After all, he was 4-1 to repeat at this time last year.

However, he missed the second half of last season with a tendon injury and it remains to be seen whether he returns as good as ever. His stable has certainly not enjoyed such a good time of things over the past year and there would be a concern on that front, too.

His stable-companion, the former Royal & SunAlliance Hurdle winner **No Refuge**, doesn't jump well enough for my liking.

One of the easiest winners at last year's Festival was **SKY'S THE LIMIT**, who defied top-weight to win the usually fiercely competitive Coral Cup with plenty to spare.

That performance suggested he would be capable of holding his own at the top level, but he got very tired in the testing ground at Aintree on his next start and had probably had enough for the season by the time Punchestown came around.

His trainer Edward O'Grady has a great record at the Cheltenham Festival and has won this race twice before, and while he's said that the chances are 50/50 that Sky's The Limit will go chasing this term, I believe there's a good chance he'll stay hurdling. Interestingly, the Irish bookmakers all have him shorter in the betting than their British counterparts.

The fitting of a visor for the first time may have been significant at Cheltenham and it wouldn't be a surprise to see his trainer

42

SKY'S THE LIMIT: could well improve into a top World Hurdle contender

again save the headgear for the big day.

Rule Supreme missed most of last year with a leg problem and will be 11 in March. His best days are probably behind him.

Refinement is an admirable mare with good Festival form, but she needs to find plenty of improvement and her stable has stronger candidates.

Another who had a good novice season but needs to find quite a lot of improvement still is **Temoin**. He didn't run his race at Aintree on his final start, but he had previously looked a promising recruit.

From the ranks of last season's Irish novice hurdlers, **Mounthenry** looks a potential candidate, but a number of those in the betting for the World Hurdle are expected to go chasing this season.

They include Nicky Henderson's **The Market Man**, Royal & SunAlliance Hurdle winner **Nicanor** and the Paul Nicholls pair **Neptune Collonges** and **Gungadu**.

Most would be of some interest, especially Nicanor, if plans to jump fences were shelved, but none can be recommended as ante-post selections.

World Hurdle

Cheltenham, 15 March 2007

	Bet365	Coral	Hills	Lads	S James	Tote	VC	Betfair
Black Jack Ketchum	**5-2**	**5-2**	**5-2**	**5-2**	2	**5-2**	**5-2**	3.55
Golden Cross	8	8	8	7	8	8	7	14
Inglis Drever	7	6	5	10	6	8	7	14
My Way De Solzen	8	6	8	10	8	-	7	16.5
Asian Maze	8	6	5	10	9	7	6	16
Mighty Man	10	8	5	7	10	8	8	13.5
Nicanor	16	-	-	-	16	20	-	42
Sky's The Limit	16	16	**20**	-	16	16	20	48
Gungadu	**20**	-	**20**	-	**20**	-	-	180
Neptune Collonges	**20**	-	**20**	-	**20**	-	-	70
Al Eile	**25**	-	-	-	20	-	-	150
Refinement	20	-	-	-	**25**	-	-	65
Fire Dragon	25	25	-	-	25	33	-	70
No Refuge	**33**	25	25	-	**33**	-	33	180

each-way 1/4 odds, 1-2-3 (except Betfair)
Others on request, prices correct at time of going to press

Gold Cup

The last two winners of the Gold Cup dominate the current market, but I wouldn't have any hesitation in preferring **War Of Attrition** over his compatriot **Kicking King**.

The 2005 victor was beaten on his first two starts last season and, although there were excuses for those defeats, he was also unimpressive in scrambling home from Monkerhostin in the King George.

A tendon injury picked up during that race prevented him seeing the track during the second half of the season and his trainer Tom Taaffe has already decided to take it easy this term, announcing plans to run him over two miles around Christmas before a final prep in January. This is off-putting and I'd rather see clear evidence he retains his ability before stepping in to back him.

War Of Attrition, a Grade 1-winning novice over two miles, silenced those who doubted his stamina by winning the race impressively last season, and he had little trouble in following up at Punchestown.

While he handles soft ground, a faster surface sees him at his best, and granted those conditions he should be the one to beat – it's certainly difficult to see how any of those behind him in the Gold Cup can reverse the form this time. At 5-1, though, he doesn't make much appeal, especially as only four horses since the second world war have won the race more than once.

Another top contender returning from a tendon injury this term is **Trabolgan**.

The 2005 Royal & SunAlliance Chase winner, who defied top-weight to win the Hennessy last year, is also likely to be lightly-raced prior to Cheltenham, with his seasonal debut unlikely to come until 2007. He gave L'Ami 7lb and a beating at Newbury and the French horse went on to finish fourth in both the King George and Gold Cup, suggesting that Nicky Henderson's charge doesn't need to improve hugely to be a major player.

With Trabolgan out, **Hedgehunter** was drafted in to represent owner Trevor Hemmings last year and ran a personal best in second. That was followed by a fine effort

WAR OF ATTRITION: can he come back and win the Gold Cup again in 2007?

Sponsored by Stan James

MISSED THAT: a strong finisher, as he showed at Punchestown last season

in the National, confirming he is both smart and tough. However, he is coming up 11 and the stats say that's too old.

Last year's third **Forget The Past** is more interesting. He didn't help his cause by hitting a few fences in the closing stages, but the good ground suited him and it's easy to see him returning to put up another good show. He has a bit to find with War Of Attrition, though, and very few placed horses go on to win the following season.

Besides, trainer Michael O'Brien believes he has a stronger candidate in the shape of **IN COMPLIANCE**. An easy winner of his first two starts over fences, he was done for toe by speedier rivals at Grade 1 level after that, but those were highly creditable efforts given his pedigree suggests he's very much a staying chaser in the making.

While he's won on soft ground, O'Brien reckons he's better on a faster surface and it's easy to see him developing into one of Ireland's main hopes come March.

Following the example of Kicking King and War Of Attrition, who were both targeted at the Arkle rather than the unforgiving Royal & SunAlliance Chase as novices, last season's renewal featured three or four who could emerge as high-class staying chasers this season.

First up is **Monet's Garden**, who, together with eventual winner Voy Por Ustedes, gave the rest a lesson in jumping and dominated the race. Though a smart hurdler, fences were always going to be the making of him,

and perhaps the surprising thing was that he had the speed to be competitive over two miles, given his final hurdles start was a win over three miles at Aintree.

On the face of it, he would look to have everything, but whether he will get 3m2f around Cheltenham is another question. He looks a likelier winner of the King George than the Gold Cup, and his trainer's belief that he really wants three miles on a flat track backs up that view.

Don't Be Shy stayed on quite well for fifth and should get three miles this season, but all his best form to date has come in very soft conditions.

Of more interest is former Festival Bumper winner **MISSED THAT**, who ran on to take sixth having made a hash of the fourth last and subsequently been outpaced.

Chopped for room when going for an ambitious run up the inside rail on the turn into the straight, he stayed on well up the hill, and everything about him suggests that he's crying out for three miles plus.

Last season he quickly developed into Ireland's top novice chaser, winning two Grade 1 races, including the Irish Arkle, and the feature of those victories and his end-of-season win at Punchestown was how well he finished his races. Once he gets a proper test of stamina he's likely to do better still, and at 25-1 he simply must be backed.

The other Arkle also-ran with Gold Cup pretensions is **Racing Demon**. Favourite at Cheltenham, he found the pace too hot over the minimum trip on decent ground, but his successes earlier in the season, coupled with his runner-up spot in the previous year's Royal & SunAlliance Hurdle clearly mark him out as potentially high-class.

He can be expected to improve for the extra, and the only significant worry I would have is his tendency to jump right. He has only run left-handed twice in his ten-race career – both at the Festival – and he was kept wide in the Arkle in anticipation of him jumping out to his right. He looks another more tailor-made for the King George.

Last season's Royal & SunAlliance was captured in fine style by **Star De Mohaison**, who made full use of his generous 10lb age allowance and won his race thanks to an accurate round of jumping. Following up at Aintree proved that was no fluke, and the application of a tongue strap was clearly of benefit. Best on a decent surface, he will have to improve quite a bit this season as he won't have the benefit of an allowance in 2007, but that is not out of the question.

Feltham winner **Darkness** was only a staying-on third in the SunAlliance after a poor round of jumping. He has won decent races despite his slowness over the fences, but he will have to improve significantly in that department to challenge for top honours.

The Listener found the ground too quick at the Festival and was outpaced. He's a smart chaser in the making and will win races this season, but he needs genuine soft ground to be seen at his best.

Commercial Flyer is potentially interesting, as he made quite an impression on his debut over fences and was strongly fancied at Cheltenham despite his relative lack of chasing experience. Pulled up after losing his action, he was one of many from the Pipe stable to fail to shine at that time and flopped again at Aintree. However, he could well prove a dark horse.

Turpin Green, who threw away the Scilly Isles Chase at Sandown when almost refusing at the last, tackled the Jewson at the Festival instead of the SunAlliance and was a bit disappointing. He ran better at Aintree, though, and although perhaps not entirely straightforward, he has plenty of talent.

Another of last season's novices with Gold Cup pretensions is **Justified**, but he surely doesn't have the stamina for the race and also has jumping problems to address.

The Pipe stable endured a Festival to forget last season, and **Celestial Gold**, who unseated at halfway on his belated reappearance in the Gold Cup, never got a chance to improve on his seventh place the previous year. He showed what he's capable of at Aintree on his next start, though, as he travelled strongly, perhaps a bit too freely in fact, before still getting the better of Gold Cup fifth Take The Stand. Lightly-raced for his age, there's no doubt that he has the ability to be a leading player this time around.

If **Kauto Star** does the business in the King George, his connections will be under pressure to go for Gold. His Champion

Gold Cup

Cheltenham, 16 March 2007

	Bet365	Coral	Hills	Lads	S James	Tote	VC	Betfair
War Of Attrition	9-2	3	9-2	5	5	7-2	4	7.2
Kicking King	8	6	6	8	6	6	6	10.5
Trabolgan	10	10	8	8	8	10	8	22
Monet's Garden	16	12	14	16	14	16	14	19
Celestial Gold	16	16	14	16	14	16	14	29
Star De Mohaison	20	16	20	16	20	20	16	23
Hedgehunter	20	14	12	20	25	16	12	34
Forget The Past	16	16	16	25	20	20	16	75
In Compliance	20	25	20	20	20	20	25	34
L'Ami	25	16	20	20	25	25	20	60
Missed That	25	20	20	25	20	25	20	29
Iris's Gift	33	25	25	33	33	33	33	120
Beef Or Salmon	40	25	33	-	33	33	33	90
Kingscliff	40	33	25	-	33	33	40	100

each-way 1/4 odds, 1-2-3 (except Betfair)
Others on application, prices correct at time of going to press

Chase supporters must be concerned.

Despite plenty of evidence from previous Gold Cups that **Beef Or Salmon** wasn't suited to the big fields, fast pace, quick ground or the course in general, enough people were prepared to give him one more chance that he was sent off favourite for the race last season. Unsurprisingly, he didn't jump well and never stood a chance.

Even Beef Or Salmon's connections seem to have given up hope of winning a Gold Cup, but it wouldn't be a total surprise if **Church Island**, who stays well and has winning course form for the same owner, developed into a lively outsider. He is also versatile with regard to ground conditions.

The same cannot be said, however, for one of his conquerors last season. **Southern Vic**, who developed into a useful novice in Ireland and has plenty of stamina, is entirely reliant on soft ground.

Injuries have blighted **Kingscliff**'s career and, while he is capable of high-class form at his best, as when beating Beef Or Salmon and Kicking King at Haydock last year, he is hardly reliable.

Lacdoudal's performance in the Ryanair Chase at the Festival and his subsequent success in the Betfred Gold Cup proved that he needs a trip these days, and on fast ground he has the potential to develop into an interesting outsider. Tough and steadily progressive, he takes his racing well and it wouldn't be a surprise to see him hit new heights this season.

Hi Cloy gets three miles but his best form is over 2m4f, while others whose stamina for the Gold Cup trip is doubtful include former Supreme Hurdle winner **Back In Front** and the ex-French **Nickname**, who revels in soft ground.

Monkerhostin, **Cornish Rebel** and **Take The Stand** can be filed in the category of those who have had their chances and aren't quite of the class required, while last season's useful novices **Idle Talk** and **Our Ben** appeal more as likelier types for valuable handicaps like the Hennessy this term.

French challenger **Mid Dancer** is a winner of 13 of his 14 career starts, his only defeat so far coming on his debut in this country in the Arkle. A smart performer over hurdles and fences across the Channel, he stays well and is very effective in soft ground, but he still has to prove he can handle British fences.

His owner also owns another prolific winner in **Cyrlight**, but appears to have a couple of stronger candidates for the Gold Cup in the shape of Forget The Past and In Compliance.

Every year one or two novices are talked up as potential candidates, but it's over 30 years since a novice won the Gold Cup and those who take their chance usually don't jump well enough and fail to complete.

Last season it was Iris's Gift; this time **Denman** and **My Way De Solzen** are among those to have received early quotes.

Neptune Collonges is already a multiple winner over fences in France and was bought as a potential Gold Cup horse, but he'll still be only six in March and it might be a year too soon for this mud-lover.

Taranis, another Paul Nicholls-trained French-bred, benefitted from a breathing operation and won on each of his four completed starts in novice company last season. He's an interesting prospect, but there are valuable handicaps to be won with him before thoughts turn to Cheltenham.

Recommended Bets

Champion Hurdle

2pts Harchibald 12-1
(Cashmans)

Champion Chase

2pts Voy Por Ustedes 8-1
(general)
1pt Foreman 16-1
(Stan James)

World Hurdle

2pts Golden Cross 10-1
(Cashmans)
1pt Sky's The Limit 25-1
(Bet Direct, Skybet)
1pt Fire Dragon 33-1
(Ladbrokes, Tote)

Gold Cup

2pts Missed That 25-1
(general)
1pt In Compliance 25-1
(general)

Prices correct at time of going to press

Ireland by Jerry M

FOR the past two seasons now the Cheltenham Gold Cup has been won by a second-season chaser who had previously shown high-class form over two miles in their novice campaign.

Both Kicking King and War Of Attrition followed that path, and while both could lock horns again at Prestbury next March, it might be wise to add *MICHAEL O'BRIEN*'s **In Compliance** to your list as he embarks on a potentially similar route.

The latter enjoyed a profitable, if truncated, season in 2005/2006, not starting off until winning a novice chase over 2m4f at Fairyhouse at the end of February with consummate ease.

His fencing was a joy to behold on a track which can test the best of jumpers, and he was equally good when winning at Leopardstown on his next start when dishing out a 20l beating to Kerryhead Windfarm.

On the strength of those wins, he was immediately upped to Grade One level for his final two outings, and while winning neither, he was by no means disgraced.

In the Powers Gold Cup at Fairyhouse he was beaten by an inspired Tony McCoy on Justified, while in the Swordlestown Cup (a race used by both Kicking King and War Of Attrition in their novice season) over two miles he was just done for toe by the super-quick Accordion Etoile, finishing a five-and-a-half-length third.

One got the feeling in those final races that, although the talent was there, the experience was not, and he will have learnt an

IN COMPLIANCE: will he step up to the Gold Cup plate this season?

AREN'T I GOOD: Accordion Etoile happy with himself having won at Punchestown

awful lot from both races.

Still only six, and having raced in only ten races thus far, the best is definitely yet to come, and there must be a very good chance that this will be the season when he comes of age and shows everyone the considerable talent he seems to possess.

His trainer, O'Brien, trained Forget The Past to finish third in last season's Gold Cup, and it's a fair bet that he holds In Compliance in higher esteem.

John Joseph Murphy's reformation of **Newmill** last season was one of the training performances of the season, and if staying at the minimum trip again this season, his challenge for back-to-back Champion Chases should not be underestimated.

However, if *PAUL NOLAN*'s **Accordion Etoile** has finally ironed out his jumping demons, he might just have enough foot to beat the lot of them.

Here we have a horse who would have been good enough to win an average Champion Hurdle; indeed he ran a great race to come fourth in the 2005 renewal only to have the misfortune to bump into Hardy Eu-

stace, Harchibald and Brave Inca, who finished just in front of him.

Switched to chasing last season, he got off to an encouraging start, winning a Grade Two at Cheltenham last November, but he never quite convinced with his fencing even in victory, and the wheels well and truly came off at Cheltenham and Aintree.

In the Arkle he took a crashing fall at the eighth, and then at Aintree he made such a horrendous blunder that it immediately ended his interest in the race, as he eventually jogged home to be sixth of seven behind Foreman.

However, the horse must be made of stern stuff, as he was then marched up to Punchestown for the Swordlestown Cup, in which he put up a much more proficient display of jumping for John Cullen to win easily by two and a half lengths from Justified.

Although a risky manoeuvre to go for that race (another fall might have damaged him pyschologically), the bravery of Paul Nolan and the horse to get back on the bike as soon as possible was rewarded and could be the turning-point.

PUBLICAN: could be good if going back novice chasing again this season

Accordion Etoile is blessed with an outstanding turn of foot on good ground or better, and as long as his jumping holds up, rates a big threat to everybody in the Champion Chase.

On the novice chasing front, it would be interesting to see *PAT FAHY*'s **Publican** given another crack over fences.

A beautiful-looking horse, he has also threatened to be very good on occasions but has never quite got it together.

Last season he gave chasing a crack, and ran some fair races in defeat behind the likes of Wild Passion, Father Matt and Major Vernon.

However, the end product always seemed to be missing, and after unshipping his rider at Leopardstown in January, he was returned to hurdles for a crack at the County Hurdle at the Cheltenham Festival, for which he was well supported.

The money went astray on that occasion, but he showed immediately afterwards what he could do, when defeating Arthur Moore's Tiger Cry by 4l in a two-mile Fairyhouse hurdle.

Interestingly, his trainer claimed that was the first time Publican had really sparkled all season.

The upside of his near misses over fences though is that he still retains his novice status for this season, and the ability is definitely in there to suggest he could become an Arkle candidate next March.

On the hurdling front, *MICHAEL HALFORD*'s **Golden Cross** looks our premier candidate for World Hurdle glory, and with last season's winner My Way De Solzen going chasing, and Baracouda having been retired, the way could be left clear for him to attain Festival success.

He got on a real roll last season, starting off with a couple of successes on the Flat last Autumn.

Then on his hurdling return in the Hatton's Grace Hurdle over 2m4f at Fairyhouse, he put up a brave effort when just beaten in a titanic struggle with Solerina after the last.

At that stage, connections might not have been sure as to his stamina capabilities, but those fears were allayed somewhat by his victory in the Boyne Hurdle at Navan a month before Cheltenham over 2m7f on soft to heavy ground.

Although that wasn't an impressive win (he went off 8-15), he's not a horse to do anything easily and it was enough to justify a trip to Cheltenham, where he aimed to provide predominantly Flat jockey Johnny Murtagh with a Festival winner. And he oh so nearly did.

Creeping around at the back for much of the race, he made a forward move four out, and despite not getting the best of runs approaching the last, he kept on well only to be denied by a head.

A similar campaign is likely this time, with the Hatton's Grace, Christmas Hurdle and the Boyne all possible targets before a revenge mission at Prestbury next March. He could be the one they all have to beat.

On the novice hurdling front, *TOM HOGAN*'s **Kalderon** appeals as a horse to do well this season.

He was smart on the Flat both in Germany and France (won at Listed level) and he made an encouraging introduction to hurdles when second to Schindler's Hunt at Leopardstown last March.

An ambitious crack at the Supreme Hurdle followed shortly afterwards, when he failed to cut much ice, perhaps predictably on only his second hurdling start.

However, his form on the Flat this summer has been solid, and he scored again in August at Tralee, winning a Listed race over a mile and beating some useful types in the process.

With the experience of last season under his belt, he should have no trouble winning his novices this season, and it will be disappointing if he doesn't end up at Cheltenham.

Two miles would be his trip as he looks to have plenty of speed, while he has won on surfaces ranging from good to genuinely soft.

Invincible Irish

Accordion Etoile
In Compliance
Kalderon

KALDERON: Listed class on the Flat, and could take high rank over hurdles

Berkshire by Downsman

A NEW jumps season is upon us and the once-dominant Lambourn area is looking forward to the new campaign with a renewed sense of optimism.

It has to be conceded that the village at the heart of the "Valley of the Racehorse" is not anything like the potent force of 20 years ago, and we have had to rely heavily on *NICKY HENDERSON* to carry the battle to the powerful West Country trainers in the high-profile events in recent years.

But his supremacy is now being challenged by *ALAN KING*'s increasingly strong Barbury Castle stable, who has just got better and better since taking up the training game, having served his apprenticeship with the late David Nicholson.

There are also changes at the heart of the Lambourn training operation after this year's purchase of the famous Mandown and Neardown gallops by the Jockey Club. They promised further investment to follow and have already embarked on an ambitious improvement scheme on Mandown.

A polytrack gallop is replacing the old wood chip at the eastern end of the site, and

COPSALE LAD: will be aiming to keep the Hennessy at Seven Barrows

AFSOUN: being sent chasing and will aim to exploit his weight allowances

this should be of great help to all the trainers in the long wet winters and dry summers.

Henderson has enjoyed a wonderful view of the building work during the summer and will be keen as anyone to see the Jockey Club's plan realised. But he is also as determined as ever for his Seven Barrows gallops to retain the number one spot, and will once again field an impressive line up of stars for the forthcoming campaign.

Trabolgan's win in the Hennessy Gold Cup was clearly the highlight of last season, but things soon went awry for Trevor Hemmings' star when heat was found in one of his tendons. It remains to be seen just when he will return to the racecourse, but the Gold Cup will be the focus of attention when he does.

The Hennessy has been ruled out, but the old sages of Seven Barrows think they have a fitting substitute in **Copsale Lad**, who improved steadily last term and is at the right end of the handicap.

Fondmort, one of the most popular chasers in training thanks to his Cheltenham exploits, will be hunting more Prestbury goodies, and expect the enigmatic **Crozan** to win a nice prize at some stage. First time out, or after a break, could be the time to catch him.

Henderson's main strength lies in novice chasers this term, and he is particularly

strong in the four-year-old department.

Afsoun was one of the leading juvenile hurdlers last term and hopes are high that he can take similar rank over fences. **Royals Darling**, somewhat disappointing last term, has the make and shape for birch, a remark which also applies to **Ostrogoth**. He has done particularly well during the summer and is a much stronger animal than at the end of last season.

Tarlac, who carries the colours of JP McManus, had problems jumping hurdles last season, but he should pay more respect to his fences and is another certain to improve. **Wogan**, a real staying type, and the classy **Temoin** are also sure to win more than their share of races.

Completing the team is **Its A Dream**. Not the easiest of rides last term, he is learning all the time and, again, will stay a trip.

Handicap hurdlers may be a little thin on the ground, but the lightly-raced **Grande Jete** remains on a favourable mark. **Wantage Road**, **Mam Ratagan** and **Ship's Hill** were all highly-rated bumper horses and should do well over timber, as will **Sir Jimmy Shand**, who has a high cruising speed and a turn of foot. Two more possible class acts are Wincanton bumper winner **Barbers Shop** and **Jean Le Poisson**, an impressive winner of a bumper at Newbury.

Henderson always does well with his

MURPHY'S CARDINAL: injury-free at last and could finally fulfil his potential

mares and fillies and both **Karello Bay**, a quality horse in bumpers last season, and the unexposed **Thief** should come to the fore in races restricted to their own sex.

Alan King could not quite match Henderson's three winners at the Festival, but his two victories from **Voy Por Ustedes** and **My Way de Solzen** were both in championship races and promise much for the future.

Voy Por Ustedes has been beaten just once over fences in six starts, and he showed admirable toughness as well as a smart turn of foot to win the Arkle Trophy.

There looks a shortage of high-class two-mile chasers at present and, if all goes well, he must be a leading player for the Queen Mother Champion Chase. He has certainly summered well in the paddocks of owner Robert Ogden.

My Way de Solzen covered himself in glory by wining the World Hurdle on ground faster than he prefers. If he takes to chasing, he will be a top stayer and a major threat in the Royal & SunAlliance Chase.

Like Henderson, King is excited about his team of novice chasers. **Penzance**, **Howle Hill** and **Il Duce** all won over fences in the spring, **Senorita Rumbalita** promises to be a leading player, and there are two new arrivals from France in **Esprit de Saint** and **Stoway**.

Both won over hurdles across the Channel, and the latter, a four-year-old, is expected to make the most of the weight allowances he receives from the older generations.

Mughas, who has already schooled well at home, and useful handicap hurdler **Pretty Star** provide further back-up in this department.

King is one of the leading trainers of juvenile hurdlers and one of his possible aces this time around could be **Pouvoir**, a winner on the Flat for Freddie Head in France. Three more names from his pool of home-grown talent are **Katchit**, **Urban Tiger** and **My Petra**.

The stable can boast a wealth of promising jumping stock in addition to their Flat recruits. Bumper horses do their bit to bolster the coffers and three names from last season are **Pangbourne**, **Wyldello** and **Apollo Lady**.

Much is expected from **Halcon Genelardais** in his second season over birch. A rugged stayer, he could well make his mark in some of the top staying events around the Christmas period and beyond.

NOEL CHANCE also has his beady eye on these events for the highly-talented but fragile **Murphy's Cardinal**. A smart novice a couple of seasons ago, leg trouble has so far prevented him realising his potential. He is back this year, however, and so far the

54

signs are encouraging.

The Berkeley House trainer has a couple of young hurdlers worth noting, and he will wear a broad smile when the very useful **Kimi** lands a deserved win. His bumper form is very solid, despite the fact he did not get his head in front last term.

Little Bit of Hush had no problem winning his bumper, and he should have no problem adding to the tally over timber, while **Moncada**, an expensive purchase from the Doncaster Sales, has the make and shape for the game. Chance is looking forward to him tackling a bumper or two.

Chance's great pal *CHARLIE MANN* has plenty of new blood in his Whitcombe House Stable and has German import **Air Force One** at the top of the list for novice hurdles.

A big, powerfully-made sort, the Lando gelding was considered good enough to run in his own country's St Leger. His best trip may be two and a half miles.

Moon Over Miami is another Pattern-class performer on the Flat and has always been the apple of his trainer's eye. He took an outing or two to find his feet over hurdles but improved steadily during the spring and won twice at Wincanton and Uttoxeter. Mann has some decent handicaps in mind and he will start off at Cheltenham in October.

Hoh Viss also proved a good money-spinner last season and looked very good when hacking up on desperate ground on the second of his three wins.

Mann confirmed that he is at his best when the ground is barely raceable so expect to see him at the height of his powers when the winter rains have taken full toll on the ground. He goes novice chasing.

Nadover showed some decent form over hurdles and it was no surprise to see him do well over fences in what proved a light campaign. He is back in great form and his trainer is enthusiastic about his chance of making the Hennessy Gold Cup line-up.

The most prestigious handicap chases are also on the agenda for **Keltic Bard**, though three miles-plus on a galloping track may stretch his stamina.

He will start off over 2m5f with the Paddy Power Gold Cup an early target. Injury prevented this highly talented gelding from realising his potential last season, but his one outing suggested a valuable heat can come his way. He has, thankfully, fully recovered from the stress fracture he sustained during that solitary appearance.

Blairgowrie looked a promising young staying chaser with Howard Johnson in the spring and is a welcome new arrival, as are the winning Irish point-to-pointers **Teamgeist** and **Duly Noted**. Both will go novice hurdling with the latter being aimed at the mares-only series.

Finally, we come to our new boy. *CARL LLEWELLYN* took over from Mark Pitman and made an immediate impact when he trained and rode Run For Paddy to victory in the Scottish National at Ayr in April.

His team for his first full season is top-heavy with novice hurdlers, with **Roll Along** topping the list of potential winners.

Having claimed two bumpers last season, he has made all the right moves physically in the summer and seems to handle any ground.

Bradley Boy failed to win in bumpers last term, but Llewellyn is equally confident about his prospects over timber, observing that it should not be too long before he loses his maiden tag.

Nightfly was not beaten far despite finishing 14th in the Festival Bumper and has pleased his trainer with his progress, as has **Joyryder**, the winner of what looked a more than decent bumper at Newbury.

Rapallo is one of the unexposed types and is worth noting for both hurdles and fences, while **Little Rocker** is another dark horse likely to improve. He will be most effective on good ground.

On the chasing front, the pick of the novices may be **Snakebite**, an easy winner of a novice hurdle at Lingfield in December. He was placed on his remaining three starts and looks a cracking prospect.

Dempsey is the star chaser in the yard and Llewellyn will be looking to win a big handicap after his narrow defeat in the Victor Chandler at Sandown in February.

Berkshire's best

Keltic Bard
Roll Along
Trabolgan

The West by Hastings

THE crowning of *PAUL NICHOLLS* as champion jump trainer last season halted the remarkable 15-title reign of Martin Pipe. It also marked the end of an era with Pipe handing over the reins at Pond House to son David.

Given the enormous strength in depth housed at Nicholls' powerful Ditcheat yard, the recent shift in the balance of power looks like widening in the years to come.

Though 2004 Champion Chase hero Azertyuiop was sadly forced to retire this summer, Nicholls still has a host of top-class inmates, including a ready-made replacement for Azertyuiop in two-mile champion-elect **Kauto Star**, who's expected to more than pay his way at the highest level.

He was a smart hurdler in France and turned heads when beating Foreman on his British bow over fences. Injury subsequently denied him a run at Cheltenham that season, and a few niggling setbacks again held him up in the last campaign, but he still managed to highlight what an awesome prospect he is when fending off Ashley Brook in the Tingle Creek at Sandown, the pair drawing clear of a decent field.

Kauto Star was then made favourite for the Queen Mother Champion Chase, but lack of experience proved his downfall on just his fifth chase start and he crashed out early on before being put away to recuperate.

Stable vibes are positives that this exciting six-year-old can take all before him this winter before bagging the big one at Cheltenham in March.

Denman made giant strides as a novice hurdler for Nicholls last season and he can continue to climb the ladder as a chaser.

The six-year-old hails from an impressive jumping family and oozed quality when running away with the prestigious Challow Hurdle at Cheltenham on New Year's Day.

He also lost no caste in defeat when losing to the classy Nicanor in the SunAlliance at the Festival in March.

KAUTO STAR: the Nicholls camp have high hopes for the two-mile star

DENMAN: lost no caste in defeat to Nicanor (left) at Cheltenham in March

Nicholls sees Denman as a three mile chaser at his most effective with juice in the ground, so expect fireworks from him over birch in the months leading up to a tilt at the Royal & SunAlliance Chase.

Leading Arkle hope **Noland** capped a magnificent first season over hurdles with a last-gasp win over top-class subsequent winner Straw Bear in the Supreme at Cheltenham.

He showed class and fighting spirit to claw back a 7l deficit on the run from the last that day. Nicholls, though, has made no secret that he believes his rising star is a chaser through and through, so it will be a major disappointment if the five-year-old cannot continue the winning spree over the larger obstacles in the months to come.

Natal is another classy hurdler expected to make waves as a chaser this winter. He ran a cracker when sixth behind stablemate Noland in the Supreme and, despite idling in front, he signed off with a Grade 2 success at Aintree in April.

He possesses enormous scope for fences, and Nicholls rates him as an exciting prospect for the campaign ahead.

A 'darker' prospect over fences is **Pirate Flagship**, who's already schooled really well over the larger obstacles at his Somerset establishment.

He ranked highly as a hurdler, finishing a gallant fourth off a mark of 122 in the County Hurdle at the Cheltenham Festival and signing off with an easy win back at Prestbury Park the following month. He's sure to be well placed to gain some early confidence-boosting successes as a novice chaser before taking on the bigger guns.

Made In Montot could well be up to bagging a valuable handicap chase for Team Nicholls this season.

He was snapped up after impressively landing a hurdle race at Auteuil. There were plausible excuses for last year's flops in the Tolworth and again on his chase debut but, despite running fresh, he found the reserves to open the account for Nicholls in a small-field novice chase in April.

A subsequent wind operation should prove beneficial and he's one to keep on your side when the ground is decent.

Another bright prospect expected to defy the handicapper this term is **Nycteos**, who gave an indication of things to come when delivering a facile success in a beginners chase at Chepstow and rallied gamely to overcome a rating of 124 on a return to the Welsh venue soon after.

He was set a stiff assignment for the hat-trick bid in the Topham at Aintree and was found out by Bechers. Back over less daunting fences, he should soon regain the winning thread.

YES SIR: a star this summer and the exciting novice looks set for big things

Kicks For Free possesses ample speed to take the two mile hurdle sphere by storm this winter and he could well represent some value in the ante-post market for the Supreme Novices at Cheltenham.

He was mightily impressive when coasting to a couple of wins in Wincanton bumpers, so it came as no surprise to see him finish a gallant third when upped into the Champion Bumper at Cheltenham.

He showed no signs of those exertions when again making the podium behind Pangbourne in a similarly hot bumper at Aintree. Expect even greater heights to be scaled as a timber-topper this season.

Well Chief looks like being one of the main flagbearers for *DAVID PIPE* in his first season in charge at Nicholashayne. The 2004 Arkle hero, who was last seen beating Azertyuiop in last year's Celebration Chase at Sandown, is firmly on the comeback trail from injury and should enjoy a successful season.

Interesting Flat recruit **Scotland Yard** can win more than his share as a juvenile hurdler for Pipe this season.

He made pleasing progress with Mark Johnston during the summer and went to the sales soon after landing his second middle-distance handicap in impressive style at Ripon in July.

Now in the hands of Pipe, he was far from disgraced when third off a stiff mark at York

and will be well schooled for the almost inevitable switch to hurdles.

PHILIP HOBBS has much to look forward to this winter, not least from the star **Detroit City**. The awesome grey was useful on the Flat and quickly developed into one of the top juveniles around, proving in a different league to the rest in the Triumph Hurdle and showing similar distain for his rivals in a strong Grade One at Aintree.

Stamina wasn't an issue on the level and, with that in mind, he could well emerge as a leading contender for the World Hurdle in March, although the Champion Hurdle remains a strong possibility.

Hobbs' Withycombe base in Somerset looks sure to enjoy plenty of success from the emerging talent **French Saulaie**.

He was bought after showing placed promise over hurdles in Southern France and, although the plan was to rough him off until fully ready in the autumn, connections found a suitable opening at Worcester in May, when he was never off the bridle in drawing well clear of his rivals.

Soft ground is the key to this promising type and, when conditions are conducive, he could well rack up a sequence in novice company.

Hobbs' highly progressive **Noble Request** can continue on the upgrade for some time to come. The five-year-old grey hasn't looked back since easily landing a Wincanton handicap hurdle in February.

Subsequent seconds in hot handicaps at Cheltenham and Aintree read really well and he highlighted his rate of improvement with successive defeats of Faasel at Sandown and Ayr.

Though he'll be rated too highly for handicaps this term, there'll be plenty of opportunities for him in graded races.

Although *PAUL BLOCKLEY* is best known for his exploits on the level, he appears to have a smart hurdler to look forward to by the name of **Is It Me**.

The Newport handler's rising star has thrived over timber since landing an ordinary Flat handicap in July. He showed off a high cruising speed and ability to jump when delivering demolition jobs at Stratford, Bangor, Sedgefield and Market Rasen over the summer and, with those positive experiences to draw upon, he can make light of the stronger opposition he'll face during winter months, hopefully culminating in a strong challenge for the Triumph.

PETER BOWEN made hay while the sun shone over the summer and his thriving Pembrokeshire yard looks sure to continue hitting the headlines courtesy of the vastly improved win-machine **Yes Sir**.

The seven-year-old has taken all before him since May, including a ready win in the valuable Summer Plate at Market Rasen.

He was even more impressive when making all and finishing in splendid isolation at Newton Abbot next time and can continue to further exploit his novice status over fences.

It's been far from plain sailing for *JONJO O'NEILL* since arriving at Jackdaws Castle, so it was pleasing to see him notch his first ton in a season there last term.

With the likes of world-beater **Black Jack Ketchum** to go to war with, he looks sure to repeat the feat this campaign.

The unbeaten stayer will be hard to oppose when he makes his eagerly-awaited reappearance.

Best of the West

Black Jack Ketchum
Kauto Star
Yes Sir

NOBLE REQUEST: leading Faasel over the final flight at Sandown

The North
by Borderer

NICKY RICHARDS has few peers when it comes to assessing the Northern jumping scene. The glory days at Greystoke are returning and they are due in no small part to **Monet's Garden**.

The dashing grey was a high-class staying hurdler and he has looked potentially even better over fences, finishing a highly creditable second to Voy Por Ustedes in the Arkle at Cheltenham in March.

He may not have been at his very best when making heavy weather of winning the Future Champions Novice Chase at Ayr in April but it was still mission accomplished.

Borderer has visited Richards during the summer and in all likelihood Monet's Garden will start his season at Ayr towards the end

of November, followed hopefully by a trip to Kempton for the King George on Boxing Day.

A decision will then be made whether to stay at three miles and aim towards the Gold Cup or revert back in distance. Regardless of the decision, the eight-year-old is a fine prospect.

Also a horse to follow from the Richards camp is **Money Trix**, who embarks on a chasing career and looks set for stardom.

A bloodless winner of his novice hurdles at Kelso and Ayr, he ran the race of his life when separating Black Jack Ketchum and Neptune Collonges at Aintree.

Yet another grey, the six-year-old could end up competing in the Royal & SunAlliance Chase, as he is considered a top-class recruit

MONET'S GARDEN: can bring the glory days back to Greystoke

Sponsored by Stan James

TURPIN GREEN: exuberant chaser with buckets of talent at his disposal

to fences.

Others to keep an eye on from the same stable are **According To John** and **Harmony Brig** who will also be jumping fences in public for the first time. Both look the types to run up a sequence in the North before contemplating something bigger.

Turpin Green is being aimed at the Hennessy Gold Cup following his good second to Star de Mohaison at Aintree.

Trevor Hemmings' charge is the type to improve with age as he attempts to erase the memories of his Sandown debacle when he looked set to score in the Grade One Scilly Isles Chase only to all but refuse at the last.

He undoubtedly possesses talent and, once his exuberance has been harnessed, a big prize awaits.

Finally, keep an eye out for Kelso bumper winner **Watch My Back** and one of many new recruits from Ireland, **Ransboro**, who was bought for 140,000gns out of Charlie Swan's yard at the Doncaster May Sales.

HOWARD JOHNSON has been busy during the summer buying new stock and he paid out 500,000gns for **Bleak House** and **Tidal Bay** at the Doncaster Sales.

The former was a Haydock bumper winner for Tom Tate, while the latter was runner-up in both his starts, including the Aintree bumper behind Pangbourne for Alaistair Charlton. Both look set for lucrative campaigns over hurdles this winter.

White Lea Farm is blessed with some exceptional talent and there is every reason to think we didn't see the best of **Bewley's Berry** last season.

The former Irish pointer looked so impressive on his chasing bow at Wetherby in November but, despite being placed in the Feltham Chase at Sandown on Boxing Day, he never quite looked the same horse thereafter.

He may prove leniently treated off a mark of 140 and can capture a good staying prize at some stage during the winter.

Hard Act To Follow and **Lennon** look other interesting prospects who will be going novice chasing this season.

The former stays particularly well and has the look of a chaser, while Lennon showed glimpses of what he could do over hurdles last year and, once again, should prove better over fences.

FERDY MURPHY was quick to acquire the services of Graham Lee once he became available and the pair must be looking forward to seeing **L'Antartique** jump fences.

The ex-Tony Mullins gelding was a winner at Haydock and Doncaster over hurdles but then split a joint at Wetherby in February and wasn't seen again. Back to full fitness, the West Witton trainer feels he could go all the way over the larger obstacles.

The six-year-old is ably backed up in the novice chase division by the mud-loving **Nine De Sivola** and **King of Confusion**.

Both appear set to be even better chasing than they were over timber. The last-named is a big, tall, rangy individual who recorded two effortless wins at Kelso during the first half of last season.

The most exciting novice hurdle prospect at Wynbury Stables is the once-raced **Supreme Builder**.

Seventh in the Grade One Championship bumper at the Punchestown Festival on his debut behind the unbeaten Leading Run, he has always shown a lot of ability at home according to his trainer and hopes are high that he will prove good enough to contest one of the Cheltenham Festival novices in March.

Amongst the more established ranks, **Joes Edge** ran a terrific race in last season's Grand National and, granted better ground, Murphy feels he is the one they will all have to beat with another year's experience behind him.

He is expected to head to Cheltenham's Paddy Power meeting in November for a tilt at the 3m3f handicap chase before being geared towards a return visit to Liverpool.

New Alco is another who ought to pay his way in staying handicap chases. A bold jumper who originated in France, he was a winner at Sedgefield over the Festive period before running some decent races in defeat.

SUE SMITH has been looking forward to the day **Patriarch Express** goes over fences for some time now and, following an injury which curtailed his season last term, the eight-year-old will now try his hand in novice chases.

A smart staying hurdler, he is arguably at

L'ANTARTIQUE: could be even better when switched to fences this year

Sponsored by Stan James

KADOUNT (far side): needs his enthusiasm rekindling by Len Lungo

his best over two and a half miles despite winning the Cleeve Hurdle at Cheltenham over three miles the previous season. A fine jumper, he will take some stopping in the North this winter and looks very much one to follow.

LEN LUNGO may not have the same firepower as the likes of Messrs Richards and Johnson but he is particularly keen on novice hurdler **The Pious Prince**.

An easy winner of his only start at Ayr, he was bought back at the Doncaster Sales to stay in the yard and reportedly ranks highly with all Lungo's previous bumper winners.

Keith Mercer, the new stable jockey at Carrutherstown, will also be aboard a new addition to the yard in **Kadount**.

A useful novice chaser for Alan King, he rather lost his way last season and has since joined Lungo. It will be fascinating to see if he can rekindle the gelding's enthusiasm.

DONALD MCCAIN JNR is a man rapidly making a name for himself and he is very enthusiastic about the campaign ahead with **Cloudy Lane**.

Another Trevor Hemmings horse, Cloudy Lane is considered a super prospect for novice chasing. He was a four-time winner over hurdles, including the final of the Fixed Brush Hurdle Series at Haydock in the spring, and he could be even better over fences.

That comment also applies to **Regal Heights,** who won in heavy ground at Carlisle before going on to tackle the likes of Senorita Rumbalita at Sandown.

Also, keep an eye out for a new recruit from France in the shape of **Maurice**. A six-year-old by Video Rock, he has some excellent form over fences but may well start the season over hurdles and has a big future.

The South
by Southerner

DOWN in deepest Sussex at the end of September a handsome bear emerged from his summer hibernation and began limbering up in readiness to gatecrash a party that has been exclusively reserved for Irish guests in recent years.

Six of the last eight Champion Hurdles have been won by runners trained in Ireland, and Irish dominance has become so complete in the Cheltenham feature that no horse trained outside of the Emerald Isle has even managed to finish in the first four in the two most recent renewals.

However, Findon trainer *NICK GIFFORD*'s **Straw Bear** made a tremendous impression during his first jumping campaign and he starts the new season as a genuine contender to break the Irish stranglehold on the hurdling crown.

The chestnut opened his account over timber at the first time of asking on a cold wet day at Leicester last January when carrying Tony McCoy to a smooth success in a well-contested two mile novice that produced several future winners, including Acambo.

McCoy was impressed and, though he tried not to get over-excited, Gifford couldn't hide his delight either.

Following another comfortable victory at Folkestone at the end of January, Straw Bear lined up for the Supreme at Cheltenham in March. Always prominent before moving into the lead two out, he looked the winner when jumping the last with a 3l advantage but he stumbled badly on landing and lost virtually all forward momentum.

He rallied in the bravest fashion but Noland, who produced a strong run up the hill, was a neck in front of him at the line.

The five-year-old regained winning ways three weeks later at the Grand National meeting at Aintree, cruising home 13l clear of the very smart Conna Castle, and though beaten into second by Iktitaf at Punchestown on his final start, there was no disgrace that day in losing to a very highly-regarded horse

STRAW BEAR: gets in too close to the last at Cheltenham in March

Sponsored by Stan James

who had missed Cheltenham and Aintree and therefore arrived by far the fresher.

Straw Bear is at his best on soft ground and there is the possibility he may not get his ideal going at the quick-draining Prestbury Park in March.

However, after the horrific casualty toll at the last Festival, Cheltenham management will surely ensure that this year's Festival gets underway on safe, easy ground and the Champion Hurdle is always run on the first day of the meeting.

While ante-post betting on a jumps race so far in advance of the event is a pretty risky business, the 14-1 available at the time of writing about Straw Bear becoming the new champ is very attractive.

He will be lightly raced this winter with probably just two – certainly no more than three – runs, before the real test in the spring. If all goes well he is sure to be much shorter on the day.

Straw Bear's association with McCoy is also likely to be maintained, given he is owned by JP McManus, meaning the reigning champion Brave Inca will be without the jockey so instrumental in his success.

Gifford could easily have more than one serious challenger for Cheltenham glory next March as the SunAlliance Chase has already been pencilled in as the long-term target for **Killaghy Castle**, who hails from the family of Gold Cup heroine Glencaraig Lady.

The good-looking gelding was clear when falling at the final flight on his debut in a 2m6f maiden hurdle at Stratford last October and made amends three weeks later when readily beating the useful pair Snakebite and Glasker Mill over 2m2f at Folkestone.

He was suffering from a splint problem when third at Chepstow in October but got back on the winning trail on his last outing of the term, landing the valuable 2m4f Sunderlands Novices Handicap Hurdle Final at Sandown in March.

Russian Around, who was not seen out last season after making a winning debut in a two mile novice hurdle at Wincanton in October and is far less exposed than his illustrious stable-companions, has the potential to be of a similarly high standard.

The rangy chestnut stayed on strongly to catch the outsider Missly close home at the Somerset course.

KILLAGHY CASTLE: wins at Sandown

The runner-up didn't do much to advertise the form subsequently, yet the third was the aforementioned Noland.

Shaka's Pearl has always been considered a chaser in the making by Gifford but he still managed to win on his second start over timber at Towcester.

He returned to the same venue for his fencing debut in May and again showed his liking for the stiff circuit, just failing by a length and a half to give the much more experienced Schoolhouse Walk 28lb.

The six-year-old was put away afterwards to strengthen up over the summer and he should be more than capable of picking up races over the larger obstacles this term.

Wee Robbie and **Witness Run** are others who may have a future over fences.

The first-named won a bumper at Plumpton on his debut at the start of last year and he got off the mark over hurdles at the third time of asking in a 2m3f novice at Newbury last December, while the lightly-raced Witness Run won a 2m novice at Towcester in March.

Gifford also has several nice types for novice hurdles this season.

Mr Nick, who came off worse in a three-way photo for a very competitive Cheltenham bumper on his racecourse bow last October, is well worth watching out for when he begins his career over timber.

Cathedral Rock and **Push The Port** also showed plenty of promise to finish in the frame on their sole outings in bumpers last term.

In 2001 *GARY MOORE* saddled 181 National Hunt runners. In 2005 the number had gone up to 452, a growing total that is testament to the Brighton trainer's success and the resultant popularity with owners.

From a punting point of view, it is interesting to note that Moore has managed to maintain his strike-rate over jumps during this increase in activity at a very creditable 14%, with more than 20% at both Plumpton and Fontwell.

Moore first schooled **Cold Turkey** over hurdles more than three years ago but the gelding was going great guns on the Flat and he didn't make his jumping bow until last November when he got up on the line to beat Kings Signal by a head in a slowly-run two mile event at Plumpton.

He had just one more outing last term at Fakenham in January when, after pulling hard in another race run at a modest gallop, he finishing a slightly disappointing third to Dance World over two miles.

Cold Turkey is at his best on the level when held up for a late run off a strong pace and is likely to show much improved form over jumps when those tactics can be employed. He is just the type to pick up a valuable handicap hurdle this winter.

Verasi collected over £28,000 for winning the 2m Listed William Hill Handicap Hurdle and very nearly added another £34,000-plus when a fast-finishing third, beaten a neck and half a length, behind Victram and stablemate **Dusky Warbler** in the Sunderlands Imperial Cup over the same course and distance in March.

Just four days later he finished a highly creditable fifth to Sky's The Limit in the 2m5f

Coral Cup at Cheltenham, staying on great guns up the hill to suggest three miles should be within his compass this season.

Dusky Warbler has proven a frustrating character over the years and, while his second in the Imperial Cup confirms he retains a great deal of talent, he is not one to get stuck into at a short price. He's far more likely to finish in the frame at good odds in a race where his chances are less obvious.

Heathcote, on the other hand, is the ideal type to follow. He was very consistent and did exceptionally well in his first season over sticks, winning three times and just failing by three-quarters of a length to give the well-regarded Onnix 11lb in a bog at Lingfield in January. Heathcote relishes easy ground and there should be plenty of paydays for him this winter.

Mr Boo was developing into a smart fencer in the spring, looking set for a four-timer until falling two out at Sandown in April. He was a decent hurdler last year and could be given a spin over timber for his confidence before resuming his promising chasing career.

DINA SMITH should be able to pick up a handicap hurdle or two with **Spear Thistle**, whose best run was a second to Sole Agent in a 2m1f maiden hurdle at Folkestone in January. The Pulborough trainer does very well with her small string and her horses are particularly worth noting when there is market support for them.

SUZY SMITH is another who does exceptionally well with limited resources.

The Lewes handler rightly earned great praise for bringing back **Golden Bay** from serious injury to land her seasonal bow at Fontwell in late January. The seven-year-old went on to win a Listed handicap at Cheltenham in April, showing great courage in a pulsating finish up the hill.

Smith also excelled with another ex-invalid, the one-eyed **Material World**, who finished third in the 2m6f totescoop6 Sandown Hurdle on her comeback in February, won the Blue Square Handicap Hurdle at Wincanton two weeks later and chased home the very smart Refinement in the 3m110yds Listed John Smith's Extra Cold Handicap Hurdle at Aintree in April on her third and final outing last term.

Material World is a wonderfully game mare, finishing out of the frame only once in 14 starts and is always worth considering.

Southern stars

Cold Turkey
Material World
Straw Bear

Sponsored by Stan James

Midlands by John Bull

Last season was a vintage one for Midlands jump racing, with the region's runners making an impact at many of the top meetings.

HENRY DALY led the way in terms of prize money, with his total of 35 winners two up on the previous year, and **Mighty Man**, who won two of his six starts, was the ace in the pack.

Despite wins at Cheltenham's December meeting and the Aintree Festival, the season could – and should – have witnessed even more glory for the French-bred gelding. At Cheltenham in January and at Sandown a month later, jockey Richard Johnson gave his mount far too much to do, although on the latter occasion his cause was not helped by being caught for room on the inside rail turning for home.

At the age of six, there's likely to be further improvement to come from this gutsy performer and another profitable season over hurdles looks on the cards.

In the chasing division, Daly's **Green Tango** is set to continue his ascent up the ladder. Beaten by Racing Demon and Cornish Sett in hot novice events at the start of last season, he won at Hereford (2m3f) and Southwell (2m) before a respectable handicap debut when seventh in the ultra-competitive Grand Annual at the Cheltenham Festival.

At Aintree, a switch to front-running tactics failed to bring dividends, but he ran out a comfortable 2l winner over Coat of Honour on his last start at Perth.

Best when held up off a strong pace, the Greensmith gelding can prove a force in the leading two mile handicaps this winter, and given his great record at Newbury's Hennessy meeting (one win and a second place from two runs) a race like the Jim Joel Memorial Trophy on Hennessy Day could

MIGHTY MAN: set for a big year after this storming victory at Aintree

be an ideal early-season target.

Another Downton Hall inmate to keep close tabs on is **Opera de Coeur**. The winner of his only race in his native France, the four-year-old won his first three starts for Daly, all in novice hurdles, including when gamely defying a double penalty on good to soft ground at Stratford in March.

As impressive as those wins were, the French-bred's best performance was in defeat.

Taking a huge step up in class in the two mile Grade 1 novice race at Aintree in April, he was up with the leaders all the way to the third-last, travelling smoothly, before eventually finishing fourth.

Although his wins to date have been at distances of around two miles, it's clear that he'll get further, and while it might be premature to suggest this talented individual can emulate Mighty Man, there's no doubt he is going the right way.

PAUL WEBBER's total of 23 winners was three down on the previous campaign, but his strike-rate did improve from 13% to 15%.

For the second year running the Banbury handler came agonisingly close to success in the valuable Cheltenham Festival bumper, with **Pressgang** filling the runner-up berth occupied by stablemate **De Soto** 12 months earlier.

Inexperience was all that defeated him that day as he hung to his whip when asked for an effort by Tom Doyle, losing at least two lengths in the process (he was only beaten a head).

Earlier he had comfortably beaten a decent field at Newbury and the Festival form was upheld by Hairy Molly running the unbeaten Leading Run to half a length at Punchestown. "He's a class act and has everything going for him to allow him to get to the top," Webber says.

Don Castille was another successful bumper performer for Webber, quickening nicely to win at 50-1 on his third start at Stratford in March.

The Royal Anthem gelding was then handed a tough assignment at Punchestown but ran with great credit on ground Webber believes had dried out too much for him to be fully effective.

He has schooled very well over fences and could be very interesting with a weight allowance over the larger obstacles, especially

OPERA DE COEUR: wins at Warwick

when there's some cut in the ground.

Now, time for a question. Which jumps handler, who has had over 200 runners, has proved the most profitable to follow blindly over the last five years?

Paul Nicholls? Philip Hobbs? Think again. The answer is Nottinghamshire-based permit holder *CHARLES POGSON*.

A £1 level stake on all Pogson's runners would have brought you a whopping profit of £133.63, and if you had concentrated solely on his runners in bumpers the total would even higher – £155.25.

Pogson, assisted by wife Katie and jockey son Adam, looks set for another good season, having assembled what he believes to be his best ever team of horses.

"**Major Catch** is the one Adam says he is most excited about riding", Pogson told *John Bull*. "He won over hurdles for us, but now goes novice chasing. He stays well, gets three miles and likes soft ground."

Reel Missile, a dual winner over hurdles the season before last, could have won three times over fences but for novicey mistakes and should take some stopping when he gets his jumping together. However, he won't be out until around Christmas after putting his leg through a fence in the summer.

"We'll give him a couple of confidence boosters over hurdles before putting him back over fences. He's still very young and has time on his side," said Pogson.

Pogson's ability to bring about vast improvement in other trainers' cast-offs has been advertised again by **Lord Baskerville**.

Claimed for £6,000 having finished second in a seller at Hexham, the Wolfhound gelding won his first three starts for his new connections, rising 37lb in the handicap, before finishing a highly creditable seventh in the valuable Summer Hurdle at Market Rasen.

He has been given a break as Pogson feels he wasn't at his best then, but he will be back in November.

Emmasflora, meanwhile, is an exciting chasing prospect. She was a three-times winner last year over hurdles, and the way she was staying on when landing a 2m4f event at Sedgefield in March suggests she'll have no problems in staying three miles.

Pogson is also excited about the return to action of **Oscardeal** and **Ravenscar**, both of whom missed last season with injury and have subsequently been fired.

Oscardeal, a 9l bumper winner in 2005, will run over the brush hurdles at Haydock before being sent chasing, while Pogson reports that Ravenscar, who won twice and was placed seven times in his last full season, will be back over fences around November.

Finally, keep an eye out for new recruit **Bronson F'Sure**, a seven-year old dual point-to-point winner in Wales, who looks sure to pay his way for Pogson under Rules.

Regular RFO readers will know that *John Bull* is a big fan of Eastnor trainer *MATT SHEPPARD*, a man who can always be relied upon to get the very best out of whatever material he has at his disposal.

Sheppard recorded 11 wins last year, two of those victories achieved by **Moorlands Again**, who should again prove a profitable horse to follow in long-distance staying chases run on soft ground.

The 11-year-old prefers going left-handed and a race he won last December at Warwick by 17l – a 0-120 3m5f handicap chase at Warwick – is once again likely to be on the agenda.

Sheppard, like Charles Pogson, is a master of wringing improvement from horses which come to him from other yards.

San Marco (16-1), Young Tot (10-1), Precious Bane (9-2) and Rabbit (9-1) all won on their first start for him and a likely sort to follow in their footsteps is **La Marette**, whose current handicap mark of 90 Sheppard should be able to exploit.

Midlands magic

Green Tango
Major Catch
Simon

REEL MISSILE: may be one to follow once he sorts his jumping out

Newmarket by Aborigine

JAMES FANSHAWE is no stranger to Cheltenham Festival glory and his exciting young chaser **Reveillez** could develop into a serious challenger for the Gold Cup.

Fanshawe has hit the hallowed unsaddling enclosure with two Champion Hurdle winners in Royal Gait (1992) and Hors La Loi III (2002) and, though he is not given to over optimism, one feels he is very sweet about this progressive seven-year-old.

Reveillez was good enough to win both on the Flat and over hurdles but, because of his size, has always looked like achieving even more over the larger obstacles.

He confirmed this point of view last season when, after a couple of encouraging placed runs, he hacked up in a confidence-booster at Folkestone before his sights were raised, and Reveillez rounded his campaign off with a scintillating display to win the Jewson at the Festival.

The powerfully-built grey justified heavy market support in this valuable event and was ridden by the champion Tony McCoy.

Despite hitting the third-last, he was always travelling well within himself and coasted home by a length and a half from Copsale Lad, with the third home 9l behind them.

The great thing about Reveillez is his accurate, reliable jumping and, as he also possesses plenty of stamina, he could make the chasing stars from the bigger yards look to their laurels.

LUCY WADHAM has the largest number of jumpers in town and suggests that we should not abandon her Grade 1-winning mare **United**.

Bought in Germany, she had a tremendous first season at the Moulton Paddocks stables alongside the mighty Godolphin empire.

United rounded her unbeaten novice campaign off with a fine performance in beating the smart Strangely Brown by 12l in the Four-Year-Old Champion Hurdle at Punchestown.

Sadly she then badly injured a tendon and, though given plenty of time to recover, seemed to lack her former sparkle last sea-

son. It is too soon to write her off yet, though, and as she has thrived during a mid-summer break she could start exploiting her dropping handicap mark in 2m4f hurdles.

Fenix has been a great servant to Team Wadham having performed with credit in top handicap company, including when second to Martin Pipe hotpot Medison in the Imperial Cup a couple of seasons ago.

It was in that race in March that he finished only 16th to Victram but it turned out that he had picked up an injury and should be excused that defeat.

He has done well physically during his enforced rest and will resume in handicap hurdle company before going novice chasing and, as he jumps soundly, he could start making up for lost time in that new sphere.

Among the other Wadham horses it could pay to keep on the right side of novice hurdler **Chaim**.

This good-looking individual started off his career winning a bumper at 25-1 at Uttoxeter despite having shown very little in his work on the heath!

He was then seriously upped in class in the big Aintree Festival bumper and, though the race probably came too soon for him, he was a creditable tenth to Pangbourne.

As is always the case with the Wadham horses he has not been hurried and this patient approach should reap its reward this season.

The plan is to go for novice hurdles and, judged on the way he has been moving in his early-season work and schooling sessions on the Links, we will be hearing a lot more of him.

Regular readers will know how many good turns **The Dark Lord** has done us both over hurdles and fences.

Sadly he picked up an injury to his stifle, which had to be operated on earlier in the year. Though he will not be hurried back, the current prognosis is favourable and there are decent chases to be won with him off his current mark in the handicap.

On the novice chasing front **Victoria's**

70

REVEILLEZ: pictured en route to a scintillating win at the Festival

Gem could be the one to follow.

This huge gelding – 16.3 hands – started off over hurdles and, though not setting the Thames on fire, he managed to win a novice hurdle at Uttoxeter in March. His work up the Al Bahathri and the Cambridge Road Polytracks indicates that we will be hearing more of him.

Another Wadham hurdler currently on the easy list is **Ken's Dream**. Good enough to have run in a Listed race at Newmarket on the Flat, he had always shown plenty of ability up on the well-appointed Links schooling grounds.

After a couple of good efforts he translated his home form into a public win at Plumpton, where he beat Classic Role handsomely by eighteen lengths. His enforced break might be a blessing in disguise as he is being scheduled for a reappearance in the spring, when he will get the faster ground he needs.

I must also put in a good word for **King's Mill**, who won on the Flat for Neil Graham. He continued to show ability when moving to the Wadham yard, despite failing to add to previous successes, and amazingly the nine-year-old is still a novice. However, that should enable his skilful handler to find a winning opening for him before he continues to ply his trade in handicaps.

JAMES EUSTACE was delighted when Jeff Smith decided against selling his St Simon Stakes winner **Orcadian** and gave him the go-ahead to run over hurdles.

The move paid off last year with a win at Market Rasen and, given his inexperience, he then ran a cracker in the Supreme Hurdle, only fading late to finish 13th behind Noland.

He has thrived during the summer and could make even more of an impact over timber this winter, especially as he loves soft ground.

Former jump jockey *VINCE SMITH* has done well under both Rules since he retired from the saddle and he has his strongest jumping team to date.

The five-year-old mare **Sweet Serenade** is a winner on the Flat at Brighton and, though that was only in a seller, her work at home suggests there are races to be won with her over timber. Though no world-beater, **Boss Mak** looks another likely winner for this well run small yard, while **Capitalise** definitely has ability and should be able to pick up a race or two over hurdles.

JEFF PEARCE, another former jump jockey, has switched mainly to the Flat but keeps one or two jumpers on the go, including the promising **Felix Rex**.

After running a 100-1 debut third at Towcester, he did enough on his final start at Newbury to suggest that there are good races to won with him.

Among the novice hurdlers likely to make an impact there is a lot to like about **Southern Tide** and a couple of young Flat horses, **Cheveley Flyer** and **Simplified**, could also pay their way at their own level.

JULIA FEILDEN always keeps a jumper or two on the go in addition to her All-Weather team in the winter and previous winner **Dance World** still figures on a handy rating. This fluent jumper goes well for Matthew Smith and never be put off from backing a horse ridden by this highly capable amateur.

JONATHAN JAY rents a yard at Henry Cecil's Warren Place training complex and he has already been on the mark with **The Bonus King** in a novice hurdle.

Though exposed, he is a still a progressive individual who should add more wins to his capable trainer's sound CV.

PAUL HOWLING is another Cecil tenant at Warren Place and expects his up-and-coming staying chaser **Penalty Clause** and **Trackattack** to help him pay some of the rent for his landlord!

Irishman *DON CANTILLON* is a master of his art and regularly rides the massive **Goblin** out on the heath. From an early stage of proceedings Cantillon told me Goblin would make a chaser and, though yet to win, it should not be long before he puts matters to rights. It could also pay to keep on the right side of dual-purpose winner **Sharaab**.

JOHN BERRY does not intend to run his versatile multiple winner **Jack Dawson** over hurdles having nursed him back to health and got a win out of him on the Flat this summer. The astute Berry singled out another Flat winner, **My Obsession**, as a possible for the winter game, though he will have to prove he jumps well enough.

Hot off the Heath

Chaim
Ken's Dream
Reveillez

Sponsored by Stan James

Hunter chasers
by Nick Watts

THE simplest way of looking at hunter chasers for the season ahead is to look at the results of last season's two big races at Cheltenham and Aintree and work outwards from there.

Many of the main protagonists come back for more the following year, so at the risk of being unoriginal, there seems little reason not to look out for **Whyso Mayo** again after his heroics of last season.

He went into the Cheltenham Foxhunter an unconsidered 20-1 shot, but his best form entitled him to serious consideration and it was no surprise to see him win as he did.

On his previous run at Leopardstown in one of the most informative races of its type in Ireland, Whyso Mayo was running a crack-

er when unseating his rider three out. The race was won by General Montcalm with Harbour Pilot in second.

Had he stood up, Whyso Mayo would definitely have been in the frame, but next time out he managed to string together a great round of jumping at Prestbury Park to win the most prestigious prize of the lot.

He confirmed that was no fluke when triumphing again at the Punchestown Festival, and as he will only be ten next year, there is no reason to assume he will not be at the top of the tree again.

Bosham Mill could manage only tenth place at Cheltenham, but that was really the only blemish in an otherwise consistent campaign.

BOSHAM MILL: had a consistent campaign last season and is one to watch

CHRISTY BEAMISH (left): doing battle with Katarino at Aintree last season

He showed he had stamina in abundance when winning over 4m1f at Cheltenham's Hunter Chase meeting last May, and he could be considered slightly unfortunate not to finish better than fourth in the Horse And Hound Cup at Stratford afterwards.

An afternoon downpour put racing in jeopardy and turned the ground into a quagmire which didn't suit Bosham Mill, and he weakened close home.

However, he bounced back with a success at Newton Abbot under Rules in the summer, and as an eight-year-old, rising nine, he has plenty of time for another crack at the top races next season, always assuming he goes back hunter chasing.

The Aintree version was won for the second year by **Katarino**, who is making a habit of just turning up for the one race, and making off with it!

It would be a tremendous feat were he to do it again, but the one to take out of the race would be **Christy Beamish**, an honourable second.

His season finished on a slightly sour note when he fell at Stratford in the John Corbet Cup (beaten at the time), but it's probable he was feeling his previous Aintree exertions.

Earlier on in the season, he had looked pretty good when defeating Horse And Hound victor Knife Edge easily at Newbury and he is most definitely one to keep on the right side of.

Of the younger brigade, Enda Bolger's **General Striker** would easily be the pick.

Only six years of age, he strung together a consistent series of efforts in the latter half of last season.

He won two consecutive races at Fairyhouse, one in February and the other in April, when he beat Beachcomber Bay (third in the Aintree Fox Hunters') by two and a half lengths.

However, he saved his best performance for last when finishing a fine second behind the aforementioned Whyso Mayo in the Champion Hunter Chase at Punchestown.

A bad mistake four out probably ruined his winning chance in that event, but he stayed on to such effect that he was beaten only 2l at the line.

That margin may have flattered him

slightly, but there is no doubting his promise, nor the fact that he has struck up a fine rapport with Nina Carberry, one of the best riders around in this type of event.

At a more ordinary level, Steve Flook's **Beauchamp Oracle** finished last season in the form of his life and is one to bear in mind when the ground is riding on top.

He wouldn't be very effective on true winter ground so may not be seen until the spring, but it could be worth the wait.

His winning spree started at Exeter in April and continued through the Cheltenham May meeting on to Huntingdon, where he completed the hat-trick in good style.

Although often described as quirky in the past, he didn't appear to show that side of his nature during his treble and looked well on the way to becoming the sort of horse he promised to be during his younger days.

Finally, it's worth stating that, although betting in hunter chases isn't everyone's cup of tea, it would be silly to dismiss them from your agenda when considering a punt.

Lack of knowledge of both horse and rider is enough to put people off, but following a few basic principles can result in success.

Jockey's abilities can vary wildly in hunter chases, and the best riders are definitely worth a length or two.

Shock results are also surprisingly rare, and even in the Aintree Fox Hunters, you have to go back to Cavalero in 1998 for the last winner at a double-figure price, so sticking with the market leaders and current form, although an obvious thing to say, will narrow down the field considerably in hunter chases and result in increased success for you, the punter.

'There is no doubting his promise, or the fact that he has struck up a fine rapport with Nina Carberry, one of the best riders around in this type of event'

NINA CARBERRY: always worth watching out for in amateur rider events

AFTER several years spent on the sand, I will be going back to where I started out and concentrating on the jumping game this winter.

The bottom line reason for this is that I feel it will be more profitable, although there are several contributory factors.

I started betting on the All-Weather because there was one meeting a day and during the winter it meant I only had to open one page of the *Racing Post* to keep myself on top of things.

The situation is very different nowadays and, though I don't know the exact figures, I am pretty sure there will be as many All-Weather races run this winter as there are jumps races…and most of them will be contested by selling platers.

With the exception of a few meetings at Kempton and Lingfield most of the All-Weather cards are inconsequential and boring.

When I start to get bored of things I lose concentration and that is fatal, so I am hoping a fresh pair of eyes will help me to be enthused and on the ball for the winter jumping.

To give me a good start I have persuaded my mate Anthony Bromley to give me a list of horses I certainly need to take note of this winter and I pass them on to you.

TEN TO FOLLOW

1) MY WAY DE SOLZEN (A King)

He is the least original of picks, but there cannot be a more likely champion staying novice chaser than this horse. He already has a Cheltenham Festival victory under his belt and already at this stage the SunAlliance Chase betting is dominated by him and Paul Nicholls' Denman. It will be intriguing when they meet.

2) OFAREL D'AIRY (P Nicholls)

Runs In the Stewart family colours and, though only second on his English debut at Wincanton in May, lots more is expected of him. He is likely to exploit his four-year-old allowance over fences this season.

3) GRANIT JACK (P Nicholls)

He was one of the top four-year-old chasers in France last year and because of that he goes novice hurdling. He runs in the One Man colours and is expected to make the grade for John Hales who has sadly had to retire Azertyuiop.

4) NEW LITTLE BRIC (P Nicholls)

He was unbeaten in hurdle races at Pau last winter and is due to go novice chasing for Paul Nicholls this winter. He is very well regarded down at Ditcheat.

5) TARANIS (P Nicholls)

He was one of the easiest handicap winners of last winter when he spreadeagled a decent field at Cheltenham in April. He was probably a fresher horse than those he beat, but it was still impressive and his early-season target is the Paddy Power Gold Cup. He may not be a handicapper at all by the season's end.

6) FRENCH SAULAIE (P Hobbs)

Philip Hobbs is hopeful that impressive Worcester novice hurdle winner French Saulaie will make further progress this winter. He beat some well regarded types in that event last May, including an odds-on shot from the Paul Nicholls yard.

TEMOIN: could provide some fun for Mick Fitzgerald in his final season riding

7) MAURICE (D McCain Jnr)

Donald McCain has already shown signs of more than filling his father's footprints and Maurice is expected to further him along the way. Bought to win the Grand National for Trevor Hemmings, he will make his seasonal reappearance in one of the brush novice hurdles at Haydock as he is still a maiden over the smaller obstacles. He is only six, but has already been a smart handicap chaser at Auteuil, so the National is definitely not just a pipedream.

8) SWING BILL (H Knight)

He won two hurdles at Pau and Auteuil and as a result was snapped up by Henrietta Knight. He is expected to be one of the young stars of her stable this winter.

9) TEMOIN (N Henderson)

He was probably over the top when he went out very quickly at Aintree last time out but he had made a big impression when winning at Sandown and Newbury. He is expected to be one of Nicky Henderson's top novice chasers this winter.

10) URBAN TIGER (A King)

He is already being talked about as a leading Triumph Hurdle candidate at Alan King's and is expected to make a winning debut in one of the better juvenile events in mid-October.

Outlook

Morning Mole
by Steve Mellish

Let's get the show on the road!

2006 saw two new names on the trophies for the Champion Hurdle and Gold Cup, Brave Inca and War Of Attrition, two thoroughly deserving winners.

Both are young enough to come back and defend their crowns this season, but with several major contenders who missed Cheltenham through injury reportedly back – and a few new kids on the block due to take them on – it won't be easy.

Brave Inca would be no certainty to confirm placings with Macs Joy, who got his revenge the following month at Punchestown. When you add to the mix the likes of Harchibald and Feathard Lady – both absentees at Cheltenham – impressive youngster Detroit City, and dark horses such as Mephisto, Desert Quest and Wellbeing, it's hard not to get excited.

The chasers are the same. War Of Attrition was mighty impressive at the Festival, but 2005 winner Kicking King is due back.

Trabolgan could challenge and novices Star De Mohaison and Monet's Garden might develop into serious contenders. Just writing those names makes me look forward to March.

The vast majority of these horses are trained in Ireland and there's no question that that's where the power in jumps racing lies at present.

The Irish took three of the big four races at Cheltenham 2006: the Gold Cup, Champion Hurdle and Queen Mother, with only My Way De Solzen (pictured right) in the World Hurdle preventing a clean sweep.

Last season proved one too far for some great champions. Best Mate sadly died, Moscow Flyer and Baracouda saw their powers wane and were honourably retired, whilst even Hardy Eustace, who went down with all guns blazing in defence of his hurdling crown, showed signs of age.

It wasn't just with the horses that the pecking order changed. After several near misses, Paul Nicholls wrested the champion trainer's crown from Martin Pipe who, with dubious timing, announced his retirement the morning of Nicholls' coronation.

Pipe's son David takes over the reins at Pond House, but it will surely take an act of God for him, or anybody else, to stop Nicholls winning the title again.

It was a more familiar story with the jockeys. McCoy dominated, whilst Ruby Walsh popped over regularly from Ireland to remind us just what a class act he is.

But ultimately racing is about the horses. I've already mentioned a few of the stars likely to figure at the 2007 Festival, and now for five more who may pay our expenses to go and watch them.

MY WAY DE SOLZEN: British winner

Morning Mole's horses to follow

DENMAN
6yo chestnut gelding
11112-

Denman lost his unbeaten record in the Royal & Sun Alliance, but he didn't take the eye beforehand. He was dull in his coat and I'm sure he wasn't at his best. He jumped less fluently than usual and lacked his normal zip. The fact he still managed to finish second says much for his class.

In his previous four starts over hurdles he'd rarely looked in danger of defeat and his victory at Cheltenham on New Year's Day was the best performance put up by a novice all season.

Reportedly hurdles are now a thing of the past and he's to be sent novice chasing this season. A big, strong sort, he's just the sort to make a top recruit. It's not hard to see him turning up in one of the big novice chases at the next Festival once again defending an unbeaten record.

Paul Nicholls

FLASH CUMMINS
6yo bay/brown gelding
07203P-

Whereas Denman will be a popular choice in horses to follow lists, Flash Cummins is a darker one, but that won't stop him paying his way.

He joined the Pipe yard from Ireland and arrived with a big reputation, having impressed in points in his native land. He

hardly set the world alight in five hurdles and one chase, but he caught my eye more than once. He's seriously well handicapped over both codes and I expect he'll be placed to advantage before long.

David Pipe

MIGHTY MAN
6yo bay gelding
912231-

Black Jack Ketchum is the horse most people expect to dominate the staying hurdling division, and after his fantastic novice season it's easy to see why, but it would be foolish to dismiss the claims of Mighty Man.

The six-year-old appeared to fall just short of top class when third in this year's World Hurdle and the way he reversed placings with the winner at Aintree suggests he's still on the up.

He used to get upset before his races, but was pretty good at Aintree and could just be growing up.

Henry Daly

OVER THE CREEK
7yo brown gelding
11012/

This son of Over The River featured in my list in last year's annual, but injury prevented him seeing the track. He's reportedly fine again now and can make up for lost time.

As a hurdler he showed plenty of stamina and a good jumping technique, just the things needed in a staying novice chaser.

David Pipe

SKIPPERS BRIG
5yo bay gelding
2-

We saw this horse only once last season, when lining up in a decent bumper at Ayr on Scottish National Day.

The fact he started at 3-1 says much for his reputation and he went a long way to justifying it by finishing second.

He can't fail to take bumpers on this form, if Lungo chooses to go that route, but being from the family of Skippers Cleuch he's bred to jump and is just the type to run up a sequence in northern novice hurdles.

Len Lungo

OVER THE CREEK: One to follow

Sponsored by Stan James

Sponsored by Stan James

Time Test with Mark Nelson

Lacdoudal is a tempter

THE 2005/06 JUMPS season presented *Time Test* followers with a huge enigma. Just how good is **Black Jack Ketchum**?

Unbeaten in two bumpers, the Jonjo O'Neill-trained gelding went on to rack up a sequence of five victories in as many starts over hurdles, ending the campaign with a Grade One success at Aintree.

Last year's novice hurdler of the year is currently the shortest price of all the ante-post favourites for Cheltenham 2007.

So, is the answer to the question 'exceptional'? Very possibly yes but, in all five outings over hurdles, he has yet to record a speed figure in excess of 48. When you consider Inglis Drever is rated 81 on my figures, you begin to realise the gulf from top novice to champion stayer is huge.

It's not that Black Jack Ketchum is slow, it's just that he's not had to come out of second gear to win convincingly on each start to date. We've simply not seen what the sev-en-year-old is capable of.

The plan at the time of writing is for Jonjo's star to reappear in Wetherby's West Yorkshire Hurdle at the end of October, the same race won by Inglis Drever last year.

That contest can't come soon enough for clockwatchers as we will hopefully find out if the beast has an engine to match the hype.

With Moscow Flyer retired, the Champion Chase crown is very much up for grabs.

Last year's victor **Newmill** won impressively but the winning time was only fair with the winner rated over 10lb below Moscow Flyer's success the year before.

I doubt whether the Irish-trained gelding will have enough improvement in him to see off a serious challenge for the crown.

If **Well Chief** returns from the sidelines in the same form he showed when landing the Victor Chandler Chase in 2005, then he's the one the others have to beat.

He clocked a great time under a welter

BLACK JACK KETCHUM (nearside): just how good is Jonjo O'Neill's stayer?

burden and found only Moscow Flyer too good in the subsequent Champion Chase in the same year.

Last year's Arkle winner **Voy Por Ustedes** also has sound claims to the crown.

He is a spectacular jumper and, although rated below both Newmill and Well Chief on my figures, should have more to offer in his second season over fences and may be capable of improving past the pair.

Second-season hurdlers tend not to progress so well, so it will be interesting to see how **Detroit City** fares this term.

The 2006 Triumph Hurdle winner managed to win four of his five starts around the minimum trip last season, despite looking in

Last season's top chasers

	Horse	Speed rating	Distance in furlongs	Going	Track	Date achieved
1	Ollie Magern	86	25	Sf	Wetherby	Oct 29 2005
2	War Of Attrition	84	26	Gd	Cheltenham	Mar 17 2006
3	Kingscliff	82	24	Gs	Haydock	Nov 19 2005
4	Kicking King	81	24	Gd	Sandown	Dec 26 2005
4	Newmill	81	16	Gd	Cheltenham	Mar 15 2006
6	Hi Cloy	80	17	Ys	Leopardstown	Dec 27 2005
6	Monkerhostin	80	24	Gd	Sandown	Dec 26 2005
8	Beef Or Salmon	79	24	Gs	Haydock	Nov 19 2005
8	Central House	79	16	Yd	Punchestown	Feb 5 2006
8	Hedgehunter	79	26	Gd	Cheltenham	Mar 17 2006
8	L'Ami	79	24	Sf	Sandown	Feb 25 2006
8	Our Vic	79	20	Hy	Lingfield	Feb 18 2006
13	Fota Island	78	17	Ys	Leopardstown	Dec 27 2005
13	Impek	78	20	Gd	Huntingdon	Nov 19 2005
15	Darkness	77	25	Gs	Cheltenham	Dec 9 2005

Last season's top hurdlers

	horse	speed rating	distance in furlongs	going	track	date achieved
1	Brave Inca	89	16	Gd	Cheltenham	Mar 14 2006
2	Harchibald	88	16	Gs	Cheltenham	Dec 10 2005
3	Macs Joy	87	16	Gd	Cheltenham	Mar 14 2006
4	Hardy Eustace	82	16	Gd	Cheltenham	Mar 14 2006
5	Inglis Drever	81	24	Gd	Newbury	Nov 26 2005
6	My Way De Solzen	80	24	Gd	Cheltenham	Mar 16 2006
6	Golden Cross	80	24	Gd	Cheltenham	Mar 16 2006
8	Baracouda	78	24	Gd	Newbury	Nov 26 2005
9	Asian Maze	77	20	Gs	Aintree	Apr 8 2006
9	Feathard Lady	77	16	Gs	Sandown	Dec 26 2005
11	Al Eile	76	16	Gd	Cheltenham	Mar 14 2006
11	Arcalis	76	16	Gd	Cheltenham	Mar 14 2006
11	Briareus	76	16	Gs	Wincanton	Feb 18 2006
11	Intersky Falcon	76	16	Gd	Wincanton	Nov 15 2005
15	Crystal D'Ainay	74	24	Gd	Newbury	Nov 26 2005
15	Newmill	74	16	Sf	Leopardstown	Dec 29 2005

need of further.

Although quoted in the ante-post lists for the Champion Hurdle, I think he will find the current band of two-mile specialists too quick.

Current champion **Brave Inca** finished runner-up to Hardy Eustace in 2005 and posted an 8lb better figure on my numbers when landing the spoils last season.

That's as good as any winner in the last five years and the current band of top-class two-milers are exactly that.

I have Brave Inca 2lb above his Punchestown conqueror **Macs Joy** and 1lb ahead of **Harchibald**, who needs to prove he retains his ability after injury. Either way, it's hard to see the 2007 Champion Hurdle going anywhere other than Ireland.

That may not be the case with the Gold Cup, though, as **Monet's Garden** looks an exceptional second-season chaser and I'm hoping connections take the staying route as opposed to the Queen Mother.

The Nicky Richards-trained grey got tapped for toe at a vital stage when beaten by Voy Por Ustedes in the Arkle, but jumped very well and had the remainder well held.

Longer distances should be his game this term and the King George is likely to be his early-season aim. Success in that event may convince connections to go for gold and, having already clocked a figure of 75 in his novice season, it shouldn't be outside his grasp as he continues to progress.

Current champion **War Of Attrition** sets the standard. His rating of 85 was a decent Gold Cup performance, within 5lb of Best Mate at his best.

That said, I had Kicking King on a figure of 86 when he won in 2005 and if Tom Taaffe's chaser can make the return from injury, it would spice up the division even more.

It's hard to analyse the Grand National because my ratings are weight-dependent.

Whilst last year's top three, **Numbersixvalverde**, **Hedgehunter** and **Clan Royal**, are all likely to be trained for a repeat bid, I find it hard to enthuse over their chances.

They're likely to be high enough in the handicap judged on their past efforts and I'd prefer to locate a less exposed runner on the off-chance he'll take to the circuit at more rewarding odds.

Lacdoudal is only small but has an engine and allayed stamina doubts when winning the Betfred Gold Cup over 3m5f on his final start of last season's campaign.

The Philip Hobbs-trained gelding is fast and clean at his obstacles and strikes me as the type to take well to the fences.

Soft ground wouldn't be ideal but, if he turns up fit and well on the day, you can expect this likeable grey to be well supported. Current quotes around the 33-1 mark would then look very appealing.

2005-2006
review

Outlook

That was the year that was
2005-2006 by Richard Williams

September

11   It's the time of year when trainers stage their public open days. Henrietta Knight parades Best Mate, who looks in excellent shape. Following the retirement of Jim Culloty, he is set to be ridden by Timmy Murphy or Tony McCoy. In Lambourn Mark Pitman and his new assistant Carl Llewellyn co-host the annual owners' open day at the famous Weathercock House, where Pitman's mother Jenny had so much success. Pitman's future is of more interest than the horses because he plans to be away a lot in Spain. He has, in his own words, some "family issues" there. He denies stories that he is being eased out, in favour of Llewellyn, by the stable's owner Malcolm Denmark. "That's rubbish," says Pitman. Denmark says: "I want the best for Mark. If he can sort out his issues, that will be the ideal solution for both of us." All of which brings to mind Shakespeare's play Hamlet, in which Marcellus says: "Something is rotten in the state of Denmark."

22   Prize-money for the Gold Cup and Champion Hurdle is increased for the first time in three years. The Gold Cup will be worth £400,000 as against the 2005 pot of £350,000. The hurdling crown is to carry £340,000 from £300,000.

28   An early setback for Paul Nicholls as Strong Flow is retired. He was a brilliant winner of the 2003 Hennessy Gold Cup but never really recovered from an injury in the Feltham.

29   The Jockey Club decides to strengthen the existing rules with respect to remounting rather than impose the outright ban called for by its own veterinary committee and some welfare organisations. The Club's regulatory board considered a ban would be "using a sledgehammer to crack a nut and was confident the welfare of the horse would remain at the forefront of owners', trainers' and jockeys' minds."

October

7   Europe's largest betting and gaming company is created when Coral Eurobet is bought by Gala, the bingo operator. The group already has 1,267 betting shops. It is the third time in seven years that Coral bookmakers have changed hands. The company was started by Polish-born Joseph Kagarlitski who, at the age of 20, used to take bets in a London billiards club.

8   Now it's Willie Mullins' turn to have a setback. His Rule Supreme is ruled out for the season with a leg problem. The Royal

86

& SunAlliance Chase winner had been considered a Gold Cup contender. Kicking King shortens to 2-1.

9   Maskul, a horse bred by the Maktoum family at Shadwell Stud, lands his second Velka Pardubicka, the 4m2f race that is held in the Czech Republic. The event is marred by a fatal injury to Irish-trained Takagi. The Ferdy Murphy-trained Luzcadou is out the back when refusing six from home, the same fence at which he refused the year before. Maskul is ridden by German jockey Dirk Fuhrmann who says: "I thought my race was over when I had to jump over the fallen Registana. My only regret is that Peter Gehm could not be here to ride Registana because of his serious injury."

17   Be My Royal remains disqualified from the 2002 Hennessy Gold Cup when the High Court backs the Jockey Club against Willie Mullins in the continuing fight to have the horse restored to the winner's roll of honour. The judge orders the trainer to pay £35,000 in legal costs immediately, although the total costs are estimated at over £100,000, given that the club employs only top lawyers. Defeated but undaunted, Mullins is expected to go back to the High Court and ask the same judge to open the way for him to mount a private law breach of contract claim against the club. The race went to Gingembre, whose owner and trainer Lavinia Taylor surely deserves some sort of reward for her patience.

18   Totesport announce that they will sponsor the big Cheltenham handicap chase which traditionally takes place in the second week of December and they will name the race in memory of Robin Cook. Jumping was the former foreign secretary's great love.

29   Some see the start of the jumps season as May 1. Others believe it doesn't properly start until the Paddy Power meeting at Cheltenham. Others settle for the Charlie Hall Chase at Wetherby, which is won this year by Ollie Magern, trained by Nigel Twiston-Davies and ridden by Carl Llewellyn. Later that night the Irish Turf Club's office at the Curragh is burned to the ground.

November

1   Britain's best-loved horse Best Mate dies at Exeter while competing in the Haldon Gold Cup. He weakens seven from home and is pulled up three from home. Within a few minutes he collapses from a heart attack. Departing from her usual policy of hiding away when Best Mate races, trainer Henrietta Knight watches from the stands and is quickly by his side. Surprisingly, she maintains her cool throughout the tragedy and is able to talk to the press. "I was proud of the horse," she says. "He looked a picture and he was enjoying what he was doing. The whole country will miss him. For me, the best moment was his third Gold Cup. Everyone said he couldn't do it but he did." Best Mate won three Cheltenham Gold Cups, two Peterborough Chases and one King George VI.

5   Northern Ireland's highest-profile meeting of the year is abandoned after two races when a security alert forces the evacuation of Down Royal. The highlight was to be a clash between War Of Attrition and Beef Or Salmon in the James Nicholson Wine Merchant Champion Chase. The crowd is ushered into the centre of the course following telephone bomb warnings and there is an unsubstantiated rumour that the calls are from the Continuity IRA. Michael Hourigan, trainer of Beef Or Salmon, maintains continuity by deciding to run Beef Or Salmon the next day at Leopardstown.

8   A betting-mad financial consultant from Swansea is jailed for 12 years for stealing £10.3 million from the Halifax to fund his gambling habit. Graham Price, 58, also had shares in 14 horses with Brian Ellison and Jamie and Julian Poulton. Price spent approximately £1.7m on betting advice – telephone tipsters and the like. But all his troubles could have been avoided if he had only subscribed to the *Racing & Football Outlook*.

17   Haydock's Lancashire Chase is renamed the Betfair Chase and given Grade

1 status. This is a result of the BHB waiving its own guidelines and allowing the race to be run under the sole banner of its sponsor. William Hill, who sponsor the Tingle Creek Chase in December, are reported to have asked Sandown if they can change the name of the William Hill Tingle Creek Chase to the William Hill Chase. Sandown declines.

19   The inaugural Betfair Chase attracts the Gold Cup winner Kicking King but he has to play third fiddle to Kingscliff and Beef Or Salmon in a race run at a sound pace on Haydock's good to soft. Kicking King drifts to 4-1 from 2-1 for Cheltenham.

21   Around 600 thoroughbreds are believed to have been slaughtered in China during the last month as Beijing shuts down its racecourse and equine centre. The racecourse opened in 2002 and was of international standard. But the businessmen behind the operation are reported to have pulled the plug because of the Chinese government's refusal to legalise gambling.

25   "He's getting better with every run," says Robert Lester, owner of Iris's Gift before the grey's run at Newbury. Iris's Gift, third-favourite for the Gold Cup, is knocked out to 20-1 when he trails in behind Darkness in a Grade 2 race. The former Stayers' Hurdle winner finds his name back in the betting for the World Hurdle, though. William Hill quote him at 10-1.

26   One of racing's most enduring partnerships, Nicky Henderson and Mick Fitzgerald, enjoy Hennessy Gold Cup success with Trabolgan. It is the trainer's first win in the race and it's a special moment for the jockey too, as he has only just returned from injury having broken a bone in his neck in July. The last horse to carry topweight to victory was Burrough Hill Lad in 1984 and Trabolgan is the new favourite for the Gold Cup at 4-1 with Ladbrokes.

December

4   That amazing racemare Solerina wins her third Hatton's Grace Hurdle at Fairyhouse and among her victims is Brave Inca, one of the market leaders for the Champion Hurdle. Solerina pips Golden Cross, the mount of Johnny Murtagh, by a short-head with Brave Inca a length and a half behind. Solerina is trained by James Bowe, who also trained another front-runner, Limestone Lad, to win the Hatton's Grace three times, although not in successive years.

5   Chancellor Gordon Brown deals a blow to bookmakers in their dispute with betting exchanges by deciding against reforming the way betting exchanges are taxed. Alan Ross, managing director of Ladbrokes, says: "Betting exchanges are paying duty on commission so in effect they can determine their own tax. If they reduce commission they reduce the amount of tax they pay."

10   A great day for Irish trainer Noel Meade (and jockey Paul Carberry), who saddles Sir Oj to win the Robin Cook Memorial Chase at Cheltenham and Harchibald to win the Bula Hurdle. Harchibald is the horse who has flattered to deceive more times than a British tennis player. But his refusal to win the Champion Hurdle back in March is wiped from the mind as he strides purposefully up the hill. Meanwhile Solerina completes another hat-trick, this time in the Grade 2 Tara Hurdle at Navan.

15   All the pent-up frustration of 47 consecutive losers ends for Martin Pipe at Exeter when Lough Derg wins the beginners chase. "I don't think I've been on the cold trainers' list before but it's not that interesting a place to be," he says. Pointing to the No. 1 sign in the winners' enclosure, he asks: "What does that say over there? Am I in the right place?"

18   A blow is dealt to Kevin Bishop's small stable as Ashley Brook, the Champion Chase contender, is put on the sidelines with a knee problem.

19   The BBC's racing coverage of horseracing is squeezed further as the corporation hands over the Midlands Grand National to Channel 4. It was unable to offer Uttoxeter's owners, Northern Racing, any more than coverage of the big race itself, which is set to be run on March 18. As a

result, the BBC's racing output in the first three months of 2006 will be two days.

20   Jumps racing loses its second headline horse within seven weeks when 11-year-old Rooster Booster, the 2003 Champion Hurdle winner, collapses and dies on the gallops. He is struck down while preparing for the Christmas Hurdle. His victory at Cheltenham, when ridden by Richard Johnson, was one of the most emphatic ever. His trainer Philip Hobbs says: "At least he died doing what he enjoyed best."

22   Paddy Power have Paul Nicholls as 4-9 to wrest the trainer's title away from Martin Pipe, who is quoted at 13-8. The champion trainer is having a poor season by his own standards and is third in the prize-money totals behind Nicholls and Hobbs. It doesn't help that Over The Creek is ruled out for the rest of the season with a setback. This comes on top of one of Pipe's worst ever Decembers in which he has trained just two winners.

23   Shock news from Sandown where officials actually take sensible precautions against the threat of frost. They lay covers on the take-off and landing sides of the fences ahead of the Boxing Day meeting three days away. Clerk of the course Andrew Cooper says: "We will be using covers which spread over an area the equivalent of at least two football pitches, although covering the whole of both the hurdle and the chase track is not, as yet, a feasible option."

26   A thrilling finish to the King George VI Chase, which is held at Sandown this year because Kempton is being redeveloped. Kicking King holds off the determined challenge of Monkerhostin to prevail by a neck, winning the race for the second year running. The two big races both fall to Irish raiders with the Christmas Hurdle going to Feathard Lady, who is trained by Colm Murphy and ridden by Ruby Walsh. Her 12l victory forces bookmakers to slash her price for the Champion Hurdle from 20-1 to 7-1.

27   In one of the most extraordinary pieces of premature celebrations ever seen on a racecourse, Roger Loughran throws away victory on Central House in the Grade 1 Paddy Power Dial-A-Bet Chase at Leopardstown. Mistaking the location of the winning post, Loughran stands up in his stirrups, waves his whip in victory at the crowd and eases his mount down to half-speed only to watch in horror as Hi Cloy and Fota Island pass by him on either side with their jockeys still riding a finish. Loughran, who had turned professional the day before, was banned for 14 days but Central House's trainer Dessie Hughes shows loyalty: "Roger thought the piece of birch at the end of the running rail was the winning post. I feel sorry for him as he is the one who will suffer most. He gets the best tune out of Central House and he will keep the ride." It's doubtful whether the punters felt so benevolent.

January

2/3/4   Punters are on the wrong end of a Mexican treble as first Harchibald is ruled out of the Champion Hurdle by Noel Meade on the Sunday and then Kicking King is scratched from the Gold Cup on Monday. On Tuesday a scan reveals that Inglis Drever has a tendon strain and he won't be defending his World Hurdle crown. Tom Taaffe explains that the injury to Kicking King's near-fore may have come from his race at Sandown and the 11-8 Gold Cup favourite "definitely" won't be back this season. Taaffe is notably firm in his assertion given the farce of his 'withdrawal' from the

Gold Cup the season before. On that occasion Conor Clarkson, his owner, told the press on March 2 that "there is no way he is going to make it". Two weeks later he won the Gold Cup.

22   Paul Nicholls makes British racing history at Wincanton when he becomes the first trainer to have six winners on a card. In doing so he pulls further clear of Martin Pipe in the trainers' table to give him a lead of £433,884. The world record of eight is held by JC Williams at Waterford Park, West Virginia in 1979. Pipe hasn't been champion trainer 15 times for nothing, though. That

morning he reveals that he has 13 runners entered in the two big novice chases at Chel-tenham. That afternoon he has a double at Haydock.

February

1   Betfair say that they want their odds to be part of a new SP should any changes be recommended in an independent review of how starting prices are formed. Labour peer Lord Donoughue is leading the Starting Price Regulatory Commission and officials at the betting exchange are keen to meet with the SPRC and discuss the matter.

5   Roger Loughran makes no mistake this time on Central House as he drives his mount out all the way to the line to land the Tied Cottage Chase at Punchestown. Loughran punches the air in delight and relief as he crosses the finishing line and he returns to the winner's enclosure amid huge cheers from the crowd. All this on his first day back from serving a 14-day ban for his Leopardstown bloomer. It is Loughran's first win as a professional jockey and Central House is cut to 8-1 from 16-1 for the Champion Chase. Loughran says: "When I messed up at Leopardstown the public were very good to me and so were Central House's owners and the boss. All of that is just a blur now and I've put it all behind me."

6   After 37 years training horses and in his final season before handing over to his son Donald, Ginger McCain is getting the hang of the job. At Sedgefield he breaks his previous record of 23 winners with a double – and there are still three months of the season to go.

10/11/12 With two days to the Totesport Trophy at Newbury and the weather looking decidedly frosty, clerk of the course Richard Osgood covers up about three acres of the course which includes the take-off and landing sites as well as the run-in. The next day prospects improve and, although a 7.30am inspection is scheduled for Saturday, a measure of the public's confidence in the meeting taking place is the betting on Betfair where it is 2-5 racing receiving the go-ahead. On Saturday the meeting is called off amidst a row about the handling of the abandonment. There are four inspections altogether at 7.30am, 11am, noon and just before 1pm. At the final inspection, conditions are improving rapidly, and the sun is breaking through. But several jockeys advise that they still consider conditions dangerous. The unfortunate thing is that, according to Newbury's managing director Mark Kershaw, the track is raceable at 2pm, shortly after the first race was scheduled. Trainer Ferdy Murphy is unhappy and erupts: "There are no problems with the track whatsoever. The jockeys should not be allowed to make these decisions." He gives his Aon Chase outsider Joes Edge a canter on the track just to prove his point. Others think that Newbury was in a no-win situation with the English weather being so unpredictable. It was left to the Outlook's *Off The Bit* to bring some sanity to the situation. "Course executives can't just hang on and guess what the weather might do . . . One simple ruling would suffice . . . If the meeting isn't fit to race by midday (for example) call it off," we said. Newbury is also far from blame-free as we question the wisdom of partially watering the track several days before a big chill is forecast. "Sheer lunacy," says the column that counts.

15   Betfair contact the Racecourse Association with an offer to supply blankets that will cover the whole of the racing part of a racecourse in order to protect the ground from frost. The only surprise is that no-one has come up with the idea before.

For Dave Nevison's top ten horses to follow for this National Hunt season see pages 76-77

Sponsored by Stan James

March

1   Newbury breaks new ground (so to speak) by becoming the first racecourse in Britain to cover up the whole area of ground used for racing on. With overnight temperatures predicted to dip below freezing and a two-day meeting scheduled for Friday and Saturday, frost-beating protective covers are laid throughout Wednesday and Thursday. The inspiration comes from the farming industry and in particular Guy Roberts, a racehorse owner, who rallies some soft-fruit growers to source sufficient industrial fleeces, together with more than 2,000 sandbags. Newbury's managing director Mark Kershaw says: "The challenge will be to get the covers back down after racing on Friday before the temperature dips low enough for frost to set in. We'll be appealing to racegoers to stay on after racing to help ground staff with this mammoth task."

3, 4   Two days of racing at Newbury (thanks to the fleeces) and a great finish to the £100,000 Vodafone Gold Cup, in which Cornish Sett and Horus dead-heat leaving Paul Nicholls and Martin Pipe to share the prizemoney. They also share a handshake afterwards despite their well-known rivalry. The TV soap scriptwriters could not have penned a better series of storylines because Cornish Sett provides Ruby Walsh with a win on his comeback ride from injury and Horus is Jamie Moore's first winner for Pipe for eight months.

10   Punters from Ireland travelling to next week's Cheltenham Festival are warned that they could face problems if entering (or even leaving if they are successful) Britain with large amounts of cash. Customs officers have the power to confiscate any money over £5,000. "Seizures are on the increase," points out the head of business crime at a Manchester law firm. "Carrying large amounts of cash could create the impression that the money is intended for criminal use and innocent punters could get caught up. It's extremely difficult to get legal aid to fight for the return of seized monies," he warns.

13   On the eve of Cheltenham there is news on the future of Weathercock House Stables in Lambourn where Jenny Pitman and her son Mark have trained. Carl Llewellyn will take over the licence from Mark Pitman, who will act as assistant trainer and split his time between Spain and Lambourn. The 40-year-old Llewellyn will carry on riding (mainly his own horses and those of Nigel Twiston-Davies) but on a reduced scale. The highlights of Pitman's nine-year spell as a trainer were Monsignor's two wins at the Cheltenham Festival and Ever Blessed's Hennessy Gold Cup victory.

14   Tony McCoy, who is no stranger to the black clouds of depression when things aren't going his way, feels the sun breaking through at Cheltenham when winning the Champion Hurdle on Brave Inca. He had gone 32 Festival races without victory until driving the Irish horse home ahead of Macs Joy and he milks his moment of triumph in front of a huge crowd. Trainer Colm Murphy says: "Tony would ride if he had no arms and no legs and Brave Inca would do the same. They are a match made in heaven." It's a triumph, too, for the Irish, who fill the first three places in the race.

15   An eventful second day of the Cheltenham Festival with Irish horses (and jockeys) hogging the headlines. Their horses win four out of the six races and one of the home team winners is trained by the Irish-born Ferdy Murphy. But it is the announcement that Moscow Flyer is to be retired that has everybody talking. As the 12-year-old comes home fifth to Newmill in the Champion Chase, the decision is taken by owner Brian Kearney. The horse will not have the opportunity to add to his record of 19 wins, two of which were Champion Chases, which brought in over £1m of earnings. "The dream has finished," said Kearney wearing a long black coat that might have summed up his mood. "It's been a great eight years." His regular pilot Barry Geraghty says: "I owe such a lot to him. He's the best horse that I have ever ridden. He was such a leg-up for my career. You could just pull him out and away you'd go."

16   Cheltenham's third day is overshadowed by the deaths of five horses bringing the Festival total to seven. Officials stress that there is no obvious pattern to the fatalities, which include two trained by Jonjo

O'Neill. Managing director Edward Gillespie says: "We came into this meeting having lost no horses here this season in eight race days. All but one were associated with falls. The ground is not fast, it is good. There is no jar and even if we wanted to water we couldn't. It's a minus-two forecast." That evening the fearless bookmaker Freddie Williams returns to his hotel in Bibury with his daughter and her boyfriend when they are stopped by a group of masked men. They smash the windows with crowbars and grab Williams' cash from the boot. Earlier that day Williams had laid JP McManus a bet of £600,000 to £100,000 on Reveillez, the horse who won the Jewson Novices' Handicap Chase. A bad day at the office for Williams.

17   St Patrick's Day at Cheltenham on day four and how fitting that Ireland achieve a one-two-three in the Cheltenham Cold Cup with War Of Attrition beating Hedgehunter and Forget The Past. The winner is ridden by 39-year-old Conor O'Dwyer who had ridden Imperial Call to win the same race ten years earlier and had also ridden Hardy Eustace to win two Champion Hurdles when he was in his late thirties. "This is better than watching TV with someone else on them. I might leave it another year or two before taking up training." Form students might like to note that Brave Inca and War Of Attrition came first and second in the Supreme Novices' Hurdle of 2004. Best Mate and Kicking King were also runners-up in the same Cheltenham race. The first two home in 2006 were Noland and Straw Bear.

20   The post-mortem on the nine equine deaths at the Cheltenham Festival continues and the finger of blame points at the four-mile National Hunt Chase in which three of the fatalities occurred. Edward Gillespie says the race had become "more difficult to defend" and promises to have a good hard look at it. But the race is a favourite target of top trainers. Martin Pipe, Jonjo O'Neill and Willie Mullins were the trainers who suffered losses, which indicates that the race is one to be taken seriously. Could the attacks on this historic race just be knee-jerk reaction? Would there have been the same reaction if the Gold Cup had claimed three? In other Festival post-mortem news, it emerges that Derrick Smith's wife Gay was robbed of her jewellery within hours of seeing her colours carried to victory by Black Jack Ketchum in the Brit Insurance Novices' Hurdle. Smith, a partner in Coolmore, had been staying with his wife in the nearby prestigious Lygon Arms Hotel.

22   Ginger McCain, who already has Amberleigh House and Ebony Light entered for the Grand National, acquires a third string to his bow in Inca Trail, who is bought by John Halewood for 110,000gns at the sales. Inca Trail is Best Mate's full-brother and McCain, never short of a quote, says: "We'll have to be quick because the horse's form will deteriorate from now on, having left Paul to come to me." McCain is having by far his best season ever numerically with 31 winners on the board. What a shame he is retiring just when he seems to be getting the hang of the game.

30 Willie Mullins drops his private law breach of contract in respect of Be My Royal's disqualification from first place in the 2002 Hennessy Gold Cup and he is not seeking recovery of the prize-money. Instead, Mullins launches a civil case at the High Court, asking the judge to make a formal declaration that the horse was the rightful winner and the disqualification unlawful.

April

6   Martin Pipe wins the Betfair Bowl Chase with Celestial Gold on the first day of Aintree but concedes the trainers' title to Paul Nicholls. Pipe acknowledges the end of an era on his website with three weeks of the season to go. Pipe, who has won the title 15 times, including the last ten consecutive seasons, trails Nicholls by £744,485 at the start of the day, although he claws back £85,530 via Celestial Gold before Nicholls adds to his advantage with Natal's victory in the Mersey Novices Hurdle. Pipe writes: "I would like to be the first person to congratulate Paul Nicholls."

6,7 One of the sub-plots to the Aintree meeting is the barring of amateur jockey Sam Waley-Cohen from riding in the Grand National because he has not ridden 15 winners. He makes a mockery of the rule by landing the Fox Hunters on Katarino on Thursday and the next day he wins the Topham Chase on Liberthine – both over the National's spruce fences. Nicky Henderson, trainer of both horses, says: "I can see why the rule is there, but I think there should, perhaps, be some flexibility." The Topham is Waley-Cohen's fifth ride over the National fences. All got round and three won.

8 It's a one-two-four for the Irish in the Grand National, the big prize going to Numbersixvalverde, named after a holday villa in Portugal's Algarve. He is trained by Martin Brassil, who visited the course 26 years earlier and has never had a runner there until today. The jockey is Niall Madden, 20, nicknamed 'Slippers' because his father Niall Madden snr was nicknamed 'Boots'. Boots had advised Slippers to stay at the back on the first circuit, which is exactly what he did before coming to tackle Ruby Walsh and Tony McCoy on Hedgehunter and Clan Royal at the last fence. The result was a belter for the bookmakers, already quids in following a successful Cheltenham. They estimate that turnover on the National was £250,000,000 and that half the bets struck were for the two 5-1 joint-favourites Clan Royal and Hedgehunter.

13 Thanks to some lobbying from Aintree's management, there will be a four-week gap between Cheltenham and Aintree in 2007. The gap is usually two or three weeks.

22 Just two weeks after taking over the reins from Mark Pitman as trainer at Lambourn's Weathercock House, Carl Llewellyn sends out his first winner, Run For Paddy in no less a race than the Scottish Grand National. He rides it too. "I'm very grateful to Mark for leaving me with such a good team of horses," says the weighing room's 40-year-old senior jockey. This win adds nicely to his two Grand National winners (Party Politics and Earth Summit) and his Wesh National winner Bindaree. Meanwhile, the race for the Order of Merit is hotting up with Steve Gollings considering giving top hurdler Royal Shakespeare his chasing debut in a Grade 2 at Sandown in a week's time. The horse finishes sixth in the Scottish Champion Hurdle and is two points ahead of Monkerhostin in the season-long competition. The latter, who trailed in a tired third at Cheltenham four days earlier, is due to line up in the same race. The Order of Merit is worth £200,000, which is the reason why both horses are being asked to go the extra mile.

24 The owners of Royal Shakespeare and Monkerhostin come to a private arrangement whereby the £200,000 Order of Merit first prize will be divided between the two camps. Neither horse will run in the Celebration Chase at Sandown.

29 On the last day of the jumps season, Paul Nicholls is crowned champion trainer and Lacdoudal wins the Betfred Gold Cup, formerly the Whitbread. But it is Martin Pipe who steals the headlines by informing the Morning Line that he is handing over to his son David with immediate effect. There's a quiver in his voice as he explains: "I've had one or two health problems recently. I'm not exactly as I'd like to be." Pipe retires as the winningmost trainer of all time in Britain over jumps with 3,927 winners. He won nearly all the big prizes including the Grand National with Miinnehoma in 1994. But the Cheltenham Gold Cup eluded him despite 31 attempts. Tony McCoy marks his 11th consecutive champion jockeys' title by riding Hasty Prince to victory in the handicap hurdle. In Ireland the champions' roll of honour includes Ruby Walsh (top jockey for the fourth time), Noel Meade (trainer) and JP McManus (owner). Nina Carberry is the leading amateur jockey.

To read what Evan Williams has planned for the season ahead see pages 232-233

May

5   Willie Mullins faces more bills from his lawyer. His latest attempt to prove that Be My Royal was the lawful winner of the 2002 Hennessy Gold Cup fails. Mr Justice Stanley Burnton delivers judgement in the High Court on the civil case heard in March saying: "The allegations have not been made out." Mullins is ordered to pay costs and refused permission to appeal. It looks like the end of a long legal saga.

6   Eight days after retiring, Martin Pipe is still training winners because his son and heir David Pipe has been unable to obtain a full trainer's licence as yet. The Pond House maestro, who is sunning himself on a Caribbean island, swept into an early lead in the new trainers' title race with a 356-1 double. He lands the two jumps races on the Haydock card including the first big race of the season, the Betfred Swinton Hurdle, with the 16-1 shot Acambo. Another retired trainer still officially training is Ginger 'Red Rum' McCain. His son Donald is being held up in the red tape surrounding trainer's licences.

8, 9 After six seasons training point-to-pointers, David Pipe is granted a trainers' licence by the Horseracing Regulatory Authority. The following day he saddles a treble in his own name, one at Kelso and two at Exeter.

15   Donald McCain is taking steps to meet the qualification requirements for a training licence by enrolling on HRA courses but it looks as if it will be at least four months before he can officially take over from his father Ginger. The form of the McCain horses has been so good in the new season (six winners up until May 13) that Ginger was numerically leading trainer for a few days.

24   Paul Carberry is sentenced to two months in jail for threatening, abusive and insulting behaviour on an aircraft last year. He set fire to a friend's newspaper with a cigarette lighter when returning from a holiday in Malaga. The Swords District Court in Dublin releases him on bail pending a likely appeal. The Grand National-winning jockey looks shocked as he is declared guilty of a breach of the peace on the Aer Lingus flight.

ACAMBO: won for Martin Pipe even after he had announced his retirement!

Sponsored by Stan James

DAVID NICHOLSON: a sad loss to the jumping game

Summer

June 8   Jockey Larry McGrath is banned for four and a half months for testing positive for cocaine on March 9. He has had six weeks on the sidelines already so, in effect, receives the maximum six-month ban.

June 13   David Johnson sends two horses to Henrietta Knight. One is a point-to-pointer from Ireland called Quarry Town. The other is from France called Swing Bill.

June 27   The BBC cuts back on its racing coverage by handing over Haydock, jumps and Flat, to Channel 4. Sir Peter O'Sullevan, the BBC's race commentator for half a century, is dismayed, saying: "The BBC covers about as many races as its namesake, the British Bathroom Centre."

August 27 David Nicholson, a towering figure in jump racing and twice champion trainer, dies aged 67. The invariably red-socked trainer won the Cheltenham Gold Cup with Charter Party but it wasn't until moving to Jackdaws Castle in 1992 that the big winners started to flow regularly. Viking Flagship won the Champion Chase for him in 1994 and 1995 while Barton Bank won him a King George. He was well known both for his explosive temper and for encouraging young talent. Jockeys such as Peter Scudamore, Richard Dunwoody and Adrian Maguire blossomed from their association with him. Alan King, who joined the Duke in 1985 and took over from him when he retired, says: "I learned just about everything from him about racing."

Outlook

Big race review
by Dylan Hill
May 2005 to April 2006

1 **Daily Star Chase (Listed) (2m6f)**
Punchestown October 20 (Good to Soft)
1 **War Of Attrition** 6-11-12   C O'Dwyer
2 **Kicking King** 7-11-12   B J Geraghty
3 **Pizarro** 8-11-12   R Walsh
7-1, 3-10f, 11-2. 3l, shd. 5 ran. 5m 44.1
Gigginstown House Stud (M Morris, IRE).

The season had barely got going in earnest when there was the first changing of the guard, not that many could have predicted it at the time, as **Kicking King**, brilliant winner of the King George and Gold Cup in 2004/05, lost out to **War Of Attrition**, who would end up succeeding him as Gold Cup winner. While War Of Attrition could have done no more than win, Kicking King still came out looking the better horse, as he jumped his rivals silly, gaining lengths at certain obstacles, but was heavily restrained to prevent him making the most of such an advantage and then blew up in the straight. The rematch promises to be one of the highlights of the new campaign.

2 **Bet365 Charlie Hall Chase (Grade 2)**
(3m1f) Wetherby October 29 (Soft)
1 **Ollie Magern** 7-11-5   C Llewellyn
2 **Kingscliff** 8-11-0   R Walford
3 **Take The Stand** 9-11-0   A Dobbin
11-4f, 10-3, 12-1. 1¹/4l, 1¹/2l. 8 ran. 6m 25.5
Mr Roger Nicholls (N Twiston-Davies, Cheltenham).

The first top-class chase of the season this side of the Irish Sea and a great performance from **Ollie Magern**, who set a strong gallop and saw off **Kingscliff** and **Take The Stand**, both of whom were making sound reappearances, in the straight. While he was bitterly disappointing subsequently, this form should not be underestimated, particularly as he was giving 5lb to his closest pursuers, and he should still be dangerous when allowed to make the running in small fields. **Grey Abbey** was pulled up, the first sign he would no longer be a force.

3 **William Hill Haldon Gold Cup Chase**
(Handicap) (Gr2) (2m1f110yds)
Exeter November 1 (Good to Soft)
1 **Monkerhostin** 8-10-5   R Johnson
2 **Kauto Star** 5-10-9   R Walsh
3 **Ashley Brook** 7-11-4   P J Brennan
10-1, 3-1, 7-4f. 4l, 9l. 11 ran. 4m 13.2
(b3.30)
Mr M G St Quinton (P Hobbs, Minehead).

Whatever the quality of the first three, this will forever be remembered for the demise of **Best Mate**, who was struggling a long way out and collapsed before the final fence having suffered a heart attack. **Monkerhostin** put in a much-improved round of jumping to exploit his lenient handicap mark and mark his development into a high-class chaser, while **Kauto Star**, who was said to need the run, and **Ashley Brook**, who appeared to be crying out for a longer trip, also shaped well. Arkle winner **Contraband** could finish only fifth after a huge mistake at the fourth.

4 **Paddy Power Gold Cup Handicap**
Chase (Grade 3) (2m4f110yds)
Cheltenham November 12 (Good to Soft)
1 **Our Vic** 7-11-7   T J Murphy
2 **Monkerhostin** 8-11-9   R Johnson
3 **Kandjar D'Allier** 7-10-7   R Thornton
4 **Fondmort** 9-11-12   M Foley
9-2f, 5-1, 14-1, 25-1. 2¹/2l, 1¹/2l, 4l. 18 ran. 5m 9.7
(a2.45)
Mr D A Johnson (M Pipe, Wellington).

Our Vic finally claimed the valuable prize he so richly deserved after his final-fence fall in the 2004 Tripleprint, extending Martin Pipe's stunning record in this race to seven winners in the last 10 years. Extremely well-in if putting in a safe round, Our Vic won as smoothly as he liked, with **Monkerhostin** never really in the race and just staying on past tired horses from the last. The only real threat turned out to be

Redemption, who fell when going well two out. Further back 2003 winner **Fondmort** ran another cracker under top-weight to finish fourth.

5 Greatwood Handicap Hurdle (Grade 3) (2m110yds)

Cheltenham November 13 (Good to Soft)

1 **Lingo** 6-10-6		A P McCoy
2 **Tramantano** 6-10-0		C Llewellyn
3 **Phar Bleu** 4-10-2		R Walsh
4 **Adamant Approach** 11-10-0		D J Casey

5-1, 50-1, 8-1, 25-1. 3¹/2l, 1¹/4l, ¹/2l. 19 ran. 3m 55.8
(a0.30)
Mr J P McManus (Jonjo O'Neill, Cheltenham).

Tragically, having put himself firmly in the Champion Hurdle picture with this win, **Lingo** turned out to have run his last race as he later died on the gallops. On a ridiculously low mark considering he was once a Supreme Hurdle favourite prior to being scratched days before the race, Lingo was just 5-1 to defy a 680-day absence and tore a competitive field apart, bounding clear from the home turn. Yet the proximity of 50-1 no-hoper **Tramantano** and poor performances from the favourite **Power Elite** and top-rated trio **Rooster Booster**, **Westender** and **Self Defense** show the form wasn't up to much.

6 Fortria Chase (Grade 2) (2m)
Navan November 13 (Soft)

1 **Central House** 8-11-12		Mr R Loughran
2 **Moscow Flyer** 11-11-12		B J Geraghty
3 **Hi Cloy** 8-11-12		Andrew J McNamara

8-1, 4-11f, 5-1. 3¹/2l, 2¹/2l. 5 ran. 4m 10.6
(b15.93)
John F Kenny (D Hughes, IRE).

Beaten by Rathgar Beau in April for his first ever defeat in a completed chase, **Moscow Flyer** suffered another shock reverse behind **Central House** on his reappearance, never able to get to the winner who benefited from an aggressive ride from Roger Loughran. Though he remained a firm favourite for the Champion Chase with Azertyuiop and Well Chief already ruled out for the season, the writing was on the wall.

7 Betfair Chase (Grade 1) (3m)
Haydock November 19 (Good to Soft)

1 **Kingscliff** 8-11-8		R Walford
2 **Beef Or Salmon** 9-11-8		P Carberry
3 **Kicking King** 7-11-8		B J Geraghty

8-1, 8-1, 4-5f. 1¹/4l, 9l. 7 ran. 6m 5.4
(a4.20)
Mr A J Sendell (R Alner, Blandford).

The inaugural running of this Grade One chase, and with it the start of the new Betfair Million – an initiative to get the best horses running against each other more often by offering £1m to a horse able to win the Betfair Chase, the King George and the Gold Cup. **Kicking King** was everyone's idea of the horse most likely to grab the bonus, but he fell at the first hurdle by finishing only third at 4-5, weakening tamely from the second-last, with a twisted shoe the explanation. Instead **Kingscliff** took the glory, ridden positively and jumping brilliantly to repel a string of challenges in the straight. The last challenger was **Beef Or Salmon**, who ran a cracker to expose the myth that he is a poor traveller – his failings in Britain are more down to poor jumping in big fields and a scarcity of soft ground opportunities. **Ollie Magern**, unable to dominate, dropped out to finish last.

8 Totesport Peterborough Chase (Grade 2) (2m4f110yds)
Huntingdon November 19 (Good)

1 **Impek** 9-11-6		A P McCoy
2 **Monkerhostin** 8-11-6		R Johnson
3 **Thisthatandtother** 9-11-10		R Walsh

5-1, 5-2f, 3-1. 5l, 3¹/2l. 11 ran. 5m 0.7
(a1.40)
Mr Jim Lewis (Miss H Knight, Wantage).

Impek had won at Aintree in October to break a 22-month duck and this confirmed his sudden improvement into a genuinely top-class chaser. Suited by forcing tactics, Impek was committed four out and went further clear in the closing stages for a fine win over **Monkerhostin**, who ran another cracker but could never get in a serious blow, and the returning Cheltenham Festival hero **Thisthatandtother**.

9 Maplewood Developments Morgiana Hurdle (Grade 2) (2m)
Punchestown November 20 (Soft)

1 **Brave Inca** 7-11-12		A P McCoy
2 **Essex** 5-11-7		R Walsh
3 **Harchibald** 6-11-12		P Carberry

11-4, 9-4, 7-4f. ¹/2l, 4l. 5 ran. 4m 14.7
(a20.46)
Novices Syndicate (C A Murphy, IRE).

Only five runners but what a prize quintet as the first three were joined by **Macs Joy** and subsequent Champion Chase hero **Newmill**. **Brave Inca** had struggled to win in 2004/05 but was straight off the mark this time, outbattling **Essex** in typically determined fashion. **Harchibald** was the victim of a strange incident between the last two as Paul Carberry asked him to go through an impossible gap on the rail and Tony McCoy not surprisingly shut the door. Newmill made a fine return in fourth, while **Macs Joy** badly needed the run.

10 Ballymore Properties Long Distance Hurdle (Grade 2) (3m110yds)
Newbury November 26 (Good)

1 **Inglis Drever** 6-11-8		G Lee
2 **Baracouda** 10-11-8		A P McCoy
3 **Crystal d'Ainay** 6-11-8		R Thornton

ARCALIS: lost his form after an impressive win in the Fighting Fifth

8-13f, 3-1, 16-1. 1¼l, 3l. 6 ran. 5m 49.3 (b12.08)
Andrea & Graham Wylie (J Howard Johnson, Crook).

Having made a successful reappearance at Wetherby, **Inglis Drever** confirmed his status as the leading light in the staying division at this stage of the season. The early pace was only steady, but **Crystal d'Ainay** pushed on into the straight and was challenged on both sides two out, Inglis Drever eventually asserting on the flat to win cosily. The time dipped under standard to confirm the immense quality of the winner, as well as **Baracouda**'s enduring class and Crystal d'Ainay's ability, with the first three miles clear of the useful **Korelo**.

11 Hennessy Cognac Gold Cup Handicap Chase (Grade 2) (3m2f110yds)

Newbury November 26 (Good)

1	**Trabolgan** 7-11-12	M A Fitzgerald
2	**L'Ami** 6-11-5	D J Casey
3	**Cornish Rebel** 8-11-11	R Walsh
4	**Comply Or Die** 6-11-7	T J Murphy

13-2, 10-1, 11-2f, 12-1. 2¹/2l, 1³/4l, 1¹/2l. 19 ran. 6m 31.7 (b8.45)
Mr Trevor Hemmings (N Henderson, Lambourn).

Far from a vintage Hennessy, with the weights and final places dominated by last season's staying novices who weren't that exceptional a bunch. Having said that, **Trabolgan** had been an impressive winner of the SunAlliance and, under top-weight, was similarly dominant here, always looking the winner in the straight even though plenty held chances. Denied an-

other run by injury, he comes into the season still a relative novice, with only five outings over fences, and promises lots of improvement. **L'Ami**, **Cornish Rebel** and **Comply Or Die** also ran terrific races, ahead of two more lightly-weighted second-season novices in **All In The Stars** and **Red Devil Robert**. Progressive young handicappers **King Harald** and **Kandjar d'Allier** were the disappointments of the race, both never in contention.

12 Pertemps 'Fighting Fifth' Hurdle (Grade 1) (2m)

Newcastle November 26 (Soft)

1	**Arcalis** 5-11-7	A Dobbin
2	**Royal Shakespeare** 6-11-7	T Scudamore
3	**The French Furze** 11-11-7	B Harding

9-4f, 8-1, 33-1. 5l, shd. 9 ran. 4m 0.6 (a8.60)
Andrea & Graham Wylie (J Howard Johnson, Crook).

This race lacked a real star at its outset but looked to have produced one as **Arcalis** oozed class to win well. Held up in rear, he travelled beautifully throughout to hit the front still on the bridle two out and quickened away gloriously on the run-in. A repeat of his performance at Cheltenham confirmed him as the best English hurdler around, though still well short of Ireland's golden generation. **Royal Shakespeare** led the rest of a modest bunch.

13 William Hill - Tingle Creek Trophy Chase (Grade 1) (2m)

Sandown December 3 (Soft)

1	**Kauto Star** 5-11-7	M A Fitzgerald
2	**Ashley Brook** 7-11-7	A P McCoy

3 Oneway 8-11-7   G Lee
5-2j, 5-2j, 4-1. 1¹/2l, 8l. 7 ran. 4m 6.8
(a20.40)
Mr Clive D Smith (P Nicholls, Shepton Mallet).

Injuries to Azertyuiop and Well Chief had left the door open for a new two-mile star to take centre stage at Sandown, and **Kauto Star** took his opportunity with an outstanding performance. Just as he had at Exeter, Kauto Star travelled and jumped with real style and easily took **Ashley Brook**'s measure after the third-last, establishing a four-length lead before idling on the run-in. The runner-up also ran a solid race, again looking likely to prove better over further, and it was a huge shame that neither was really seen again – Ashley Brook missed the rest of the season and Kauto Star lasted only three fences at Cheltenham. The other fancied runners, **Oneway** and **Monkerhostin**, ran well without troubling the principals.

14 Ballymore Properties Hatton's Grace Hurdle (Grade 1) (2m4f)
Fairyhouse December 4 (Heavy)
1 **Solerina** 8-11-7   G T Hutchinson
2 **Golden Cross** 6-11-12   J P Murtagh
3 **Brave Inca** 7-11-12   A P McCoy
6-4, 7-1, 11-8f. shd, 1¹/2l. 5 ran. 5m 4.2
(a7.08)
John P Bowe (J Bowe, IRE).

These race conditions suit **Solerina** down to the ground, but she was pushed all the way to gain her third straight win in the race by **Golden Cross**, with **Brave Inca**'s sloppy round of jumping relegating him to third. Solerina even fell half a length down after the last but fought back thrillingly to land the spoils over Golden Cross, who hadn't run for 21 months over hurdles prior to this but began his preparations for a crack at the World Hurdle.

15 Robin Cook Memorial Gold Cup Handicap Chase (Grade 3) (2m5f)
Cheltenham December 10 (Good to Soft)
1 **Sir Oj** 8-10-0   P Carberry
2 **Le Passing** 6-10-9   J Tizzard
3 **Lacdoudal** 6-11-3   R Johnson
4 **Brooklyn Breeze** 8-10-9   A Dobbin
16-1, 20-1, 8-1, 20-1. 1l, 5l, shd. 16 ran. 5m 15.0
(a1.50)
Mr Brian Keenan (N Meade, IRE).

An incident-packed race produced a highly unsatisfactory result, except for in-running backers of **Sir Oj**, who looked out with the washing two out but stormed up the hill to catch the weakening **Le Passing** in the dying strides. Le Passing had been left clear only when **Thisthatandtother** took a crashing fall at the third-last, taking down **Fondmort** with him as both were creeping into contention.

Therealbandit and **Scots Grey** were also badly affected when still in with a squeak, while the other market principal, **Our Vic**, ran no sort of race and was pulled up.

16 Totesport Bula Hurdle (Grade 2) (2m1f)
Cheltenham December 10 (Good to Soft)
1 **Harchibald** 6-11-8   P Carberry
2 **Intersky Falcon** 8-11-0   A P McCoy
3 **Faasel** 4-11-4   A Dobbin
10-11f, 14-1, 9-2. 1³/4l, 5l. 9 ran. 4m 0.3
(b3.20)
Mr D P Sharkey (N Meade, IRE).

Harchibald's last run at Cheltenham as injury subsequently ruled him out of the Champion, and a tantalising one when it comes to considering the new campaign. Having travelled with his customary ease, Harchibald finally managed to storm up the hill, giving weight all round, and while the opposition wasn't in the same league as the likes of Brave Inca it was enough at the time to make him Champion Hurdle favourite. **Intersky Falcon** ran a great race, and **Faasel** confirmed he had progressed past his Triumph Hurdle conqueror **Penzance** (fourth) while falling short of the best.

17 Stan James Christmas Hurdle (Grade 1) (2m110yds)
Sandown December 26 (Good to Soft)
1 **Feathard Lady** 5-11-0   R Walsh
2 **Self Defense** 8-11-7   M A Fitzgerald
3 **Royal Shakespeare** 6-11-7   T Scudamore
6-4f, 13-2, 12-1. 12l, 3l. 7 ran. 3m 55.2
(a2.38)
Lord Of The Ring Syndicate (C A Murphy, IRE).

Feathard Lady emerged as yet another potential Irish superstar with this massively impressive performance, exposing the woeful lack of British talent. An unbeaten novice in 2004 before injury ruled her out for almost a year, Feathard Lady had twice won well in lesser company and passed her first major test with remarkable ease, bursting clear with a stunning turn of foot and value for more than the 12 length margin. On this evidence she would have been bang in the frame at Cheltenham but for another injury blow. **Self Defense** and **Royal Shakespeare** ran decent races but fall well short of top-class, **Akilak** became another second-season juvenile to be found out, and **Intersky Falcon** was disappointing.

18 Stan James King George VI Chase (Grade 1) (3m110yds)
Sandown December 26 (Good)
1 **Kicking King** 7-11-10   B J Geraghty
2 **Monkerhostin** 8-11-10   T Scudamore
3 **Impek** 9-11-10   A P McCoy
11-8f, 22-1, 13-2. nk, 5l. 9 ran. 6m 11.9
(a16.65)

Mr Conor Clarkson (T Taaffe, IRE).

Kicking King made it back-to-back King Georges but was far from at his best, perhaps inevitably after a troubled preparation, and may even have lost out in two or three more strides. Indeed, as the runners passed the second winning post, Tom Scudamore thought he had won on the fast-finishing **Monkerhostin**, who flew up the hill, running the race of his life stepped up in trip. For nearly all of the three miles Kicking King had looked in complete command, but he failed to quicken away from his rivals having headed long-time leader Impek two out and was hanging on desperately at the line. Another soon ruled out of Cheltenham by injury, it remains to be seen whether he can again match his 2004/05 peak. **Impek** ran a cracker, pulling away from two high-class yardsticks in **L'Ami** and **Royal Auclair**. The disappointments were **Kingscliff**, who was never going and was pulled up, and **Ollie Magern**.

19 Skybet.com Rowland Meyrick Handicap Chase (Grade 3) (3m1f)

Wetherby December 26 (Soft)
1 **Therealbandit** 8-10-6   A Glassonbury (10)
2 **Take The Stand** 9-10-12   B Harding
3 **My Will** 5-10-4   J Tizzard
9-1, 6-1, 11-4f. 1¹/2l, 15l. 10 ran. 6m 38.5
Mr D A Johnson (M Pipe, Wellington).

The combination of soft ground and a searching gallop led to half the field being pulled up, including the veteran **Grey Abbey**, who was subsequently retired. While not quite the force many felt he was during his novice season, **Therealbandit** showed he remains highly talented, seeing off the persistent challenge of **Take The Stand**, who also ran a blinder on unsuitable ground. **My Will** paid the price for some costly jumping errors.

20 Totesport Long Walk Hurdle (Grade 1) (3m)

Chepstow December 27 (Good to Soft)
1 **My Way de Solzen** 5-11-7   R Thornton
2 **Neptune Collonges** 4-11-7   R Walsh
3 **Starzaan** 6-11-7   T J Murphy
12-1, 6-1, 66-1. 5l, 12l. 8 ran. 5m 55.1
(a19.06)
B Winfield,A Longman,J Wright & C Fenton (A King, Barbury Castle).

A decisive change in the staying division, with 2-5 favourite **Inglis Drever** eclipsed and subsequent Cheltenham winner **My Way de Solzen** coming good. Inglis Drever, well beaten when falling two out, remains the best stayer on the book after his previous efforts, and it was a shame injury denied him the chance to prove this at the Festival. With Inglis Drever out of the way, My Way de Solzen and the four-year-old novice **Neptune Collonges** were

the next best in the market, and so it proved, with My Way de Solzen's career-best effort enough to beat the dour stayer.

21 Coral Welsh National Handicap Chase (Grade 3) (3m5f110yds)

Chepstow December 27 (Good to Soft)
1 **L'Aventure** 6-10-4   L Aspell
2 **Heros Collonges** 10-10-11   C Williams
3 **Cornish Rebel** 8-11-12   R Walsh
4 **Crystal d'Ainay** 6-11-0   R Thornton
14-1, 25-1, 9-2j, 12-1. dis, nk, 1³/4l. 18 ran. 7m 38.9
(a4.60)
Mr C J Harriman (P Nicholls, Shepton Mallet).

The usual slog, with **L'Aventure** the last one standing. The mare just about had the measure of long-time leader **One Knight** when he took a crashing fall at the last, while **Sir Rembrandt** also held every chance when he came down at the first in the straight. That helped L'Aventure to an extremely easy win, with the rest nowhere – **Heros Collonges** just took second from **Cornish Rebel** and **Crystal d'Ainay**, taken back over fences, while **Comply Or Die** ran a shocker and was pulled up.

22 Paddy Power Dial-A-Bet Chase (Grade 1) (2m1f)

Leopardstown December 27 (Good to Soft)
1 **Hi Cloy** 8-11-12   Andrew J McNamara
2 **Fota Island** 9-11-12   A P McCoy
3 **Central House** 8-11-12   Mr R Loughran
8-1, 9-1, 11-4. ³/4l, 1¹/2l. 5 ran. 4m 16.0
(b4.88)
Mrs S McCloy (M Hourigan, IRE).

The unfortunate Roger Loughran provided one of the enduring images of the season as he sat up in the saddle and punched the air with glee having seemingly steered **Central House** to a brilliant victory – only to discover he had celebrated 100 yards too early. In the confusion Central House was passed by **Hi Cloy** and **Fota Island**, and it is tough to say who was the moral winner out of Central House and Hi Cloy, who was slightly down but finishing fast. Amid the drama another major story was overshadowed, with **Moscow Flyer** suffering a third successive defeat. Though beaten less than five lengths in fourth, by now he was looking more and more past his best.

23 Lexus Chase (Grade 1) (3m)

Leopardstown December 28 (Good to Soft)
1 **Beef Or Salmon** 9-11-12   P Carberry
2 **War Of Attrition** 6-11-12   C O'Dwyer
3 **Forget The Past** 7-11-12   D N Russell
9-10f, 11-4, 11-2. 4l, 11l. 5 ran. 6m 23.1
(b22.14)
B J Craig (M Hourigan, IRE).

A fabulous performance from **Beef Or Salmon**,

who toyed with a top-class field and eased effortlessly clear, further proof that he is desperately tough to beat in soft-ground, small-field races at Leopardstown. Ultimately, though, the best Gold Cup trial came from **War Of Attrition**, who stayed on well enough at his first crack at three miles and wasn't best suited by the going. **Forget The Past** was later reported to have burst blood vessels in third but still managed to beat **Hedgehunter**, who was having his first run over fences since the Grand National and clearly needed it.

24 Bewleyshotels.com December Festival Hurdle (Grade 1) (2m)
Leopardstown December 29 (Soft)
1 **Brave Inca** 7-11-12   A P McCoy
2 **Harchibald** 6-11-12   P Carberry
3 **Newmill** 7-11-12   Andrew J McNamara
9-4, 9-10f, 40-1. 3l, 4¹/2l. 5 ran. 4m 2.9
(b3.36)
Novices Syndicate (C A Murphy, IRE).

The same five horses who had produced a corker in the Morgiana Hurdle met again here with an almost identical result, only **Essex** letting the side down with a sub-standard effort. **Harchibald** had been backed into odds-on after his Bula win, but he could never get on terms with **Brave Inca**, who continued to gel with Tony McCoy. Having tracked **Newmill**, he was driven to the front between the last two and stayed on strongly on the run-in. **Macs Joy** was far from disgraced in fourth.

25 Totesport Classic Handicap Chase (Grade 3) (3m5f)
Warwick January 14 (Soft)
1 **Eurotrek** 10-10-9   R Walsh
2 **Sir Rembrandt** 10-11-7   A Thornton
3 **Control Man** 8-10-7   A Glassonbury (7)
6-1, 10-1, 10-1. 15l, 1¹/2l. 13 ran. 7m 35.2
(a18.75)
Mr Paul Green (P Nicholls, Shepton Mallet).

Remarkably, the injury-prone **Eurotrek** was having only his fifth run over fences here but absolutely toyed with a field of seasoned handicappers, bolting clear in the straight for a hugely impressive win having travelled sweetly throughout. **Sir Rembrandt** had failed to complete in his previous four starts but stayed on to take second from the front-running **Control Man**, while **Crystal d'Ainay**'s fourth was further confirmation that, while a high-class hurdler, he surely won't match those feats over fences. **Joaaci** was sent off the 3-1 favourite after an impressive handicap win at Cheltenham on New Year's Day but was brought down early.

26 Pierse Handicap Hurdle (0-145) (2m)
Leopardstown January 15 (Heavy)
1 **Studmaster** 6-10-3   T P Treacy

L'AVENTURE: has the Welsh National at her mercy as the slog takes its toll

2 **No Where To Hyde** 6-10-8   A P McCoy
3 **Pom Flyer** 6-10-11   K T Coleman (5)
4 **Charlies First** 6-10-0   O Casey (7)
12-1, 6-1, 25-1, 25-1. 2^1/2l, 2^1/2l, 3^1/2l. 27 ran.
4m 14.8
 (a8.54)
Mothership Racing Club (Mrs J Harrington, IRE).

A massively competitive field as ever, with 27 going to post for Ireland's biggest betting heat, yet they were well strung out at the line. **Studmaster** led the way in blistering fashion, bursting clear in the straight, while **No Where To Hyde** also finished well having been given too much to do. However, as impressive as the pair looked, the heavy ground looks to have had a lot to do with it, as both subsequently flopped at Cheltenham – No Where To Hyde tragically taking a fatal fall – and the form hasn't worked out.

27 Commhoist Logistics Champion Hurdle Trial (Grade 2) (2m)
Haydock January 21 (Heavy)
1 **Al Eile** 6-11-12   T J Murphy
2 **Mister McGoldrick** 9-11-4   P Whelan
3 **Faasel** 5-11-8   A Dobbin

5-1, 4-1, 2-1f. nk, 5l. 7 ran. 4m 11.9
 (a27.10)
Mr M A Ryan (J Queally, IRE).

Al Eile provided another sad indictment of the dearth of quality in British hurdlers. He hardly represents the cream of the Irish challenge but was still good enough to see off **Mister Mc-Goldrick**, primarily known for his chasing exploits, in a terrific battle from the last. This was also his first run for seven months. **Faasel** again couldn't quite live up to his lofty billing in third, while brilliant Fighting Fifth winner **Arcalis** was pulled up having reportedly lost his action when absolutely clouting the third-last.

28 Peter Marsh Handicap Chase (Grade 2) (3m)
Haydock January 21 (Heavy)
1 **Ebony Light** 10-10-4   S J Craine (5)
2 **Kingscliff** 9-11-10   R Walford
3 **Truckers Tavern** 11-10-4   D O'Meara
33-1, 5-2, 10-1. 9l, 14l. 5 ran. 6m 37.7
 (a36.50)
Mr Roger Bellamy (D McCain, Cholmondeley).

A bizarre result as 33-1 shot **Ebony Light** won from 22lb out of the handicap as each of his

AL EILE: jumping en route to winning the Haydock Champion Hurdle Trial

rivals failed to act on the heavy going. Ebony Light simply galloped them into submission as **Kingscliff**, running in snatches and tailed off at one point, disappointed again and **Lord Transcend**, exhausted by his pursuit of the winner, was pulled up between the last two.

29 AIG Europe Champion Hurdle (Grade 1) (2m)

Leopardstown January 29 (Good to Soft)

1	**Brave Inca** 8-11-10	A P McCoy
2	**Macs Joy** 7-11-10	B J Geraghty
3	**Golden Cross** 7-11-10	J P Murtagh

6-5f, 13-2, 6-1. 1l, 4l. 7 ran. 4m 0.2
(b6.06)
Novices Syndicate (Colm A Murphy, IRE).

The Champion Hurdle picture really took shape here, as **Brave Inca** took over favouritism from the well-beaten **Hardy Eustace** in a finish virtually identical to Cheltenham. Brave Inca was given a typically positive ride by Tony McCoy and pulled out more when strongly pressed in the straight by **Macs Joy**, who had appeared to be travelling the better, for a terrific win. Macs Joy also produced by far his best run of the season, knuckling down well and even getting back at Brave Inca at the line. There were two more hugely encouraging runs behind, with **Golden Cross** third over a highly inadequate trip and former SunAlliance favourite **Sadlers Wings** defying a 22-month absence to finish fourth – unfortunately injury would soon intervene again. Hardy Eustace was never really going well and dropped out tamely two out, after which he was found to be all wrong.

30 HBLB Cleeve Hurdle (Grade 2) (3m)

Sandown February 4 (Good)

1	**Fire Dragon** 5-11-0	P McCoy
2	**Mighty Man** 6-11-4	R Johnson
3	**Westender** 10-11-4	T J Murphy

16-1, 15-8f, 28-1. 2l, 1½l. 12 ran. 5m 54.3
Mrs Gay Smith (Jonjo O'Neill, Cheltenham).

Several promising young stayers went to post and it was the youngest of all, **Fire Dragon**, who won under an excellent front-running ride from Tony McCoy, ending a frustrating run of seconds in handicaps. While his win shouldn't be underestimated – as it clearly was when he was sent off a ridiculous 40-1 in the World Hurdle – the horse to take out of the race was **Mighty Man**, who relished his first attempt at three miles and was an unlucky loser, finishing fast having lost lengths when trying an ambitious run up the inside rail. **Patriarch Express** ran a blinder on his reappearance, showing up well until lack of fitness told, but **No Refuge** was a poor fifth.

31 Victor Chandler Handicap Chase (Grade 2) (2m)

Sandown February 4 (Good to Firm)

1	**Tysou** 9-11-2	M A Fitzgerald
2	**Dempsey** 8-11-12	A Tinkler
3	**Kalca Mome** 8-10-7	R Johnson

10-1, 11-2, 25-1. 2l, 3l. 10 ran. 3m 50.1
(a3.70)
Mr W J Brown (N Henderson, Lambourn).

A sub-standard renewal of this traditionally top-class handicap as top-weight **Dempsey** was rated only 150 and a novice, **Hoo La Baloo**, was sent off 9-4 favourite. With Hoo La Baloo found wanting, it was a veteran of the handicap scene who had his moment of glory as **Tysou** wore down Dempsey in the straight under a patient ride. Dempsey came out comfortably best of those who had forced the pace, suggesting he could well be capable of better, and **Kalca Mome** was another to come from out the back having been badly outpaced.

32 Hennessy Cognac Gold Cup (Grade 1) (3m)

Leopardstown February 12 (Good to Soft)

1	**Beef Or Salmon** 10-11-12	P Carberry
2	**Hedgehunter** 10-11-12	D J Casey
3	**Native Upmanship** 13-11-12	C O'Dwyer

2-5f, 10-3, 50-1. 12l, 7l. 7 ran. 6m 30.1
(b15.14)
B J Craig (M Hourigan, IRE).

A desperate renewal of what is usually a top-class race. There were only two serious contenders and the forecast was duly landed as **Beef Or Salmon** continued his love affair with Leopardstown, overcoming a huge blunder five out to stretch clear of **Hedgehunter** on the run-in. The runner-up jumped well in front without having any answer to the winner's turn of foot, but the fact **Native Upmanship** took third says it all.

33 Red Mills Trial Hurdle (Grade 2) (2m)

Gowran Park February 18 (Soft)

1	**Macs Joy** 7-11-11	B J Geraghty
2	**Asian Maze** 7-11-6	P Carberry
3	**Ground Ball** 9-11-6	C O'Dwyer

2-5f, 13-2, 25-1. 4½l, 1½l. 4 ran. 3m 55.8
(a2.43)
Mac's J Racing Syndicate (Mrs J Harrington, IRE).

This was all about fine-tuning for Cheltenham, and connections would have been delighted with the performances of both **Macs Joy** and **Asian Maze**. Asian Maze was making her first appearance since April and set a good pace, before Macs Joy moved smoothly to the head of affairs three out and pulled clear with ease, maintaining the upward curve of his entire season with a first win. Asian Maze dropped to last once headed but stayed on again to pass **Ground Ball** and the disappointing **Essex**.

34 Red Square Vodka Gold Cup Handicap Chase (Grade 3) (3m4f110yds)
Haydock February 18 (Heavy)

1 **Ossmoses**	9-10-0	R McGrath
2 **Model Son**	8-10-7	P Merrigan (5)
3 **Sir Rembrandt**	10-11-5	W Marston

14-1, 25-1, 12-1. 15l, 8l. 14 ran. 7m 19.8 (a15.15)

Mr D M Forster (D M Forster, Darlington).

As in the Peter Marsh, heavy ground around Haydock led to another funny result, with lightly-weighted pair **Ossmoses** and **Model Son** able to dominate under their small burdens. Among the rest only the brave **Sir Rembrandt** managed to stay remotely within touching distance, and the first five in the market all failed to complete, including favourite **What A Native** and **Joaaci**, who took a heavy fall when well adrift.

35 Ascot Totesport Chase (Grade 1) (2m4f110yds)
Lingfield February 18 (Heavy)

1 **Our Vic**	8-11-7	T J Murphy
2 **My Will**	6-11-7	J Tizzard
3 **Fondmort**	10-11-7	M A Fitzgerald

2-1f, 10-3, 5-1. 6l, 2l. 7 ran. 5m 17.7 (a12.25)

Mr D A Johnson (M Pipe, Wellington).

Our Vic isn't generally one to trust at 2-1, but fortunately for favourite backers he was on a going day and won in terrific style. Jumping well in front, Our Vic's only cause for concern came from a loose horse as his rivals could never get close to him, **My Will** and **Fondmort** both finishing well-beaten. This was another example of his enormous ability, but another flop at Cheltenham was a reminder that he is hard to catch right.

36 Totesport.com National Spirit Hurdle (Grade 2) (2m4f)
Fontwell February 19 (Heavy)

1 **My Way de Solzen**	6-11-11	R Thornton
2 **Dancing Bay**	9-11-3	M A Fitzgerald
3 **Sporazene**	7-11-3	Christian Williams

10-11f, 12-1, 12-1. 9l, 9l. 6 ran. 5m 9.8

B Winfield,A Longman,J Wright & C Fenton (A King, Barbury Castle).

Further confirmation of **My Way de Solzen**'s development into a leading World Hurdle contender, though he had little to beat once the heavy ground led to **Fire Dragon** being withdrawn. He did it the hard way from the front and put his rivals firmly in their place, **Dancing Bay** not up to this in second and **Sporazene**, on his second attempt over a trip, again failing to convince.

37 Osmosis Ireland Limited Bobbyjo Chase (3m1f)
Fairyhouse February 25 (Soft)

1 **Forget The Past**	8-11-10	B J Geraghty
2 **Garivonnian**	11-11-6	M Ferris
3 **Marcus de Berlais**	9-11-3	D J Casey

4-9f, 9-1, 16-1. 8l, 13l. 9 ran. 7m 4.0

S Mulryan (M J O'Brien, IRE).

Forget The Past had fallen off the radar as a Gold Cup contender when breaking blood vessels in the Lexus, but this win – his second in a week after a similar event at Gowran Park – saw him head to Cheltenham as a lively dark horse. This was a good win on unsuitably testing ground, with National types **Garivonnian** and **Marcus de Berlais** easily seen off.

38 Racing Post Handicap Chase (Grade 3) (3m110yds)
Sandown February 25 (Soft)

1 **Innox**	10-11-0	A P McCoy
2 **L'Ami**	7-11-12	A Duchene (5)
3 **My Will**	6-11-4	J Tizzard

8-1, 8-1, 8-1. 2¹/2l, ¹/2l. 15 ran. 6m 19.8 (a24.55)

Mr John P McManus (F Doumen, FRANCE).

Always one of the highlights of the season but a very different race on testing ground at Sandown rather than round the sharp bends of Kempton, with more staying types brought into play and Grand National hope **Innox** coming out on top. Always prominent, Innox hit the front for the second time three out and stayed on strongly up the hill to repel a host of challengers. Top-weight **L'Ami** ran magnificently in second, just falling short of the top prize he deserves, as did **My Will**. Favourite **Ladalko** and 100-1 shot Ballycassidy were the others in the mix, while the immensely frustrating but talented **Risk Accessor** again blotted his copybook by running out when delivering what may have been a winning run at the last.

39 Smurfit Kappa Champion Hurdle Challenge Trophy (Grade 1) (2m110yds)
Cheltenham March 14 (Good to Soft)

1 **Brave Inca**	8-11-10	A P McCoy
2 **Macs Joy**	7-11-10	B J Geraghty
3 **Hardy Eustace**	9-11-10	C O'Dwyer

7-4f, 13-2, 11-2. 1l, 3¹/2l. 18 ran. 3m 50.0 (b5.50)

Novices Syndicate (Colm A Murphy, IRE).

A richly deserved championship success for **Brave Inca**, who had been the dominant hurdler and confirmed his narrow superiority over **Macs Joy** from the Irish version. Yet again, though, he did things the hard way and those who took the 7-4 would not have been sitting comfortably in the early stages as he was pushed along and received reminders around halfway. But he was back on the bridle coming down the hill, disputing the running with **Hardy Eustace**, and was always just about holding Macs Joy in the straight after Hardy

BRAVE INCA: leading Hardy Eustace and Macs Joy up the Cheltenham hill

Eustace had cried enough. Macs Joy loomed up ominously approaching the last but couldn't get past the gutsy winner, nonetheless running an awesome race, and Hardy Eustace produced a monumental attempt at a third successive crown after his interrupted preparation. Nothing else ever stood a chance, though **Al Eile** ran on into fourth to make it a 1-2-3-4 for the Irish – and conceivably it could have been seven with Harchibald and Feathard Lady injured and **Asian Maze** falling. **Arcalis** was comfortably best of the British challenge, a close enough fifth, with **Briareus** and **Faasel** not up to the task.

40 **William Hill Trophy Handicap Chase (Grade 3) (3m110yds)**

Cheltenham March 14 (Good to Soft)
1 **Dun Doire** 7-10-9   R Walsh
2 **Juveigneur** 9-11-5   M A Fitzgerald
3 **Irish Hussar** 10-11-12   M Foley
4 **Model Son** 8-10-13   P Merrigan (5)
7-1, 16-1, 66-1, 14-1. 2l, 1¹/4l, 1¹/2l. 21 ran. 6m 12.1
(b9.40)
Dunderry Racing Syndicate (A J Martin, IRE).

Festival specialists **Juveigneur** and **Irish Hussar** looked to have the race between them in the straight, but both were powerless against **Dun Doire**'s finishing burst. The rapidly improving novice, raised 50lb for five straight wins prior to this, seemingly held no chance when 20l down at the top of the hill, and again when 6l down at the last. But he flew up the run-in

to nail the leading pair comfortably enough in the end. Juveigneur almost won at back-to-back Festivals but the other story of the race was 66-1 shot Irish Hussar, lightly-raced due to injury problems but a huge talent when right. **Moulin Riche**, a well-backed 100-30 favourite, was pulled up.

41 **Queen Mother Champion Chase (Grade 1) (2m)**

Cheltenham March 15 (Good)
1 **Newmill** 8-11-10   A J McNamara
2 **Fota Island** 10-11-10   A P McCoy
3 **Mister McGoldrick** 9-11-10 D Elsworth
16-1, 4-1, 50-1. 9l, 1¹/2l. 12 ran. 3m 51.4
(b10.68)
Ms M T Hayes (John Joseph Murphy, IRELAND).

Half the field failed to complete, including the 7-4 favourite **Kauto Star**, so with leading players in Well Chief, Azertyuiop, Ashley Brook and Contraband already missing it would be easy to dismiss **Newmill**'s victory. Yet that would be grossly unfair as this was a stunning performance by Newmill, who may well have beaten them all anyway. John Joseph Murphy did a brilliant job with his stable star, nursing him back to form over hurdles after he had lost his confidence chasing, and he decimated the field, making virtually all the running and not giving his backers a moment of doubt. **Mister McGoldrick** was the last horse to stay with him and paid the price up the hill, losing second to **Fota Island**, who came from well off the pace.

MY WAY DE SOLZEN: neck and neck with Golden Cross (left) at the final flight

Central House also stayed on having been badly outpaced, while **Moscow Flyer**, clearly nothing like as good as in previous years, still bowed out on a high with a brave fifth. Kauto Star's early fall also took out lively outsider **Dempsey**, while **River City**, the 2004 Arkle third making his seasonal debut, was absolutely cruising when he unseated his rider four out.

42 **Coral Cup Handicap Hurdle (Grade 3) (2m5f)**

Cheltenham March 15 (Good)
1 **Sky's The Limit** 5-11-12   B J Geraghty
2 **Strangely Brown** 5-11-8   B C Byrnes (5)
3 **Dom d'Orgeval** 6-11-12   R Johnson
4 **Phar Bleu** 5-11-6   R Walsh
11-1, 25-1, 20-1, 10-1. 4l, ³/4l, nk. 30 ran. 5m 2.5
(b5.15)
Mr Raymond J Rooney (E O'Grady, IRE).

Five-year-olds have an awful record in the race, while the difficulties horses at the top of the handicap face in these massively competitive Festival handicaps are widely known. All of which suggests **Sky's The Limit** could be a bit special, for this was a breathtaking win. He cruised into contention on the bridle and wasn't remotely extended in bolting clear on the flat, despite his welter burden. **Strangely Brown** ran a great race in second to make it a 1-2 for the Irish, while **Dom d'Orgeval** and **Phar Bleu** led the home challenge, the latter defying a recent wind operation and possibly needing the run. Favourite **No Where To Hyde**, runner-up in the Pierce Hurdle, fell fatally at the last.

43 **Ryanair Chase (Grade 2) (2m5f)**
Cheltenham March 16 (Good)
1 **Fondmort** 10-11-0   M A Fitzgerald

2 **Lacdoudal** 7-11-0   R Johnson
3 **Impek** 10-11-3   A P McCoy
10-3j, 20-1, 10-3j. 1¹/4l, hd. 11 ran. 5m 3.0 (b10.50)
Mr W J Brown (N Henderson, Lambourn).

This race might as well have been created with **Fondmort** specifically in mind, a real 2m5f specialist around Cheltenham with wins in the two major end-of-year handicaps here in 2003 and a string of top Festival efforts behind him, and this win showed age had not diminished his power. Fondmort headed **Impek** turning for home, bursting into a 4l lead, but the line only just came in time as he tired up the hill with **Lacdoudal** closing in rapidly and Impek delivering a renewed challenge. This trio pulled well clear of **My Will** in fourth, while **Our Vic** weakened badly in the straight having shown up for a long way.

44 **Ladbrokes World Hurdle (Grade 1) (3m)**
Cheltenham March 16 (Good)
1 **My Way de Solzen** 6-11-10   R Thornton
2 **Golden Cross** 7-11-10   J Murtagh
3 **Mighty Man** 6-11-10   R Johnson
8-1, 5-1, 4-1f. hd, 4l. 20 ran. 5m 38.2 (b1.80)
B Winfield, A Longman, J Wright & C Fenton (A King, Barbury Castle).

With **Baracouda** far from disgraced in fifth but unquestionably past his best and reigning champion **Inglis Drever** absent, it was time for a new breed of stayers to stake their claims to the throne, and **My Way de Solzen** just prevailed in a classic. Five horses still held every chance at the last – the first three plus **Fire Dragon** and Baracouda – but only My Way

Sponsored by Stan James

de Solzen and **Golden Cross** were able to really quicken up the hill. The two then had a strange battle, Golden Cross jinking away from his opponent and losing ground before rallying while My Way de Solzen idled and hung right. **Mighty Man** and Fire Dragon ran as well as they were entitled to after their recent Sandown running and are both progressive horses, which cannot be said of Baracouda, retired after his fine effort.

45 Racing Post Plate Handicap Chase (Grade 3) (2m5f)

Cheltenham March 16 (Good)
1 **Non So** 8-11-3		M A Fitzgerald
2 **Kelrev** 8-11-1		S Thomas
3 **Graphic Approach** 8-11-6		A P McCoy
4 **Roman Ark** 8-10-12		G Lee

14-1, 50-1, 11-1, 33-1. 9l, 7l, hd. 24 ran. 5m 5.2
(b8.30)
ROA Dawn Run Partnership (N Henderson, Lambourn).

Non So's starting price of 14-1 showed punters had lost faith in his ability to jump round after a string of expensive failures, but he remained a seriously well-handicapped horse over fences and duly won with remarkable ease. Stablemate **Saintsaire** set a blistering gallop, with the result that few really got into it, and Non So was always clearly travelling the best. He was finally given his best between the last two and bolted clear of **Kelrev**, who crept into contention and came a similar distance clear of the rest. Saintsaire was out on his feet when falling at the last, while **Le Passing** was an eye-catching fast finisher.

46 Totesport Cheltenham Gold Cup (Grade 1) (3m2f110yds)

Cheltenham March 17 (Good)
1 **War Of Attrition** 7-11-10		C O'Dwyer
2 **Hedgehunter** 10-11-10		R Walsh
3 **Forget The Past** 8-11-10		B J Geraghty

15-2, 16-1, 9-1. 2½l, 7l. 22 ran. 6m 31.7
(b13.55)
Gigginstown House Stud (M Morris, IRE).

One of the most wide open Gold Cups ever, lacking an obvious favourite, with the result that 22 were encouraged to take their chance, but none stood a chance against the brilliant **War Of Attrition**. The Irish had long felt he was a serious horse, making him favourite for the 2005 Arkle, and he more than proved it here. With his stamina still just about unproven, he was given a patient ride, keeping to the wide outside and never putting a foot wrong. He made smooth headway to challenge **Forget The Past** passing the bypassed third-last and pulled out plenty when tackled by **Hedgehunter** in the straight, always looking the winner. Young and

progressive, he is clearly a force to be reckoned with. Hedgehunter ran the race of his life in second, also benefiting from a flawless round of jumping and a patient ride. There was a big gap to the rest, led by Forget The Past and **L'Ami**, both of whom were handy throughout, and solid yardsticks **Take The Stand** and **Sir Rembrandt** confirmed their love of the conditions, finishing well in touch. They were split by **Monkerhostin**, who paid the price for some sloppy jumps but stuck on well up the hill, and **Cornish Rebel** was another running well when hitting the fourth-last badly and dropping out. The big disappointments were **Kingscliff**, not the same horse since his Betfair Chase win at Haydock, and in particular **Beef Or Salmon**, who was said to be never travelling by Paul Carberry. **Celestial Gold** took a heavy fall early on, while **Iris's Gift** was nowhere near fluent enough and was pulled up.

47 Vincent O'Brien County Handicap Hurdle (Grade 3) (2m1f)

Cheltenham March 17 (Good)
1 **Desert Quest** 6-10-10		R Walsh
2 **Noble Request** 5-10-11		R Johnson
3 **Adamant Approach** 12-10-13		R J Kiely (7)
4 **Pirate Flagship** 7-10-1		P J Brennan

4-1j, 25-1, 50-1, 10-1. 2½l, 3½l, 1l. 29 ran. 3m 52.7
(b10.80)
Mrs M Findlay (P Nicholls, Shepton Mallet).

This race's timing as the last race of the Cheltenham Festival makes it virtually the biggest betting heat of the year, and **Desert Quest** made sure it went the punters' way. A novice who had raced in handicap company for most of the season, rattling up four wins in the process, Desert Quest arrived officially 3lb well-in and more importantly on a clear upward curve. He was mightily impressive again, cruising into contention two out and only needing to be pushed out to burst clear up the hill with a supreme turn of foot. The similarly progressive **Noble Request** beat the rest out of sight, from 50-1 veteran **Adamant Approach**. Pierse Hurdle winner **Studmaster**, the other joint-favourite, was only 10th.

48 John Smith's Conservative Club Liverpool Hurdle (Grade 2) (3m110yds)

Aintree April 6 (Good)
1 **Mighty Man** 6-11-6		R Johnson
2 **My Way de Solzen** 6-11-10		R Thornton
3 **No Refuge** 6-11-10		G Lee

11-4, 6-4f, 16-1. 7l, 13l. 12 ran. 6m 5.5
(a10.25)
Mr E R Hanbury (H Daly, Ludlow).

Mighty Man, aided by a 4lb pull, comprehensively reversed Cheltenham form with **My Way de Solzen**, suggesting he could prove the best of this season's young stayers. The pair were utterly dominant, but Mighty Man benefited from being ridden closer to the pace than usual, always going well, and had the World Hurdle hero's measure as they drew clear from two out. My Way de Solzen ran another great race, while **No Refuge** saw out the trip better than he had previously but simply wasn't good enough. **Fire Dragon** dropped out quickly in the closing stages and was pulled up.

49 Betfair Bowl Chase (Grade 2) (3m1f)
Aintree April 6 (Good)

1 **Celestial Gold** 8-11-8		T J Murphy
2 **Take The Stand** 10-11-2		A Dobbin
3 **L'Ami** 7-11-8		A P McCoy

8-1, 6-1, 5-2f. 7l, 2¹/2l. 9 ran. 6m 27.8 (a16.30)
Mr D A Johnson (M Pipe, Wellington).

A massively impressive performance from **Celestial Gold**, putting him firmly in the picture for this season's Gold Cup. Not surprisingly, given his reappearance had been cut short by an early fall at Cheltenham, Celestial Gold jumped exuberantly and seemed to expend plenty of energy as Timmy Murphy, determined to hold him up, pulled him back after every fence. He remained buried in the pack until shaken up to chase down **Take The Stand** and **L'Ami** between the last two, jumped the last far better than Take The Stand, and duly eased clear on the run-in. Celestial Gold had already shown the rare combination of speed and stamina in 2004 when doubling up in the Paddy Power and the Hennessy, and this was a step closer to the required form as well. Take The Stand and L'Ami ran typical races – both are close to the best but Take The Stand was let down by his jumping and L'Ami lacked tactical speed when the principals quickened. **Monkerhostin** looked over the top for the season, **Ollie Magern** disappointed yet again, and **Beef Or Salmon** fell early on.

50 John Smith's Melling Chase (Grade 1) (2m4f)
Aintree April 7 (Good)

1 **Hi Cloy** 9-11-10		A J McNamara
2 **Fota Island** 10-11-10		A P McCoy
3 **Mariah Rollins** 8-11-3		R Walsh

14-1, 4-1, 40-1. 3/4l, 13l. 11 ran. 5m 7.3 (a12.70)
Mrs Susan McCloy (M Hourigan, IRE).

Much like the Champion Chase, this was a real catalogue of errors, with more than half the field failing to complete as the effects of Cheltenham and a searching gallop caught most of them out. However, **Hi Cloy** has always been a horse with immense ability and there was no fluke about his win. He may even have been suited by being held up for longer as he hit the front

four out and looked to be idling on the run-in, still doing just enough to hold off the consistent **Fota Island**. Otherwise the race was about those who didn't make it round – **Central House** and **Impek** paid the price for their forcing tactics, **Fondmort** and **River City** dropped out quickly after bad blunders, and **Mister McGoldrick** didn't run his race.

51 Scottish And Newcastle Aintree Hurdle (Grade 1) (2m4f)
Aintree April 8 (Good)

1 **Asian Maze** 7-11-0		R Walsh
2 **Hardy Eustace** 9-11-7		C O'Dwyer
3 **Sky's The Limit** 5-11-7		B J Geraghty

4-1, 5-2f, 11-4. 17l, 7l. 9 ran. 5m 7.8 (a21.80)
Mrs C A Moore (T Mullins, IRE).

Asian Maze produced arguably the best performance of the season with this stunning victory. Connections will always face a dilemma over whether to tackle 2m or 3m at Cheltenham, but she is the undisputed number one over 2m4f after absolutely destroying a top-class field. Thomas Mullins' mare set off at a furious tempo, jumping brilliantly, yet as they turned for home it was hard to believe she wouldn't pay the price, especially with **Hardy Eustace** and **Sky's The Limit** close enough. However, the youngster was the first to crack and Hardy Eustace couldn't keep up either, allowing Asian Maze to fittingly roar home in splendid isolation. Hardy Eustace looked to run reasonably up to form, and Sky's The Limit is certainly worth another chance in top-class company. **Kawagino** was the only other horse to finish within hailing distance – another great effort after he had finished seventh in the Champion Hurdle at 500-1 to blow his handicap mark apart.

52 John Smith's Grand National Handicap Chase (Grade 3) (4m4f)
Aintree April 8 (Good to Soft)

1 **Numbersixvalverde** 10-10-8		N P Madden
2 **Hedgehunter** 10-11-12		R Walsh
3 **Clan Royal** 11-10-10		A P McCoy
4 **Nil Desperandum** 9-10-7		T P Treacy

11-1, 5-1j, 5-1j, 33-1. 6l, 1¹/4l, shd. 40 ran. 9m 41.0 (a1m2.60)
Mr O B P Carroll (M Brassil, IRE).

A classy renewal of the world's most valuable steeplechase and a quality finish to match as **Numbersixvalverde** just had too much for the well-backed **Hedgehunter** and **Clan Royal**. The rain came just in time for Numbersixvalverde, campaigned specifically for the race since winning the 2005 Irish National, and he ran out a decisive winner after four looked to hold every chance at the last. Having crept slowly into contention, he was going well on the heels of the leaders in the latter stages and was produced perfectly at the final fence, when he saw out the trip better than anyone. Hedgehunter, though, lost nothing in defeat, only his welter burden in testing conditions denying him back-to-back Nationals. He has not stopped improving in the last few seasons. Clan Royal may have missed his time, though, as he just fell short once more. **Nil Desperandum**, another race specialist after his sixth in 2005, completed the leading quartet, who were well clear of **Risk Accessor** and **Puntal**. The only major hard-luck story was **Ballycassidy**, clear and still going well when he fell at Valentine's on the second circuit.

53 Powers Whiskey Irish Grand National (3m5f)

Fairyhouse April 17 (Good)

1 **Point Barrow** 8-10-8	P A Carberry
2 **Oulart** 7-10-1	R Loughran (3)
3 A New Story 8-10-6	Andrew J McNamara
4 American Jennie 8-10-7	D N Russell

20-1, 10-1, 16-1, 16-1. 1l, 8l, 1¹/2l. 26 ran. 7m 41.7
(b38.33)
Mrs P Clune Hughes (P Hughes, IRE).

Not a patch on the English version now the Irish have rediscovered their love of Aintree, particularly as most of the fancied runners failed to perform. The exception was **Oulart**, still a maiden over fences but well-weighted on his hurdling form, but he could never quite get to **Point Barrow**, who was sent on before the fourth-last and saw off all his pursuers in determined style. Only eight and winning for the first time since a useful novice campaign in 2004/05, he could go on from this. **Dun Doire**, on a seven-timer after Cheltenham, could never get in contention and finished seventh.

54 Gala Casinos Daily Record Scottish National Hcp Chase (Grd3) (4m1f)

Ayr April 22 (Good)

1 **Run For Paddy** 10-10-2	C Llewellyn
2 Ladalko 7-10-1	R Walsh
3 Royal Emperor 10-11-4	D Elsworth
4 Idle Talk 7-10-11	J M Maguire

33-1, 7-1j, 50-1, 8-1. shd, ¹/2l, 10l. 30 ran. 8m 35.1
(a26.70)
Mr B Perkins (C Llewellyn, Upper Lambourn).

It is remarkable how often this 4m1f marathon goes right down to the wire, and this was another example as **Run For Paddy** beat **Ladalko** and **Royal Emperor** in a thriller. The first three were all held up early on with Royal Emperor first to work his way into contention, hitting the front five out. Ladalko came past him approaching the last, but Run For Paddy had left his run latest of all and just scraped home.

Ladalko remains the most progressive horse in the race but is starting to rack up the losses, while the most honourable performance came from Royal Emperor, who had been done few favours by the handicapper.

55 Kerrygold Champion Chase (Grade 1) (2m)

Punchestown April 25 (Good)

1 **Newmill** 8-11-12	Andrew J McNamara
2 Fota Island 10-11-12	A P McCoy
3 Central House 9-11-12	R Loughran

5-4f, 9-4, 6-1. 15l, ³/4l. 6 ran. 4m 6.3
(b7.89)
Mrs Mary T Hayes (J J Murphy, IRE).

If the nature of the Champion Chase had led anyone to question **Newmill**'s quality, he answered those critics emphatically with another crushing win. Newmill led at a strong pace from start to finish and none of his rivals ever got close, with the win in the bag a long way out despite at least three serious mistakes, confirming he will take some deposing even against the likes of Azertyuiop, Well Chief and Kauto Star. **Fota Island** and **Central House** were probably both below their best at the end of a long season, as were **Mariah Rollins** and **Sir Oj**.

56 Punchestown Guinness Gold Cup (Grade 1) (3m1f)

Punchestown April 26 (Good)

1 **War Of Attrition** 7-11-12	C O'Dwyer
2 Beef Or Salmon 10-11-12	T J Murphy
3 Hi Cloy 9-11-12	Andrew J McNamara

4-5f, 9-2, 15-2. 2¹/2l, 1¹/2l. 6 ran. 6m 17.7
(b10.73)
Gigginstown House Stud (M Morris, IRE).

War Of Attrition confirmed his status as an excellent Gold Cup winner with this follow-up, also showing his adaptability having been forced to make his own running. Conor O'Dwyer elected to do so at a pedestrian pace before gradually winding up the tempo on the final circuit. He produced a breathtaking leap at the third-last as **Hi Cloy** and **Beef Or Salmon** challenged, enabling him to win fairly comfortably in the end. Beef Or Salmon returned to form somewhere near his best in second, just lacking the pace to go with the winner in the straight, while Hi Cloy and **Watson Lake**, both stepping into unknown territory over three miles, coped well enough without seriously threatening. **Forget The Past** was tailed off, his jumping having fallen apart.

57 Whitewater Champion Stayers' Hurdle (Grade 1) (3m)

Punchestown April 27 (Good)

1 **Asian Maze** 7-11-7	R Walsh
2 Kerryhead Windfarm 8-11-12	A J McNamara
3 Fire Dragon 5-11-10	D N Russell

8-13f, 100-1, 12-1. 4¹/₂l, ¹/₂l. 12 ran. 5m 44.2 (b9.84)

Mrs C A Moore (T Mullins, IRE).

Though not quite as visually spectacular as her Aintree romp, **Asian Maze** signed off for the season with another outstanding win – further evidence that she is a real star. Perhaps mindful of the trip, Ruby Walsh didn't ask the mare for another flat-out gallop throughout but still made it a true test and, as he increased the tempo four out, he soon had all bar **Fire Dragon** beaten. Fire Dragon eventually gave best as well, and in the end Asian Maze was chased home by **Kerryhead Windfarm**, whose proximity need not detract from the form as she always seems to overperform in top company. Fire Dragon suffered for trying to chase Asian Maze but confirmed himself a top-class stayer, beating the rest out of sight. **Sky's The Limit** was well below par.

58 Acc Bank Champion Hurdle (Grade 1) (2m)

Punchestown April 28 (Good)

1 **Macs Joy** 7-11-12		B J Geraghty
2 **Brave Inca** 8-11-12		A P McCoy
3 **Hardy Eustace** 9-11-12		C O'Dwyer

11-4, 4-5f, 4-1. 4l, 1l. 4 ran. 3m 51.8 (b2.44)

Mac's J Racing Syndicate (Mrs J Harrington, IRE).

Barry Geraghty stole the race with an enterprising ride on **Macs Joy**, setting this hold-up horse alight three out to turn the tables on his Champion Hurdle conqueror **Brave Inca**. The race had panned out as expected, with **Hardy Eustace** leading but hassled all the time by Brave Inca, until Geraghty played his surprise hand on Macs Joy, soon opening up a 5l lead which he was never going to relinquish. Whether Macs Joy will be able to repeat this superiority promises to be one of the most fascinating questions of this season – certainly Tony McCoy cannot claim to have been simply caught cold, as Macs Joy's turn of foot when he quickened clear was awesome, yet the proximity of Hardy Eustace, and more so **Essex**, suggests the champion was not at his peak.

59 Betfred Million Hurdle (2m110yds)

Sandown April 28 (Good)

1 **Noble Request** 5-11-8		R Johnson
2 **Faasel** 5-11-4		A Dobbin
3 **Intersky Falcon** 9-11-4		M A Fitzgerald
3 **Penzance** 5-11-4		R Thornton

2-1f, 9-4, 11-1, 15-2. 1¹/₂l, 1l, dht. 8 ran. 3m 46.8 (b6.02)

Mrs Karola Vann (P Hobbs, Minehead).

Noble Request had gone from strength to strength all season and rounded things off in fine style, pointing the way towards a Champion Hurdle campaign. He had won a similar contest at Ayr the previous week but had plenty more on his plate here with **Faasel** 15lb better off for a 5l beating, which indicates Noble Request's rapid rate of improvement into a genuinely high-class hurdler and Faasel's lack of resolution – he was travelling best by far two out before finding little. **Arcalis** finished his season under a cloud with a team fifth, having disappointed when favourite in the Ayr contest.

60 Betfred Gold Cup Handicap Chase (Grade 3) (3m5f110yds)

Sandown April 29 (Good to Firm)

1 **Lacdoudal** 7-11-5		R Johnson
2 **Eric's Charm** 8-10-7		L Aspell
3 **My Will** 6-11-2		R Walsh
4 **Liberthine** 7-10-6		Mr S Waley-Cohen (7)

10-1, 8-1, 8-1, 10-1. 1¹/₄l, hd, 10l. 18 ran. 7m 18.9 (a8.20)

Mrs R J Skan (P Hobbs, Minehead).

The traditional finale to the season and an absolutely storming contest, with the finish fought out by three well-fancied young horses. Many had long felt **Lacdoudal** had been crying out for a stamina test and they were proved right as he produced a memorable performance, jumping spectacularly and racing clear of the opposition in the straight before the pack closed in again as he idled on the run-in. **Eric's Charm** and **My Will** ran great races in defeat, as did fifth-placed **Therealbandit**, who jumped left throughout and looked desperate for easier ground. The massively frustrating **One Knight**, yet again failed to complete, falling on the final circuit when going well.

LACDOUDAL: winning at Sandown

Big-race index

All horses placed or commented on in our big-race review section, with race numbers

Adamant Approach 5, 47	Hi Cloy 6, 22, 50, 56
Akilak..17	Hoo La Baloo 31
Al Eile 27, 39	Idle Talk 54
All In The Stars.......................................11	Impek 8, 18, 43, 50
American Jennie 53	Inglis Drever 10, 20
A New Story 53	Innox 38
Arcalis 12, 27, 39, 59	Intersky Falcon 16, 17, 59
Ashley Brook 3, 13	Iris's Gift 46
Asian Maze 33, 39, 51, 57	Irish Hussar 40
Ballycassidy 38, 52	Joaaci 25, 34
Baracouda 10, 44	Juveigneur 40
Beef Or Salmon 7, 23, 32, 46, 49, 56	Kalca Mome 31
Best Mate...3	Kandjar D'allier 4, 11
Brave Inca 9, 14, 24, 29, 39, 58	Kauto Star 3, 13, 41
Briareus 39	Kawagino...51
Brooklyn Breeze 15	Kelrev 45
Celestial Gold 46, 49	Kerryhead Windfarm 57
Central House 6, 22, 41, 50, 55	Kicking King 1, 7, 18
Charlies First 26	King Harald...11
Clan Royal 52	Kingscliff 2, 7, 18, 28, 46
Comply Or Die 11, 21	Korelo 10
Contraband 3	Lacdoudal 15, 43, 60
Control Man 25	Ladalko 38, 54
Cornish Rebel 11, 21, 46	L'Ami 11, 18, 38, 46, 49
Crystal d'Ainay 10, 21, 25	L'Aventure 21
Dancing Bay 36	Le Passing 15, 45
Dempsey 31, 41	Liberthine 60
Desert Quest 47	Lingo 5
Dom d'Orgeval 42	Lord Transcend 28
Dun Doire 40, 53	Macs Joy 9, 24, 29, 33, 39, 58
Ebony Light 28	Marcus de Berlais 37
Eric's Charm 60	Mariah Rollins 50, 55
Essex 9, 24, 33, 58	Mighty Man 30, 44, 48
Eurotrek 25	Mister McGoldrick 27, 41, 50
Faasel 16, 27, 39, 59	Model Son 34, 40
Feathard Lady 17	Monkerhostin 3, 4, 8, 13, 18, 46, 49
Fire Dragon 30, 44, 48, 57	Moscow Flyer 6, 22, 41
Fondmort 4, 15, 35, 43, 50	Moulin Riche...40
Forget The Past 23, 37, 46, 56	My Way de Solzen 20, 36, 44, 48
Fota Island 22, 41, 50, 55	My Will 19, 35, 38, 43, 60
Garvivonnian 37	Native Upmanship 32
Golden Cross 14, 29, 44	Neptune Collonges 20
Graphic Approach 45	Newmill 9, 24, 41, 55
Grey Abbey 2, 19	Nil Desperandum 52
Ground Ball 33	Noble Request 47, 59
Harchibald 9, 16, 24	Non So 45
Hardy Eustace 29, 39, 51, 58	No Refuge 30, 48
Hedgehunter 23, 32, 46, 52	No Where To Hyde 26, 42
Heros Collonges 21	Numbersixvalverde 52

Ollie Magern	2, 7, 18, 49
One Knight	21, 60
Oneway	13
Ossmoses	34
Oulart	53
Our Vic	4, 15, 35, 43
Patriarch Express	30
Penzance	16, 59
Phar Bleu	5, 42
Pirate Flagship	47
Pizarro	1
Point Barrow	53
Pom Flyer	26
Puntal	52
Red Devil Robert	11
Redemption	4
Risk Accessor	39, 52
River City	41, 50
Roman Ark	45
Rooster Booster	5
Royal Auclair	18
Royal Emperor	54
Royal Shakespeare	12, 17
Run For Paddy	54
Sadlers Wings	29
Saintsaire	45
Scots Grey	15
Self Defense	5, 17
Sir Oj	15, 55
Sir Rembrandt	21, 25, 34, 46
Sky's The Limit	42, 51, 57
Solerina	14
Sporazene	36
Starzaan	20
Strangely Brown	42
Studmaster	26, 47
Take The Stand	2, 19, 46, 49
The French Furze	12
Therealbandit	15, 19, 60
Thisthatandtother	8, 15
Trabolgan	11
Tramantano	5
Truckers Tavern	28
Tysou	31
War Of Attrition	1, 23, 46, 56
Watson Lake	56
Westender	5, 30
What A Native	34

SIR REMBRANDT: a standing dish in many of the season's top staying chases

Outlook

Top novices
by Dylan Hill

1 **Anglo Irish Bank Novice Hurdle (Grade 2) (2m110yds)**
Cheltenham November 11 (Good to Soft)
1 **Boychuk** 4-11-0 R Johnson
2 **Buena Vista** 4-11-7 T J Murphy
3 **Two Miles West** 4-11-7 A P McCoy
8-1, 9-4f, 7-2. 2l, 2¹/2l. 10 ran. 4m 1.6
(a6.10)
Mrs D L Whateley (P Hobbs, Minehead).

The first really competitive novice hurdle of the year, bringing together most of the best early-season novices. It was also an eye-catching victory from **Boychuk**, who was badly outpaced down the hill but made up several lengths in the straight to win readily. However, as this performance suggested, he will need much further to be seen at his best and failed to win again. The two to take out of the race were Martin Pipe's front-running **Buena Vista**, ultra-tough and consistent, and the staying-on fifth **Natal**.

2 **Concord At Jet.com Juvenile Hurdle (Grade 2) (2m110yds)**
Cheltenham November 12 (Good to Soft)
1 **Fair Along** 3-10-12 R Johnson
2 **Afsoun** 3-10-12 M Foley
3 **Kasbah Bliss** 3-11-6 A Duchene
11-2, 3-1f, 4-1. 3l, 8l. 13 ran. 4m 2.1
(a6.60)
Mr Alan Peterson (P Hobbs, Minehead).

A high-class field of juveniles were torn apart by **Fair Along**, who set a fierce gallop and was 15 lengths clear at the top of the hill. Though he hit the second-last, he still had enough in the tank to run on strongly for an impressive win. Only **Afsoun** managed to live with the winner, though French raider **Kasbah Bliss** also ran well under his 8lb penalty, and subsequent events would prove all three to be very smart individuals.

3 **Independent Newspaper Novice Chase (Grade 2) (2m)**
Cheltenham November 13 (Good to Soft)
1 **Accordion Etoile** 6-11-5 J Cullen
2 **Tamarinbleu** 5-11-5 A P McCoy
3 **Albuhera** 7-11-5 R Walsh
5-2f, 3-1, 9-2. shd, 6l. 10 ran. 3m 58.0
(b4.08)
Banjo Syndicate (P Nolan, IRE).

This looked a phenomenal Arkle trial, with **Accordion Etoile** and **Tamarinbleu** leaving a quality field in their wake and enjoying a terrific battle up the hill. Accordion Etoile wasn't particularly fluent – a problem that could still stop him reaching the top – but he showed a brilliant turn of foot to reel in Tamarinbleu on the flat and is a real class act. Tamarinbleu lost nothing in defeat, especially on his chasing debut, and though not suited by the hurly-burly of the Arkle, he remains a potentially under-rated horse. **Albuhera** soon translated his hurdles form in third but couldn't match the first two.

4 **Unicoin Homes Novice Chase (Grade 2) (3m)**
Newbury November 25 (Good)
1 **Darkness** 6-11-2 B Fenton
2 **Iris's Gift** 8-11-9 A P McCoy
3 **Unleash** 6-11-2 R Johnson
14-1, 4-7f, 16-1. 13l, shd. 7 ran. 5m 53.8
(b6.20)
Lady Lloyd-Webber (C Egerton, Chaddleworth).

Iris's Gift began the season as one of the most fascinating horses to follow, but this defeat said much about his future prospects. Clumsy over his fences, Iris's Gift could never get into his customary galloping rhythm as a result and was put firmly in his place – after falling at Warwick and flopping in the Gold Cup, his progress will again be watched with great interest. The demise of the favourite led to some silly antepost prices being knocked about for **Darkness**, but this was still a quality performance.

5 **Sodexho Prestige Henry VIII Novice Chase (Grade 2) (2m)**
Sandown December 3 (Soft)
1 **Racing Demon** 5-11-10 T J Murphy
2 **Hoo La Baloo** 4-10-13 M A Fitzgerald
3 **Cerium** 4-10-13 Christian Williams

6-4f, 6-1, 4-1. 4l, 10l. 7 ran. 4m 6.1
 (a19.70)
Mrs T P Radford (Miss H Knight, Wantage).

Henrietta Knight had lost one superstar in November with the tragic death of Best Mate, but this was the emergence of another. **Racing Demon**, an unlucky loser in the SunAlliance Hurdle in 2005, was held up as **Hoo La Baloo** set a furious pace but made effortless headway in the latter stages and won with plenty to spare. The Paul Nicholls pair Hoo La Baloo and **Cerium** appeared to run right up to form, suggesting this was a top-class effort for only his second run over fences.

6 Bet at Bluesquare.com Royal Bond Novice Hurdle (Grade 1) (2m)
Fairyhouse December 4 (Heavy)
1 **Iktitaf** 4-11-7   P Carberry
2 **O'Muircheartaigh** 5-11-12   B J Geraghty
3 **Mounthenry** 5-11-12   D N Russell
7-1, 4-5f, 5-1. 5l, 3¹/2l. 8 ran. 4m 2.3
 (a1.01)
Mrs P Sloan (N Meade, IRE).

A surprise result as **Iktitaf**, unplaced off 109 in a Listowel handicap in September but progressive since, found lots more improvement to upset the odds-on **O'Muircheartaigh**. It was no fluke either as he left a field packed with decent novices well strung out, and he would certainly have been hard to beat in the Supreme but for injury. O'Muircheartaigh had looked excellent in winning at Navan on his debut but had his limitations exposed.

7 Brit Insurance Novice Hurdle (Grade 2) (3m)
Cheltenham December 10 (Good to Soft)
1 **Black Jack Ketchum** 6-11-7   A P McCoy
2 **Gungadu** 5-11-0   Christian Williams
3 **Amicelli** 6-11-7   R Johnson
4-6f, 5-1, 10-1. 2l, 24l. 6 ran. 5m 56.1
 (a16.10)
Mrs G Smith (Jonjo O'Neill, Cheltenham).

Black Jack Ketchum had built up a decent reputation with four wins in lesser company and it went into overdrive after this hugely impressive win in his stiffest test to date. Held up in rear, he cruised through on the bridle to challenge the useful **Gungadu** at the last and was in command the second he was shaken up on the flat. He went straight to the Festival looking a banker for the three-miler.

8 Durkan New Homes Novice Chase (Grade 1) (2m1f)
Leopardstown December 26 (Good to Soft)
1 **Missed That** 6-11-12   D J Casey
2 **Wild Passion** 5-11-10   P Carberry
3 **Kill Devil Hill** 5-11-10   J L Cullen
10-1, 7-2, 6-1. 1¹/2l, 25l. 8 ran. 4m 12.1
 (b8.78)

114

Mrs Violet O'Leary (W P Mullins, IRE).

With the exception of Accordion Etoile, all the best two-mile Irish novices were in action for this Boxing Day showpiece, although only two, **Missed That** and **Wild Passion**, managed to get seriously involved. Missed That had failed to impress on his chasing debut at Thurles but put that right in a ding-dong battle, leading on the home turn and fighting back again close home having been headed on the run-in. **Justified**, sent off as short as 5-4 after two clearcut wins, crashed out at the first, **Mansony** fell at the last when a close third, and **Kill Devil Hill** and **Arteea** were disappointing.

9 Stan James Feltham Novice Chase (Grade 1) (3m110yds)
Sandown December 26 (Good)
1 **Darkness** 6-11-7   A P McCoy
2 **Zabenz** 8-11-7   R Walsh
3 **Bewleys Berry** 7-11-7   A Dobbin
13-8f, 8-1, 7-2. 3l, hd. 5 ran. 6m 16.2
 (a20.95)
Lady Lloyd-Webber (C Egerton, Chaddleworth).

An odd race as **Darkness** looked out with the washing at one point before finishing with a right old rattle to storm past **Zabenz** and **Bewleys Berry**. Hugely impressive when beating Iris's Gift at Newbury, and again in following up at Cheltenham earlier in the month, Darkness was nowhere near as good over his fences and only ever got on terms in the straight to pull away from Zabenz, who had looked like the winner in front, and another thorough stayer in Bewleys Berry. He seemingly needs soft ground to put in a good round.

10 At The Races 1.2 Million Viewers Finale Juvenile Hurdle (2m110yds)
Chepstow December 27 (Good to Soft)
1 **Blue Shark** 3-11-0   M A Fitzgerald
2 **Turko** 3-11-0   R Walsh
3 **Patman Du Charmil** 3-11-0 Antony Evans
7-1, 11-10f, 40-1. 8l, 11l. 15 ran. 3m 58.0
 (a2.05)
Mr Trevor Hemmings (N Henderson, Lambourn).

Despite its Grade One status, this race is often an unreliable guide as most young horses find the stamina demands beyond them, and once more the field was well strung out. However, **Blue Shark** could well be a cut above average as he arrived from France with a big reputation and showed a good turn of foot to race away from the 11-10 favourite **Turko**. Nicky Henderson was unable to get another run into him but he remains one to follow. Turko owed his short price to a close second behind Afsoun but that run soon proved to be overrated.

11 stanjames.com Challow Novice Hurdle (Grade 1) (2m4f110yds)

Cheltenham January 1 (Good to Soft)

1 **Denman** 6-11-7		R Walsh
2 **The Cool Guy** 6-11-7		C Llewellyn
3 **Boychuk** 5-11-7		R Johnson

5-2f, 7-2, 3-1. 21l, ³/4l. 8 ran. 4m 59.5 (a10.50)

Mr Paul K Barber & Mrs M Findlay (P Nicholls, Shepton Mallet).

The emergence of a potential superstar as **Denman** stormed to a brilliant wide-margin win. Sent off at 5-2 with a trio of previous winners – **Boychuk**, **The Cool Guy** and **It's a Dream** – also challenging for favouritism, Denman never gave any of them a chance, powering away in the straight to become a strong favourite for Cheltenham as the rest battled for places. The opposition probably didn't amount to much but this was still pretty special.

12 Unicoin Homes 'Dipper' Novice Chase (Grade 2) (2m5f)

Cheltenham January 1 (Good to Soft)

1 **The Listener** 7-11-11		A Thornton
2 **Napolitain** 5-10-8		Christian Williams
3 **Star De Mohaison** 5-10-12		M A Fitzgerald

8-11f, 20-1, 4-1. ³/4l, 1¹/4l. 7 ran. 5m 22.2 (a8.70)

Old Moss Farm (R Alner, Blandford).

The Listener came into this race on a hat-trick after impressive wins at Exeter and Windsor and cemented his reputation as one of the best staying novices around by giving weight all round to a decent field. The Listener buckled down well under pressure after a slowly-run race, and had anyone been told afterwards they had seen the SunAlliance winner few would have doubted it was him. Yet **Star de Mohaison**, well beaten by The Listener at Exeter, got significantly closer this time and was also staying on strongly in the closing stages having lost his position earlier on.

13 Anglo Irish Bank Corporate Treasury Tolworth Hurdle (Grd 1) (2m110yds)

Sandown January 7 (Soft)

1 **Noland** 5-11-7		Christian Williams

THE LISTENER: put in an exhibition round at Cheltenham on New Year's Day

2 **Whispered Promises** 5-11-7   J P McNamara
3 **Albarino** 7-11-7   T Scudamore
6-4f, 15-2, 9-1. 5l, 9l. 5 ran. 4m 6.7
(a13.88)
Mr J Hales (P Nicholls, Shepton Mallet).

Noland had little to beat in a desperately weak renewal, made weaker by the failures of his main market rivals **Lennon** and **Compton Bolter** to reproduce their smart form in other spheres of the game. However, Noland still won with great authority, stamping his authority in the race by powering clear of a couple of decent sorts.

14 Paddy Fitzpatrick Memorial Novice Chase (Grade 2) (2m5f)

Leopardstown January 15 (Heavy)
1 **Nickname** 7-11-5   C O'Dwyer
2 **Father Matt** 8-11-5   B J Geraghty
3 **Romaha** 10-11-5   L J Fleming
evensf, 10-3, 100-1. 11l, 5l. 6 ran. 6m 2.7
(a26.29)
Mrs Claudia Jungo-Corpataux (M Brassil, IRE).

Few horses made such a favourable impression all season as **Nickname** did here, trotting up for the second time in two weeks after a breathtaking display of jumping. As a dual Grade One winner in France, he is clearly a huge talent and simply pulverised the opposition. While his absence at Cheltenham probably made little difference to the outcome given he looks to be far better on soft ground, this marks him out as one to follow.

15 Intercasino.co.uk Novice Chase (Grade 2) (2m)

Lingfield January 21 (Soft)
1 **Foreman** 8-11-3   A P McCoy
2 **Le Volfoni** 5-10-13   J Tizzard
3 **Marcel** 6-11-3   R Greene
11-8, evensf, 9-1. 3l, 12l. 4 ran. 4m 7.8
(a11.00)
Mr John P McManus (T Doumen, FRANCE).

Former Champion Hurdle fourth **Foreman** got his career back on track with an excellent defeat of the well-regarded **Le Volfoni**. Tried twice over fences in 2004 prior to an unsuccessful return to hurdling in France, Foreman was the outsider against his younger rival in a virtual match but won almost as he pleased, jumping well on unsuitably soft ground and quickening up nicely on the run-in.

16 Baileys Arkle Perpetual Challenge Cup Novice Chase (Grade 1) (2m1f)

Leopardstown January 29 (Good to Soft)
1 **Missed That** 7-11-12   D J Casey
2 **Arteea** 7-11-12   Andrew J McNamara
3 **Justified** 7-11-12   A P McCoy
3-1, 25-1, 5-2. ³/4l, 9l. 7 ran. 4m 16.8
(b4.08)

Mrs Violet O'Leary (W P Mullins, IRE).

A disappointing race with 11-8 favourite **Nickname** pulled up after breaking blood vessels and **Justified** below his best. On their day both might have beaten **Missed That**, who was all out to wear down **Arteea**, yet the winner had produced a similarly dour victory over Wild Passion at Christmas and is admirably tough to make up for his slight lack of class. Arteea also came into this a seriously underrated horse.

17 Anthony Baker Juvenile Novice Hurdle (2m110yds)

Sandown February 4 (Good)
1 **Detroit City** 4-11-3   R Johnson
2 **Royals Darling** 4-11-3   M A Fitzgerald
3 **Linnet** 4-10-5   P Carberry
2-1, 11-8f, 20-1. 7l, 1¹/2l. 9 ran. 3m 56.9
(a4.08)
Mr Terry Warner (P Hobbs, Minehead).

Not the strongest of races but an eye-catching performance from **Detroit City**. Niggled to dispute the lead down the back straight, he stormed clear of Royals Darling once shaken up in the straight to become the new favourite for the Triumph.

18 Totesport.com Scilly Isles Novice Chase (Grade 1) (2m4f110yds)

Sandown February 4 (Good to Firm)
1 **Napolitain** 5-10-12   A P McCoy
2 **Turpin Green** 7-11-6   A Dobbin
3 **Stance** 7-11-6   J E Moore
3-1, 9-4, 16-1. nk, 21l. 4 ran. 5m 7.9
(a11.67)
The Stewart Family (P Nicholls, Shepton Mallet).

Only four runners but plenty of drama, all at the final fence when **Turpin Green**, with the race at his mercy, was spooked and tried to run out. Tony Dobbin forced him over the obstacle and then coaxed a fabulous renewed effort, from a virtual standing start, which nearly reeled in the reprieved **Napolitain** and proved him the clear moral winner. Napolitain is short of true Grade One class and will find things difficult under his penalty, while **Albuhera** ran no sort of race.

19 Blue Square Casino Kingmaker Novice Chase (Grade 2) (2m)

Wincanton February 18 (Soft)
1 **Voy Por Ustedes** 5-11-1   R Thornton
2 **Hoo La Baloo** 5-11-4   S Thomas
3 **Dictum** 8-11-3   T Scudamore
10-11f, 6-5, 25-1. 2¹/2l, dis. 4 ran. 3m 59.5
(a3.75)
Sir Robert Ogden (A King, Barbury Castle).

This was a virtual match between two classy novices and they managed to produce a real cracker. **Voy Por Ustedes** had rattled up three short-priced wins before the New Year and always just had the edge, comfortably holding **Hoo La Baloo** up the straight despite minor mistakes at the last two fences to set himself up perfectly for a crack at the Arkle.

20 RPSport Sports Adonis Juvenile Novice Hurdle (Grade 1) (2m110yds)

Sandown February 25 (Soft)

1 **Kasbah Bliss** 4-11-5		A Duchene
2 **Blazing Bailey** 4-11-2		R Thornton
3 **Twist Magic** 4-11-5		Christian Williams

2-1f, 5-2, 11-2. 1¹/2l, dis. 8 ran. 4m 5.1 (a12.28)

Mr Henri de Pracomtal (F Doumen, FRANCE).

Traditionally the strongest trial for the Triumph, this lacked its normal strength in depth but still threw up another leading contender in French raider **Kasbah Bliss**. The combination of a fierce gallop and testing ground led to the field being well strung out – a distance separated **Blazing Bailey** and **Twist Magic** – so Kasbah Bliss's stamina looks his major forte and he asserted well from two out to beat the previously unbeaten Blazing Bailey.

21 Anglo Irish Bank Supreme Novice Hurdle (Grade 1) (2m110yds)

Cheltenham March 14 (Good)

1 **Noland** 5-11-7		R Walsh
2 **Straw Bear** 5-11-7		A P McCoy
3 **Buena Vista** 5-11-7		T J Murphy

6-1, 11-1, 14-1. nk, 1¹/4l. 20 ran. 3m 54.5 (b1.00)

Mr J Hales (P Nicholls, Shepton Mallet).

Noland had several major factors to overcome here yet won in the most remarkable fashion, passing a string of horses on the run-in to get up close home. A slow early pace made it difficult for those coming off the pace, including Noland, particularly when he was outpaced down the hill and misjudged the third-last to leave himself in a seemingly hopeless position. However, he absolutely flew after turning for home, gobbling up the hill to deny **Straw Bear** in the shadow of the post. Yet perhaps the biggest factor against Noland had been Paul Nicholls' dire record in Festival novice hurdles, with Ditcheat's finest always beaten by more precocious types before stepping up a level over fences. The future is exciting for Noland if his progress follows that pattern, and he certainly could be an even better recruit to chasing. Straw Bear would also have wanted a better gallop and lost all momentum when walking through the last after he had looked set to quicken clear. **Buena Vista** was a game third having dictated the pace from two more top prospects in **Sublimity** and **Sweet Wake**, a shade disappointing given he started at 5-2 but that was more the result of gallops talk rather than anything achieved in two straightforward

wins. **Rasharrow**, **O'Muircheartaigh** and **Quatre Heures** were other well-fancied flops.

22 Irish Independent Arkle Challenge Trophy Chase (Grade 1) (2m)

Cheltenham March 14 (Good)

1 **Voy Por Ustedes** 5-11-2		R Thornton
2 **Monet's Garden** 8-11-7		A Dobbin
3 **Foreman** 8-11-7		A P McCoy

15-2, 8-1, 5-1. 1¹/4l, 5l. 14 ran. 3m 52.3 (b9.78)

Sir Robert Ogden (A King, Barbury Castle).

A high-class Arkle and, in pulling clear of such a good field, **Voy Por Ustedes** and **Monet's Garden** suggested they have it in them to graduate to bigger things this season. With four five-year-olds winning in eight years now with their controversial allowance, Voy Por Ustedes clearly had an advantage, but he still deserves enormous credit. Jumping brilliantly, he was the only horse able to latch on to the front-running Monet's Garden without being taken off his feet and pulled clear on the run-in. Connections of Monet's Garden had been torn between the Arkle and the SunAlliance, and he justified their decision with a spectacular display of jumping out in front. Several top-class staying types have floundered in this speed test - **Racing Demon** was another this year - which emphasises his quality and he could be a leading Gold Cup horse one day. **Foreman** and **Wild Passion** fought out third to frank the form, Foreman coming from off the pace to pass the more forceful Wild Passion up the hill, while **Don't Be Shy** was a never-nearer fifth. **Missed That** and Racing Demon were next, the latter clearly capable of better, while **Accordion Etoile** was travelling well when falling around halfway.

23 Royal & SunAlliance Novice Hurdle (Grade 1) (2m5f)

Cheltenham March 15 (Good)

1 **Nicanor** 5-11-7		P Carberry
2 **Denman** 6-11-7		R Walsh
3 **Refinement** 7-11-0		A P McCoy

17-2, 11-10f, 11-2. 2¹/2l, 6l. 17 ran. 5m 1.0 (b6.65)

Mr D P Sharkey (N Meade, IRE).

Several big bets went down as **Denman**, the banker of the meeting for many punters after his Challow Hurdle romp, lost out to **Nicanor**. In fairness Denman could have done no more, taking up the running after the second-last and galloping strongly to the line. However, Nicanor, despite having a bit to find on the book, was always travelling sweetly in behind and quickened up well on the flat for a cosy win, justifying Noel Meade's high opinion of him. Both are expected to go chasing soon and Denman, like Noland and so many other Paul Nicholls inmates, looks the more

HAIRY MOLLY (near side): all out to beat Pressgang in the Champion Bumper

guaranteed to improve for the transition. Only five were given any chance in the betting and two of the others, **Refinement** and **Mr Nosie**, filled the next two places to give the form a solid look. **Mr Pointment**, a close fifth, was the only other horse to get a sniff, with French raider **Zaiyad** a disappointing ninth.

24 Royal & SunAlliance Chase (Grade 1) (3m110yds)

Cheltenham March 15 (Good)

1 **Star De Mohaison** 5-10-8		B J Geraghty
2 **Idle Talk** 7-11-4		J M Maguire
3 **Darkness** 7-11-4		P J Brennan

14-1, 33-1, 11-2. 6l, 11l. 15 ran. 6m 9.0 (b12.50)

Sir Robert Ogden (P Nicholls, Shepton Mallet).

The usual catalogue of mishaps, with only seven out of 15 getting round and **Star de Mohaison** winning primarily because he was the only horse to put in anything approaching a decent round. Yet another French recruit making the most of five-year-old weight allowances, Star de Mohaison moved smoothly to the front four out and was left in total control two fences later by the fall of **Back In Front**. He eventually won easily from the staying-on **Idle Talk** and **Darkness** but probably had little to beat given the carnage behind. Indeed, Darkness put in perhaps the worst round of all and was never a serious factor, but he at least stayed on his feet, unlike early casualty **Our Ben** and second-last fallers **The Listener** and Back In Front. The Listener was going nowhere at the time, but Back In Front was the surprise of the race,

running a stormer on only his only second start over fences, and he would have been a good second stamina permitting. **Commercial Flyer**, the 9-2 favourite after a sole win at Taunton, lost his action and was pulled up four out before being asked a serious question.

25 Weatherbys Champion Bumper Standard Open NH Flat Race (Grd1) (2m110yds)

Cheltenham March 15 (Good)

1 **Hairy Molly** 6-11-5		P Carberry
2 **Pressgang** 4-10-11		T Doyle
3 **Kicks For Free** 5-11-5		M A Fitzgerald

33-1, 20-1, 5-1. hd, 1³/4l. 23 ran. 3m 46.7 (b6.78)

F T B Syndicate (J Crowley, IRE).

The market could not have got this more wrong with a 33-1 winner in **Hairy Molly** and third-placed **Kicks For Free** the only horse in the top nine priced in single figures. However, the result still upheld a couple of Champion Bumper trends, with Hairy Molly the 11th Irish winner out of 14 and **Pressgang** maintaining Paul Webber's great record in the race. For the second successive year, though, Webber had to settle for second as Pressgang, looking all over the winner, hung badly right and then jinked left in the final furlong to allow Hairy Molly a lead he couldn't quite get back. Kicks For Free ran well, but Willie Mullins' pair **Equus Maximus** and **Ballytrim** were the major disappointments back in 12th and 13th. It's hard to see Hairy Molly as a great champion, although he ran well again at Punchestown when

Sponsored by Stan James

a close second to the unbeaten Leading Run, while ninth-placed **Pangbourne** turned the form upside-down when winning at Aintree.

26 JCB Triumph Hurdle (Grade 1) (2m1f)
Cheltenham March 17 (Good)

1 **Detroit City** 4-11-0	R Johnson
2 **Fair Along** 4-11-0	P J Brennan
3 **Blazing Bailey** 4-11-0	R Thornton

7-2f, 25-1, 14-1. 5l, 1l. 17 ran. 3m 51.2 (b12.30)
Mr Terry Warner (P Hobbs, Minehead).

A course-record time from **Detroit City** as the ground dried out, so while his performance wasn't the prettiest it was still out of the top drawer. Pushed along at halfway and jumping left throughout, he was helped by stable-mate **Fair Along** making it a true test of stamina with the entire field off the bridle at the top of the hill. Fair Along was still in front at that point and clung on to his lead until approaching the last, but Detroit City was in hot pursuit and stayed on stoutly up the hill. Fair Along ran a blinder in second, though he might have been collared had the closing **Breathing Fire** not fallen at the last, and Blazing Bailey was a good third. This quartet come out clear best with some sizeable gaps behind, though **Afsoun**, who sweated up badly beforehand, had his excuses in fifth and **Kasbah Bliss** fell at the fourth Irish hope **Mister Hight** was a poor eighth.

27 Brit Insurance Novice Hurdle (Grade 2) (3m)
Cheltenham March 17 (Good)

1 **Black Jack Ketchum** 7-11-7	A P McCoy
2 **Powerstation** 6-11-7	D N Russell
3 **Travino** 7-11-7	B J Geraghty

evensf, 9-1, 6-1. 9l, 3l. 19 ran. 5m 38.3 (b1.70)
Mrs Gay Smith (Jonjo O'Neill, Cheltenham).

Only the second running of this race and it is clearly still finding its feet as there was hardly any strength in depth, a couple of fairly exposed Irish stayers providing the only serious opposition to **Black Jack Ketchum**. Yet that shouldn't take anything away from the winner, who was absolutely brilliant once again. Put away for this since his Cheltenham win in December, he never gave his backers a moment of worry as he cruised alongside **Travino** two out firmly on the bridle and only needed to be pushed out on the run-in to burst well clear with a truly breathtaking turn of foot. **Powerstation** just emerged best of the Irish, staying on past the front-running Travino, but nothing else was really in this class.

28 The Sportsman Anniversary 4-Y-O Novice Hurdle (Grade 1) (2m110yds)
Aintree April 6 (Good)

| 1 **Detroit City** 4-11-0 | R Johnson |

| 2 **Premier Dane** 4-11-0 | A Dobbin |
| 3 **Afsoun** 4-11-0 | M A Fitzgerald |

3-1f, 20-1, 7-2. 8l, 3l. 13 ran. 4m 1.4 (a8.75)
Mr Terry Warner (P Hobbs, Minehead).

Further evidence of **Detroit City**'s quality as he became the first juvenile in 27 years to complete the Cheltenham/Aintree double, despite the track and the run of the race not really suiting him. Perhaps because **Fair Along** was patently not the same horse as in the Triumph, the early pace was far from furious and Detroit City again had to be driven to hit the front early in the straight. However, he then put serious distance between himself and the rest of the field, maintaining a relentless gallop for an awesome win. **Premier Dane** ran his best race in second ahead of **Afsoun**, who was a shade disappointing given there were no obvious excuses this time.

29 John Smith's Mildmay Novice Chase (Grade 2) (3m1f)
Aintree April 7 (Good)

1 **Star De Mohaison** 5-11-0	B J Geraghty
2 **Turpin Green** 7-11-5	A Dobbin
3 **Copsale Lad** 9-11-5	M Foley

11-4f, 8-1, 8-1. 2l, 2l. 15 ran. 6m 32.2 (a20.70)
Sir Robert Ogden (P Nicholls, Shepton Mallet).

Surprisingly, this was every bit as much of a mess as the SunAlliance , with only six out of 15 getting round, but at least most of the major players made it, headed by Cheltenham hero **Star de Mohaison**. The five-year-old carried a 5lb penalty to detract from his age allowance but was still comfortably best, jumping his rivals silly and pulling out more when pressed on the run-in after he had idled between the last two. He was again impressive, though **Turpin Green** and **Copsale Lad** both look useful stayers rather than top-class types. The main disappointment was **Commercial Flyer**, forgiven his Festival flop but never a factor again and pulled up when tailed off in the straight.

30 Citroen C6 Sefton Novice Hurdle (Grade 1) (3m110yds)
Aintree April 7 (Good to Soft)

1 **Black Jack Ketchum** 7-11-4	A P McCoy
2 **Money Trix** 6-11-4	A Dobbin
3 **Neptune Collonges** 5-11-4	Chris Williams

8-13f, 12-1, 8-1. 5l, ½l. 11 ran. 6m 19.1 (a23.85)
Mrs Gay Smith (Jonjo O'Neill, Cheltenham).

For some reason this produced a far stronger field than the equivalent race at Cheltenham, with Long Walk Hurdle second **Neptune Collonges** and Nicky Richards' unexposed **Money Trix** added to the mix, yet **Black Jack Ketchum** won with even more effortless authority. This was a total demolition job as Black Jack Ketchum was never off the bridle, even when making his only mistake two out, and quickened clear on the run-in, prompting Jonjo O'Neill to describe him as the best horse he has trained. Money Trix stepped up massively on wins at Kelso and Ayr to mark himself down as a fine prospect, passing Neptune Collonges for second. **Powerstation** was a long way back in fourth, placing the form at a very high level.

31 John Smith's Imagine Appeal Top Novice Hurdle (Grade 2) (2m110yds)

Aintree April 7 (Good to Soft)

1 **Straw Bear** 5-11-3	A P McCoy
2 **Conna Castle** 7-11-3	B J Geraghty
3 **The Duke's Speech** 5-11-0	J M Maguire

2-1f, 9-2, 100-1. 13l, 5l. 16 ran. 4m 2.4 (a9.75)

Mr John P McManus (N Gifford, Findon).

A weak renewal with only one of the Supreme principals asked out again and his main rival, County Hurdle winner **Desert Quest**, running no sort of race, but this was still an exceptional performance from **Straw Bear**. He cruised up to the leaders on the home turn and soon put

the result beyond doubt, storming further and further clear with extravagant leaps over the final three hurdles to suggest he had more in the tank. He had looked slightly unlucky at Cheltenham, and this confirmed it. Irish raider **Conna Castle** ran a solid race in second, comfortably beating the rest, but, all in all, they were a modest bunch.

32 John Smith's Maghull Novice Chase (Grade 1) (2m)

Aintree April 8 (Good to Soft)

1 **Foreman** 8-11-4	A P McCoy
2 **Voy Por Ustedes** 5-11-1	R Thornton
3 **Le Volfoni** 5-11-1	J Tizzard

4-1, 10-11f, 40-1. 1l, 13l. 7 ran. 4m 12.3 (a17.42)

Mr John P McManus (T Doumen, FRANCE).

Voy Por Ustedes had beaten **Foreman** hands down in the Arkle, but in different conditions Foreman appeared to turn the tables fair and square in a cracking duel. A speed test clearly suited the French raider, who was quick enough to win a slowly-run Irish Champion Hurdle in his time, and though Voy Por Ustedes held every chance of maintaining his unbeaten run, jumping to the front still going well three out, Foreman moved upsides at the last and

QUATRE HEURES (far side): early on in the big juvenile at Punchestown

was just stronger on the run-in. Given a lot to do at the Festival, he is clearly even closer to the best than that run implied. **Le Volfoni** was well beaten in third, ahead of a disappointing **Hoo La Baloo** under unusual hold-up tactics, while **Accordion Etoile** was cruising in rear when he hit the fourth-last hard and was pulled up.

33 Powers Gold Cup (Grade 1) (2m4f)
Fairyhouse April 16 (Good to Soft)

1 **Justified** 7-11-9		A P McCoy
2 **In Compliance** 6-11-9		B J Geraghty
3 **The Railway Man** 7-11-9		D N Russell

5-1, 7-4f, 10-1. 3l, 20l. 8 ran. 4m 59.2 (b32.54)

Braybrook Syndicate (E Sheehy, IRE).

A top-class novice chase but weakened by the falls of **Missed That** and **Wild Passion** before halfway. Nonetheless, this was still a great performance from **Justified**, restoring his reputation as a leading player in this sphere as he made all the running and saw out the trip well on his first attempt. Justified also lowered the colours of **In Compliance** for the first time over fences, the runner-up having recorded two bloodless wins just before Cheltenham but too late to justify an Arkle entry. He ran well enough in second, pulling well clear of the rest.

34 VC Bet Champion Novice Hurdle (Grade 1) (2m)
Punchestown April 25 (Good)

1 **Iktitaf** 5-11-11		R Walsh
2 **Straw Bear** 5-11-11		A P McCoy
3 **Jazz Messenger** 6-11-12		D F O'Regan

8-1, 8-11f, 20-1. 7l, 1¹/2l. 7 ran. 3m 50.5 (b3.74)

Mrs P Sloan (N Meade, IRE).

While Aintree suggested **Straw Bear** was the true winner of the Supreme, this suggested the best two-mile novice might not have even been in the field. **Iktitaf**, winner of the Royal Bond before Christmas, had been injured at Fairyhouse in February and missed Cheltenham, but this confirmed him as another top-class novice as he left Straw Bear for dead, travelling ominously well behind him turning in before quickening clear before the last. Straw Bear had jumped to the front four out and had his other rivals in trouble but, with **Jazz Messenger** and **Sublimity** not beaten far, this looked a repeat of his Cheltenham form rather than the apparent improvement from Aintree. It remains to be seen just how good he is. However, Supreme favourite **Sweet Wake** certainly looks to have been over-hyped after a poor run in sixth.

35 tote.ie Champion Four-Year-Old Hurdle (Grade 1) (2m)
Punchestown April 27 (Good)

1 **Quatre Heures** 4-11-0		M A Fitzgerald
2 **Artist's Muse** 4-10-9		D N Russell
3 **Breathing Fire** 4-11-0		R M Power

9-2, 13-2, 11-4. 8l, 1¹/2l. 8 ran. 3m 52.0 (b2.24)

John Mc's Winchester Syndicate (W P Mullins, IRE).

A terrific performance by **Quatre Heures**, the best all season by any juvenile other than the outstanding Detroit City. Disappointing in the Supreme, Quatre Heures restored his reputation in devastating style, easing into contention three out when clearly travelling best and quickly storming clear when asked to assert before the last. With 9-4 favourite **Mister Hight** and **Breathing Fire**, a final-flight faller at Cheltenham, both running well – Mister Hight fell at the last, badly hampering Breathing Fire and relegating him to third – the form is rock-solid and shouldn't be detracted by Quatre Heures' subsequent flops in France.

36 Swordlestown Cup Novice Chase (Grade 1) (2m)
Punchestown April 27 (Good)

1 **Accordion Etoile** 7-11-12		J L Cullen
2 **Justified** 7-11-12		A P McCoy
3 **In Compliance** 6-11-12		B J Geraghty

9-4, 13-8f, 3-1. 2¹/2l, 3l. 6 ran. 4m 2.5 (b11.69)

Banjo Syndicate (P Nolan, IRE).

Accordion Etoile finally put in a clear round to establish himself as the best of the Irish novices, even if jumping errors may continue to dog him. Surprisingly assured over his fences, he was always close enough to the front-running **Justified** and quickened up nicely in the straight for a decent win. Justified beat **In Compliance** by exactly the same margin he had at Fairyhouse, suggesting both ran pretty much to form (the latter, in particular, is expected to improve over further).

JUSTIFIED: beating In Compliance

Novice index

All horses placed or commented on in our novice review section, with race numbers

Accordion Etoile 3, 22, 32, 36
Afsoun 2, 26, 28
Albarino 13
Albuhera 3, 18
Amicelli 7
Arteea 16
Artist's Muse 35
Back In Front..................................24
Ballytrim.......................................25
Bewleys Berry 9
Black Jack Ketchum 7, 27, 30
Blazing Bailey 20, 26
Blue Shark 10
Boychuk 1, 11
Breathing Fire 26, 35
Buena Vista 1, 21
Cerium 5
Commercial Flyer 24, 29
Compton Bolter...............................13
Conna Castle 31
Copsale Lad 29
Darkness 4, 9, 24
Denman 11, 23
Desert Quest 31
Detroit City 17, 26, 28
Dictum 19
Don't Be Shy 22
Equus Maximus.................................25
Fair Along 2, 26, 28
Father Matt 14
Foreman 15, 22, 32
Gungadu 7
Hairy Molly 25
Hoo La Baloo 5, 19, 32
Idle Talk 24
Iktitaf 6, 34
In Compliance 33, 36
Iris's Gift 4
It's A Dream....................................11
Jazz Messenger 34
Justified 8, 16, 33, 36
Kasbah Bliss 2, 20, 26
Kicks For Free 25
Kill Devil Hill 8
Le Volfoni 15, 32
Lennon..13
Linnet 17
Marcel 15

Missed That 8, 16, 22, 33
Mister Hight................................26, 35
Monet's Garden 22
Money Trix 30
Mounthenry 6
Mr Nosie 23
Mr Pointment...................................23
Napolitain 12, 18
Natal 1
Neptune Collonges 30
Nicanor 23
Nickname 14, 16
Noland 13, 21
O'Muircheartaigh 6, 21
Our Ben 24
Pangbourne.....................................25
Patman Du Charmil 10
Powerstation 27, 30
Premier Dane 28
Pressgang 25
Quatre Heures 21, 35
Racing Demon 5, 22
Rasharrow 21
Refinement 23
Romaha 14
Royals Darling 17
Stance 18
Star De Mohaison 12, 24, 29
Straw Bear 21, 31, 34
Sublimity..................................21, 34
Sweet Wake 21, 34
Tamarinbleu 3
The Cool Guy 11
The Duke's Speech 31
The Listener 12, 24
The Railway Man 33
Travino 27
Turko 10
Turpin Green 18, 29
Twist Magic 20
Two Miles West 1
Unleash 4
Voy Por Ustedes 19, 22, 32
Whispered Promises 13
Wild Passion 8, 22, 33
Zabenz 9
Zaiyad..23

Trainer Statistics

Race type

	Hurdles				Chases			
	W	R	%	£1 stake	W	R	%	£1 stake
Handicap	17	120	14	-40.94	29	190	15	-27.42
Selling	1	3	33	-1.43	0	0	-	-
Claiming	1	1	100	+3.33	0	0	-	-
Novice	44	125	35	+3.80	28	92	30	-10.54
Maiden	8	24	33	+2.90	3	4	75	+1.93

Jockeys

	Hurdles				Chases				Bumpers			
	W	R	%	£1 stake	W	R	%	£1 stake	W	R	%	£1 stake
R Walsh	36	98	37	+20.79	23	90	26	+2.26	4	15	27	-2.83
C Williams	18	91	20	-24.37	12	89	13	-44.10	2	13	15	-6.75
L Heard	10	50	20	-13.42	7	43	16	-6.58	3	9	33	-2.41
J Tizzard	0	7	-	-7.00	7	34	21	-15.81	0	0	-	-
B Geraghty	2	5	40	+0.00	3	7	43	+13.08	0	0	-	-
A McCoy	1	6	17	-4.33	3	7	43	+2.57	0	0	-	-
P Brennan	1	4	25	-2.27	3	15	20	-8.62	0	2	-	-2.00
Mr J Snowden	0	0	-	-	2	6	33	-1.79	0	0	-	-
S Thomas	1	1	100	+0.67	1	6	17	-4.09	0	0	-	-
M Fitzgerald	1	3	33	-1.64	1	5	20	-1.50	0	1	-	-1.00
Mr C Sweeney	0	0	-	-	2	9	22	-1.25	0	0	-	-
L Aspell	0	0	-	-	1	1	100	+14.00	0	0	-	-

By month

	Hurdles				Chases				Bumpers			
	W	R	%	£1 stake	W	R	%	£1 stake	W	R	%	£1 stake
May 2005	7	19	37	+13.07	7	17	41	+6.68	0	2	-	-2.00
June	2	6	33	-0.45	2	10	20	-4.50	1	3	33	+1.33
July	1	3	33	-0.38	1	7	14	-3.75	0	1	-	-
August	2	5	40	+5.83	0	3	-	-	1	1	100	+2.50
September	0	1	-	-1.00	1	4	25	+9.00	0	0	-	-
October	7	30	23	-7.03	8	34	24	-9.66	0	0	-	-
November	8	34	24	-15.07	10	57	18	-14.75	0	8	-	-8.00
December	11	41	27	-4.84	12	50	24	+8.17	2	3	67	+1.42
January 2006	13	34	38	+10.93	7	32	22	+1.72	1	10	10	-6.00
February	8	32	25	-18.60	7	33	21	-16.92	2	4	50	-1.41
March	6	30	20	-8.31	7	32	22	-0.06	2	7	29	-0.83
April	6	38	16	-12.02	6	53	11	-27.59	0	5	-	-5.00

By horse

	Wins	Runs	%	Win prize	Total Prize
Star de Mohaison	4	6	67	144,952.50	152,291.80
Noland	4	5	80	105,849.48	106,584.48
Kauto Star	1	3	33	71,275.00	85,178.50
Napolitain	4	9	44	65,296.96	80,269.96
My Will	0	9	-	0.00	79,261.49
Neptune Collonges	4	7	57	53,739.53	74,879.15
L'Aventure	1	6	17	57,020.00	73,782.72
Desert Quest	5	10	50	67,322.39	72,917.19
Natal	5	9	56	55,387.99	70,368.99
Hoo La Baloo	3	8	38	44,338.20	69,971.76
Darrias	6	12	50	51,852.05	66,156.05
Ladalko	1	7	14	10,359.46	65,125.44
Le Volfoni	4	11	36	30,732.96	62,362.53
Denman	4	5	80	38,084.17	59,474.17

All runners

	Wins	Runs	%	2nd	3rd	4th	Win prize	Total prize	£1 Stake
Chase	68	334	20	58	33	30	919,772.84	1,501,907.07	-56.67
Hurdle	71	273	26	34	33	36	626,435.57	868,215.75	-37.85
Bumpers	9	44	20	11	5	2	17,414.41	32,251.50	-19.00
TOTAL	148	651	23	103	71	68	1,563,622.82	2,402,374.32	-113.51

Paul Nicholls

A stroll to the title for Nicholls as he stormed past the £2m mark in prize money, despite stable star Azertyuiop missing the campaign and heir apparent Kauto Star only seeing the racecourse three times.

Interestingly, for a trainer best known for his chasers, Nicholls' hurdlers went better last season, boasting an impressive 26 per cent strike-rate.

On the jockey front, the contrast between Ruby Walsh and Christian Williams couldn't be greater, with Walsh well in profit on Nicholls horses and Williams massively down.

Course records

	Hurdles				Chases				Bumpers			
	W	R	%	£1 stake	W	R	%	£1 stake	W	R	%	£1 stake
Aintree	1	16	6	-11.50	4	31	13	-16.63	0	3	-	-3.00
Ayr	0	5	-	-5.00	0	7	-	-7.00	0	0	-	-
Bangor	1	5	20	-3.92	0	4	-	-4.00	0	0	-	-
Cheltenham	8	37	22	+3.14	5	53	9	-15.75	0	3	-	-3.00
Chepstow	7	30	23	-9.34	5	17	29	+5.87	1	5	20	-3.33
Doncaster	1	1	100	+3.00	0	6	-	-6.00	0	0	-	-
Exeter	3	17	18	-10.25	1	15	7	-10.50	0	2	-	-2.00
Fakenham	0	1	-	-1.00	1	2	50	+1.00	0	0	-	-
Folkestone	2	4	50	-0.42	1	3	33	-1.09	0	1	-	-1.00
Fontwell	0	5	-	-5.00	2	7	29	-4.52	1	2	50	-0.64
Haydock	1	4	25	-2.82	1	6	17	-4.27	0	0	-	-
Hereford	2	6	33	-1.68	2	3	67	+1.88	0	1	-	-1.00
Huntingdon	2	3	67	+0.98	1	6	17	-4.39	0	0	-	-
Leicester	0	0	-	-	1	3	33	-1.60	0	0	-	-
Lingfield	1	5	20	-3.39	2	7	29	+2.00	0	0	-	-
Ludlow	1	5	20	-2.00	3	6	50	+4.32	0	2	-	-2.00
Market Rasen	0	1	-	-1.00	1	5	20	-2.63	0	0	-	-
Musselburgh	0	2	-	-2.00	0	0	-	-	0	0	-	-
Newbury	4	11	36	+3.88	7	20	35	+10.88	0	1	-	-1.00
Newton Abbot	2	5	40	+4.13	1	8	13	-0.70	0	0	-	-
Plumpton	0	2	-	-2.00	1	7	14	-5.09	0	1	-	-1.00
Sandown	3	15	20	-7.50	7	26	27	-8.02	0	0	-	-
Southwell	1	1	100	+1.25	0	1	-	-1.00	0	0	-	-
Stratford	3	8	38	+6.30	4	13	31	+0.75	0	0	-	-
Taunton	5	15	33	-3.93	2	17	12	-9.25	1	7	14	-2.50
Uttoxeter	0	3	-	-3.00	0	5	-	-5.00	0	0	-	-
Warwick	2	6	33	-0.25	3	8	38	+4.60	0	1	-	-1.00
Wetherby	1	2	50	-0.60	1	5	20	-1.25	0	0	-	-
Wincanton	14	44	32	+5.31	10	33	30	+17.73	4	7	57	+2.64
Windsor	1	4	25	-1.25	0	1	-	-1.00	0	0	-	-
Worcester	5	10	50	+12.03	2	9	22	+10.00	2	8	25	-0.17

Race type

	Hurdles				Chases			
	W	R	%	£1 stake	W	R	%	£1 stake
Handicap	34	177	19	+25.64	20	204	10	-71.67
Selling	0	1	-	-1.00	0	0	-	
Novice	30	149	20	-16.35	13	63	21	-19.01
Maiden	7	44	16	-0.43	1	1	100	+2.25

Jockeys

	Hurdles				Chases				Bumpers			
	W	R	%	£1 stake	W	R	%	£1 stake	W	R	%	£1 stake
R Johnson	52	231	23	+12.70	29	172	17	-33.27	2	23	9	-14.63
P Brennan	7	50	14	+6.00	10	667	15	-23.17	0	6	-	-6.00
T O'Brien	3	17	18	-7.58	2	15	13	+2.50	1	1	100	+1.75
R Stephens	4	30	13	-6.00	0	12	-	-12.00	0	1	-	-1.00
N Felihy	0	0	-	-	1	1	100	+2.25	0	0	-	-
A McCoy	1	3	33	+0.50	0	1	-	-1.00	0	0	-	-
A Honeyball	0	0	-	-	0	1	-	-1.00	0	0	-	-
A Tinkler	0	0	-	-	0	1	-	-1.00	0	0	-	-

By month

	Hurdles				Chases				Bumpers			
	W	R	%	£1 stake	W	R	%	£1 stake	W	R	%	£1 stake
May 2005	3	20	15	-7.25	3	18	17	-7.00	0	1	-	-1.00
June	3	15	20	+5.00	2	13	15	-8.18	0	0	-	-
July	4	15	27	-0.50	3	11	27	+7.50	0	0	-	-
August	4	18	22	+3.50	5	13	38	+19.63	0	0	-	-
September	3	12	25	+1.75	1	7	14	-5.64	0	0	-	-
October	13	42	31	+10.79	6	30	20	-8.37	1	4	25	+1.50
November	5	36	14	-6.93	3	45	7	-25.50	1	5	20	-2.13
December	4	33	12	-16.56	6	30	20	-3.52	0	4	-	-4.00
January 2006	3	34	9	-6.09	0	24	-	-24.00	0	4	-	-4.00
February	5	36	14	-6.17	2	17	12	-4.50	0	1	-	-1.00
March	8	33	24	-0.08	4	32	13	-17.04	1	9	11	-4.00
April	11	44	25	+13.14	6	36	17	-0.07	0	4	-	-4.00

By horse

	Wins	Runs	%	Win prize	Total Prize
Lacdoudal	3	9	33	133,742.12	189,582.22
Monkerhostin	1	8	13	37,063.00	144,734.60
Detroit City	4	5	80	133,576.50	133,576.50
Noble Request	3	7	43	71,625.00	96,223.50
Tamango	4	12	33	50,645.32	59,233.92
Fair Along	2	6	33	27,252.11	53,347.11
Wellbeing	3	5	60	38,919.60	39,970.10
Boychuk	3	7	43	25,660.00	36,494.50
Motorway	4	8	50	34,580.39	35,704.39
Amicelli	4	9	44	19,652.55	32,105.05
Zabenz	1	8	13	4,560.70	31,748.43
Croix de Guerre	3	10	30	23,210.40	29,703.20
Supreme Prince	1	6	17	18,858.60	27,886.60
Willie John Daly	1	7	14	23,877.34	25,996.98
Double Honour	1	8	13	13,506.46	25,172.74
Drumbeater	4	8	50	20,553.05	23,946.43
McBain	2	7	29	21,269.00	23,636.75
Kalca Mome	1	9	11	16,265.00	22,986.34
Unleash	1	8	13	4,104.75	20,428.45

All runners

	Wins	Runs	%	2nd	3rd	4th	Win prize	Total prize	£1 Stake
Chase	42	280	15	39	36	33	446,091.11	829,087.88	-76.68
Hurdle	67	347	19	39	39	28	598,664.73	784,817.00	-10.39
Bumpers	3	32	9	4	4	5	13,637.47	18,760.18	-20.88
TOTAL	112	659	17	82	79	66	1,058,393.31	1,632,665.06	-107.95

Philip Hobbs

A cracking season for Hobbs, crowned by Lacdoudal's victory in the Betfred Gold Cup.

Handicap hurdles are a Hobbs speciality, his 34 winners in that sphere showing a £25 profit to £1 level stakes.

There are few strong jockey trends with so many Hobbs inmates being partnered by stable no. 1 Richard Johnson, but follow anything Hobbs runs at Newton Abbot, where his horses turned over a good profit over hurdles and fences.

However, his record in bumpers was very poor last year with just three winners out of 32.

Course records

	Hurdles				Chases				Bumpers			
	W	R	%	£1 stake	W	R	%	£1 stake	W	R	%	£1 stake
Aintree	3	11	27	+2.57	0	14	-	-14.00	0	1	-	-1.00
Ayr	1	2	50	+2.50	1	5	20	-0.50	0	0	-	-
Bangor	2	9	22	+2.00	2	6	33	+0.36	1	2	50	+0.75
Catterick	0	1	-	-1.00	0	1	-	-1.00	0	0	-	-
Cheltenham	6	26	23	+4.23	0	34	-	-34.00	1	5	20	-2.13
Chepstow	6	22	27	+0.66	0	5	-	-5.00	1	3	33	+2.50
Doncaster	1	1	100	+3.50	1	2	50	+1.25	0	0	-	-
Exeter	4	30	13	-7.81	10	25	40	+13.25	0	1	-	-1.00
Fakenham	0	0	-	-	0	2	-	-2.00	0	0	-	-
Folkestone	0	3	-	-3.00	0	0	-	-	0	0	-	-
Fontwell	0	7	-	-7.00	1	4	25	+0.00	0	1	-	-1.00
Haydock	2	11	18	-5.67	3	6	50	+13.50	0	3	-	-3.00
Hereford	1	12	8	-10.56	3	7	43	+4.36	0	1	-	-1.00
Huntingdon	1	6	17	-3.25	1	9	11	-4.50	0	0	-	-
Kelso	0	0	-	-	0	1	-	-1.00	0	0	-	-
Leicester	1	2	50	+1.50	0	1	-	-1.00	0	0	-	-
Lingfield	0	0	-	-	0	4	-	-4.00	0	0	-	-
Ludlow	2	17	12	-12.25	1	9	11	-4.00	0	0	-	-
Market Rasen	4	14	29	+11.25	1	9	11	-5.75	0	0	-	-
Newbury	5	19	26	+6.00	0	19	-	-19.00	0	3	-	-3.00
Newton Abbot	6	27	22	+23.17	6	19	32	+16.92	0	0	-	-
Perth	2	4	50	+2.75	1	2	50	-0.47	0	0	-	-
Plumpton	0	7	-	-7.00	1	2	50	+0.25	0	1	-	-1.00
Sandown	2	11	18	-5.00	3	19	16	+0.50	0	0	-	-
Stratford	4	13	31	+11.25	2	10	20	+9.00	0	1	-	-1.00
Taunton	4	23	17	-0.31	1	9	11	-7.20	0	2	-	-2.00
Towcester	0	3	-	-3.00	2	3	67	+6.83	0	1	-	-1.00
Uttoxeter	3	10	30	+8.00	0	7	-	-7.00	0	0	-	-
Warwick	0	8	-	-8.00	0	5	-	-5.00	0	1	-	-1.00
Wetherby	0	1	-	-1.00	0	1	-	-1.00	0	0	-	-
Wincanton	2	23	9	-10.50	1	29	3	-19.00	0	3	-	-3.00
Windsor	0	3	-	-3.00	0	0	-	-	0	0	-	-
Worcester	5	21	24	-1.42	1	11	9	-7.50	0	1	-	-1.00

Race type

	Hurdles				Chases			
	W	R	%	£1 stake	W	R	%	£1 stake
Handicap	24	200	12	-46.54	19	171	11	-54.92
Selling	0	4	-	-4.00	0	0	-	-
Novice	31	182	17	-37.88	16	62	26	+3.62
Maiden	6	45	13	-12.31	0	1	-	-1.00

Jockeys

	Hurdles				Chases				Bumpers			
	W	R	%	£1 stake	W	R	%	£1 stake	W	R	%	£1 stake
A McCoy	43	212	20	-6.54	22	134	16	-35.36	4	20	20	-1.75
N Fehily	5	52	10	-28.46	2	28	7	-10.50	2	4	50	+4.00
Mr A Berry	1	16	6	-14.39	2	6	33	+10.83	2	15	13	-10.02
J Moore	4	19	21	+12.63	0	13	-	-13.00	0	0	-	-
M Fitzgerald	2	31	6	-1.00	2	5	40	+3.60	0	0	-	-
Mr J P Magnier	0	0	-	-	0	0	-	-	3	5	60	+4.50
S Walsh	1	10	10	-5.50	2	3	67	+12.00	0	0	-	-
Mr J T McNamara	0	1	-	-1.00	2	5	40	-1.04	0	0	-	-
B Harding	0	5	-	-5.00	2	14	14	-1.25	0	0	-	-

By month

	Hurdles				Chases				Bumpers			
	W	R	%	£1 stake	W	R	%	£1 stake	W	R	%	£1 stake
May 2005	1	11	9	-9.80	5	8	63	+8.92	0	0	-	-
June	2	19	11	-10.25	1	13	8	-10.90	0	1	-	-1.00
July	6	32	19	-4.56	2	15	13	-2.75	1	1	100	+2.00
August	2	21	10	-11.00	4	21	19	-2.75	1	2	50	+1.50
September	1	11	9	-2.00	2	18	11	-9.50	2	4	50	+3.23
October	12	48	25	+2.20	3	34	9	-23.77	1	5	20	-1.75
November	5	49	10	-24.83	5	35	14	-2.75	2	13	15	-4.25
December	7	36	19	-14.07	2	25	8	-15.50	0	3	-	-3.00
January 2006	4	48	8	-6.42	2	19	11	+1.00	1	4	25	-2.00
February	9	57	16	+0.24	4	22	18	-0.04	1	4	25	+3.50
March	4	49	8	-24.75	3	21	14	-15.17	2	6	33	-0.50
April	6	30	20	+8.89	1	15	7	+0.00	0	4	-	-4.00

By horse

	Wins	Runs	%	Win prize	Total Prize
Black Jack Ketchum	5	5	100	125,446.62	125,446.62
Clan Royal	1	4	25	5,204.80	80,938.80
Refinement	6	7	86	65,595.37	76,305.37
Bold Bishop	2	6	33	48,336.58	52,529.80
Fire Dragon	2	8	25	27,611.50	51,584.11
Iris's Gift	3	6	50	31,107.75	38,038.31
Feel The Pride	4	10	40	26,469.01	33,077.26
Risk Accessor	0	8	-	0.00	33,049.00
Intersky Falcon	0	7	-	0.00	30.207.50
Lingo	1	1	100	28,510.00	28,510.00
Millenaire	3	7	43	23,699.56	24,069.56
Be My Better Half	1	8	13	12,526.00	22,561.61
Ursis	2	4	50	19,315.25	20,190.25
Tigers Lair	3	4	75	17,830.50	19,120.50
Olaso	1	3	33	13,012.00	17,831.50
Englishtown	2	4	50	7,606.30	17,532.70
Nor'Nor'East	2	5	40	14,285.21	15,965.42
Hasty Prince	1	8	13	12,526.00	14,944.00

Sponsored by Stan James

All runners

	Wins	Runs	%	2nd	3rd	4th	Win prize	Total prize	£1 Stake
Chase	35	247	14	39	24	14	249,409.10	491,363.11	-67.72
Hurdle	59	417	14	44	38	40	486,649.54	675,311.11	-102.35
Bumpers	11	47	23	5	3	6	23,346.09	27,941.16	-6.27
TOTAL	105	711	15	88	65	60	759,404.73	1,194,615.38	-176.34

Jonjo O'Neill

A relatively disappointing season for O'Neill, with the loss of form of Iris's Gift and the tragic demise of Lingo. Several strongly fancied runners were turned over, resulting in a loss of £176 to £1 level stakes.

There are promising signs for the future, and not just in the shape of Black Jack Ketchum.

O'Neill's novice chasers showed a healthy 26 per cent strike-rate and turned over a small profit, and his record in bumpers was excellent with 11 wins out of 46.

Tony McCoy shows a significant loss in chases.

Course records

	Hurdles				Chases				Bumpers			
	W	R	%	£1 stake	W	R	%	£1 stake	W	R	%	£1 stake
Aintree	2	9	22	-3.64	0	14	-	-14.00	0	2	-	-2.00
Ayr	0	1	-	-1.00	0	1	-	-1.00	0	0	-	-
Bangor	2	14	14	-10.18	2	11	18	-7.47	0	1	-	-1.00
Carlisle	4	7	57	+13.75	1	6	17	+6.00	0	2	-	-2.00
Cartmel	0	2	-	-2.00	0	1	-	-1.00	0	0	-	-
Cheltenham	4	26	15	-8.83	4	23	17	+8.00	0	3	-	-3.00
Chepstow	3	17	18	-9.77	1	9	11	-7.00	0	4	-	-4.00
Doncaster	1	1	100	+1.63	1	1	100	+2.75	0	0	-	-
Exeter	3	18	17	+4.20	0	7	-	-7.00	0	1	-	-1.00
Fakenham	1	6	17	-4.27	0	2	-	-2.00	0	0	-	-
Folkestone	1	5	20	-3.27	1	5	20	+0.50	0	1	-	-1.00
Fontwell	0	12	-	-12.00	1	6	17	+0.00	0	1	-	-1.00
Haydock	2	15	13	-6.50	0	3	-	-3.00	2	4	50	+4.00
Hereford	1	6	17	+9.00	0	0	-	-	1	3	33	-0.75
Hexham	0	2	-	-2.00	0	1	-	-1.00	0	1	-	-1.00
Huntingdon	3	18	17	-4.33	1	10	10	-7.38	0	1	-	-1.00
Leicester	0	7	-	-7.00	4	11	36	+13.50	0	0	-	-
Lingfield	1	3	33	+6.00	0	4	-	-4.00	0	0	-	-
Ludlow	1	14	7	-12.27	1	4	25	-0.25	0	2	-	-2.00
Market Rasen	2	25	8	-18.25	3	22	14	-11.75	2	2	100	+6.50
Newbury	0	15	-	-15.00	1	6	17	+2.00	2	3	67	+3.00
Newcastle	1	3	33	+4.50	0	2	-	-2.00	0	0	-	-
Newton Abbot	3	13	23	+1.00	1	5	20	+4.00	1	1	100	+2.50
Perth	0	2	-	-2.00	0	2	-	-2.00	0	1	-	-1.00
Plumpton	2	16	13	+27.00	0	5	-	-5.00	1	1	100	+6.50
Sandown	5	18	28	+22.56	0	7	-	-7.00	0	0	-	-
Sedgefield	0	1	-	-1.00	1	1	100	+0.33	0	0	-	-
Southwell	0	6	-	-6.00	2	11	18	+1.00	0	1	-	-1.00
Stratford	3	14	21	+5.53	4	16	25	-0.15	0	2	-	-2.00
Taunton	0	6	-	-6.00	1	3	33	+5.00	0	0	-	-
Towcester	2	10	20	-5.65	0	1	-	-1.00	0	1	-	-1.00
Uttoxeter	5	25	20	+1.38	0	9	-	-9.00	0	1	-	-1.00
Warwick	0	9	-	-9.00	2	9	22	-5.63	0	0	-	-
Wetherby	4	16	25	-3.13	1	10	10	-8.17	0	0	-	-
Wincanton	1	14	7	-12.56	0	1	-	-1.00	0	2	-	-2.00
Windsor	0	3	-	-3.00	0	0	-	-	0	0	-	-
Worcester	2	38	5	-30.25	2	18	11	-3.00	2	6	33	+2.50

Race type

	Hurdles				Chases			
	W	R	%	£1 stake	W	R	%	£1 stake
Handicap	19	107	18	-4.42	12	88	14	+17.83
Claiming	0	1	-	-1.00	0	0	-	
Novice	27	101	27	+1.54	2	30	7	-21.00
Maiden	2	16	13	-7.63	0	2	-	-2.00

Jockeys

	Hurdles				Chases				Bumpers			
	W	R	%	£1 stake	W	R	%	£1 stake	W	R	%	£1 stake
M Fitzgerald	24	104	23	-10.80	12	56	21	+23.67	8	21	38	+12.14
M Foley	8	30	27	+15.50	3	33	9	-17.67	3	8	38	+17.00
A Tinkler	2	30	7	-20.50	2	22	9	+3.00	3	13	23	-2.00
A McCoy	3	9	33	-2.71	0	1	-	-1.00	1	1	100	+0.73
Mr J Snowden	0	2	-	-2.00	3	4	75	+6.38	0	0	-	
Mr T Greenall	1	3	33	-0.75	0	0	-		2	3	67	+13.50
S Curling	1	13	8	-7.00	0	3	-	-3.00	2	3	67	+0.93
C Studd	2	7	29	+4.00	0	0	-		0	0	-	
Mr S Waley-C	0	4	-	-4.00	1	9	11	+8.00	1	1	100	+1.00
B Geraghty	1	1	100	+6.00	0	0	-		0	0	-	

By month

	Hurdles				Chases				Bumpers			
	W	R	%	£1 stake	W	R	%	£1 stake	W	R	%	£1 stake
May 2005	2	13	15	-2.50	0	0	-		2	2	100	+7.00
June	0	1	-	-1.00	0	0	-		1	2	50	-0.09
July	0	0	-		0	1	-	-1.00	0	0	-	
August	0	0	-		0	0	-		0	1	-	-1.00
September	0	1	-	-1.00	0	0	-		0	0	-	
October	3	9	33	+6.50	1	2	50	+2.33	1	3	33	-
November	5	20	25	-4.13	3	22	14	-3.50	3	9	33	+0.33
December	9	36	25	+5.35	5	20	25	+4.00	1	4	25	+6.00
January 2006	8	28	29	+11.46	4	18	22	+3.83	2	4	50	+0.50
February	9	34	26	+0.44	2	14	14	+1.00	3	4	75	+11.23
March	5	36	14	-12.00	5	21	24	+25.71	5	12	42	+19.83
April	3	23	13	-11.38	1	27	4	-10.00	2	11	18	-2.50

By horse

	Wins	Runs	%	Win prize	Total Prize
Fondmort	2	6	33	108,338.00	125,190.00
Liberthine	1	6	17	62,630.00	72,098.00
Trabolgan	1	1	100	71,275.00	71,275.00
Afsoun	2	5	40	30,043.60	51,992.60
Non So	1	4	25	42,765.00	49,080.10
Copsale Lad	2	5	40	12,607.92	45,347.12
Greenhope	1	3	33	42,765.00	43,111.50
Tysou	2	6	33	36,210.82	39,319.16
Blue Shark	1	1	100	28,510.00	28,510.00
The Market Man	2	3	67	23,831.60	27,821.51
Shining Strand	2	10	20	10,350.00	18,086.25
All Star	1	5	20	13,812.23	17,983.63
Juveigneur	0	5	-	0.00	17,112.00
Karello Bay	2	3	67	16,310.60	16,809.85
Tessanoora	2	5	40	11,060.20	16,133.24
Tarlac	2	5	40	12,322.20	15,840.20
First Love	3	44	75	15,135.65	15,135.65

All runners

	Wins	Runs	%	2nd	3rd	4th	Win prize	Total prize	£1 Stake
Chase	21	129	16	12	14	17	445,904.70	589,368.14	+18.37
Hurdle	44	208	21	23	25	17	291,494.04	407,105.48	-15.26
Bumper	20	53	38	9	4	2	54,336.81	61,662.95	+40.30
TOTAL	85	390	22	44	43	36	791,735.55	1,058,136.57	+43.42

Nicky Henderson

Astonishingly, having £1 blind on all Henderson horses last season would have yielded a £43 profit – clearly he is never a man to rule out of calculations.

Henderson also loves to lay one out for a chase at Cheltenham and his record in them is awesome, with a £31.67 profit to £1 level stakes over the Cheltenham fences. He would have been in profit even if Greenhope hadn't come storming up the hill to land the Grand Annual.

He also does well at Sandown and Chepstow, reinforcing the view that Henderson is a man for the top tracks.

Course records

	Hurdles				Chases				Bumpers			
	W	R	%	£1 stake	W	R	%	£1 stake	W	R	%	£1 stake
Aintree	0	7	-	-7.00	1	12	8	+5.00	0	4	-	-4.00
Ayr	1	4	25	+0.50	0	3	-	-3.00	0	1	-	-1.00
Bangor	0	4	-	-4.00	0	2	-	-2.00	2	3	67	+10.00
Carlisle	0	0	-	-	0	1	-	-1.00	0	0	-	-
Cheltenham	2	24	8	-16.13	6	27	22	+31.67	1	2	50	+3.00
Chepstow	1	4	25	+4.00	1	1	100	+4.00	1	1	100	+2.50
Doncaster	0	3	-	-3.00	0	3	-	-3.00	0	1	-	-1.00
Exeter	1	5	20	-3.39	1	3	33	+1.50	0	0	-	-
Fakenham	1	2	50	+0.25	0	0	-	-	0	3	-	-3.00
Folkestone	3	4	75	+5.83	0	1	-	-1.00	1	1	100	+4.50
Fontwell	1	8	13	-3.50	0	2	-	-2.00	1	2	50	+6.00
Haydock	0	4	-	-4.00	0	5	-	-5.00	0	3	-	-3.00
Hereford	1	5	20	-2.38	0	0	-	-	0	2	-	-2.00
Huntingdon	5	11	45	+4.49	0	7	-	-7.00	1	1	100	+0.83
Kelso	0	2	-	-2.00	0	0	-	-	0	0	-	-
Leicester	0	1	-	-1.00	0	2	-	-2.00	0	0	-	-
Lingfield	1	6	17	+0.00	2	7	29	-0.67	0	0	-	-
Ludlow	4	14	29	+15.00	0	3	-	3.00	2	4	50	+4.50
Market Rasen	1	1	100	+4.00	0	0	-	-	0	0	-	-
Newbury	6	28	21	-2.28	1	14	7	-6.50	1	6	17	+11.00
Newton Abbot	1	2	50	+4.00	0	0	-	-	0	0	-	-
Perth	0	1	-	-1.00	0	1	-	-1.00	0	0	-	-
Plumpton	4	5	80	+8.00	0	2	-	-2.00	1	1	100	+1.50
Sandown	5	21	24	+4.21	3	14	21	+3.88	1	3	33	+3.00
Southwell	0	5	-	-5.00	1	3	33	+1.00	1	1	100	+0.73
Stratford	0	4	-	-4.00	0	2	-	-2.00	1	3	33	-1.09
Taunton	2	6	33	+3.13	0	2	-	-2.00	0	1	-	-1.00
Towcester	1	3	33	+1.00	0	2	-	-2.00	1	2	50	+3.50
Uttoxeter	1	5	20	-1.50	0	2	-	-2.00	0	0	-	-
Warwick	0	7	-	-7.00	2	2	100	+15.00	1	2	50	+0.50
Wetherby	1	1	100	+3.50	0	1	-	-1.00	0	0	-	-
Wincanton	0	6	-	-6.00	2	4	50	+3.50	2	2	100	+4.23
Windsor	0	2	-	-2.00	1	1	100	+1.00	0	0	-	-
Worcester	1	3	33	+2.00	0	0	-	-	2	3	67	+1.60

Race type

	Hurdles				Chases			
	W	R	%	£1 stake	W	R	%	£1 stake
Handicap	12	105	11	-45.30	7	78	9	-1.50
Selling	1	2	50	+1.75	0	0	-	-
Claiming	0	1	-	-1.00	0	0	-	-
Novice	19	125	15	+22.32	10	32	31	+14.53
Maiden	2	19	11	-13.28	0	0	-	-

Jockeys

	Hurdles				Chases				Bumpers			
	W	R	%	£1 stake	W	R	%	£1 stake	W	R	%	£1 stake
R Thornton	25	176	14	+11.28	13	83	16	-14.06	8	26	31	+32.43
W Hutchison	5	49	10	-25.38	3	20	15	+9.83	0	14	-	-14.00
Mr G Tumelty	4	13	31	+0.75	0	2	-	-2.00	2	10	20	+3.25
A McCoy	0	0	-	-	1	1	100	+1.20	0	0	-	-
P Brennan	0	0	-	-	1	1	100	+8.00	0	1	-	-1.00
W Marston	1	3	33	+5.00	0	0	-	-	0	0	-	-
J McCarthy	0	1	-	-1.00	0	0	-	-	0	0	-	-
L Heard	0	0	-	-	0	1	-	-1.00	0	0	-	-

By month

	Hurdles				Chases				Bumpers			
	W	R	%	£1 stake	W	R	%	£1 stake	W	R	%	£1 stake
May 2005	1	11	9	-6.50	0	5	-	-5.00	1	2	50	+5.00
June	0	5	-	-5.00	0	4	-	-4.00	0	0	-	-
July	0	3	-	-3.00	0	1	-	-1.00	0	0	-	-
August	0	3	-	-3.00	1	3	33	+5.00	0	0	-	-
September	0	4	-	-4.00	0	1	-	-1.00	0	0	-	-
October	5	14	36	+8.91	0	1	-	-1.00	1	1	100	+5.00
November	6	31	19	-13.09	2	23	9	-18.55	2	12	17	-6.55
December	5	28	18	+9.75	3	16	19	+9.33	1	6	17	+4.00
January 2006	7	40	18	+55.35	2	16	13	-3.50	1	6	17	-2.75
February	6	40	15	-7.44	4	14	29	-2.88	3	8	38	+2.98
March	2	38	5	-26.80	3	9	33	+11.13	0	9	-	-9.00
April	2	27	7	-17.75	1	15	7	-11.00	1	8	13	+21.00

By horse

	Wins	Runs	%	Win prize	Total Prize
My Way de Solzen	3	5	60	185,009.00	212,932.00
Voy Por Ustedes	5	6	83	118,926.02	142,455.02
Nyrche	3	10	30	31,336.49	74,557.85
Halcon Genelardais	3	6	50	41,311.72	46,210.76
Blazing Bailey	2	5	40	7,807.20	36,270.90
Senorita Rumbelita	3	6	50	25,230.14	28,669.64
Mughas	1	6	17	13,012.00	26,451.34
Pangbourne	3	6	50	23,383.00	24,069.97
Yardbird	2	5	40	19,422.36	22,018.26
Kandjar d'Allier	1	6	17	5,530.10	21,818.60
Crystal d'Ainay	0	6	-	-	20,020.20
Wyldello	1	4	25	2,192.64	14,556.24
Sharajan	0	5	-	-	14,075.10
Howle Hill	0	5	-	-	12,627.95
Five Colours	1	4	25	4,228.90	12,495.90
Pretty Star	1	4	25	12,404.49	12,404.49
First de la Brunie	2	6	33	10,774.60	12,012.28
The Hairy Lemon	3	6	50	10,474.33	11,676.83

All runners

	Wins	Runs	%	2nd	3rd	4th	Win prize	Total prize	£1 Stake
Chase	18	111	16	14	12	10	235,298.04	373,672.85	-1.03
Hurdle	35	251	14	38	25	25	343,936.25	535,215.61	-18.35
Bumper	10	53	19	9	6	6	36,917.29	58,553.49	+18.68
TOTAL	63	415	15	61	43	41	616,151.58	967,441.95	-0.70

Alan King

King's season was lit up by the Festival success of Voy Por Ustedes and My Way de Solzen, taking him desperately close to the £1m mark in prize money.

It was a respectable season all round for King, particularly as he had his fair share of seconds as well, and he ended it only fractionally down to level stakes.

He is particularly proficient with his novices – both hurdlers and chasers register a decent profit – and the success of King's bumper horses last season suggests this is a trend which may well continue in the forthcoming campaign.

Course records

	Hurdles				Chases				Bumpers			
	W	R	%	£1 stake	W	R	%	£1 stake	W	R	%	£1 stake
Aintree	0	8	-	-8.00	0	5	-	-5.00	1	3	33	+26.00
Ayr	1	1	100	+4.50	1	4	25	+0.00	0	0	-	-
Bangor	1	9	11	-4.50	0	3	-	-3.00	0	0	-	-
Cheltenham	1	26	4	-17.00	1	13	8	-4.50	0	1	-	-1.00
Chepstow	2	9	22	+6.20	0	3	-	-3.00	0	1	-	-1.00
Doncaster	1	5	20	+3.00	0	1	-	-1.00	0	1	-	-1.00
Exeter	1	13	8	-9.75	2	6	33	-2.18	0	1	-	-1.00
Fakenham	0	2	-	-2.00	0	2	-	-2.00	1	4	25	-2.27
Folkestone	1	6	17	-1.00	0	2	-	-2.00	2	4	50	+5.25
Fontwell	4	13	31	+7.41	0	1	-	-1.00	1	3	33	-0.80
Haydock	1	6	17	-1.00	0	2	-	-2.00	1	2	50	+4.00
Hereford	5	19	26	+42.37	0	2	-	-2.00	0	3	-	-3.00
Huntingdon	1	9	11	+6.00	1	10	10	-5.00	3	5	60	+11.50
Leicester	2	6	33	-1.00	1	3	33	-0.38	0	0	-	-
Lingfield	1	2	50	+8.00	0	2	-	-2.00	0	4	-	-4.00
Ludlow	0	10	-	-10.00	0	1	-	-1.00	0	0	-	-
Market Rasen	0	5	-	-5.00	0	1	-	-1.00	0	0	-	-
Newbury	0	8	-	-8.00	1	5	20	+4.00	0	2	-	-2.00
Newton Abbot	0	3	-	-3.00	1	2	50	+6.00	0	0	-	-
Plumpton	0	7	-	-7.00	1	2	50	+0.50	0	2	-	-2.00
Sandown	1	10	10	-3.50	0	5	-	-5.00	0	2	-	-2.00
Southwell	1	4	25	+0.00	1	2	50	+21.00	0	1	-	-1.00
Stratford	0	3	-	-3.00	0	3	-	-3.00	0	0	-	-
Taunton	2	6	33	+0.60	0	2	-	-2.00	0	0	-	-
Towcester	2	6	33	+17.75	0	0	-	-	0	2	-	-2.00
Uttoxeter	0	10	-	-10.00	0	7	-	-7.00	1	3	33	+4.00
Warwick	6	12	50	+5.28	3	8	38	+2.03	0	3	-	-3.00
Wetherby	0	5	-	-5.00	1	3	33	-1.17	0	1	-	-1.00
Wincanton	1	23	4	-12.00	4	10	40	+21.66	0	5	-	-5.00
Windsor	0	1	-	-1.00	0	0	-	-	0	0	-	-
Worcester	0	4	-	-4.00	0	1	-	-1.00	0	0	-	-

Race type

	Hurdles				Chases			
	W	R	%	£1 stake	W	R	%	£1 stake
Handicap	14	102	14	-2.38	22	142	15	+8.58
Selling	1	3	33	+14.00	0	0	-	-
Claiming	0	2	-	-2.00	0	0	-	-
Novice	12	79	15	-15.43	6	26	23	+6.65
Maiden	1	12	8	-8.75	0	3	-	-3.00

Jockeys

	Hurdles				Chases				Bumpers			
	W	R	%	£1 stake	W	R	%	£1 stake	W	R	%	£1 stake
D Elsworth	15	104	14	-20.05	27	128	21	+52.53	1	11	9	-5.50
D O'Meara	3	7	43	+11.50	3	19	16	-8.63	0	1	-	-1.00
P Whelan	5	21	24	+32.00	1	18	6	-14.00	0	3	-	-3.00
M O'Connell	2	16	13	-6.50	0	2	-	-2.00	1	6	17	+11.00
A Adams	0	3	-	-3.00	0	0	-	-	1	6	17	-1.50
B Keniry	0	1	-	-1.00	0	0	-	-	0	0	-	-
K Johnson	0	0	-	-	0	1	-	-1.00	0	0	-	-
L McGrath	0	0	-	-	0	1	-	-1.00	0	0	-	-
L Aspell	0	0	-	-	0	1	-	-1.00	0	0	-	-
M Bradburne	0	0	-	-	0	1	-	-1.00	0	0	-	-

By month

	Hurdles				Chases				Bumpers			
	W	R	%	£1 stake	W	R	%	£1 stake	W	R	%	£1 stake
May 2005	1	15	7	-10.50	3	15	20	-0.63	0	1	-	-1.00
June	2	10	20	-2.42	3	7	43	+6.88	0	1	-	-1.00
July	0	8	-	-8.00	0	8	-	-8.00	0	1	-	-1.00
August	1	6	17	+2.50	3	16	19	-2.92	0	3	-	-3.00
September	0	5	-	-5.00	2	3	67	+23.50	1	2	50	+2.50
October	0	14	-	-14.00	5	18	28	+16.25	0	3	-	-3.00
November	2	15	13	+15.00	7	30	23	+22.75	0	10	-	-10.00
December	1	24	4	-21.13	2	24	8	-15.70	0	5	-	-5.00
January 2006	3	18	17	-3.50	1	18	6	-12.00	0	2	-	-2.00
February	7	21	33	+32.38	0	17	-	-17.00	1	3	33	+14.00
March	3	16	19	-7.25	2	9	22	-1.13	0	3	-	-3.00
April	6	21	29	+18.37	3	21	14	-3.10	1	4	25	+1.50

By horse

	Wins	Runs	%	Win prize	Total Prize
Mister McGoldrick	1	10	10	28,845.00	84,532.20
St Matthew	2	5	40	58,341.00	58,741.03
Ross Comm	5	10	50	54,115.60	56,806.10
Little Big Horse	3	9	33	47,180.64	55,852.64
Royal Emperor	1	6	17	22,915.20	43,751.20
Town Crier	2	8	25	29,843.00	35,658.00
Undeniable	2	6	33	18,581.14	28,572.32
Bushido	3	8	38	18,434.00	19,449.00
Corlande	2	6	33	19,032.00	19,032.00
Presumptuous	2	4	50	18,983.40	18,983.40
Rebel Rhythm	2	7	29	10,785.03	18,070.53
Oso Magic	3	8	38	14,550.66	15,521.06
Supreme Breeze	1	6	17	13,127.24	15,477.27
Smiths Landing	1	1	100	14,882.80	14,882.80
Better Days	0	9	-	-	14,721.41
Darina's Boy	2	6	33	6,987.00	11,475.50
Sharp Belline	2	8	25	9,654.90	12,418.76

Sponsored by Stan James

All runners

	Wins	Runs	%	2nd	3rd	4th	Win prize	Total prize	£1 Stake
Chase	31	191	16	26	23	15	296,314.19	464,568.55	+3.91
Hurdle	26	183	14	19	16	13	182,348.54	243,104.20	-13.55
Bumper	3	38	8	0	3	7	5,337.00	6,232.97	-11.00
TOTAL	60	412	15	45	42	35	483,999.73	713,905.72	-20.64

Sue Smith

Sue and Harvey Smith are a traditional National Hunt partnership, and most of their horses come into their own over fences.

Bumper horses and novice hurdlers generally come up short – only three of their 38 bumper runners made the first two last season, an absolutely shocking record – but it pays to follow their chasers, particularly when Dominic Elsworth is in the saddle.

Elsworth on Smith chasers showed a £52 profit to £1 level stakes last year.

Mister McGoldrick would have boosted the stable coffers even more but for some near misses.

Course records

	Hurdles				Chases				Bumpers			
	W	R	%	£1 stake	W	R	%	£1 stake	W	R	%	£1 stake
Aintree	0	6	-	-6.00	0	9	-	-9.00	0	1	-	-1.00
Ayr	0	3	-	-3.00	0	5	-	-5.00	0	0	-	-
Bangor	0	10	-	-10.00	1	8	13	-3.00	0	4	-	-4.00
Carlisle	3	9	33	+5.25	3	9	33	+11.25	0	0	-	-
Cartmel	0	4	-	-4.00	2	5	40	+2.38	0	0	-	-
Catterick	2	15	13	-8.75	0	8	-	-8.00	0	7	-	-7.00
Cheltenham	0	1	-	-1.00	0	3	-	-3.00	0	0	-	-
Doncaster	0	5	-	-5.00	0	5	-	-5.00	0	0	-	-
Exeter	0	0	-	-	0	2	-	-2.00	0	0	-	-
Haydock	2	13	15	+24.00	1	9	11	+3.00	0	4	-	-4.00
Hexham	1	4	25	+0.50	1	4	25	+11.00	1	2	50	+2.50
Huntingdon	0	1	-	-1.00	1	6	17	-2.75	0	0	-	-
Kelso	2	6	33	+0.12	2	7	29	+3.50	0	0	-	-
Leicester	0	0	-	-	0	1	-	-1.00	0	0	-	-
Lingfield	0	0	-	-	0	1	-	-1.00	0	0	-	-
Market Rasen	3	23	13	+3.88	5	16	31	+22.28	1	3	33	+2.50
Newbury	0	1	-	-1.00	1	4	25	+13.00	0	0	-	-
Newcastle	1	7	14	-4.00	3	9	33	+2.50	0	1	-	-1.00
Perth	0	2	-	-2.00	0	1	-	-1.00	0	0	-	-
Sandown	0	3	-	-3.00	0	3	-	-3.00	0	0	-	-
Sedgefield	3	17	18	+7.25	1	16	6	-10.50	1	5	20	+12.00
Southwell	2	7	29	+8.00	1	15	7	-11.25	0	1	-	-1.00
Stratford	0	0	-	-	1	2	50	+2.50	0	0	-	-
Towcester	0	0	-	-	0	1	-	-1.00	0	0	-	-
Uttoxeter	2	11	18	-2.75	0	6	-	-6.00	0	2	-	-2.00
Warwick	0	1	-	-1.00	0	2	-	-2.00	0	0	-	-
Wetherby	3	23	13	-12.38	5	24	21	+3.30	0	4	-	-4.00
Worcester	2	11	18	+2.33	3	10	30	+3.71	0	4	-	-4.00

Race type

	Hurdles				Chases			
	W	R	%	£1 stake	W	R	%	£1 stake
Handicap	19	124	15	+9.99	33	211	16	-27.86
Novice	9	76	12	-30.09	14	48	29	+17.35
Maiden	3	19	16	-3.25	1	4	25	-2.39

Jockeys

	Hurdles				Chases				Bumpers			
	W	R	%	£1 stake	W	R	%	£1 stake	W	R	%	£1 stake
S Thomas	12	104	12	-21.50	29	148	20	-32.93	1	12	8	-9.75
P O'Neill	8	32	25	-2.42	6	34	18	+7.50	0	3	-	-3.00
L Treadwell	4	18	22	+2.16	2	6	33	+9.50	1	2	50	+13.00
A O'Keeffe	2	34	6	-27.00	5	45	11	-11.00	0	0	-	-
Mr W Biddick	0	2	-	-2.00	2	9	22	+4.50	0	0	-	-
N Fehily	1	1	100	+12.00	0	0	-	-	0	0	-	-
P Kinsella	1	1	100	+3.00	0	0	-	-	0	0	-	-
T O'Brien	1	1	100	+3.00	0	0	-	-	0	0	-	-
A McCoy	0	2	-	-2.00	1	2	50	+0.88	0	0	-	-
L Stephens	1	3	33	+31.00	0	6	-	-6.00	0	0	-	-

By month

	Hurdles				Chases				Bumpers			
	W	R	%	£1 stake	W	R	%	£1 stake	W	R	%	£1 stake
May 2005	2	14	14	-6.00	3	15	20	-1.13	0	0	-	-
June	1	4	25	+2.00	2	7	29	+2.50	0	0	-	-
July	1	8	13	-3.67	1	2	50	+0.10	0	0	-	-
August	1	2	50	+2.00	0	1	-	-1.00	0	0	-	-
September	1	4	25	+0.00	0	0	-	-	0	0	-	-
October	0	9	-	-9.00	1	16	6	-10.50	2	4	50	+13.25
November	2	15	13	+1.25	6	37	16	-3.79	0	1	-	-1.00
December	8	34	24	+17.00	10	35	29	+7.65	0	5	-	-5.00
January 2006	3	30	10	-21.75	8	39	21	-9.27	0	2	-	-2.00
February	5	27	19	+6.25	7	37	19	-10.12	0	1	-	-1.00
March	2	27	7	+22.00	4	34	12	-3.50	0	4	-	-4.00
April	3	24	13	-16.84	3	30	10	-1.50	0	0	-	-

By horse

	Wins	Runs	%	Win prize	Total Prize
Mon Mome	4	9	44	38,555.51	51,526.09
Bleu Superbe	1	10	10	10,057.92	35,622.09
Lorient Express	5	9	56	30,344.12	34,306.32
Kelrev	1	6	17	10,608.02	29,279.52
De Blanc	3	10	30	15,346.60	23,986.14
Gods Token	3	5	60	22,039.07	22,160.87
Jolly Boy	5	10	50	19,452.37	20,057.84
Lord Olympia	2	9	22	13,959.00	20,042.91
Schuh Shine	2	5	40	16,863.56	18,535.49
Sonevafushi	2	7	29	14,313.20	15,567.50
Nephite	2	9	22	13,711.75	15,284.06
Avitta	2	8	25	10,099.46	15,208.69
Magico	2	5	40	12,036.10	14,328.10
Kelly	2	2	100	14,287.00	14,287.00
Misty Dancer	1	5	20	12,676.00	13,971.00
Flying Enterprise	1	8	13	12,920.56	13,548.76
Tribal Dancer	1	12	8	6,506.00	13,212.63

All runners

	Wins	Runs	%	2nd	3rd	4th	Win prize	Total prize	£1 Stake
Chase	45	256	18	41	19	23	293,406.86	453,251.01	-33.55
Hurdle	30	202	15	21	22	18	133,502.61	197,194.51	-7.76
Bumper	2	17	12	5	1	0	5,436.40	12,121.62	+0.25
TOTAL	77	475	16	67	42	41	432,345.87	662,567.14	-41.06

Venetia Williams

Williams certainly casts her net wide in the pursuit of winners last season as she was represented at every racecourse in the country to make up for a lack of star names, exemplified by the fact Mon Mome won more prize money than any other horse.

Doncaster was probably the happiest hunting ground, as 50 per cent of Williams' runners hit the mark for a tidy profit.

Sam Thomas rides the majority of Williams horses but didn't have the most success last season, and punters are best advised focusing on Williams when Liam Treadwell is up.

Course records

	Hurdles				Chases				Bumpers			
	W	R	%	£1 stake	W	R	%	£1 stake	W	R	%	£1 stake
Aintree	2	4	50	+8.00	1	6	17	+2.50	1	1	100	+14.00
Ayr	1	1	100	+12.00	0	4	-	-4.00	0	0	-	-
Bangor	2	11	18	-1.00	0	6	-	-6.00	0	1	-	-1.00
Carlisle	0	2	-	-2.00	0	2	-	-2.00	0	0	-	-
Cartmel	0	2	-	-2.00	0	2	-	-2.00	0	0	-	-
Catterick	0	0	-	-	0	1	-	-1.00	0	0	-	-
Cheltenham	0	9	-	-9.00	1	17	6	-10.00	0	2	-	-2.00
Chepstow	2	11	18	-4.50	1	8	13	+3.00	0	0	-	-
Doncaster	1	2	50	+13.00	2	4	50	+5.00	0	0	-	-
Exeter	4	14	29	+6.75	0	8	-	-8.00	0	0	-	-
Fakenham	0	3	-	-3.00	1	10	10	-5.50	0	0	-	-
Folkestone	0	4	-	-4.00	3	7	43	+2.37	0	1	-	-1.00
Fontwell	0	14	-	-14.00	4	12	33	-1.10	0	0	-	-
Haydock	2	9	22	+15.00	2	12	17	-2.63	0	0	-	-
Hereford	0	6	-	-6.00	2	10	20	+5.00	0	0	-	-
Huntingdon	1	5	20	-1.00	4	9	44	+23.50	0	0	-	-
Kelso	0	1	-	-1.00	0	2	-	-2.00	0	0	-	-
Leicester	1	9	11	-5.25	1	7	14	-4.75	0	0	-	-
Lingfield	0	2	-	-2.00	0	4	-	-4.00	0	0	-	-
Ludlow	4	7	57	+17.50	0	14	-	-14.00	0	1	-	-1.00
Market Rasen	0	4	-	-4.00	0	6	-	-6.00	0	0	-	-
Musselburgh	1	1	100	+0.50	0	0	-	-	0	0	-	-
Newbury	0	8	-	-8.00	1	11	9	-5.50	0	1	-	-1.00
Newcastle	0	0	-	-	0	1	-	-1.00	0	0	-	-
Newton Abbot	1	5	20	-0.67	0	1	-	-1.00	0	0	-	-
Perth	0	2	-	-2.00	1	2	50	+3.00	0	0	-	-
Plumpton	0	5	-	-5.00	4	7	57	+8.90	1	3	33	-0.7
Sandown	0	8	-	-8.00	3	14	21	+7.33	0	1	-	-1.0
Southwell	1	3	33	-1.00	0	4	-	-4.00	0	0	-	-
Stratford	0	5	-	-5.00	1	3	33	+1.50	0	1	-	-1.00
Taunton	0	7	-	-7.00	2	6	33	+3.00	0	0	-	-
Towcester	2	8	25	+29.25	6	17	35	+7.13	0	2	-	-2.00
Uttoxeter	1	8	13	-4.75	2	14	14	-5.40	0	0	-	-
Warwick	2	4	50	+2.50	1	5	20	+0.00	0	2	-	-2.00
Wetherby	0	5	-	-5.00	0	5	-	-5.00	0	0	-	-
Wincanton	1	10	10	-8.09	1	11	9	-8.63	0	1	-	-1.00
Windsor	0	2	-	-2.00	1	3	33	-1.27	0	0	-	-
Worcester	1	1	100	+3.00	0	1	-	-1.00	0	0	-	-

Race type

	Hurdles				Chases			
	W	R	%	£1 stake	W	R	%	£1 stake
Handicap	11	76	14	+25.00	5	39	13	-7.75
Selling	0	1	-	-1.00	0	0	-	-
Claiming	1	2	50	+1.00	0	0	-	-
Novice	20	131	15	-63.07	6	35	17	-8.10
Maiden	3	15	20	-2.56	2	2	100	+13.00

Jockeys

	Hurdles				Chases				Bumpers			
	W	R	%	£1 stake	W	R	%	£1 stake	W	R	%	£1 stake
G Lee	28	145	19	-49.33	9	55	16	-8.51	2	9	22	-2.13
B Hughes	6	44	14	+32.00	0	1	-	-1.00	3	8	38	+16.12
A Dobbin	3	7	43	-0.93	2	6	33	+4.07	0	0	-	-
A Dempsey	0	21	-	-21.00	2	6	33	+2.00	0	0	-	-
J Tizzard	1	1	100	+1.25	0	0	-	-	0	0	-	-
R Johnson	0	2	-	-2.00	1	2	50	+1.75	0	0	-	-
P Buchanan	0	2	-	-2.00	1	6	17	-1.00	0	0	-	-
A McCoy	0	1	-	-1.00	0	0	-	-	0	0	-	-
J Crowley	0	0	-	-	0	1	-	-1.00	0	0	-	-
Mr M O'Hare	0	0	-	-	0	1	-	-1.00	0	0	-	-

By month

	Hurdles				Chases				Bumpers			
	W	R	%	£1 stake	W	R	%	£1 stake	W	R	%	£1 stake
May 2005	1	7	14	+0.00	0	1	-	-1.00	0	0	-	-
June	0	0	-	-	0	0	-	-	0	0	-	-
July	0	1	-	-1.00	0	0	-	-	0	0	-	-
August	1	2	50	+7.00	0	2	-	-2.00	0	0	-	-
September	1	5	20	-2.00	0	4	-	-4.00	0	0	-	-
October	2	12	17	-7.00	0	6	-	-6.00	0	2	-	-2.00
November	8	40	20	-4.60	4	14	29	+8.57	0	2	-	-2.00
December	10	44	23	-14.54	5	18	28	+4.08	0	1	-	-1.00
January 2006	10	38	26	-7.38	4	12	33	+7.90	1	3	33	-1.39
February	1	32	3	-6.00	0	7	-	-7.00	0	3	-	-3.00
March	1	21	5	-17.00	1	5	20	+0.00	3	3	100	+20.88
April	3	26	12	+4.50	1	11	9	-7.25	1	4	25	+1.50

By horse

	Wins	Runs	%	Win prize	Total Prize
Arcalis	1	5	20	45,072.00	55,753.33
Coat Of Honour	2	5	40	46,214.67	48,124.67
Inglis Drever	2	3	67	46,008.00	46,008.00
No Refuge	1	4	25	22,915.20	31,484.20
Kinburn	3	3	100	22,861.63	22,861.63
Covent Garden	1	2	50	16,927.63	16,927.63
Lennon	2	5	40	12,647.67	16,240.20
Bewleys Berry	1	5	20	3,854.80	16,141.54
Masafi	2	5	40	10,025.74	15,238.04
Kasthari	1	5	20	8,000.70	14,753.98
Island Faith	1	3	33	13,363.32	13,363.32
Ortolan Bleu	1	3	33	9,355.62	12,334.27
Hard Act To Follow	2	3	67	11,470.07	11,470.07
Supreme Leisure	1	6	17	6,506.00	10,787.40
Scotmail	2	5	40	8,174.78	10,558.78
Circassian	1	5	20	5,465.04	10,382.88
Iron Man	1	4	25	6,506.00	10,210.56

All runners

	Wins	Runs	%	2nd	3rd	4th	Win prize	Total prize	£1 Stake
Chase	15	81	19	10	8	5	91,691.62	151,120.88	-7.69
Hurdle	38	232	16	22	12	18	319,837.50	406,478.29	-52.01
Bumper	5	18	28	3	2	2	9,387.24	11,710.03	+12.99
TOTAL	58	331	18	35	22	25	420,916.36	569,309.20	-46.72

Howard Johnson

A step backwards for Johnson, as Arcalis, No Refuge and Inglis Drever – the three Graham Wylie horses who had won at Cheltenham in 2005 – all failed to live up to expectations.

Indeed, Johnson failed to train a single winner at HQ out of 20 runners and was also none from 12 at Sandown.

Having said that, Johnson's handicap hurdlers had an exceptional record, returning a profit of £25 to £1 level stakes, particularly at Wetherby.

It also paid to follow Johnson's occasional bumper runners, with five out of 18 successful.

Course records

	Hurdles				Chases				Bumpers			
	W	R	%	£1 stake	W	R	%	£1 stake	W	R	%	£1 stake
Aintree	1	9	11	-3.00	0	2	-	-2.00	0	2	-	-2.00
Ayr	1	9	11	-6.50	2	10	20	-1.25	1	1	100	+16.00
Bangor	0	0	-	-	0	2	-	-2.00	0	0	-	-
Carlisle	4	9	44	+1.07	2	11	18	-5.43	1	2	50	+2.50
Cartmel	1	2	50	+7.00	0	0	-	-	0	0	-	-
Catterick	4	12	33	-4.02	0	1	-	-1.00	1	1	100	+0.62
Cheltenham	0	14	-	-14.00	0	6	-	-6.00	0	0	-	-
Chepstow	0	4	-	-4.00	0	1	-	-1.00	0	0	-	-
Doncaster	0	7	-	-7.00	1	1	100	+2.25	0	1	-	-1.00
Haydock	2	10	20	-1.47	1	5	20	+3.50	0	0	-	-
Hexham	1	10	10	+2.00	0	2	-	-2.00	0	0	-	-
Huntingdon	0	6	-	-6.00	0	3	-	-3.00	0	0	-	-
Kelso	0	11	-	-11.00	0	1	-	-1.00	0	0	-	-
Market Rasen	2	10	20	-6.80	2	6	33	+4.50	1	2	50	+0.38
Musselburgh	4	18	22	-11.03	2	3	67	+11.33	0	2	-	-2.00
Newbury	1	3	33	-1.39	0	0	-	-	0	0	-	-
Newcastle	2	11	18	-2.75	0	2	-	-2.00	0	0	-	-
Perth	2	11	18	+14.00	0	3	-	-3.00	1	1	100	+4.50
Sandown	0	8	-	-8.00	0	4	-	-4.00	0	0	-	-
Sedgefield	5	39	13	-20.14	3	8	38	+11.00	0	4	-	-4.00
Southwell	0	3	-	-3.00	0	1	-	-1.00	0	1	-	-1.00
Uttoxeter	0	0	-	-	0	1	-	-1.00	0	0	-	-
Warwick	0	1	-	-1.00	0	0	-	-	0	0	-	-
Wetherby	7	24	29	+33.25	2	8	25	-4.60	0	1	-	-1.00
Windsor	1	1	100	+1.75	0	0	-	-	0	0	-	-

DREAM TEAM: But Graham Lee (left) has since left the Johnson-Wylie unit

Race type

	Hurdles				Chases			
	W	R	%	£1 stake	W	R	%	£1 stake
Handicap	17	113	15	-11.68	7	26	27	+11.67
Selling	1	8	13	-1.00	0	1	-	-1.00
Claiming	0	2	-	-2.00	0	0	-	-
Novice	20	74	27	+2.26	6	17	35	+6.47
Maiden	3	16	19	-7.11	0	1	-	-1.00

Jockeys

	Hurdles				Chases				Bumpers			
	W	R	%	£1 stake	W	R	%	£1 stake	W	R	%	£1 stake
A Dobbin	25	98	26	-2.98	8	26	31	-8.74	4	12	33	+5.00
Miss R D'son	5	17	29	+16.20	3	6	50	+1.79	1	4	25	-1.75
B Harding	4	46	9	-16.00	2	13	15	-1.50	2	6	33	+6.00
A McCoy	1	1	100	+2.50	0	0	-	-	0	0	-	-
A Dempsey	0	0	-	-	1	1	100	+14.00	0	0	-	-
E Williams	0	5	-	-5.00	0	0	-	-	1	2	50	+2.00
Mr C Callow	0	1	-	-1.00	1	4	25	-1.38	0	2	-	-2.00
S Marshall	1	8	13	+0.50	0	0	-	-	0	1	-	-1.00
F Davis	0	12	-	-12.00	0	0	-	-	0	0	-	-
G Lee	0	2	-	-2.00	0	0	-	-	0	1	-	-1.00

By month

	Hurdles				Chases				Bumpers			
	W	R	%	£1 stake	W	R	%	£1 stake	W	R	%	£1 stake
May 2005	3	16	19	+3.50	2	5	40	+0.13	2	3	67	+4.25
June	2	11	18	+1.50	0	3	-	-3.00	1	1	100	+2.00
July	2	7	29	-0.33	0	2	-	-2.00	0	0	-	-
August	1	4	25	-2.33	2	2	100	+4.63	0	1	-	-1.00
September	0	7	-	-7.00	1	3	33	-0.25	0	0	-	-
October	2	13	15	-5.00	0	1	-	-1.00	1	2	50	+0.50
November	2	23	9	-9.50	3	5	60	+7.40	0	3	-	-3.00
December	4	23	17	-1.38	1	4	25	-1.38	1	2	50	+7.00
January 2006	9	29	31	+24.22	1	2	50	-0.33	1	4	25	+2.50
February	3	18	17	-8.50	2	8	25	-3.21	0	3	-	-3.00
March	4	16	25	-7.31	1	8	13	-6.09	2	7	29	+0.00
April	2	22	9	-17.77	2	6	33	+10.29	0	3	-	-3.00

By horse

	Wins	Runs	%	Win prize	Total Prize
Monet's Garden	3	4	75	37,185.45	67,131.45
Faasel	0	6	-	0.00	40,614.41
Premier Dane	1	4	25	12,572.40	39,195.40
Turpin Green	1	5	20	7,351.78	38,404.85
Direct Access	1	3	33	33,804.00	33,804.00
Money Trix	3	4	75	9,932.00	29,183.00
The French Furze	1	4	25	13,152.30	21,648.30
According To John	4	4	100	20.838.27	20,838.27
Harmony Brig	3	6	50	12,594.30	19,997.52
Possextown	2	5	40	14,335.68	19,831.68
Rayshan	1	2	50	14,197.75	14,867.75
Native Coral	2	4	50	11,564.17	14,282.44
Bohemian Spirit	3	6	50	11,768.18	14,139.45
Jazz d'Estruval	1	1	100	13,584.52	13,584.52
Rising Generation	1	13	8	4,901.00	12,457.08
Ever Present	2	4	50	8,635.42	10,498.63
Ben Britten	2	3	67	9,084.50	9,950.10

All runners

	Wins	Runs	%	2nd	3rd	4th	Win prize	Total prize	£1 Stake
Chase	15	51	29	11	5	3	124,569.20	208,043.06	+3.17
Hurdle	36	197	18	26	22	14	181,614.60	336,439.98	-26.78
Bumper	8	29	28	4	4	2	15,781.16	21,260.29	+6.25
TOTAL	59	277	21	41	31	19	321,964.96	565,743.33	-17.36

Nicky Richards

From a significantly smaller pool of runners than those above him in the list, this was an excellent season for Richards, who boasted a 21 per cent strike-rate and a level-stakes profit in both chases and bumpers .

Hexham was a happy hunting ground, as were Kelso and Carlisle, although Richards trained only one winner apiece at Cheltenham and Sandown.

Of course, that could change this season with Monet's Garden likely to contest the top races.

Amateur pilot Rose Davidson has also done very well, including winning the Lanzarote.

Course records

	Hurdles				Chases				Bumpers			
	W	R	%	£1 stake	W	R	%	£1 stake	W	R	%	£1 stake
Aintree	1	12	8	-5.00	0	3	-	-3.00	0	1	-	-1.00
Ayr	7	32	22	-6.41	3	7	43	-2.41	2	7	29	+5.00
Bangor	0	3	-	-3.00	1	1	100	+2.50	1	2	50	+3.00
Carlisle	2	7	29	+6.88	2	3	67	+0.29	1	2	50	+0.50
Cartmel	1	5	20	+1.00	0	3	-	-3.00	0	0	-	-
Catterick	0	2	-	-2.00	0	0	-	-	1	1	100	+3.00
Cheltenham	1	6	17	+7.00	0	6	-	-6.00	0	2	-	-2.00
Haydock	1	12	8	-8.75	0	0	-	-	0	2	-	-2.00
Hexham	2	11	18	+4.50	1	3	33	+12.00	1	3	33	+0.00
Huntingdon	0	2	-	-2.00	0	0	-	-	0	0	-	-
Kelso	9	27	33	+13.97	1	5	20	-2.38	0	2	-	-2.00
Leicester	0	1	-	-1.00	0	0	-	-	0	0	-	-
Ludlow	1	1	100	+4.00	0	0	-	-	0	0	-	-
Market Rasen	0	4	-	-4.00	0	3	-	-3.00	0	0	-	-
Musselburgh	2	9	22	+2.50	2	2	100	+2.29	0	3	-	-3.00
Newcastle	4	14	29	-0.29	1	2	50	+7.00	0	0	-	-
Perth	3	27	11	-18.67	4	7	57	+4.88	1	1	100	+1.25
Sandown	0	2	-	-2.00	0	1	-	-1.00	0	2	-	-2.00
Sedgefield	1	9	11	-6.00	0	3	-	-3.00	1	1	100	+5.50
Southwell	0	2	-	-2.00	0	1	-	-1.00	0	0	-	-
Uttoxeter	1	2	50	+1.50	0	1	-	-1.00	0	0	-	-
Warwick	0	1	-	-1.00	0	0	-	-	0	0	-	-
Wetherby	0	6	-	-6.00	0	0	-	-	0	0	-	-

Race type

	Hurdles				Chases			
	W	R	%	£1 stake	W	R	%	£1 stake
Handicap	5	92	5	-48.50	18	164	11	-12.50
Selling	0	3	-	-3.00	0	1	-	-1.00
Claiming	1	2	50	+1.50	0	0	-	
Novice	16	122	13	-50.89	7	51	14	-6.92
Maiden	4	20	20	-5.59	1	3	33	+3.50

Jockeys

	Hurdles				Chases				Bumpers			
	W	R	%	£1 stake	W	R	%	£1 stake	W	R	%	£1 stake
C Llewellyn	17	109	16	-37.88	14	113	12	-3.50	0	13	-	-13.00
A Evans	5	47	11	-10.59	6	52	12	-6.50	0	2	-	-2.00
M Goldstein	1	18	6	-10.50	1	4	25	-2.17	4	6	67	+43.50
S Crawford	1	10	10	-4.00	0	0	-	-	4	20	20	-2.63
Mr D England	0	2	-	-2.00	3	12	25	+2.75	0	0	-	-
B Wharfe	0	12	-	-12.00	1	4	25	+5.00	1	4	25	+13.00
T Scudamore	0	7	-	-7.00	1	8	13	-4.75	0	1	-	-1.00
A McCoy	0	1	-	-1.00	0	0	-	-	0	0	-	-
W Marston	0	1	-	-1.00	0	0	-	-	0	0	-	-
T Siddall	0	9	-	-9.00	0	8	-	-8.00	0	0	-	-

By month

	Hurdles				Chases				Bumpers			
	W	R	%	£1 stake	W	R	%	£1 stake	W	R	%	£1 stake
May 2005	0	6	-	-6.00	2	7	29	+8.00	0	3	-	-3.00
June	1	6	17	-2.50	1	5	20	+8.00	0	0	-	-
July	0	3	-	-3.00	2	4	50	+13.00	0	1	-	-1.00
August	0	5	-	-5.00	0	1	-	-1.00	1	1	100	+3.50
September	2	4	50	+2.41	0	1	-	-1.00	0	0	-	-
October	9	24	38	+15.90	6	32	19	-8.25	0	10	-	-10.00
November	1	26	4	-18.50	2	33	6	-27.92	2	6	33	+13.50
December	4	31	13	-13.90	5	26	19	+14.50	1	6	17	+4.00
January 2006	2	23	9	-14.50	2	23	9	-1.00	2	7	29	-0.13
February	4	36	11	-12.89	5	26	19	+17.00	1	2	50	+24.00
March	0	29	-	-29.00	0	29	-	-29.00	1	6	17	+3.00
April	1	26	4	-11.00	1	17	6	-12.50	1	4	25	+4.00

By horse

	Wins	Runs	%	Win prize	Total Prize
Ollie Magern	1	6	17	45,750.00	54,854.00
Rimsky	2	10	20	21,001.00	32,703.90
Bob The Builder	3	9	33	18,864.12	22,780.27
Patman du Charmil	2	7	29	6,814.29	20,777.79
Va Vavoom	2	12	17	14,193.12	18,254.49
Miss Shakira	3	9	33	14,578.76	17,249.56
The Cool Guy	2	3	67	8,659.76	17,215.76
Baby Run	1	1	100	15,004.00	15,004.00
Jeremy Cuddle Duck	3	6	50	13,241.05	14,045.05
Naunton Brook	2	8	25	12,018.00	13,868.00
Day Of Claies	2	7	29	12,122.00	13,151.91
Redemption	0	9	-	-	12,410.00
Bilyandi	1	10	10	5,204.80	11,074.42
Tramantano	0	3	-	-	10,695.00
Florida Dream	2	8	25	10,214.42	10,572.47
No Guarantees	1	6	17	4,879.50	10,401.70
Lord Maizey	1	5	20	9,682.59	10,078.59

All runners

	Wins	Runs	%	2nd	3rd	4th	Win prize	Total prize	£1 Stake
Chase	26	206	13	6	11	25	194,192.32	246,814.13	-22.17
Hurdle	24	220	11	24	22	20	114,549.02	216,004.04	-98.98
Bumper	9	46	20	6	3	1	18,121.15	23,683.95	+37.88
TOTAL	59	472	13	36	36	46	326,862.49	486,502.12	-83.27

Nigel Twiston-Davies

The season peaked early for Twiston-Davies, with Ollie Magern's win in the Charlie Hall his biggest victory of the year.

That was followed by a shocking run of form in March, when only one of his 64 runners were successful, contributing to an equally dire set of statistics for Cheltenham – one out of 51.

Things are set to look different for Twiston-Davies, with regular pilot Carl Llewellyn moving into management.

Marc Goldstein and Antony Evans look set to fight it out for No. 1, and on this evidence Goldstein could be the man.

Course records

	Hurdles				Chases				Bumpers			
	W	R	%	£1 stake	W	R	%	£1 stake	W	R	%	£1 stake
Aintree	1	8	13	-4.25	1	10	10	-6.00	0	1	-	-1.00
Ayr	0	0	-	-	0	1	-	-1.00	0	0	-	-
Bangor	1	5	20	-2.13	0	4	-	-4.00	1	4	25	+0.50
Carlisle	1	5	20	-2.80	0	3	-	-3.00	0	0	-	-
Cartmel	0	0	-	-	0	1	-	-1.00	0	0	-	-
Cheltenham	0	17	-	-17.00	1	29	3	-20.00	0	5	-	-5.00
Chepstow	4	18	22	+0.50	3	12	25	+6.25	2	6	33	-0.63
Exeter	1	7	14	-3.50	0	5	-	-5.00	0	2	-	-2.00
Fakenham	0	1	-	-1.00	0	1	-	-1.00	0	0	-	-
Folkestone	0	1	-	-1.00	0	1	-	-1.00	0	1	-	-1.00
Haydock	3	9	33	+14.57	1	9	11	+8.00	2	3	67	+27.00
Hereford	0	8	-	-8.00	2	8	25	+8.25	0	0	-	-
Hexham	0	0	-	-	0	1	-	-1.00	0	0	-	-
Huntingdon	0	14	-	-14.00	1	12	8	-3.00	1	1	100	+9.00
Leicester	0	4	-	-4.00	3	9	33	+1.58	0	0	-	-
Lingfield	0	4	-	-4.00	0	3	-	-3.00	0	0	-	-
Ludlow	0	15	-	-15.00	4	14	29	+10.50	1	5	20	+12.00
Market Rasen	1	6	17	+5.00	3	4	75	+21.50	0	0	-	-
Newbury	0	9	-	-9.00	0	13	-	-13.00	0	2	-	-2.00
Newcastle	2	2	100	+7.12	0	3	-	-3.00	0	0	-	-
Newton Abbot	0	2	-	-2.00	0	2	-	-2.00	0	0	-	-
Perth	3	11	27	-1.09	0	3	-	-3.00	0	0	-	-
Plumpton	0	3	-	-3.00	0	0	-	-	0	0	-	-
Sandown	0	6	-	-6.00	0	1	-	-1.00	0	1	-	-1.00
Southwell	0	0	-	-	0	2	-	-2.00	0	0	-	-
Stratford	1	1	100	+4.50	0	2	-	-2.00	0	0	-	-
Taunton	1	5	20	+3.00	0	5	-	-5.00	0	0	-	-
Towcester	2	12	17	+5.00	2	8	25	+0.25	1	4	25	+4.00
Uttoxeter	2	8	25	-3.43	2	14	14	-6.25	0	3	-	-3.00
Warwick	1	10	10	-8.47	0	5	-	-5.00	0	4	-	-4.00
Wetherby	0	8	-	-8.00	1	8	13	-4.25	1	2	50	+7.00
Wincanton	0	8	-	-8.00	1	5	20	+16.00	0	0	-	-
Windsor	0	2	-	-2.00	0	1	-	-1.00	0	0	-	-
Worcester	0	11	-	-11.00	1	7	14	+2.00	0	2	-	-2.00

Trainer profiles, including Irish king Noel Meade, pages 6-16 and 21-31

Top trainers 2005-06 by winners

All runs				First time out			Horses*		
Won	Ran	%	Trainer	Won	Ran	%	Won	Ran	%
148	651	23	P Nicholls	37	158	23	79	158	50
112	661	17	P Hobbs	21	155	14	66	155	43
112	880	13	M Pipe	30	195	15	71	195	36
105	712	15	Jonjo O'Neill	28	187	15	64	187	34
85	390	22	N Henderson	30	119	25	59	119	50
77	475	16	Miss V Williams	17	112	15	47	112	42
63	415	15	A King	15	108	14	37	108	34
63	452	14	G L Moore	19	94	20	48	94	51
60	414	14	Mrs S J Smith	6	105	6	38	105	36
59	277	21	N Richards	23	92	25	38	92	41
59	334	18	J Howard Johnson	21	117	18	46	117	39
59	473	12	N Twiston-Davies	24	116	21	42	116	36
57	343	17	E Williams	16	93	17	37	93	40
57	519	11	R C Guest	13	92	14	34	92	37
45	387	12	F Murphy	7	95	7	25	95	26
41	315	13	P Bowen	13	82	16	25	82	30
38	353	11	R Alner	12	81	15	28	81	35
36	304	12	D McCain	6	55	11	21	55	38
35	273	13	H Daly	8	75	11	20	75	27
34	262	13	T George	11	67	16	24	67	36
32	269	12	K G Reveley	9	63	14	19	63	30
32	331	10	B Powell	6	90	7	22	90	24
30	197	15	Miss E Lavelle	10	52	19	19	52	37
29	337	9	I Williams	8	93	9	20	93	22
28	157	18	P Haslam	8	40	20	20	40	50
28	191	15	J Jefferson	5	40	13	15	40	38
28	245	11	Miss H Knight	4	75	5	15	75	20
27	227	12	L Lungo	8	69	12	19	69	28
24	198	12	C L Tizzard	5	40	13	16	40	40
23	154	15	Mrs H Dalton	7	50	14	15	50	30
23	159	14	P R Webber	12	66	18	19	66	29
23	184	13	C Mann	5	62	8	16	62	26
22	302	7	J Mullins	6	62	10	19	62	31
21	85	25	C Egerton	7	26	27	11	26	42
21	173	12	J Frost	6	45	13	12	45	27
20	183	11	O Sherwood	5	49	10	16	49	33
19	94	20	J J Quinn	4	30	13	11	30	37
19	134	14	M Pitman	9	45	20	16	45	36
18	177	10	M D Hammond	4	46	9	13	46	28
18	209	9	R Phillips	9	63	14	15	63	24
18	219	8	M Harris	1	44	2	14	44	32
17	82	21	V Dartnall	6	27	22	12	27	44
17	150	11	M Todhunter	5	40	13	9	40	23
16	116	14	R Ford	1	30	3	7	30	23
15	80	19	G A Swinbank	7	37	19	9	37	24
15	122	12	J Old	3	42	7	12	42	29
15	240	6	M Scudamore	4	64	6	11	64	17
14	89	16	N Gifford	4	29	14	10	29	34
14	93	15	C Tinkler	6	28	21	12	28	43
14	104	13	Mrs L Wadham	5	28	18	12	28	43
14	113	12	J Spearing	1	34	3	7	34	21

*Shows how many individual horses ran for the yard last season, and how many won at least once

Top trainers 2005-06 by prize money

Total prizemoney	Trainer	Win prizemoney	Wins	Class 1-3			Class 4-6		
				Won	Ran	%	Won	Ran	%
2,487,494	P Nicholls	1,550,827	148	30	170	18	47	148	32
1,636,948	P Hobbs	1,058,293	112	19	121	16	52	251	21
1,584,719	M Pipe	1,090,893	112	14	144	10	54	361	15
1,197,167	Jonjo O'Neill	761,179	105	16	108	15	45	296	15
1,025,048	N Henderson	757,326	85	11	61	18	17	76	22
970,424	A King	616,124	63	6	47	13	20	116	17
790,457	Mrs S J Smith	483,133	60	10	49	20	22	184	12
666,058	Miss V Williams	431,973	77	5	49	10	35	162	22
573,291	J Howard Johnson	423,973	59	10	52	19	22	109	20
566,422	N Richards	321,232	59	4	22	18	22	115	19
493,498	R Alner	309,488	38	4	34	12	16	145	11
492,984	G L Moore	323,559	63	4	45	9	30	207	14
484,228	N Twiston-Davies	323,503	59	5	53	9	30	165	18
484,008	P Bowen	286,467	41	6	45	13	24	158	15
461,459	F Murphy	299,490	45	3	50	6	21	170	12
456,830	R C Guest	320,344	57	5	33	15	36	338	11
399,140	M Brassil	399,140	1	0	0	0	0	0	0
399,095	E Williams	304,020	57	2	17	12	36	210	17
389,664	H Daly	240,702	35	3	21	14	11	96	11
360,877	Miss H Knight	243,175	28	4	24	17	10	94	11
323,980	T George	168,325	34	1	22	5	19	125	15
308,611	M Morris	228,080	1	0	0	0	0	0	0
281,979	C Egerton	212,895	21	4	11	36	6	25	24
275,464	K G Reveley	169,619	32	1	25	4	14	119	12
265,192	D McCain	192,496	36	0	16	0	14	134	10
259,595	Miss E Lavelle	166,528	30	0	20	0	18	87	21
257,468	C Mann	161,135	23	2	26	8	14	89	16
256,023	F Doumen	110,533	4	1	11	9	0	0	0
255,642	W P Mullins	0	0	0	3	0	0	0	0
251,609	I Williams	151,102	29	1	17	6	16	184	9
219,154	C L Tizzard	113,065	24	1	10	10	15	98	15
217,537	O Sherwood	115,962	20	2	10	20	8	73	11
216,961	J Spearing	164,285	14	2	5	40	5	59	8
211,516	N Meade	170,098	3	2	5	40	0	0	0
209,635	J Mullins	102,191	22	0	12	0	9	144	6
204,438	B Powell	125,592	32	0	18	0	14	158	9
202,683	Colm A Murphy	202,683	1	0	0	0	0	0	0
190,517	P Haslam	107,921	28	0	11	0	19	79	24
188,095	L Lungo	130,258	27	1	25	4	15	101	15
185,984	S Gollings	101,074	13	3	17	18	8	60	13
183,166	Nick Williams	137,918	11	1	13	8	6	38	16
180,895	J Jefferson	126,111	28	1	11	9	13	97	13
167,368	John Joseph Murphy	165,358	1	0	0	0	0	1	0
167,282	P R Webber	109,293	23	3	23	13	8	51	16
161,588	M Pitman	96,675	19	2	12	17	7	44	16
154,795	N Gifford	115,800	14	0	5	0	8	39	21
150,273	Miss L Russell	72,062	12	0	15	0	3	141	2
143,583	T Taaffe	114,040	1	1	4	25	0	1	0
134,922	N Chance	93,142	11	0	6	0	4	15	27
132,767	J J Quinn	97,199	19	2	15	13	11	43	26
130,782	Mrs L Wadham	70,747	14	1	10	10	4	41	10

Top jockeys 2005-06

all rides			chases		hurdles		Jockey	best trainer	for best trainer	
W	R	%	W	R	W	R			W	R
178	831	21	67	304	111	527	**A P McCoy**	Jonjo O'Neill	69	367
167	914	18	63	341	104	573	**R Johnson**	P Hobbs	83	428
108	750	14	33	250	75	500	**G Lee**	J H Johnson	39	209
92	516	18	31	170	61	346	**A Dobbin**	N Richards	37	136
87	565	15	38	201	49	364	**T J Murphy**	M Pipe	44	268
76	544	14	38	221	38	323	**Christian Williams**	P Nicholls	32	193
73	605	12	26	208	47	397	**R Thornton**	A King	46	285
69	236	29	26	100	43	136	**R Walsh**	P Nicholls	63	203
62	372	17	17	107	45	265	**M A Fitzgerald**	N Henderson	44	181
60	558	11	33	230	27	328	**P J Brennan**	P Hobbs	17	123
58	540	11	27	250	31	290	**A Thornton**	R Alner	21	170
57	479	12	24	170	33	309	**T Doyle**	P R Webber	21	121
55	400	14	32	188	23	212	**S Thomas**	Miss V Williams	42	265
55	547	10	19	182	36	365	**L Aspell**	O Sherwood	16	134
52	441	12	19	153	33	288	**N Fehily**	C Mann	19	114
52	443	12	14	140	38	303	**J E Moore**	G L Moore	28	207
46	321	14	29	146	17	175	**D Elsworth**	Mrs S J Smith	43	244
45	445	10	15	153	30	292	**W Hutchinson**	A King	8	83
42	388	11	18	157	24	231	**J M Maguire**	T George	16	145
40	394	10	18	152	22	242	**C Llewellyn**	N Twiston-Davies	31	235
40	398	10	17	152	23	246	**R McGrath**	K G Reveley	13	108
39	297	13	15	101	24	196	**P Hide**	G L Moore	28	147
39	351	11	27	179	12	172	**J Tizzard**	C L Tizzard	18	146
37	299	12	11	94	26	205	**W Kennedy**	G Harker	9	28
36	393	9	12	134	24	259	**K J Mercer**	F Murphy	19	186
35	417	8	17	159	18	258	**M Bradburne**	H Daly	8	108
35	474	7	17	169	18	305	**T Scudamore**	M Pipe	11	124
31	209	15	18	99	13	110	**M Foley**	N Henderson	14	71
31	239	13	15	90	16	149	**P C O'Neill**	Miss V Williams	14	68
30	360	8	14	155	16	205	**Paul Moloney**	E Williams	13	68
29	201	14	4	47	25	154	**P Merrigan**	P Haslam	11	52
28	205	14	9	64	19	141	**L Heard**	P Nicholls	20	102
26	284	9	5	68	21	216	**A Tinkler**	N Henderson	7	65
26	341	8	9	133	17	208	**B Harding**	N Richards	8	65
25	231	11	5	55	20	176	**J Crowley**	K G Reveley	7	37
25	240	10	8	67	17	173	**S J Craine**	D McCain	19	146
25	386	6	8	140	17	246	**J P McNamara**	R Brookhouse	6	28
24	226	11	11	81	13	145	**R Garritty**	J J Quinn	9	38
23	158	15	5	53	18	105	**T J O'Brien**	P Hobbs	6	33
23	160	14	7	54	16	106	**B Fenton**	Miss E Lavelle	16	95
23	332	7	10	83	13	249	**D C Costello**	G A Swinbank	5	35
21	218	10	13	100	8	118	**T J Dreaper**	F Murphy	10	79
21	220	10	5	61	16	159	**T Greenall**	M W Easterby	8	123
20	263	8	6	87	14	176	**F Keniry**	G M Moore	7	105
20	343	6	12	96	8	247	**O Nelmes**	B Ryall	5	13
19	148	13	13	63	6	85	**D Jacob**	D Keane	8	72
19	306	6	4	72	15	234	**W Marston**	D Wintle	8	67
19	393	5	12	168	7	225	**P Buchanan**	Miss L Russell	11	233
18	249	7	6	73	12	176	**J Mogford**	J C Tuck	5	39
17	136	13	6	56	11	80	**D R Dennis**	I Williams	9	68
17	187	9	14	93	3	94	**D O'Meara**	H Hogarth	8	49

Big Races, Fixtures and Track Facts

148

Fixtures

Key - **Jumps**, *Jumps evening*, Flat, *Flat evening*

October

1 Sunday..**Kelso**, **Market Rasen**, **Uttoxeter**
2 Monday ....Pontefract, Windsor, Wolverhampton
3 Tuesday..................................Catterick, **Huntingdon**, Leicester
4 Wednesday ....**Exeter**, Nottingham, **Towcester**
5 Thursday.....................................Lingfield, **Wincanton**, **Worcester**
6 Friday...**Carlisle**, York
7 Saturday...................................Ascot, **Bangor**, **Chepstow**, **Hexham**, York
8 Sunday...Bath, Musselburgh
9 Monday....................................Ayr, Windsor, Wolverhampton
10 Tuesday...................................Leicester, Newbury, Newcastle
11 Wednesday.................................Lingfield, **Uttoxeter**, **Wetherby**
12 Thursday....................................**Ludlow**, Newmarket, Southwell
13 Friday...Brighton, Newmarket, Redcar
14 Saturday ....Catterick, **Kempton**, Newmarket, **Stratford**
15 Sunday..**Carlisle**, **Hereford**
16 Monday ....**Plumpton**, Pontefract, Windsor
17 Tuesday ....Bath, **Exeter**, Lingfield
18 Wednesday.............................Nottingham, **Worcester**, Yarmouth
19 Thursday ....Brighton, **Haydock**, **Ludlow**
20 Friday ....Doncaster, **Fakenham**, Newbury
21 Saturday........................**Chepstow**, Doncaster, **Kelso**, **Aintree**, Newbury
22 Sunday......................................**Aintree**, **Towcester**, **Wincanton**
23 Monday.....................................Kempton, Leicester, Lingfield
24 Tuesday......................................Catterick, **Cheltenham**, Yarmouth
25 Wednesday ....**Cheltenham**, Nottingham, **Sedgefield**
26 Thursday ....Lingfield, **Stratford**, **Taunton**
27 Friday ....Newmarket, **Uttoxeter**, **Wetherby**
28 Saturday ....**Ascot**, Ayr, Newmarket, **Wetherby**, *Wolverhampton*
29 Sunday...**Carlisle**, Kempton
30 Monday ....**Plumpton**, **Warwick**, Wolverhampton
31 Tuesday ....Catterick, **Exeter**, Southwell, Wolverhampton

November

1 Wednesday ....**Chepstow**, **Huntingdon**, Kempton, Nottingham
2 Thursday ....**Haydock**, Southwell, **Towcester**, Wolverhampton
3 Friday ....Musselburgh, **Fontwell**, **Hexham**, Wolverhampton
4 Saturday ....Doncaster, **Kelso**, **Sandown**, **Wincanton**, *Wolverhampton*
5 Sunday ....**Hereford**, **Market Rasen**
6 Monday ....**Carlisle**, Kempton, Wolverhampton
7 Tuesday ....**Exeter**, **Kempton**, **Sedgefield**, Wolverhampton
8 Wednesday.........................**Bangor**, Kempton, **Lingfield**, Wolverhampton
9 Thursday...Lingfield, **Ludlow**, **Taunton**
10 Friday ....**Cheltenham**, **Newcastle**, Southwell, Wolverhampton
11 Saturday ...**Cheltenham**, Kempton, **Uttoxeter**, **Wetherby**, *Wolverhampton*
12 Sunday...**Carlisle**, **Cheltenham**, **Fontwell**
13 Monday ....**Leicester**, Lingfield
14 Tuesday.....................**Fakenham**, **Folkestone**, Southwell, Wolverhampton
15 Wednesday ....**Hexham**, Kempton, Southwell, **Warwick**

16	Thursday	......................................**Hereford**, **Market Rasen**, **Wincanton**
17	Friday	...................................**Ascot**, **Exeter**, **Kelso**, Wolverhampton
18	Saturday	............**Ascot**, **Haydock**, **Huntingdon**, Lingfield, *Wolverhampton*
19	Sunday	....**Aintree**, **Plumpton**, **Towcester**
20	Monday	....**Ludlow**, Southwell, Wolverhampton
21	Tuesday	.........................**Kempton**, **Sedgefield**, Southwell, Wolverhampton
22	Wednesday	...............................**Chepstow**, Kempton, **Lingfield**, **Wetherby**
23	Thursday	....**Carlisle**, **Taunton**, **Uttoxeter**
24	Friday	........................**Musselburgh**, Kempton, **Newbury**, Wolverhampton
25	Saturday	......Kempton, **Newbury**, **Newcastle**, **Towcester**, *Wolverhampton*
26	Sunday	....**Fontwell**, **Leicester**, **Newbury**
27	Monday	....**Folkestone**, Kempton, Wolverhampton
28	Tuesday	....**Hereford**, Lingfield, Southwell
29	Wednesday	....**Ayr**, **Catterick**, Kempton, **Plumpton**
30	Thursday	..............................**Leicester**, **Market Rasen**, **Wincanton**

December

1	Friday	.....................................**Exeter**, Lingfield, **Sandown**, Wolverhampton
2	Saturday	................**Chepstow**, Kempton, Newbury, **Sandown**, **Wetherby**,
		....*Wolverhampton*
3	Sunday	....**Kelso**, **Warwick**
4	Monday	....**Fakenham**, Lingfield, Wolverhampton
5	Tuesday	......................................**Fontwell**, **Sedgefield**, Southwell
6	Wednesday	....**Hexham**, Kempton, **Leicester**
7	Thursday	........................**Huntingdon**, **Ludlow**, **Taunton**, Wolverhampton
8	Friday	........................**Cheltenham**, **Doncaster**, Kempton, Wolverhampton
9	Saturday	...........................**Cheltenham**, **Doncaster**, **Lingfield**, Southwell,
		....*Wolverhampton*
10	Sunday	....**Musselburgh**
11	Monday	....**Ayr**, **Plumpton**, Wolverhampton

ASCOT: jumps racing finally returns to the Berkshire venue this season

 Sponsored by Stan James

12	Tuesday	**Folkestone, Sedgefield**, Southwell
13	Wednesday	**Bangor**, Lingfield, **Newbury**, Wolverhampton
14	Thursday	**Catterick, Exeter**, Southwell
15	Friday	**Ascot**, Kempton, **Uttoxeter**, Wolverhampton
16	Saturday	**Ascot, Haydock**, Lingfield, **Newcastle**
18	Monday	Kempton, **Taunton**, Wolverhampton
19	Tuesday	**Ayr**, Lingfield, Southwell
20	Wednesday	**Musselburgh, Fakenham**, Kempton, Lingfield
21	Thursday	**Exeter, Ludlow**, Southwell
22	Friday	**Hereford**, Kempton, Lingfield, Wolverhampton
23	Saturday	**Doncaster, Fontwell, Hereford**, Newbury
26	Tuesday	**Huntingdon, Kempton, Market Rasen, Sedgefield, Towcester, Wetherby, Wincanton**, Wolverhampton
27	Wednesday	**Chepstow, Kempton**, Southwell, **Wetherby**, Wolverhampton
28	Thursday	**Catterick, Leicester**, Southwell ·
29	Friday	**Newbury**, Southwell, **Taunton**, Wolverhampton
30	Saturday	**Ascot, Musselburgh, Haydock**, Lingfield

January

1	Monday	**Catterick, Cheltenham, Exeter**, Southwell
2	Tuesday	**Ayr, Folkestone**, Southwell
3	Wednesday	Lingfield, **Wetherby**
4	Thursday	**Fontwell, Lingfield**, Wolverhampton
5	Friday	**Musselburgh, Newcastle**, Wolverhampton
6	Saturday	**Chepstow, Haydock**, Kempton, Lingfield, **Sandown**
7	Sunday	**Plumpton**, Southwell
8	Monday	**Ludlow, Taunton**, Wolverhampton
9	Tuesday	**Leicester, Sedgefield**, Southwell
10	Wednesday	Kempton, Lingfield, **Wincanton**
11	Thursday	**Catterick, Hereford**, Southwell
12	Friday	**Huntingdon, Kelso**, Wolverhampton
13	Saturday	**Kempton**, Lingfield, **Warwick, Wetherby**, Wolverhampton
14	Sunday	**Carlisle**
15	Monday	**Fakenham, Plumpton**, Wolverhampton
16	Tuesday	**Folkestone**, Southwell, Wolverhampton
17	Wednesday	Lingfield, **Newbury, Newcastle**
18	Thursday	**Ludlow, Taunton**
19	Friday	**Chepstow, Musselburgh**, Wolverhampton
20	Saturday	**Ascot, Haydock**, Lingfield, **Wincanton**
21	Sunday	**Towcester**, Wolverhampton
22	Monday	**Ayr**, Kempton, Wolverhampton
23	Tuesday	**Leicester, Sedgefield**, Southwell
24	Wednesday	**Catterick, Huntingdon**, Lingfield
25	Thursday	**Fontwell, Warwick**
26	Friday	**Hereford, Lingfield**, Wolverhampton
27	Saturday	**Cheltenham**, Lingfield, **Southwell, Uttoxeter**
28	Sunday	**Kelso**, Kempton, Wolverhampton
29	Monday	Lingfield, **Ludlow**, Wolverhampton
30	Tuesday	**Folkestone**, Southwell, **Taunton**
31	Wednesday	**Leicester**, Lingfield, **Newcastle**

February

| 1 | Thursday | **Towcester, Wincanton** |

2	Friday	**Catterick**, **Chepstow**, Wolverhampton
3	Saturday	Lingfield, **Sandown**, **Stratford**, **Wetherby**
4	Sunday	**Musselburgh**, **Fontwell**, Kempton
5	Monday	**Hexham**, Lingfield, Wolverhampton
6	Tuesday	**Market Rasen**, **Sedgefield**, Southwell
7	Wednesday	**Carlisle**, Lingfield, **Ludlow**
8	Thursday	**Huntingdon**, Southwell, **Taunton**
9	Friday	**Bangor**, **Kempton**, Wolverhampton
10	Saturday	**Ayr**, Lingfield, **Newbury**, **Warwick**, *Wolverhampton*
11	Sunday	**Exeter**, **Hereford**, Southwell
12	Monday	**Plumpton**, **Wetherby**, Wolverhampton
13	Tuesday	**Folkestone**, **Newcastle**, Southwell
14	Wednesday	**Musselburgh**, **Leicester**, Lingfield
15	Thursday	**Chepstow**, **Kelso**, Southwell
16	Friday	**Fakenham**, **Sandown**, Wolverhampton
17	Saturday	**Ascot**, **Haydock**, Lingfield, **Uttoxeter**, **Wincanton**
18	Sunday	**Fontwell**, **Towcester**
19	Monday	**Carlisle**, Lingfield, **Market Rasen**
20	Tuesday	**Sedgefield**, Southwell, **Taunton**
21	Wednesday	**Lingfield**, **Ludlow**, Wolverhampton
22	Thursday	**Haydock**, **Huntingdon**
23	Friday	**Sandown**, **Warwick**, Wolverhampton
24	Saturday	**Chepstow**, **Kempton**, Lingfield, **Newcastle**
25	Sunday	**Exeter**
26	Monday	**Hereford**, **Plumpton**, Wolverhampton
27	Tuesday	**Catterick**, **Leicester**, Lingfield
28	Wednesday	**Folkestone**, Southwell, **Wetherby**

March

1	Thursday	Lingfield, **Ludlow**, **Taunton**
2	Friday	**Ayr**, **Newbury**, Wolverhampton
3	Saturday	**Kelso**, **Kempton**, **Newbury**, **Southwell**
4	Sunday	**Bangor**, **Huntingdon**
5	Monday	**Hereford**, Wolverhampton
6	Tuesday	**Exeter**, **Newcastle**, Southwell
7	Wednesday	**Catterick**, **Fontwell**, Lingfield
8	Thursday	**Carlisle**, **Lingfield**, **Wincanton**
9	Friday	**Ayr**, **Leicester**, **Sandown**
10	Saturday	**Ayr**, **Chepstow**, **Sandown**, Wolverhampton
11	Sunday	**Market Rasen**, **Warwick**
12	Monday	**Plumpton**, **Stratford**, **Taunton**
13	Tuesday	**Cheltenham**, **Sedgefield**, Southwell
14	Wednesday	**Cheltenham**, **Huntingdon**, Wolverhampton
15	Thursday	**Cheltenham**, **Hexham**
16	Friday	**Cheltenham**, **Fakenham**, Lingfield
17	Saturday	Lingfield, **Newcastle**, **Uttoxeter**, **Wetherby**
18	Sunday	**Carlisle**, **Fontwell**
19	Monday	**Market Rasen**, Southwell, **Wincanton**
20	Tuesday	**Exeter**, Southwell, **Warwick**
21	Wednesday	**Chepstow**, Kempton, **Lingfield**
22	Thursday	**Ayr**, **Ludlow**, Southwell
23	Friday	Lingfield, **Newbury**, Wolverhampton
24	Saturday	**Bangor**, Kempton, Lingfield, **Newbury**, *Wolverhampton*
25	Sunday	**Taunton**, **Worcester**
26	Monday	Kempton, **Plumpton**, **Stratford**

27	Tuesday	Lingfield, **Sedgefield**
28	Wednesday	**Kempton**, Southwell, **Towcester**
29	Thursday	**Hereford**, Lingfield, **Towcester**
30	Friday	**Ascot**, Lingfield, Wolverhampton
31	Saturday	**Ascot**, Kempton, Newcastle, **Uttoxeter**

April

1	Sunday	**Hexham, Newton Abbot**
2	Monday	**Kelso**, Lingfield, Southwell
3	Tuesday	Folkestone, **Wetherby**
4	Wednesday	Catterick, Lingfield, Nottingham
5	Thursday	**Ludlow, Wincanton**, Wolverhampton
7	Saturday	**Carlisle, Haydock**, Kempton, **Newton Abbot**
8	Sunday	Musselburgh, **Plumpton, Towcester**
9	Monday	Musselburgh, **Fakenham, Huntingdon, Plumpton**, **Sedgefield**, Warwick, Yarmouth
10	Tuesday	**Chepstow, Fontwell**, Pontefract
11	Wednesday	Bath, **Exeter, Hereford**
12	Thursday	Leicester, **Aintree, Taunton**
13	Friday	Folkestone, **Aintree**, Southwell
14	Saturday	**Chepstow**, Lingfield, **Aintree**, Newcastle
15	Sunday	**Kelso, Market Rasen, Worcester**
16	Monday	**Wetherby**, Windsor, Wolverhampton
17	Tuesday	**Exeter**, Nottingham, Warwick
18	Wednesday	Beverley, **Cheltenham**, Newmarket
19	Thursday	**Cheltenham**, Newmarket, Ripon
20	Friday	**Ayr**, Newbury, *Taunton*, Thirsk
21	Saturday	**Ayr, Bangor**, Newbury, *Nottingham*, Thirsk, *Wolverhampton*
22	Sunday	**Stratford, Wincanton**
23	Monday	**Hexham, Plumpton**, Pontefract, *Sedgefield*, *Windsor*
24	Tuesday	*Bath*, Folkestone, Southwell, *Towcester*, Wolverhampton
25	Wednesday	Catterick, Epsom, *Kempton*, **Perth**, *Worcester*
26	Thursday	Beverley, **Fontwell**, **Perth**, *Southwell*
27	Friday	*Chepstow, **Newton Abbot**, Perth*, Sandown, Wolverhampton
28	Saturday	*Haydock*, Leicester, **Market Rasen**, Ripon, Sandown, *Wolverhampton*
29	Sunday	Brighton, **Ludlow, Wetherby**
30	Monday	Lingfield, *Southwell*, **Towcester**, *Windsor*, Wolverhampton

May

1	Tuesday	Bath, *Sedgefield*, Southwell, **Wincanton**, *Wolverhampton*
2	Wednesday	Ascot, *Cheltenham*, Nottingham, Pontefract
3	Thursday	Folkestone, **Hereford**, *Huntingdon*, Redcar
4	Friday	*Bangor*, Musselburgh, *Fontwell*, Lingfield, **Southwell**
5	Saturday	Goodwood, *Hexham*, Newmarket, Thirsk, **Uttoxeter**, *Worcester*
6	Sunday	Hamilton, Newmarket, Salisbury
7	Monday	Kempton, Newcastle, Warwick, Windsor
8	Tuesday	*Catterick*, Chepstow, *Exeter*, **Kelso**, Southwell
9	Wednesday	Beverley, Chester, **Fakenham**, *Kelso*, *Kempton*
10	Thursday	Chester, Goodwood, **Newton Abbot**, *Wetherby*
11	Friday	Chester, *Hamilton*, Lingfield, Nottingham, **Wincanton**
12	Saturday	Ascot, Haydock, **Hexham**, Lingfield, Nottingham, *Thirsk*, *Warwick*

13 Sunday ....**Plumpton**, **Uttoxeter**, **Worcester**
14 Monday ....Redcar, Southwell, *Towcester*, *Windsor*, Wolverhampton
15 Tuesday ......Brighton, *Huntingdon*, Newcastle, *Newton Abbot*, Southwell
16 Wednesday ....*Bath*, **Exeter**, **Fontwell**, *Perth*, York
17 Thursday ....*Folkestone*, *Ludlow*, **Perth**, Salisbury, York
18 Friday ....*Hamilton*, *Aintree*, Newbury, Newmarket, York
19 Saturday ......**Bangor**, Newbury, Newmarket, Thirsk, *Uttoxeter*, **Worcester**
20 Sunday..**Fakenham**, **Market Rasen**, Ripon
21 Monday ......Bath, Musselburgh, **Newton Abbot**, *Windsor*, *Wolverhampton*
22 Tuesday ....Beverley, *Leicester*, Lingfield, Southwell, *Towcester*
23 Wednesday ....Ayr, *Huntingdon*, **Kelso**, Lingfield, *Sedgefield*
24 Thursday.................**Bangor**, Goodwood, Newcastle, *Salisbury*, *Southwell*
25 Friday ....Goodwood, Haydock, Newmarket, *Pontefract*, **Stratford**
26 Saturday ....Beverley, *Cartmel*, Catterick, Haydock, Newmarket, **Stratford**
27 Sunday...**Fontwell**, Newmarket, **Uttoxeter**
28 Monday.....................Carlisle, **Cartmel**, Chepstow, Leicester, Redcar
29 Tuesday ....Chepstow, *Hexham*, Leicester, Redcar, *Sandown*
30 Wednesday ....*Beverley*, Brighton, **Cartmel**, *Southwell*, Yarmouth
31 Thursday...................................Ayr, *Sandown*, *Sedgefield*, Yarmouth

June

1 Friday........................*Bath*, Catterick, Epsom, *Goodwood*, Wolverhampton
2 Saturday..............Musselburgh, Epsom, Folkestone, **Hexham**, *Newcastle*,
....*Wolverhampton*, **Worcester**
3 Sunday...Brighton, **Hereford**, **Southwell**
4 Monday ....Carlisle, Leicester, *Thirsk*, *Windsor*
5 Tuesday...*Fontwell*, Lingfield, Ripon, *Southwell*
6 Wednesday ....*Kempton*, Lingfield, Nottingham, *Ripon*, **Sedgefield**
7 Thursday ....Hamilton, Haydock, **Newton Abbot**, *Sandown*, **Uttoxeter**
8 Friday......................Brighton, Catterick, Goodwood, *Haydock*, **Towcester**
9 Saturday.............Musselburgh, Goodwood, Haydock, *Lingfield*, *Newbury*,
....Windsor
10 Sunday...Bath, **Perth**, **Stratford**
11 Monday..................**Newton Abbot**, *Pontefract*, *Windsor*, Wolverhampton
12 Tuesday ....*Chester*, Redcar, Salisbury, **Worcester**
13 Wednesday ....Beverley, Brighton, *Hamilton*, *Kempton*, Nottingham
14 Thursday.....................*Fontwell*, Lingfield, Newbury, **Uttoxeter**, Yarmouth
15 Friday ....*Chepstow*, *Goodwood*, **Market Rasen**, Sandown, York
16 Saturday ....Bath, **Hexham**, *Leicester*, *Lingfield*, Sandown, York
17 Sunday...Folkestone, Salisbury, **Stratford**
18 Monday......................................Carlisle, **Hereford**, *Warwick*, *Windsor*
19 Tuesday...Ascot, *Newton Abbot*, Thirsk, *Yarmouth*
20 Wednesday ....Ascot, Hamilton, *Kempton*, *Ripon*, **Worcester**
21 Thursday...................................Ascot, Ripon, Southwell, *Towcester*
22 Friday...........................Ascot, Ayr, *Goodwood*, *Newmarket*, Redcar
23 Saturday.....................Ascot, Ayr, *Haydock*, *Lingfield*, Newmarket, Redcar
24 Sunday ....**Hexham**, Pontefract, Warwick
25 Monday ....*Chepstow*, Musselburgh, *Windsor*, Wolverhampton
26 Tuesday ....Beverley, Brighton, *Newbury*, **Newton Abbot**
27 Wednesday ....*Bath*, Carlisle, *Kempton*, Salisbury, **Worcester**
28 Thursday ....*Hamilton*, *Leicester*, Newcastle, Warwick
29 Friday ....Folkestone, **Market Rasen**, *Newcastle*, *Newmarket*,
....Wolverhampton
30 Saturday ....Chester, *Lingfield*, Newcastle, Newmarket, Windsor,
....*Wolverhampton*

Big-race dates

October

14 Kempton Park	Huntingdon Gold Cup Handicap Chase
21 Chepstow	Persian War Novice Hurdle
21 Chepstow	Silver Trophy Handicap Hurdle
22 Aintree	Wigan Handicap Chase
28 Ascot	Coloroll United House Handicap Chase
28 Wetherby	B365 Charlie Hall Chase
28 Wetherby	John Smith's West Yorkshire Hurdle
31 Exeter	William Hill Haldon Gold Cup Handicap Chase

November

4 Wincanton	totescoop6 Rising Stars Novice Chase
4 Wincanton	totesport Elite Handicap Hurdle
4 Wincanton	Badger Ales Trophy Handicap Chase
10 Cheltenham	Anglo-Irish Bank Sharp Novice Hurdle
11 Cheltenham	Jet UK Juvenile Hurdle
11 Cheltenham	Paddy Power Gold Cup Handicap Chase
12 Cheltenham	Independent Newspaper Novice Chase
12 Cheltenham	Greatwood Handicap Hurdle
17 Ascot	Blue Square Ascot Hurdle
18 Ascot	Blue Square First National Bank Handicap Chase
18 Haydock Park	Betfair Lancashire Chase
18 Huntingdon	totesport Peterborough Chase
19 Aintree	totesport Becher Handicap Chase
24 Newbury	Worcester Novice Chase
25 Newbury	Ballymore Properties Long Distance Hurdle
25 Newbury	Hennessy Cognac Gold Cup Handicap Chase
25 Newcastle	Pertemps 'Fighting Fifth' Hurdle
25 Newcastle	Rehearsal Handicap Chase
26 Newbury	Stan James Fulke Walwyn Novice Chase

December

1 Sandown Park	William Hill Winter Novice Hurdle
2 Sandown Park	William Hill Tingle Creek Trophy Chase
2 Sandown Park	Sodexho Prestige Henry VIII Novice Chase
8 Cheltenham	Mears Group Handicap Chase
9 Cheltenham	Brit Insurance Bristol Novice Hurdle
9 Cheltenham	totesport Bula Hurdle
9 Cheltenham	Ember Gold Cup Handicap Chase
9 Lingfield Park	Ember Novice Chase
9 Lingfield Park	Summit Junio Hurdle
15 Ascot	Noel Novice Chase
16 Ascot	totesport.com Long Walk Hurdle
16 Ascot	Anglo Irish Bank Kennel Gate Novice Hurdle
26 Kempton Park	Stan James Christmas Hurdle

26 Kempton Park ....Stan James Feltham Novice Chase
26 Kempton Park ....Stan James King George VI Chase
26 Kempton Park...Stan James Wayward Lad Novice Chase
26 Wetherby ....Skybet.com Rowland Meyrick Handicap Chase
27 Chepstow...........................At The Races Red Button Betting Finale Juvenile Hurdle
27 Chepstow ....Coral Welsh National Handicap Chase
27 Wetherby ....Skybet.com Castleford Chase
29 Newbury..stanjamesuk.com Challow Novice Hurdle

January

1 Cheltenham..Unicoin Homes "Dipper" Novice Chase
1 Cheltenham ....Unicoin Homes Handicap Chase
6 Sandown Park.......................................Anglo Irish Bank Tolworth Novice Hurdle
13 Kempton Park ....totesport Lanzarote Handicap Hurdle
13 Warwick ....totesport Classic Handicap Chase
20 Ascot...Victor Chandler Handicap Chase
20 Ascot ....intercasino.co.uk Lightning Novice Chase
20 Haydock Park ....Commhoist Logistics Champion Hurdle Trial
20 Haydock Park...............................Anglo Irish Bank Rossington Main Novice Hurdle
20 Haydock Park ....Peter Marsh Handicap Chase
27 Cheltenham ....Byrne Bros Cleeve Hurdle
27 Cheltenham.......................................Letheby & Christopher Cotswold Chase
27 Cheltenham..Wragge & Co Finesse Juvenile Hurdle
27 Cheltenham...Ladbrokes Trophy Handicap Chase
27 Southwell ....Brit Insurance River Don Novice Hurdle
27 Southwell..Skybet Great Yorkshire Handicap Chase

February

3 Sandown Park ....totesport.com Scilly Isles Novice Chase
3 Sandown Park ....totescoop6 Sandown Handicap Hurdle
3 Sandown Park ....Agfa Hurdle
3 Sandown Park...Agfa Diamond Handicap Chase
3 Wetherby..totepool Towton Novice Chase
10 Newbury..Aon Chase
10 Newbury ....totepool Game Spirit Chase
10 Newbury ....totesport Gold Trophy Handicap Hurdle
10 Warwick ....Blue Square Kingmaker Novice Chase
17 Ascot...Ascot totesport Chase
17 Ascot...totepool Reynoldstown Novice Chase
17 Haydock Park ....Brit Insurance Prestige Novice Hurdle
17 Haydock Park ....Red Square Vodka Gold Cup Handicap Chase
17 Uttoxeter..Singer & Friedlander Handicap Chase
17 Wincanton...Bathwick Tyres Kingwell Hurdle
18 Fontwell Park...totesport.com National Spirit Hurdke
22 Haydock Park ....Rendlesham Hurdle
24 Kempton Park ....Anglo Irish Bank Dovecote Novice Hurdle
24 Kempton Park...Racing Post Pendil Novice Chase
24 Kempton Park ....RPSport No 1 for Sports Betting Adonis Juvenile Hurdle

24 Kempton Park ....Racing Post Handicap Chase
24 Newcastle ....totesport Eider Handicap Chase

March

3 Kelso..totepool Premier Kelso Novice Hurdle
3 Kelso................Ashleybank Investments Scottish Borders National Handicap Chase
3 Newbury ....Vodafone Gold Cup Handicap Chase
10 Sandown Park ....Sunderlands Imperial Cup Handicap Hurdle
13 Cheltenham........................Irish Independent Arkle Challenge Trophy Novice Chase
13 Cheltenham ....Anglo Irish Bank Supreme Novice Hurdle
13 Cheltenham ....Smurfit Kappa Champion Hurdle Challenge Trophy
13 Cheltenham ....William Hill Trophy Handicap Chase
14 Cheltenham..Queen Mother Champion Chase
14 Cheltenham..Royal & SunAlliance Novice Chase
14 Cheltenham..Royal & SunAlliance Novice Hurdle
14 Cheltenham ....Weatherbys Champion Bumper
14 Cheltenham ....Coral Cup Handicap Hurdle
15 Cheltenham ....Lads World Hurdle
15 Cheltenham ....Ryanair Festival Trophy Chase
15 Cheltenham ....Racing Post Plate Handicap Chase
16 Cheltenham..JCB Triumph Juvenile Hurdle
16 Cheltenham..totesport Cheltenham Gold Cup Chase
16 Cheltenham..Brit Insurance Novice Hurdle
16 Cheltenham......Johnny Henderson Grand Annual Challenge Cup Handicap Chase
16 Cheltenham..Vincent O'Brien County Handicap Hurdle
17 Uttoxeter ....John Smith's Midlands Grand National Handicap Chase

April

12 Aintree ....Sportsman Anniversary Juvenile Hurdle
12 Aintree..Betfair Bowl Chase
12 Aintree..John Smith's Liverpool Long Distance Hurdle
12 Aintree..Citroen C4 Mersey Novice Hurdle
12 Aintree..John Smith's Red Rum Handicap Chase
13 Aintree..John Smith's Melling Chase
13 Aintree..Citroen C6 Sefton Novice Hurdle
13 Aintree..John Smith's Mildmay Novice Chase
13 Aintree..John Smith's Imagine Appeal Top Novice Hurdle
13 Aintree................................John Smith's and Spar Topham Trophy Handicap Chase
14 Aintree..John Smith's Maghull Novice Chase
14 Aintree ....Scottish and Newcastle Aintree Hurdle
14 Aintree ....John Smith's Grand National Handicap Chase
18 Cheltenham ....Faucets for Mira Showers Silver Trophy Handicap Chase
21 Ayr................................Ashleybank Investments Future Champion Novice Chase
21 Ayr................................Samsung Electronics Scottish Champion Hurdle (Handicap)
21 Ayr................Gala Casinos Daily Record Scottish Grand National Handicap Chase
27 Sandown Park ....Betfred Million Hurdle
28 Sandown Park ....Betfred Celebration Chase
28 Sandown Park..Betfred Gold Cup Handicap Chase

Outlook

Big race records

Year	Form	Winner	Age-weight	Trainer	Jockey	SP	Ran

Charlie Hall Chase (3m110yds) Wetherby

Year	Form	Winner	Age-weight	Trainer	Jockey	SP	Ran
1996	-	**One Man**	8-11-10	G Richards	R Dunwoody	8-11f	4
1997	-	**One Man**	9-11-10	G Richards	R Dunwoody	4-7f	4
1998	-5	**Strath Royal**	12-11-3	O Brennan	M Brennan	14-1	5
1999	-	**See More Business**	9-11-12*b*	P Nicholls	M Fitzgerald	11-4j	6
2000	-	**See More Business**	10-11-12*b*	P Nicholls	M Fitzgerald	1-3f	4
2001	-13	**Sackville**	8-11-5	F Crowley	D Casey	5-1	9
2002	-	**Marlborough**	10-11-0	N Henderson	M Fitzgerald	7-2	8
2003	-	**Ballybough Rasher**	8-11-0	J H Johnson	G Lee	40-1	6
2004	-	**Grey Abbey**	10-11-6	J H Johnson	G Lee	5-1	6
2005	-	**Ollie Magern**	7-11-5	N Twiston-Davies	C Llewellyn	11-4f	8

Traditionally a race for small fields, and while Ollie Magern last year was the first winning favourite since 2000 it has still proven profitable to focus on those near the front of the market with only two winners returning bigger than 5-1 in the last ten years. At this stage of the season a good proportion of the runners may be some way short of peak fitness, and it must pay to look for trainers who can be relied on to have their horse ready, or horses who have already had a run. The small fields mean front-runners can often get their own way, as Grey Abbey and Ollie Magern did in the last two years.

Paddy Power Gold Cup (2m4f110yds) Cheltenham

Year	Form	Winner	Age-weight	Trainer	Jockey	SP	Ran
1996	-	**Challenger Du Luc**	6-10-2*b*	M Pipe	R Dunwoody	7-1	12
1997	-F2	**Senor El Betrutti**	8-10-0	S Nock	J Osborne	33-1	9
1998	-	**Cyfor Malta**	5-11-3	M Pipe	A McCoy	3-1f	12
1999	-1	**The Outback Way**	9-10-0	V Williams	N Williamson	9-1	14
2000	-	**Lady Cricket**	6-10-13*b*	M Pipe	A McCoy	5-1f	15
2001	-1	**Shooting Light**	8-11-3*v*	M Pipe	A McCoy	9-4f	14
2002	-	**Cyfor Malta**	9-11-9	M Pipe	B Geraghty	16-1	15
2003	-	**Fondmort**	7-10-13	N Henderson	M Fitzgerald	3-1f	9
2004	-	**Celestial Gold**	6-10-2	M Pipe	T Murphy	12-1	14
2005	-	**Our Vic**	7-11-7	M Pipe	T Murphy	9-2f	18

AKA 'The Thomas Pink', 'The Murphys','The Mackeson'. A Martin Pipe benefit in the last ten years, with seven winners coming from his Nicholashayne yard. Most of them have been well fancied, but Celestial Gold was still 16-1 in 2004 and Our Vic was a drifter last year. It will be fascinating to see if David Pipe can maintain his father's grand tradition in this race. Course form is a must as, of the last ten winners, only Senor El Betrutti and Our Vic (third in that year's SunAlliance) hadn't previously won at Cheltenham.

Blue Square Gold Cup H'cap Chase (2m3f110yds) Ascot

Year	Form	Winner	Age-weight	Trainer	Jockey	SP	Ran
1996	-2112	**Strong Promise**	5-10-5	G Hubbard	K Gaule	6-4f	8

Sponsored by Stan James

1997	-1	**Simply Dashing**	6-11-10	T Easterby	R Dunwoody	4-1	11
1998	-11	**Red Marauder**	8-10-11	N Mason	R Guest	5-1	11
1999	-	**Nordance Prince**	8-10-9	V Williams	R Johnson	8-1	11
2000	-2	**Upgrade**	6-11-8	M Pipe	A McCoy	7-4j	4
2001	-	**Wahiba Sands**	8-10-4	M Pipe	A McCoy	4-1	4
2002		*Abandoned*					
2003	-1	**Iris Royal**	7-10-4	N Henderson	M Foley	13-2	5
2004	-1	**Massac**	5-11-6	A King	R Thornton	4-1j	10
2005		*Abandoned*					

AKA 'The First National Bank Gold Cup'. Confined to chasers who are either novices or just out of their novice season, this race has consequently thrown up some real future champions in the past and is also famous for Best Mate just failing to give 20lb to Wahiba Sands in 2001. However, it has seriously lost its profile in recent years (Massac was a modest winner at Windsor in 2004) and it remains to be seen whether the return to Ascot this year will revive its fortunes.

Hennessy Cognac Gold Cup H'cap Chase (3m2f) Newbury

1996	-11	**Coome Hill**	7-10-0	W Dennis	J Osborne	11-2	11
1997	-1	**Suny Bay**	8-11-8	C Brooks	G Bradley	9-4f	14
1998	-1	**Teeton Mill**	9-10-5	V Williams	N Williamson	5-1	16
1999	-1	**Ever Blessed**	7-10-0	M Pitman	T Murphy	9-2f	13
2000	-2	**King's Road**	7-10-7	N Twiston-Davies	J Goldstein	7-1	17
2001	-	**What's Up Boys**	7-10-12	P Hobbs	P Flynn	14-1	14
2002	-3	**Gingembre**	8-10-13	L Taylor	A Thornton	16-1	25

EPIC: Wahiba Sands beats Best Mate in the First National Bank Gold Cup

2003	-F1	**Strong Flow**	6-11-0	P Nicholls	R Walsh	5-1jf	21
2004	-1	**Celestial Gold**	6-10-5	M Pipe	T Murphy	9-4f	14
2005	-	**Trabolgan**	7-11-12	N Henderson	M Fitzgerald	13-2	19

Just about the most high-quality handicap of the season, won by some very special horses in the past. This often goes to improving second-season chasers, a description which applied to Ever Blessed, King's Road, What's Up Boys, Celestial Gold and Trabolgan (when the first six home were just out of their novice season), while the ultra-impressive Strong Flow was a novice when he won. Be My Royal was also a winning novice in 2002, but was subsequently disqualified after a banned substance was found in his sample. Relatively low weights are favoured, usually taking a true great to win with lots of weight.

Fighting Fifth Hurdle (2m) Newcastle

1996*	-122121	**Space Trucker**	5-10-4	J Harrington	J Shortt	5-2	8
1997*	-15	**Star Rage**	7-11-2	M Johnston	D Gallagher	6-1	8
1998	-	**Dato Star**	7-11-8	J M Jefferson	L Wyer	13-8f	6
1999	-	**Dato Star**	8-11-8	J M Jefferson	L Wyer	4-9f	9
2000	-	**Barton**	7-11-0	T Easterby	A Dobbin	8-13f	6
2001	-	**Landing Light**	6-11-8	N Henderson	M Fitzgerald	4-5f	5
2002	-11	**Intersky Falcon**	5-11-8	J O'Neill	L Cooper	11-10f	6
2003	-71	**The French Furze**	9-11-0	N Richards	B Harding	25-1	8
2004	-31	**Harchibald**	5-11-7	N Meade	P Carberry	9-4jf	8
2005	-	**Arcalis**	5-11-7	J H Johnson	T Dobbin	9-4f	9

*run as a limited handicap

A brief and unsuccessful experiment to turn this into a limited handicap in the 90s appears to be having a lasting effect as it is struggling to re-establish itself as a leading Champion Hurdle trial. Having said that, it is usually won by a top-class hurdler but against a small and modest field, and punters would be unwise in looking beyond the obvious – Arcalis made it seven winning favourites out of eight last season.

Tingle Creek Trophy Chase (2m) Sandown

1996	-121	**Sound Man**	8-11-7	E O'Grady	R Dunwoody	10-11f	4
1997	-P	**Ask Tom**	8-11-7	T Tate	R Garritty	6-1	7
1998	-2	**Direct Route**	7-11-7	J H Johnson	N Williamson	7-1	10
1999	-1	**Flagship Uberalles**	5-11-7	P Nicholls	J Tizzard	100-30	6
2000*	-	**Flagship Uberalles**	6-11-7	N Chance	R Johnson	3-1f	7
2001	-	**Flagship Uberalles**	7-11-7	P Hobbs	R Widger	7-2	6
2002	-	**Cenkos**	8-11-7	P Nicholls	R Walsh	6-1	6
2003	-1	**Moscow Flyer**	9-11-7	J Harrington	B Geraghty	6-4f	7
2004	-1	**Moscow Flyer**	10-11-7	J Harrington	B Geraghty	2-1	7
2005	-2	**Kauto Star**	5-11-7	P Nicholls	M Fitzgerald	5-2jf	7

**run at Cheltenham

Changed from a handicap to a conditions event ahead of the 1994 renewal and has been getting better and better ever since, now rivalling the Champion Chase in terms of quality. The 2004 renewal was just about the best in the race's history, when Moscow Flyer won an epic against Well Chief and Azertyuiop. Remarkably, no winner has returned bigger than 7-1 in the last ten years, and that was on the only occasion when the field was bigger than seven. Only four horses older than nine have ever triumphed.

William Hill H'cap Hurdle (2m) Sandown

| 1996 | -111125 | **Make A Stand** | 5-10-5 | M Pipe | G Tormey (3) | 9-1 | 15 |
| 1997 | -0545 | **Major Jamie** | 6-10-0 | A Moore | R Walsh | 25-1 | 21 |

Sponsored by Stan James

1998	-22253	**Polar Prospect**	5-10-0	P Hobbs	G Tormey	16-1	13
1999	-21	**Copeland**	4-10-5*b*	M Pipe	D Casey	7-1	12
2000		*Abandoned*					
2001	-1431	**Rob Leach**	4-9-12*b*	G L Moore	F Keniry (3)	14-1	11
2002	-	**Spirit Leader**	6-10-0	J Harrington	N Williamson	9-2	12
2003	-111	**Overstrand**	4-10-6	M Reveley	R Walsh	9-1	14
2004	-11	**Monte Cinto**	4-10-5	P Nicholls	R Walsh	8-1	21
2005	-1	**Verasi**	4-10-13	G Moore	J Moore	12-1	19

Often run on dead ground or going with some give, exaggerating the effect of weight carried, so top-weights have an even worse record than in other competitive handicaps. Since 1999 only one winner (Spirit Leader) had failed to win on his previous outing, making this more straightforward for punters. The biggest-priced winner in that period, Rob Leach, was also a major gamble.

Robin Cook Memorial Gold Cup Chase (2m5f) Cheltenham

1996	-3	**Addington Boy**	8-11-10	G Richards	A Dobbin	7-4f	10
1997	-F21	**Senor El Betrutti**	8-11-3	S Nock	G Bradley	9-1	9
1998	-3	**Northern Starlight**	7-10-1	M Pipe	A McCoy	15-2	13
1999	-P11	**Legal Right**	6-10-13	J O'Neill	R Johnson	6-1	9
2000	-2	**Go Roger Go**	8-11-0	E O'Grady	N Williamson	7-1	12
2001		*Abandoned*					
2002	-3	**Fondmort**	6-10-5	N Henderson	M Fitzgerald	5-1	9
2003	-11	**Iris Royal**	7-10-13	N Henderson	M Fitzgerald	7-1	17
2004	-132	**Monkerhostin**	7-10-2	P Hobbs	R Johnson	4-1	13
2005	-54	**Sir Oj**	8-10-0	N Meade	P Carberry	16-1	16

AKA 'The Massey-Ferguson', 'The Tripleprint'. Not surprisingly, the Paddy Power Gold Cup, held at the same venue four weeks earlier, is traditionally the most useful guide to this event, as in the mid-Nineties Senor El Betrutti did the double and Addington Boy and Another Coral stepped up on placed efforts. But, apart from 2004 when Paddy Power second Monkerhostin won, the race hasn't had a look-in, suggesting those with protected handicap marks are the ones to focus on. A prior outing is essential, and not necessarily a winning one.

Bula Hurdle (2m1f) Cheltenham

1996	-111	**Large Action**	8-11-8	O Sherwood	J Osborne	5-4f	7
1997	.	**Relkool**	8-11-0	D Nicholson	R Johnson	8-1	8
1998	-	**Relkeel**	9-11-8	D Nicholson	A Maguire	8-1	5
1999	.-	**Relkeel**	10-11-8	A King	R Johnson	13-2	7
2000	-3	**Geos**	5-11-4	N Henderson	M Fitzgerald	14-1	8
2001		*Abandoned*					
2002	-11	**Rooster Booster**	8-11-4	P Hobbs	R Johnson	11-8f	9
2003	24FF112141	**Rigmarole**	5-11-4*t*	P Nicholls	R Thornton	25-1	7
2004	-12	**Back In Front**	7-11-8	E J O'Grady	D N Russell	5-2f	7
2005	-13	**Harchibald**	6-11-8	N Meade	P Carberry	10-11f	9

Not a great race for trends, with winners aged between five and ten, plus three winning favourites mixed in with a couple of outsiders. Generally it seems best to have had a couple of runs to reach peak fitness, and a Cheltenham specialist is vital – of the last 10 winners only Geos and Harchibald hadn't previously won at Prestbury Park (Geos had never run, and Harchibald had come second in a Champion Hurdle).

Long Walk Hurdle (3m1f110yds) Ascot

1996	-12	**Ocean Hawk**	4-11-7	N Twiston-Davies	C Llewellyn	7-1	6

1997	-5	**Paddy's Return**	5-11-7	F Murphy	N Williamson	8-1	7
1998	-1	**Princeful**	7-11-7	J Pitman	R Dunwoody	11-4f	11
1999	-3	**Anzum**	8-11-7	A King	R Johnson	4-1	6
2000	-	**Baracouda**	5-11-7	F Doumen	T Doumen	11-4	9
2001	-1	**Baracouda**	6-11-7	F Doumen	T Doumen	2-5f	5
2002	-23	**Deano's Beeno**	10-11-7	M Pipe	A McCoy	14-1	5
2003	-1	**Baracouda**	8-11-7	F Doumen	T Doumen	2-7f	6
2004*	-1	**Baracouda**	9-11-7	F Doumen	A P McCoy	8-13f	8
2005**	-2	**My Way de Solzen**	5-11-7	A King	R Thornton	12-1	8

*run at Windsor
**run at Chepstow

A top-quality Grade One hurdle and a massive pointer to Cheltenham. Of the last nine winners, only the high-class Deano's Beeno didn't also bag a Stayers' (or World) Hurdle crown at some point in his career, and he would have lost out to Baracouda but for a shambolic Thierry Doumen ride in 2002. Four-year-olds struggle but still fare better than they do at Cheltenham, with Silver Wedge and Ocean Hawk successful in the 90s.

Silver Cup H'cap Chase (3m110yds) Ascot

1996	-412	**Go Ballistic**	7-10-0	J O'Shea	A McCoy	4-1f	9
1997	-71	**Cool Dawn**	9-10-5	R Alner	A Thornton	5-2f	6
1998	-12	**Torduff Express**	7-10-0	P Nicholls	N Williamson	9-2	7
1999	-4F	**Tresor de Mai**	5-11-1b	M Pipe	A McCoy	10-1	9
2000	-	**Legal Right**	7-12-0	J O'Neill	N Williamson	7-1	7
2001	-11	**Shooting Light**	8-11-6v	M Pipe	A McCoy	5-2f	9
2002	-6	**Behrajan**	7-11-12	H Daly	R Johnson	7-1	7
2003	-2	**Horus**	8-10-1	M Pipe	J Moore (3)	11-2	8
2004	-134	**Spring Grove**	9-10-11	R Alner	A Thornton	8-1	8
2005		*Abandoned*					

AKA 'The SGB', 'The Betterware Gold Cup'. The traditional centrepiece of Ascot's big December meeting and another race to have suffered badly from the two-year closure of the Berkshire track. Indeed, it was even downgraded to Listed status for Spring Grove's win at Windsor in 2004 before being abandoned last year. In its time, though, it has been won by some top-class horses, including subsequent Gold Cup winner Cool Dawn in 1997.

King George VI Chase (3m) Kempton

1996*	-1	**One Man**	8-11-10	G Richards	R Dunwoody	8-13f	5
1997	-31	**See More Business**	7-11-10	P Nicholls	A Thornton	10-1	8
1998	-11	**Teeton Mill**	9-11-10	V Williams	N Williamson	7-2	9
1999	-1	**See More Business**	9-11-10b	P Nicholls	M Fitzgerald	5-2	9
2000	-1	**First Gold**	7-11-10	F Doumen	T Doumen	5-2	9
2001	-31	**Florida Pearl**	9-11-10	W Mullins	A Maguire	8-1	8
2002	-1	**Best Mate**	7-11-10	H Knight	A McCoy	11-8f	10
2003	-111	**Edredon Bleu**	11-11-10t	H Knight	J Culloty	25-1	12
2004	-121	**Kicking King**	6-11-10	T J Taffe	B Geraghty	3-1	13
2005**	-23	**Kicking King**	7-11-10	T J Taffe	B Geraghty	11-8f	9

*run at Sandown in January 1997
**run at Sandown

A race which the best performers often manage to win several times, with One Man, See More Business and Kicking King all multiple winners since the days of the legendary Desert Orchid. Francois Doumen has won this race five times with four different horses and is

Sponsored by Stan James

clearly a trainer whose horses should never be ruled out. Kempton's sharp three miles provides less of a stamina test than other major tracks, particularly Cheltenham, so those who have just failed to see out the Gold Cup trip often make amends here, such as One Man and Florida Pearl. There were also stamina doubts about Kicking King prior to his first win, while Edredon Bleu was a two mile performer stepping into the unknown.

Christmas Hurdle (2m) Kempton

1996		Abandoned					
1997	-230	**Kerawi**	4-11-7	N Twiston-Davies	C Llewellyn	4-1	5
1998	-P2	**French Holly**	7-11-7	F Murphy	A Thornton	5-2	5
1999	-1	**Dato Star**	8-11-7	J M Jefferson	L Wyer	11-8f	4
2000	-31	**Geos**	5-11-7	N Henderson	M Fitzgerald	9-4	7
2001	-1	**Landing Light**	6-11-7	N Henderson	M Fitzgerald	5-4f	5
2002	-11	**Intersky Falcon**	5-11-7b	J O'Neill	C Swan	Evensf	6
2003	-13	**Intersky Falcon**	6-11-7b	J O'Neill	L Cooper	11-4	6
2004	-311	**Harchibald**	5-11-7	N Meade	P Carberry	8-11f	7
2005	-11	**Feathard Lady**	5-11-0	C Murphy	R Walsh	6-4f	7

This sharp two miles is ideal for young, improving types, and each of the last six winners were aged five or six while two older winners, French Holly and Dato Star, both won on unusually testing ground. A couple of prep runs, preferably winning ones, is the norm and as a result Kerawi was the biggest-priced winner in the last ten years at just 4-1.

Welsh National H'cap Chase (3m5f110yds) Chepstow

1996		Abandoned					
1997	-55	**Earth Summit**	9-10-13b	N Twiston-Davies	T Jenks	25-1	14
1998	-2	**Kendal Cavalier**	8-10-0	N Hawke	B Fenton	14-1	14
1999	-11	**Edmond**	7-10-0	H Daly	R Johnson	4-1	16
2000	-42	**Jocks Cross**	9-10-4	V Williams	B Crowley	14-1	19
2001	-14	**Supreme Glory**	8-10-0	P Murphy	L Aspell	10-1	13
2002	-4	**Mini Sensation**	9-10-4	J O'Neill	A Dobbin	8-1	16
2003	-F2	**Bindaree**	9-10-9	N Twiston Davies	C Llewellyn	10-1	14
2004	-1	**Silver Birch**	7-10-1	P Nicholls	R Walsh	4-1f	14
2005	-64	**L'Aventure**	6-10-4	P Nicholls	L Aspell	14-1	18

As with most staying handicap chases that are often run in the mud, horses at the foot of the weights are massively favoured, to the extent that punters should not rule out anything from out of the weights. Kendal Cavalier was 13lb 'wrong' in 1997, Supreme Glory 3lb 'wrong' in 2001, and Dom Samourai, from 5lb out of the handicap, would have won in 1997 given a few more strides. Only three winners have carried 11st10lb or more in more than 50 runnings, and Silver Birch was a rare winning favourite in 2004.

Rowland Meyrick Chase (3m1f) Wetherby

1996		Abandoned					
1997	-2111	**Strath Royal**	11-10-10	O Brennan	M Brennan	3-1	4
1998	-U14121	**Random Harvest**	9-9-11	M Reveley	A Dempsey (3)	9-4	4
1999		Abandoned					
2000		Abandoned					
2001	-332	**Behrajan**	6-11-10	H Daly	M Bradburne	5-2f	12
2002		Abandoned					
2003	-P	**Gunner Welburn**	11-10-0	A Balding	R McGrath	10-1	8
2004	-44	**Truckers Tavern**	9-11-2	F Murphy	K J Mercer	8-1	7
2005	-00	**Therealbandit**	8-10-6	M Pipe	A Glassonbury	9-1	10

A race that has often been disrupted by small fields and abandonments, so it's hard to be bullish about any particular trends, particularly given the last three winners looked to be either past their best or bang out of form. This may not take much winning in general.

Pierse H'cap Hurdle (2m) Leopardstown

1997	-02	**Master Tribe**	7-10-4	J Pitman	N Williamson	16-1	23
1998	-	**Graphic Equaliser**	6-10-0	A Moore	C O'Dwyer	5-1f	20
1999	-005	**Archive Footage**	7-11-8b	P Mullins	D Evans	25-1	25
2000	-215	**Mantles Prince**	6-9-12	P Hughes	F Berry	12-1	14
2001	-2	**Grinkov**	6-10-7	P Hughes	C Swan	11-2	24
2002	-54	**Adamant Approach**	8-11-1	W Mullins	R Walsh	8-1	26
2003	-2	**Xenophon**	7-10-11	A Martin	M Fitzgerald	12-1	28
2004	-01	**Dromlease Express**	6-10-4	C Byrnes	J Allen (7)	6-1jf	19
2005	-	**Essex**	5-10-8p	M J P O'Brien	B Geraghty	5-1f	21
2006	-1252132	**Studmaster**	6-10-3	Mrs J Harrington	T Treacy	12-1	27

AKA 'The Ladbroke'. Ireland's hottest handicap and they like to keep the prize at home – there has only been one British winner in 20 years (Master Tribe in 1997). The strongest trends won't rule out that much of the field, but the winners tend to be either five, six or seven (Adamant Approach was only the third older winner in 2002 and no four-year-old has won since 1977) running off a fairly low weight. Favourites had had a dismal record until the last two years before Dromlease Express and Essex scored in 2004 and 2005.

Tote Gold Trophy H'cap Hurdle (2m110yds) Newbury

1997	-25111	**Make A Stand**	6-11-7	M Pipe	A McCoy	6-1	18
1998	-26	**Sharpical**	6-11-1b	N Henderson	M Fitzgerald	10-1	14
1999	-242	**Decoupage**	7-11-0	C Egerton	J McCarthy	6-1	18
2000	-132	**Geos**	5-11-3	N Henderson	M Fitzgerald	15-2	17
2001	-31	**Landing Light**	6-10-2	N Henderson	M Fitzgerald	4-1f	20
2002	-21	**Copeland**	7-11-7v	M Pipe	A McCoy	13-2	16
2003	-2315	**Spirit Leader**	7-10-0	J Harrington	N Williamson	14-1	27
2004	-2	**Geos**	9-10-9	N Henderson	M Foley	16-1	25
2005	-2611	**Essex**	5-11-6	M J P O'Brien	B Geraghty	4-1f	25
2006		*Abandoned*					

AKA 'The Schweppes'. Between 1970 and 1996 only three winners carried more than 11st, but the pattern has changed remarkably since then. The increase in prize money, making this Europe's richest handicap hurdle, has encouraged more genuine Champion Hurdle horses to take their chance, with the result that many of the supposed 'plot' horses race from out of the handicap and six out of the last nine winners were near the top of the handicap. Rooster Booster deserved to make it seven in 2004 but was just edged out by Geos after the greatest weight-carrying performance of the modern age. The Lanzarote Hurdle, run at Kempton in January, is traditionally the best trial, generally among the lower weights, but 2002 winner Copeland had been second in that race and Non So, winner of the Lanzarote in 2003, went on to finish second to Spirit Leader.

Eider National H'cap Chase (4m1f) Newcastle

1997	-511	**Seven Towers**	8-11-8	M Reveley	P Niven	2-1f	12
1998	-1P14	**Domaine de Pron**	7-10-0	L Taylor	R Supple	9-2	11
1999	-003201P	**Hollybank Buck**	9-10-11t	A Martin	F Flood	10-1	15
2000	-23P21	**Scotton Green**	9-10-2	T Easterby	L Wyer	8-1	16
2001	-121	**Narrow Water**	8-11-5t	F Murphy	A Maguire	6-1	12
2002	-301	**This Is Serious**	8-11-2	C Swan	A Dobbin	4-1f	15
2003		*Abandoned*					
2004	-22P217	**Tyneandthyneagain**	9-11-12p	R Guest	H Oliver	28-1	20

| 2005 | | Abandoned | | | | | |
| 2006 | -0FP2 | **Philson Run** | 10-11-6 | N Williams | G Lee | 10-1 | 17 |

AKA 'The Northern National'. Though regarded as a Grand National pointer, this is a race for dour stayers who lack the pace and class for Aintree. Interestingly, the last four winners – Narrow Water, This Is Serious, Tyneandthyneagain and Philson Run – have carried more than 11st to victory.

Racing Post H'cap Chase (3m) Kempton

1997	-42	**Mudahim**	11-10-2	J Pitman	R Farrant	14-1	9
1998	-113U2	**Super Tactics**	10-10-10	R Alner	A Thornton	4-1	7
1999	-63411	**Dr Leunt**	8-11-5	P Hobbs	R Dunwoody	3-1f	8
2000	-131	**Gloria Victis**	6-11-10	M Pipe	R Johnson	100-30f	13
2001	-321	**Young Spartacus**	9-11-0	H Daly	R Johnson	9-1	15
2002	-2221	**Gunther McBride**	7-10-3	P Hobbs	R Johnson	5-1	14
2003	-211111	**La Landiere**	8-11-7	R Phillips	W Marston	5-1j	14
2004	-235	**Marlborough**	12-11-12	N Henderson	R Walsh	8-1	11
2005	-1F2F41	**Farmer Jack**	9-11-12	P Hobbs	R Johnson	5-1	16
2006*	-11	**Innox**	10-11-0	F Doumen	A McCoy	8-1	15

*run at Sandown

Once again it's remarkable how many horses manage to defy welter burdens to win this top prize – Gloria Victis, Marlborough and Farmer Jack all carried 11st 10lb or more to victory, and four others defied in excess of 11st. There's little for trends followers in terms of age (Gloria Victis was six when he won in 2000, Marlborough 12 in 2004, and every other age in between has been successful too). Clearly it's wrong to look beyond the first few in the betting with Mudahim the last winner returned at double figures, and Richard Johnson knows his way around Kempton's three miles better than any rider having won four of the last six runnings to be held at the venue.

Red Square Vodka Gold Cup H'cap Chase (3m4f) Haydock

1997	-5	**Suny Bay**	10-10-8	C Brooks	J Osborne	7-2	5
1998	-121242	**Dom Samourai**	7-10-0	M Pipe	C Maude	10-1	15
1999	-22412U	**Young Kenny**	8-10-0	P Beaumont	B Powell	9-1	13
2000	-1421	**The Last Fling**	10-11-1	S Smith	S Durack	5-1	7
2001	-U21	**Frantic Tan**	9-10-4	N Twiston-Davies	C Llewellyn	7-2f	18
2002		Abandoned					
2003	-	**Shotgun Willy**	9-11-12	P Nicholls	R Walsh	10-1	17
2004	-1452	**Jurancon II**	7-10-6	M Pipe	J Elliott (5)	10-1	10
2005	-1	**Forest Gunner**	11-10-10	R Ford	P Buchanan(3)	12-1	11
2006	-G13	**Ossmoses**	9-10-0	D Forster	R McGrath	14 1	14

AKA 'The Greenalls', 'The De Vere Gold Cup'. This race is usually run on soft and can prove a real test of stamina, too much for most of the market leaders in recent years. The consensus is that Haydock's drop fences are a good preparation for Aintree, and recent winners Shotgun Willy, Jurancon II and Forest Gunner all went off pretty short prices at Aintree without success, which suggests the race is overrated as a trial.

Sunderlands Imperial Cup H'cap Hurdle (2m) Sandown

1997	-4141	**Carlito Brigante**	5-10-0	P Webber	J Osborne	10-1	18
1998	-403	**Blowing Wind**	5-11-10	M Pipe	A McCoy	5-1f	15
1999	-00	**Regency Rake**	7-10-7	A Moore	A Maguire	7-1	9
2000	-P	**Magic Combination**	7-10-0	B Curley	D Casey	11-1	18
2001	-213	**Ibal**	5-9-9	N Smith	B Hitchcott	16-1	23

CLASS: Well Chief hits the front two out in the 2004 Arkle from Kicking King

2002	-2221	**Polar Red**	5-11-1*v*	M Pipe	A McCoy	6-4f	16
2003	-25053141	**Korelo**	5-11-6	M Pipe	A McCoy	9-4f	17
2004	-62	**Scorned**	9-10-3	A Balding	B Fenton	14-1	23
2005	-18311	**Medison**	5-10-1	M Pipe	T Murphy	9-2f	19
2006	-00013P	**Victram**	6-10-3	A McGuinness	A Lynch	8-1	21

This falls on the eve of Cheltenham and, with the sponsors putting up a bonus for horses winning here as well as at Cheltenham, a strong and competitive field is always assured. Martin Pipe was the master in this race, winning three of the last five runnings, again giving his son David plenty to live up to. Five-year-olds also have an outstanding record, with six of them successful in the last ten years.

Supreme Novices' Hurdle (2m110yds) Cheltenham

1997	-11	**Shadow Leader**	6-11-8	C Egerton	J Osborne	5-1	16
1998	-31	**French Ballerina**	5-11-3	P Flynn	G Bradley	10-1	30
1999	-111	**Hors La Loi III**	4-11-0	M Pipe	A McCoy	9-2	20
2000	-11	**Sausalito Bay**	6-11-8	N Meade	P Carberry	14-1	15
2001		*Abandoned*					
2002	-1111	**Like-A-Butterfly**	8-11-3	C Roche	C Swan	7-4f	28
2003	-211	**Back In Front**	6-11-8	E O'Grady	N Williamson	3-1f	19
2004	-111	**Brave Inca**	6-11-7	C Murphy	B Cash	7-2f	19
2005	-111143	**Arcalis**	5-11-7	J H Johnson	G Lee	20-1	20
2006	-3111	**Noland**	5-11-7	P Nicholls	R Walsh	6-1	20

Punters looked to have sorted this one out at the start of the century by following the Irish money, with Like-A-Butterfly, Back In Front and Brave Inca three winning favourites in a row and making it six winners in ten years for the raiders. However, surprise winner Arcalis threw a spanner in the works and Noland was a real blow for trends followers – not only was he English, he was also trained by Paul Nicholls (whose record with novices at this meeting is generally wretched), had won the Tolworth Hurdle at Sandown (which tends to be a terrible guide) and came from off the pace (front-runners have traditionally fared best here). Watch this space.

Arkle Chase (2m) Cheltenham

| 1997 | -112 | **Or Royal** | 6-11-8*b* | M Pipe | A McCoy | 11-2 | 9 |

Sponsored by Stan James

1998	-11311	**Champleve**	5-11-0	M Pipe	A McCoy	13-2	16
1999	-221211	**Flagship Uberalles**	5-11-0	P Nicholls	J Tizzard	11-1	14
2000	-111	**Tiutchev**	7-11-8	N Henderson	M Fitzgerald	8-1	12
2001		*Abandoned*					
2002	-111F	**Moscow Flyer**	8-11-8	J Harrington	B Geraghty	11-2	12
2003	-111	**Azertyuiop**	6-11-8	P Nicholls	R Walsh	5-4f	9
2004	-151	**Well Chief**	5-11-3	M Pipe	A McCoy	9-1	16
2005	-2213	**Contraband**	7-11-3	M Pipe	T Murphy	9-1	19
2006	-1111	**Voy Por Ustedes**	5-11-2	A King	R Thornton	15-2	14

A typical Arkle winner tends to be relatively well fancied with plenty of wins under his belt earlier in the season, yet favourites still have an awful record. Plenty of high-class horses have been turned over, with only Azertyuiop doing the business, and the reason tends to be punters focusing too much on horses likely to come into their own over further. French-breds have a great record, helping to bring the average winning age lower and lower and five-year-olds look particularly interesting now with their weight allowance.

Champion Hurdle (2m110yds) Cheltenham

1997	-1251111	**Make A Stand**	6-12-0	M Pipe	A McCoy	7-1	17
1998	-1111	**Istabraq**	6-12-0	A O'Brien	C Swan	3-1f	18
1999	-1111	**Istabraq**	7-12-0	A O'Brien	C Swan	4-9f	14
2000	-1211	**Istabraq**	8-12-0	A O'Brien	C Swan	8-15f	12
2001		*Abandoned*					
2002	-2331	**Hors La Loi III**	7-12-0*t*	J Fanshawe	D Gallagher	10-1	15
2003	-1111	**Rooster Booster**	9-12-0	P Hobbs	R Johnson	9-2	17
2004	-2722	**Hardy Eustace**	7-11-10*b*	D Hughes	C O'Dwyer	33-1	14
2005	-2331	**Hardy Eustace**	8-11-10*b*	D Hughes	C O'Dwyer	7-2jf	14
2006	-1311	**Brave Inca**	8-11-10	C Murphy	A McCoy	7-4f	18

The new golden era of Irish hurdling has heralded a rapid change for trends followers. Whereas the success of Royal Gait and Alderbrook as novice Flat recruits encouraged many to tread the same path in the 90s, recent winners have been older with plenty of form and experience to their name. Therefore look for horses seven or older with four or more runs to their name in the present campaign, and last-time-out winners have an astonishing record with 20 out of 23 fitting this statistic.

William Hill National Hunt H'cap Chase (3m110yds) Cheltenham

1997	-P1P	**Flyer's Nap**	11-11-2	R Alner	D Bridgwater	20-1	14
1998	-642F4	**Unguided Missile**	10-11-10	G Richards	P Carberry	10-1	13
1999	-16	**Betty's Boy**	10-10-2	K Bailey	N Williamson	25-1	18
2000	-PU12	**Marlborough**	8-10-3	N Henderson	M Fitzgerald	11-2	12
2001		*Abandoned*					
2002	-133	**Frenchman's Creek**	8-10-5	H Morrison	P Carberry	8-1	23
2003	-131	**Youlneverwalkalone**	9-10-11	C Roche	B Geraghty	7-1	18
2004	-31U21	**Fork Lightning**	8-10-5	A King	R Thornton	7-1	11
2005	-8803F43	**Kelami**	7-10-2t	F Doumen	R Thornton	8-1	20
2006	-511111	**Dun Doire**	7-10-9	A Martin	R Walsh	7-1	21

AKA 'The Ritz Club'. After some older, heavily-weighted winners in the 90s, winners now look easier to find in this competitive handicap. A strong stayer is absolutely essential as only two of the last 13 winners lacked previous winning form at three miles or further, and both had previously been placed over that trip on soft ground. Runners carrying less than 11st also look to have a distinct advantage, as do horses aged between seven and nine. Favourites have a shocking record (two winners in the last three decades) but the last six winners were all priced between 11-2 and 8-1 so look for a fancied horse.

Royal & SunAlliance Novices' Hurdle (2m5f) Cheltenham

1997	-2111	Istabraq	5-11-7	A O'Brien	C Swan	6-5f	17
1998	-1111	French Holly	7-11-7	F Murphy	A Thornton	2-1f	18
1999	-11111	Barton	6-11-7	T Easterby	L Wyer	2-1f	18
2000	-11111	Monsignor	6-11-7	M Pitman	N Williamson	5-4f	14
2001		Abandoned					
2002	-1	Galileo	6-11-7	T George	J Maguire	12-1	14
2003	-51112	Hardy Eustace	6-11-7	D Hughes	K Kelly	6-1	19
2004	-12	Fundamentalist	6-11-7	N Twiston-Davies	C Llewellyn	12-1	15
2005	-310121	No Refuge	5-11-7	J H Johnson	G Lee	17-2	20
2006	-1F221	Nicanor	5-11-7	N Meade	P Carberry	17-2	17

Often throws up a supposed good thing and generally one worth backing – Istabraq, French Holly, Barton and Monsignor were all winning favourites between 1997 and 2000. However, short-priced defeats for Pizarro and Denman in recent times have muddied the picture somewhat. It remains wise to follow well-fancied horses who were first or second last time out and have at least four runs to their name over hurdles.

Royal & SunAlliance Novices' Chase (3m1f) Cheltenham

1997	-1U31	Hanakham	8-11-4	R Hodges	R Dunwoody	13-2	14
1998	-11	Florida Pearl	6-11-4	W Mullins	R Dunwoody	11-8f	10
1999	-U2511	Looks Like Trouble	7-11-4	N Chance	P Carberry	16-1	14
2000	-212	Lord Noelie	7-11-4	H Knight	J Culloty	9-2	9
2001		Abandoned					
2002	-21F2	Hussard Collonges	7-11-4	P Beaumont	R Garritty	33-1	19
2003	-1311	One Knight	7-11-4	P Hobbs	R Johnson	15-2	9
2004	-F1332	Rule Supreme	8-11-4	W Mullins	D Casey	25-1	10
2005	-122	Trabolgan	7-11-4	N Henderson	M Fitzgerald	5-1	9
2006	-1231	Star de Mohaison	5-10-8	P Nicholls	B Geraghty	14-1	9

Not a great race for trends, with plenty of upsets in recent times (such as Hussard Collonges and Rule Supreme) as well as some fancied winners. You would think the best rule would be to follow a quality jumper, but One Knight and Rule Supreme have both taken this prize despite being two of the dodgiest jumpers around. Ultimately the best rule is to go with a French-bred boasting bags of stamina.

Queen Mother Champion Chase (2m) Cheltenham

1997	-	Martha's Son	10-12-0	T Forster	R Farrant	9-1	6
1998	-1151	One Man	10-12-0	G Richards	B Harding	7-2	8
1999	-1	Call Equiname	9-12-0	P Nicholls	M Fitzgerald	7-2	13
2000	-5133	Edredon Bleu	8-12-0t	H Knight	A McCoy	7-2	9
2001		Abandoned					
2002	-1	Flagship Uberalles	8-12-0	P Hobbs	R Johnson	7-4f	12
2003	-1U11	Moscow Flyer	9-12-0	J Harrington	B Geraghty	7-4f	11
2004	-221	Azertyuiop	7-11-10	P Nicholls	R Walsh	15-8	8
2005	-111	Moscow Flyer	11-11-10	J Harrington	B Geraghty	6-4f	8
2006	-431	Newmill	8-11-10	J J Murphy	A McNamara	16-1	12

Newmill was only the fourth winner in over 40 runnings to return at a double-figure price, and while it would be wrong to say that was easy to predict it was nonetheless forecast in the pages of the *RFO* – Nick Watts tipped Newmill ante-post at 100-1! Newmill was also the first winner since Martha's Son in 1997 to return bigger than 7-2, so it generally pays to look for the obvious and back one of the market leaders. Proven form at Cheltenham is a massive plus – the winners of the previous season's renewal or the Arkle Trophy often follow up.

Coral Cup (2m5f) Cheltenham

1997	-121	Big Strand	8-10-0	M Pipe	Jamie Evans	16-1	28
1998	-585	Top Cees	8-10-0	L Ramsden	B Fenton	11-1	21
1999	-6	Khayrawani	7-11-3	C Roche	F Berry	16-1	30
2000	-11P3	What's Up Boys	6-10-3	P Hobbs	P Flynn (3)	33-1	26
2001		Abandoned					
2002	-54U	Ilnamar	6-10-5	M Pipe	R Greene	25-1	27
2003	-21	Xenophon	7-11-0	A Martin	M Fitzgerald	4-1f	27
2004	-134231	Monkerhostin	7-10-8	P Hobbs	R Johnson	13-2	27
2005	-1626	Idole First	6-10-10	Miss V Williams	B Geraghty	33-1	29
2006	-50121	Sky's The Limit	5-11-12	E O'Grady	B Geraghty	11-1	30

The Irish love to lay one out for this, but with constant bickering over how their raiders are assessed by the handicapper it is tough to know when their horses have been nicely treated and when they are best left alone. For example, they had four of the first five in 1998, the first five in 1999, a massively-punted winner in 2003 in Xenophon and the first two (well clear of the remainder) last year. Yet it's far from one-way traffic, with six British winners in the last nine runnings, and both Martin Pipe and Philip Hobbs are race specialists. Sky's The Limit was the first ever winning five-year-old.

Fulke Walwyn Kim Muir H'cap Chase (3m110yds) Cheltenham

1997	-3322	King Lucifer	8-11-5	D Nicholson	Mr R Thornton (5)	7-2	11
1998	-23242225	In Truth	10-9-9	S Gollings	Mr S Durack (5)	20-1	14
1999	-1	Celtic Giant	9-10-0	L Lungo	Mr B Gibson (3)	20-1	22
2000	-212341	Honey Mount	9-9-12	R Alner	Mr R Walford (5)	8-1	23
2001		Abandoned					
2002	-1	The Bushkeeper	8-11-2	N Henderson	Mr D Crosse	9-2f	23
2003	-	Royal Predica	9-10-13	M Pipe	Mr S McHugh (7)	33-1	23
2004	-42P9	Maximize	10-10-6	M Pipe	Mr D Edwards	40-1	22
2005	-31522	Juveigneur	8-11-7	N Henderson	Mr R Burton	12-1	24
2006	-P3621P	You're Special	9-10-12	F Murphy	Mr R Harding	33-1	21

A desperately tough handicap, with three of the last four winners coming in at 33-1 or 40-1. Having said that, two were trained by Martin Pipe and the other by Ferdy Murphy, so no punter should have ruled them out completely – horsemanship counts for plenty in this amateur race and the best jockeys tend to be attached to top yards, so don't discount anything from a traditional jumping stable. Light weights are also favoured, although King Lucifer, The Bushkeeper and Juveigneur carried over 11st to victory in the last 10 years.

Weatherbys Champion Bumper (2m110yds) Cheltenham

1997	-1	Florida Pearl	5-11-6	W Mullins	R Dunwoody	6-1	25
1998	-1	Alexander Banquet	5-11-6	W Mullins	R Walsh	9-1	25
1999	-134	Monsignor	5-11-6	M Pitman	B Powell	50-1	25
2000	-1	Joe Cullen	5-11-6	W Mullins	C Swan	14-1	17
2001		Abandoned					
2002	-1	Pizarro	5-11-6	E O'Grady	J Spencer	14-1	23
2003	-12	Liberman	5-11-6	M Pipe	A McCoy	2-1f	25
2004	-311	Total Enjoyment	5-10-12	T Cooper	J Culloty	7-1	24
2005	-11	Missed That	6-11-5	W Mullins	R Walsh	7-2f	24
2006	-2131	Hairy Molly	6-11-5	J Crowley	P Carberry	33-1	23

Bonanza time for the Irish, winners of 11 of the last 14 runnings. Willie Mullins has led the way in jaw-dropping style, with five of the last ten winners from Wither Or Which in 1996 to Missed That in 2005, but that statistic tends to be plugged so heavily on the day that his runners can now be poor value. Five-year-olds dominated this in the early years, but Missed That and Hairy Molly have since redressed the balance for six-year-olds.

Ryanair Festival Trophy (2m5f) Cheltenham

1997*	-1111	**Sparky Gayle**	7-11-3	C Parker	B Storey	3-1f	10
1998*	-321112	**Cyfor Malta**	5-10-8	M Pipe	A McCoy	9-4f	8
1999*	-1331	**Stormyfairweather**	7-11-3	N Henderson	M Fitzgerald	9-1	10
2000*	-P	**Stormyfairweather**	8-11-12	N Henderson	M Fitzgerald	11-2	8
2001		*Abandoned*					
2002*	-F11	**Royal Auclair**	5-10-11	M Pipe	A McCoy	2-1f	11
2003*	-2111111	**La Landiere**	8-10-12	R Phillips	R Johnson	5-4f	9
2004*	-2111121P	**Our Armageddon**	7-11-5	R Guest	L McGrath	9-1	7
2005	-222	**Thisthatandtother**	9-11-3	P Nicholls	R Walsh	9-2	12
2006	-4B13	**Fondmort**	10-11-0	N Henderson	M Fitzgerald	100-30jf	11

Run as the Cathcart Chase, open only to novices or second-season novices

Opening up this race to all sorts in 2005 as part of the new four-day Festival has changed it completely, with Thisthatandtother and Fondmort not surprisingly both older than any other recent winner when it was confined to novices or second-season novices. They did, however, maintain the fine record of horses near the front end of the market.

World Hurdle (3m) Cheltenham

1997*	-0213	**Karshi**	7-11-10	H Knight	J Osborne	20-1	17
1998*	-24124	**Princeful**	7-11-10	J Pitman	R Farrant	16-1	9
1999*	-752	**Anzum**	8-11-10	D Nicholson	R Johnson	40-1	12
2000*	-12	**Bacchanal**	6-11-10	N Henderson	M Fitzgerald	11-2	10
2001		*Abandoned*					
2002*	-111	**Baracouda**	7-11-10	F Doumen	T Doumen	13-8f	16
2003*	-12	**Baracouda**	8-11-10	F Doumen	T Doumen	9-4j	11
2004*	-2	**Iris's Gift**	7-11-10	J O'Neill	B Geraghty	9-2	10
2005	-2211	**Inglis Drever**	6-11-10	J H Johnson	G Lee	5-1	12
2006	-211	**My Way de Solzen**	6-11-10	A King	R Thornton	8-1	20

Raced over 3m1f

There seems a slim career-window in which a horse can win this; six or seven-year-olds are ideal. No five-year-old has ever won and only three eight-year-olds have scored, including the great Baracouda, who was thrice outspeeded by younger rivals (Iris's Gift, Inglis Drever and My Way de Solzen) when attempting further wins. Winners tend to have run well in some of the season's major staying hurdles, particularly the Long Walk Hurdle, and the last six hadn't been out of the first two all season.

Racing Post Plate H'cap Chase (2m4f110yds) Cheltenham

1997	-6P492	**Terao**	11-10-7	M Pipe	T Murphy	20-1	13
1998	-33111	**Super Coin**	10-10-10	R Lee	N Williamson	7-1	14
1999	-111	**Majadou**	5-11-0	M Pipe	A McCoy	7-4f	18
2000	-24P1	**Dark Stranger**	9-10-3b	M Pipe	R Johnson	14-1	18
2001		*Abandoned*					
2002	-P5	**Blowing Wind**	9-10-9	M Pipe	R Walsh	25-1	21
2003	-	**Young Spartacus**	10-10-9	H Daly	R Johnson	16-1	19
2004	-322141	**Tikram**	7-10-0	G Moore	T Murphy	16-1	12

Sponsored by Stan James

| 2005 | -2384 | **Liberthine** | 6-10-1 | N Henderson | S Waley-Cohen(7) | 25-1 | 22 |
| 2006 | -433 | **Non So** | 8-11-3 | N Henderson | M Fitzgerald | 14-1 | 24 |

AKA 'The Mildmay of Flete'. A terrible race for punters as, with so many top handicaps at Cheltenham over this trip over the course of a season, many of the leading contenders are far too well exposed, allowing rivals with far from obvious claims to make hay. Because of this the last six winners were 14-1 or bigger, although with only Non So carrying over 11st (a reasonable 11-3) punters can at least focus on the bottom of the handicap. Martin Pipe and Nicky Henderson have been the trainers to follow.

National Hunt Chase Challenge Cup (4m) Cheltenham

1997	-P221314	**Flimsy Truth**	11-12-7	M Weston	Mr M Harris	33-1	23
1998	-11	**Wandering Light**	9-12-7	T Forster	Mr R Wakley	10-1	24
1999	-514314	**Deejaydee**	7-12-0	M Hourigan	Mr A Martin	13-2	21
2000	-F24U2	**Relaxation**	8-12-0	H Daly	Mr M Bradburne	8-1	21
2001		*Abandoned*					
2002	-32232212	**Rith Dubh**	10-11-11b	J O'Neill	Mr JT McNamara	10-1	26
2003	-FF342	**Sudden Shock**	8-11-7	J O'Neill	Mr D Cullen	25-1	24
2004	-2212	**Native Emperor**	8-11-11	J O'Neill	Mr R Widger	5-1jf	22
2005	-22F4	**Another Rum**	7-11-7	I A Duncan	Mr M J O'Hare	40-1	20
2006	-5361	**Hot Weld**	7-11-11	F Murphy	Mr R Harding	33-1	22

A staying novice chase for amateur riders, this is a strange race to have anywhere, never mind the Festival, and it's by no means a safe vehicle for heroic gambling, underlined by hot favourite Stormez's short-priced defeat in 2003 and the subsequent long-shots Another Rum and Hot Weld storming home. Six of the last seven winners were aged seven or eight and all had plenty of chasing experience having run at least four times in the campaign.

Pertemps Final H'cap Hurdle (3m1f110yds) Cheltenham

1997	-31F1	**Pharanear**	7-11-9	D Nicholson	R Thornton (5)	14-1	24
1998	-111	**Unsinkable Boxer**	9-10-12	M Pipe	A McCoy	5-2f	24
1999	-250	**Generosa**	6-10-1	J L Hassett	N Williamson	12-1	24
2000	-341551	**Rubhahunish**	9-11-2	N Twiston-Davies	C Llewellyn	8-1	24
2001		*Abandoned*					
2002	-341	**Freetown**	6-11-2	L Lungo	A Dobbin	20-1	24
2003	-	**Inching Closer**	6-11-2	J O'Neill	B Geraghty	6-1f	24
2004	-380P6	**Creon**	9-10-0p	J O'Neill	T Murphy	50-1	24
2005	-4421102	**Oulart**	6-10-2	D T Hughes	P Carberry	10-1	22
2006	-50505	**Kadoun**	9-11-7	M O'Brien	T Ryan (3)	50-1	24

AKA 'The Ladbroke Casinos' and many other names due to rapid change of sponsors. Another race in which, after a decent spell of success for punters, the bookmakers have hit back in recent years with the 50-1 successes of Creon and Kadoun. The general rule has been in-form horses with recent winning form carrying over 11st, thereby missing out all the bad-value supposed 'plot' horses laid out for the race. But after those two skinners, who knows where to look next?!

Triumph Hurdle (2m1f) Cheltenham

1997	-111	**Commanche Court**	4-11-0	T Walsh	N Williamson	9-1	28
1998	-P151	**Upgrade**	4-11-0	N Twiston-Davies	C Llewellyn	14-1	25
1999	-111	**Katarino**	4-11-0	N Henderson	M Fitzgerald	11-4f	23
2000	-41	**Snow Drop**	4-10-9	F Doumen	T Doumen	7-1f	28
2001		*Abandoned*					
2002	-1	**Scolardy**	4-11-0	W Mullins	C Swan	16-1	28

2003	-01141B41	Spectroscope	4-11-0	J O'Neill	B Geraghty	20-1	27
2004	-331	Made In Japan	4-11-0	P Hobbs	R Johnson	20-1	23
2005	-111	Penzance	4-11-0	A King	R Thornton	9-1	23
2006	-011	Detroit City	4-11-0	P Hobbs	R Johnson	7-2f	17

Incredibly, each of the last nine winners had won on their most recent outing, so that should narrow the race down for punters immediately, although it's hard to rule out too many more with a couple of recent 20-1 winners mixed in with a few winning favourites. There has been a pronounced recent trend against home-breds, which was flagged up in the *RFO* ahead of the 2002 running when all nine home-breds missed the frame. However, Penzance (successful in 2005), Chief Yeoman (second in 2004) and Blazing Bailey (third in 2006) have started to redress the balance since.

Cheltenham Gold Cup (3m2f110yds) Cheltenham

1997	-4F	Mr Mulligan	9-12-0	N Chance	A McCoy	20-1	14
1998	-0111P	Cool Dawn	10-12-0	R Alner	A Thornton	25-1	17
1999	-4103	See More Business	9-12-0b	P Nicholls	M Fitzgerald	16-1	12
2000	-31P1	Looks Like Trouble	8-12-0	N Chance	R Johnson	9-2	12
2001		*Abandoned*					
2002	-122	Best Mate	7-12-0	H Knight	J Culloty	7-1	18
2003	-11	Best Mate	8-12-0	H Knight	J Culloty	13-8f	15
2004	-21	Best Mate	9-11-10	H Knight	J Culloty	8-11f	10
2005	-1211	Kicking King	7-11-10	T Taaffe	B Geraghty	4-1f	15
2006	-1152	War Of Attrition	7-11-10	M Morris	C O'Dwyer	15-2	22

Best Mate joined the immortals of steeplechasing and became the first triple winner since Arkle (1964-66). Given no horse had even doubled up since L'Escargot in the early 70s, it was a monumental achievement (if testament to his durability rather than his class) and underlines the difficulties of keeping a horse at the peak of his powers season after season – War Of Attrition followers have been warned. Following the Best Mate days, Kicking King made it another winning favourite in 2005, but outsiders have a fine record of winning and reaching the frame, bolstered by the placed performances in recent renewals of Truckers Tavern, Harbour Pilot (twice), Sir Rembrandt and Hedgehunter in recent years. All of those shared a wealth of stamina, so don't rule out any slow boats. Prior to that Cool Ground in 1992 and Cool Dawn in 1998 won at 25-1, while Mr Mulligan was 20-1 in 1997, while short-priced favourites who have bitten the dust in recent years include Florida Pearl (5-2), See More Business (9-4), One Man (11-8), Jodami (6-4), The Fellow (5-4) and Carvills Hill (Evens). Any runner older than ten can be discounted and only French-bred six-year-olds stand a chance – The Fellow was beaten a short-head in 1991, while the ill-fated Gloria Victis was still in the front rank when falling two out in 2000. But for War Of Attrition being wrong at one stage last season, the last five winners hadn't been out of the first two all season.

Christie's Foxhunter Chase (3m2f110yds) Cheltenham

1997	-	Fantus	10-12-0	R Barber	Mr T Mitchell	10-1	18
1998	-1111	Earthmover	7-12-0	R Barber	Mr J Tizzard	3-1	11
1999	-1	Castle Mane	7-12-0	Caroline Bailey	Mr B Pollock	9-2	24
2000	-21	Cavalero	11-12-0	H Manners	Mr A Charles-Jones	16-1	24
2001		*Abandoned*					
2002	-3	Last Option	10-12-0	R Tate	Mrs F Needham	20-1	20
2003	-1	Kingscliff	6-12-0	S Alner	Mr R Young	11-4f	24
2004	-1P2	Earthmover	13-12-0	P Nicholls	Miss A Goschen	14-1	24
2005	-U1	Sleeping Night	9-12-0	P Nicholls	Mr C J Sweeney	7-2f	24
2006	-4U	Whyso Mayo	9-12-0	R Hurley	Mr D Murphy	20-1	24

Hunter chasers are often hard to get fit and keep fit, so the best trend is to look for a horse with a run in the last couple of weeks, not necessarily a winning one, coming at the end of a relatively light campaign under Rules. Horses in the West Country also have a phenomenal record, although Whyso Mayo was a rare Irish winner last year having been flagged up as one to follow in this guide at the start of the season.

Grand Annual H'cap Chase (2m110yds) Cheltenham

1997	-434	Uncle Ernie	12-11-4	J Fitzgerald	G Bradley	20-1	16
1998	-4111	Edredon Bleu	6-11-6	H Knight	A McCoy	7-2f	17
1999	-F3	Space Trucker	8-10-1	J Harrington	J Barry	7-2f	15
2000	-111	Samakaan	7-10-11	V Williams	N Williamson	9-2f	16
2001		Abandoned					
2002	-321	Fadoudal Du Cochet	9-10-0	A Moore	D Casey	6-1	18
2003	-2231	Palarshan	5-10-0	H Daly	M Bradburne	8-1	21
2004	-614	St Pirran	9-10-1	P Nicholls	R Walsh	4-1f	21
2005	-3212	Fota Island	9-10-1 2oh	M Morris	P Carberry	7-1f	24
2006	-5	Greenhope	8-10-11	N Henderson	A Tinkler	20-1	23

Lightly-weighted horses are an absolute must in this contest, with the last seven winners all carrying less than 11st – five carried either 10st or 10-1. Novices also have an exceptional record in this race, with Samakaan, Palarshan and Fota Island all successful in their first season over fences following Sound Reveille in the mid-90s. Victory last time out is a plus but not essential.

County H'cap Hurdle (2m1f) Cheltenham

1997	-43364	Barna Boy	9-10-12	N Henderson	R Dunwoody	14-1	20
1998	-724831	Blowing Wind	5-11-8	M Pipe	A McCoy	15-8f	27
1999	-152	Sir Talbot	5-10-0	J Old	T Murphy	10-1	28
2000	-04811	Master Tern	5-10-3	J O'Neill	A Dobbin	9-2f	21
2001		Abandoned					
2002	-55422	Rooster Booster	8-11-1	P Hobbs	R Johnson	8-1	21
2003	-23151	Spirit Leader	7-11-7	J Harrington	B Geraghty	10-1	28
2004	-1238	Sporazene	5-10-13	P Nicholls	R Walsh	7-1f	23
2005	-0P660048	Fontanesi	5-10-0 5oh	M Pipe	T Murphy	16-1	30
2006	-221U1131	Desert Quest	6-10-10	P Nicholls	R Walsh	4-1jf	29

Unlike the Coral Cup, this has been a rotten race for the Irish with only Spirit Leader in 2003 rounding off the Festival on a good note for the raiders in recent times. Five-year-olds have an outstanding record, unlike most other Festival hurdles, with five of the last eight winners.

Betfair Bowl Chase (3m1f) Aintree

1997	-25322	Barton Bank	11-11-5	D Nicholson	D Walsh	100-30	5
1998	-12112	Escartefigue	6-11-13	D Nicholson	R Johnson	11-2	8
1999	-12644	Macgeorge	9-11-5	R Lee	A Maguire	11-1	5
2000	-1114	See More Business	10-12-0b	P Nicholls	M Fitzgerald	5-4f	4
2001	-3211112	First Gold	8-12-0	F Doumen	T Doumen	7-4f	7
2002	-31140	Florida Pearl	10-11-12	W Mullins	B Geraghty	5-2	6
2003	-373P	First Gold	10-11-2b	F Doumen	T Doumen	14-1	7
2004	-422F3	Tiutchev	11-11-12	M Pipe	A McCoy	11-2	8
2005	-115	Grey Abbey	11-11-12	J H Johnson	G Lee	7-2	8
2006	-U	Celestial Gold	8-11-8	M Pipe	T Murphy	8-1	9

AKA 'The Martell Cup'. A dramatic uplift in prizemoney improved the quality of this race greatly around the turn of the decade as Florida Pearl won almost twice as much in 2002 as Macgeorge had three years earlier, but it still struggles to attract Cheltenham principals. Aintree's Mildmay course is flat and sharp, similar to Kempton except for being left-handed; horses who run well at the Sunbury track are likely to do similarly well here. Four of the last seven to succeed were all previous King George winners, and Tiutchev was runner-up to Edredon Bleu in 2004. Dual winner Docklands Express was also a dual winner of Kempton's Racing Post Chase.

Grand National H'cap Chase (4m4f) Aintree

1997	-23112	**Lord Gyllene**	9-10-0	S Brookshaw	A Dobbin	14-1	36
1998	-55165	**Earth Summit**	10-10-5b	N Twiston-Davies	C Llewellyn	7-1f	37
1999	-580541	**Bobbyjo**	9-10-0	T Carberry	P Carberry	10-1	32
2000	-875493	**Papillon**	9-10-12	T Walsh	R Walsh	10-1	40
2001	-14552F	**Red Marauder**	11-10-11	N Mason	R Guest	33-1	40
2002	-753367	**Bindaree**	8-10-4	N Twiston-Davies	J Culloty	20-1	40
2003	3P631364	**Monty's Pass**	10-10-7	J Mangan	B Geraghty	16-1	40
2004	-342P5	**Amberleigh House**	12-10-10	D McCain	G Lee	16-1	39
2005	-924061	**Hedgehunter**	9-11-1	W Mullins	R Walsh	7-1f	40
2006	-04B443	**Numbersixvalverde**	10-10-8	M Brassil	N Madden	11-1	40

Efforts by the handicapper to attract more and more class horses have led to the weights becoming more bunched in recent years, so more horses carry over 11st and few, if any, are ever out of the handicap. However, with only Hedgehunter (11-1 in 2005) carrying a reasonably significant burden to victory it still pays to focus on those near the foot of the weights. Forget the old adage about class horses with winning form over 2m4f; even with the modified fences, this race is a severe test of stamina and proven ability to last home over 3m or further is essential. Look for horses who've run with credit in other major staying handicaps – Earth Summit had won the Welsh and Scottish Nationals, Bobbyjo and Papillon had been first and second (9l clear) in the 1998 Irish National, Monty's Pass was a Kerry National winner, and Numbersixvalverde was an Irish National winner as well. Be careful with Hennessy form as Newbury winners Suny Bay and What's Up Boys were beaten by the handicapper. Don't back at starting price but take the best available odds 'with a run' in the days before the race, and don't be put off backing more than one – this is a race in which bad luck can easily strike down a single, carefully-chosen selection.

Scottish Grand National H'cap Chase (4m120yds) Ayr

1997	-102	**Belmont King**	9-11-10	P Nicholls	A McCoy	16-1	17
1998	-34F15	**Baronet**	8-10-0	D Nicholson	A Maguire	7-1	18
1999	-22412U11	**Young Kenny**	8-11-10	P Beaumont	B Powell	5-2f	15
2000	-12111	**Paris Pike**	8-11-0	F Murphy	A Maguire	5-1j	18
2001	-2P4	**Gingembre**	7-11-2	L Taylor	A Thornton	12-1	30
2002	-36P4P5	**Take Control**	8-10-6	M Pipe	R Walsh	20-1	18
2003	-31223	**Ryalux**	10-10-5	A Crook	R McGrath	15-2	19
2004	-611	**Grey Abbey**	10-11-12	J H Johnson	G Lee	12-1	28
2005	-1222P1	**Joes Edge**	8-9-11 (5oh)	F Murphy	K J Mercer	20-1	20
2006	-10402	**Run For Paddy**	10-10-2	C Llewellyn	C Llewellyn	33-1	30

The first rule is to avoid runners who had a hard race in the Grand National – Shotgun Willy, a distant fifth behind Ryalux two season ago after pulling up at Aintree, was just another example of a horse too tired by recent exertions to produce his best form here. Seven of the last 18 winners carried the minimum of 10st, ranging up to 17lb out of the handicap, and several others had barely any more, although class horses can carry big weights to victory, Young Kenny and Grey Abbey being two examples. The ground can be on the fast side, Gingembre's year being a notable example, so soft-ground midwinter form may prove redundant.

Sponsored by Stan James

Irish Grand National H'cap Chase (3m5f) Fairyhouse

1997	-42161	**Mudahim**	11-10-5	J Pitman	J Titley	13-2	20
1998	-102	**Bobbyjo**	8-11-3	T Carberry	P Carberry	8-1	22
1999	-8493F30	**Glebe Lad**	7-10-0	M O'Brien	T Rudd	8-1cf	18
2000	-332B	**Commanche Court**	7-11-4	T Walsh	R Walsh	14-1	24
2001	-7119F61	**Davids Lad**	7-10-0t	A Martin	T Murphy	10-1	19
2002	-5312F1	**The Bunny Boiler**	8-9-9	N Meade	R Geraghty	12-1	17
2003	-P24	**Timbera**	9-10-12t	D Hughes	J Culloty	11-1	21
2004	-UP34	**Granit d'Estruval**	10-10-0	F. Murphy	B Harding	33-1	28
2005	-8231513	**Numbersixvalverde**	9-10-1 (1ow)	M Brassil	R Walsh	9-1	26
2006	-60006	**Point Barrow**	8-10-8	P Hughes	P Carberry	20-1	26

Flashing Steel, Commanche Court and, going further back, Desert Orchid have demonstrated that classy types can win this despite hefty burdens – indeed, 11 winners since the war have carried 11st10lb and above to victory – but lightweights dominate just the same. It took until 1985 for a British-trained horse to win this race and the record has barely been improved since, although Ferdy Murphy did provide the shock winner in 2004 with Granit d'Estruval. Young, improving chasers are the order of the day, with Commanche Court, Davids Lad and Numbersixvalverde all going on to bigger things.

Betfred Gold Cup H'cap Chase (3m5f) Sandown

1997	-P12	**Harwell Lad**	8-10-0	R Alner	Mr R Nuttall	14-1	9
1998	-3224F3	**Call It A Day**	8-10-10	D Nicholson	A Maguire	8-1	19
1999	-20	**Eulogy**	9-10-0	R Rowe	B Fenton	14-1	19
2000	-2412112	**Beau**	7-10-9	N Twiston-Davies	C Llewellyn	6-1c	20
2001	-FFP52	**Ad Hoc**	7-10-4	P Nicholls	R Walsh	14-1	25
2002	32143356	**Bounce Back**	6-10-9	M Pipe	A McCoy	14-1	20
2003	-51233U	**Ad Hoc**	9-10-10	P Nicholls	R Walsh	7-1	16
2004	-1211415UU	**Puntal**	8-11-4t	M Pipe	D Howard (3)	25-1	18
2006	-16134022	**Lacdoudal**	7-11-5	P Hobbs	R Johnson	10-1	18

AKA 'The Whitbread'. As in so many staying chases, lightweights are favoured – 11 of the last 17 winners have carried 10st6lb or less. However, the fast ground that usually exists at such a late stage of the season also gives the quality horses more of a chance, as Puntal and Lacdoudal showed. Six of the last 16 winners had run in the Grand National, but Mr Frisk remains the only horse ever to win both races.

THUMBS UP: Numbersixvalverde completes the Irish/Aintree National double

Track Facts

YOU WANT course statistics? Look no further – this section contains all the numbers you'll need, for every jumps track in the country.

Course by course, we've set out four-year trainer and jockey statistics, favourites records, winning pointers and three-dimensional racecourse maps, plus details of how to get there and every fixture date for the new season.

Following this (page 222), we've got details of course record times, plus standard times for each track – by comparing the time of any race this season with the relevant standard time, you should get an indication of the quality of that race.

Note that we have been unable to produce standard times in a very small number of cases, as there have not been enough recent races over the trip at the track in question.

See also our statistical assessment of last season's records from Britain's top 10 trainers (page 123).

AINTREE	177-178
ASCOT	179
AYR	180
BANGOR	181
CARLISLE	182
CARTMEL	183
CATTERICK	184
CHELTENHAM	185-187
CHEPSTOW	188
DONCASTER	189
EXETER	190
FAKENHAM	191
FOLKESTONE	192
FONTWELL	193
HAYDOCK	194
HEREFORD	195
HEXHAM	196
HUNTINGDON	197
KELSO	198
KEMPTON	199
LEICESTER	200
LINGFIELD	201
LUDLOW	202
MARKET RASEN	203
MUSSELBURGH	204
NEWBURY	205
NEWCASTLE	206
NEWTON ABBOT	207
PERTH	208
PLUMPTON	209
SANDOWN	210
SEDGEFIELD	211
SOUTHWELL	212
STRATFORD	213
TAUNTON	214
TOWCESTER	215
UTTOXETER	216
WARWICK	217
WETHERBY	218
WINCANTON	219
WINDSOR	220
WORCESTER	221

AINTREE

How to get there - Road: M6, M62, M57, M58. Rail: Liverpool Lime St + taxi

Features: The LH 2m2f giant triangular Grand National course is perfectly flat. Inside it, the sharp LH Mildmay course is 1m4f in circumference.

2006-07 Fixtures: Oct 21, 22, Nov 19, Apr 12, 13, 14

Winning Pointers: Jonjo O'Neill performs comfortably best of the big guns here, with an excellent strike-rate of nearly 17 per cent. In contrast, Paul Nicholls wins with just 9.3 per cent. No jockey rides the National course as well as Ruby Walsh – or indeed the Mildmay course – though Sam Waley-Cohen is putting together a remarkable record.

Trainers	Wins-Runs	%	Hurdles	Chases	£1 level stks
P Bowen	6-24	25.0	4-12	1-10	+10.75
Mrs H Dalton	3-15	20.0	2-5	1-8	+1.50
L Lungo	3-16	18.8	2-12	0-1	+0.38
N Richards	5-29	17.2	5-23	0-3	+11.25
Jonjo O'Neill	16-95	16.8	8-48	6-39	-8.94
R Ford	3-20	15.0	0-8	3-11	-2.00
Miss V Williams	8-60	13.3	5-23	2-34	+7.50
J Howard Johnson	6-52	11.5	4-30	2-19	-23.43
A King	4-39	10.3	2-24	0-11	+16.25
N Twiston-Davies	5-51	9.8	1-20	3-25	+16.37
H Daly	3-31	9.7	3-13	0-15	-17.25
F Murphy	3-32	9.4	1-8	2-23	-18.25
Miss H Knight	3-32	9.4	0-10	3-16	-9.50
P Nicholls	11-118	9.3	3-27	8-86	-44.75

Jockeys	Wins-Rides	%	£1 level stks	Best Trainer	W-R
S Waley-Cohen	3-7	42.9	+20.83	R Waley-Cohen	2-3
Antony Evans	3-10	30.0	+26.00	J Spearing	1-1
A McCoy	18-85	21.2	+5.57	Jonjo O'Neill	5-22
R Walsh	14-71	19.7	+53.50	P Nicholls	8-52
L Cooper	4-22	18.2	+8.13	Jonjo O'Neill	4-22
P J Brennan	4-24	16.7	+9.38	K Bishop	1-1
B J Geraghty	6-38	15.8	-12.33	Mrs J Harrington	2-4
A Dobbin	9-73	12.3	-11.87	N Richards	5-20
T Doyle	3-28	10.7	-7.00	R Lee	1-6
R Johnson	9-85	10.6	-40.93	H Daly	3-15
R Thornton	5-57	8.8	+11.75	A King	3-32
G Lee	9-104	8.7	-42.93	J Howard Johnson	6-46
C Llewellyn	4-48	8.3	-29.63	N Twiston-Davies	3-37
T J Murphy	5-71	7.0	-16.25	J Queally	2-3
D Elsworth	3-55	5.5	-26.00	Mrs S J Smith	3-47

Mildmay hurdles

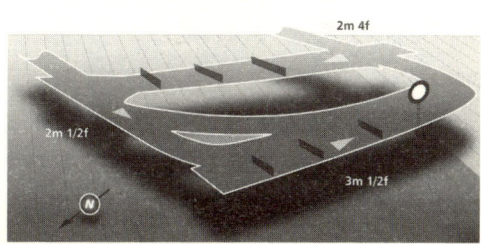

Favourites

Chase	24.0%	-£10.18
Hurdle	24.8%	-£25.87
Overall	24.4%	-£36.05

Sponsored by Stan James

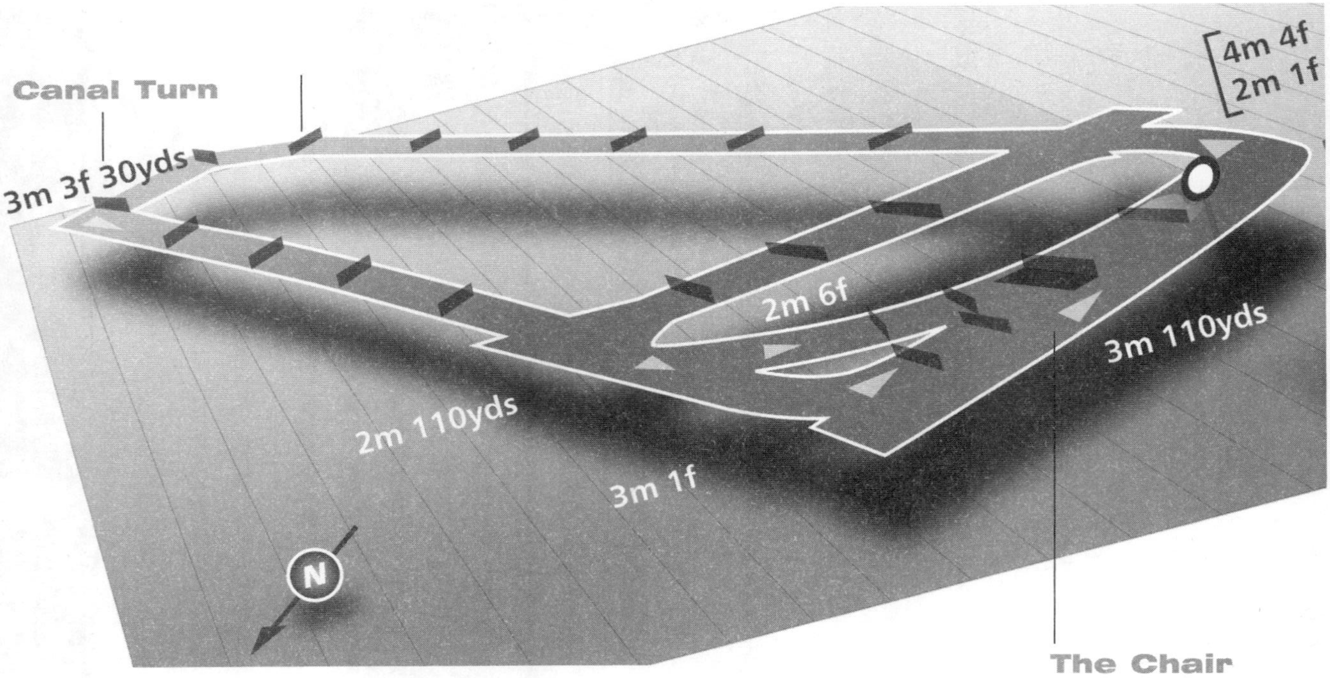

Grand National and Mildmay chase courses

4m 4f
2m 1f

3m 110yds

The Chair

2m 6f

3m 1f

2m 110yds

N

Canal Turn

3m 3f 30yds

Sponsored by Stan James

ASCOT

How to get there – Road: M4 junction 6 or M3 junction 3 on to A332.
Rail: Frequent service from Reading or Waterloo
Features: RH
2006-07 fixtures: Oct 28, Nov 17, 18, Dec 15, 16, 30, Jan 20, Feb 17, Mar 30, 31
Pointers: Several trainers now retired understandably top Ascot's five-year stats given there has been no racing for two years, but they are still worth a look as Francois Doumen, Martin Pipe and Mark Pitman all remain heavily involved in the operations of Thierry Doumen, David Pipe and Carl Llewellyn respectively.

Chases

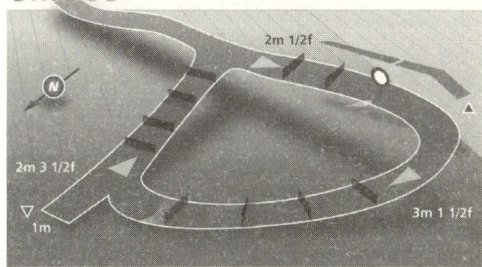

Hurdles

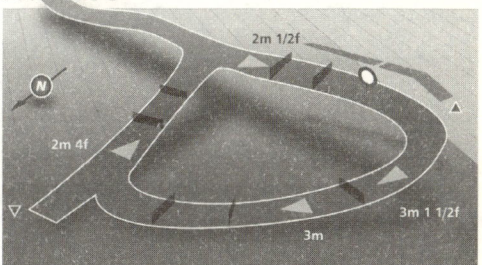

Favourites

Chase	41.7%	+£3.54
Hurdle	24.2%	-£28.74
Overall	31.6%	-£25.19

Trainers	Wins-Runs	%	Hurdles	Chases	£1 level stks
F Doumen	3-6	50.0	3-5	0-1	-1.21
J Gifford	3-10	30.0	3-6	0-4	+62.00
R Alner	4-16	25.0	2-9	2-6	+21.33
H Daly	4-16	25.0	1-4	3-10	+20.25
M Pipe	19-78	24.4	10-45	8-30	+5.87
I Williams	4-18	22.2	1-13	2-3	+15.75
M Pitman	4-19	21.1	1-8	3-9	+9.25
N Henderson	8-44	18.2	4-20	3-21	+30.50
Miss V Williams	5-31	16.1	2-14	3-17	+46.88
G L Moore	3-20	15.0	3-19	0-0	-0.37
Jonjo O'Neill	5-35	14.3	1-20	2-11	-18.40
P Nicholls	3-26	11.5	1-10	2-16	-18.54
P Hobbs	6-53	11.3	2-33	4-18	-31.75

Jockeys	Wins-Rides	%	£1 level stks	Best Trainer	W-R
W L Morgan	3-6	50.0	+4.77	Miss P Robson	2-2
D R Dennis	3-6	50.0	+16.75	I Williams	3-5
T Doumen	3-7	42.9	-2.21	F Doumen	3-6
A McCoy	19-59	32.2	+18.53	M Pipe	16-40
M Batchelor	3-13	23.1	+10.50	M Bradstock	2-4
L Cooper	3-15	20.0	-5.40	Jonjo O'Neill	3-15
R Johnson	8-49	16.3	+18.75	P Hobbs	4-28
R Walsh	4-25	16.0	-7.54	P Nicholls	3-20
J Culloty	4-31	12.9	-6.25	Miss H Knight	2-15
A Thornton	3-24	12.5	-7.34	R Alner	2-7
L Aspell	5-41	12.2	+32.96	J Gifford	2-2
M Fitzgerald	4-45	8.9	-0.50	N Henderson	4-32
B Fenton	3-35	8.6	-19.67	Miss E Lavelle	2-8

AYR

Whitletts Road Ayr KA8 0JE
Tel: 01292 264179

How to get there – Road: south from Glasgow on A77 or A75, A70, A76. Rail: Ayr

Features: LH 1m4f oval, easy turns, slight uphill finish

2006-07 Fixtures: Nov 29, Dec 11, 19, Jan 2, 22, Feb 10, Mar 2, 9, 10, 22, Apr 20, 21

Winning Pointers: Richard Phillips tends to make the long trip north count, whereas the most successful local trainers are Howard Johnson and Nicky Richards. Tony Dobbin's strike-rate is absolutely sensational given his volume of rides.

Chases

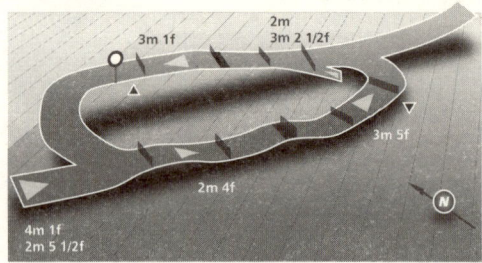

Hurdles

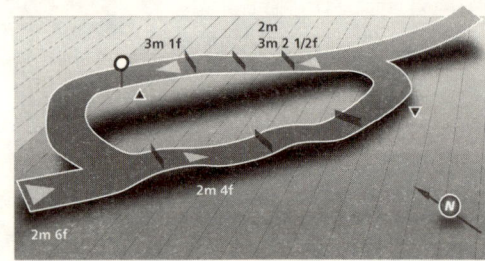

Favourites

Chase	39.6%	+£1.48
Hurdle	35.5%	-£24.62
Overall	37.3%	-£23.13

Trainers	Wins-Runs	%	Hurdles	Chases	£1 level stks
R Phillips	3-9	33.3	2-6	1-3	-2.97
T Tate	3-9	33.3	3-7	0-0	+3.50
J Howard Johnson	16-55	29.1	8-27	7-23	+28.06
N Richards	37-132	28.0	21-81	12-33	+15.41
P Hobbs	5-19	26.3	2-4	2-14	+5.00
J Jefferson	5-20	25.0	2-9	2-8	+23.73
L Lungo	42-173	24.3	19-102	16-44	-11.76
Jonjo O'Neill	3-13	23.1	2-5	1-8	+2.00
A King	3-14	21.4	2-6	1-7	-2.25
Mrs K Walton	3-15	20.0	3-8	0-3	-8.13
P Niven	3-15	20.0	2-12	0-0	+11.80
J Wade	3-15	20.0	3-5	0-8	+7.50
J Bewley	3-15	20.0	1-7	2-7	+22.33

Jockeys	Wins-Rides	%	£1 level stks	Best Trainer	W-R
W L Morgan	3-6	50.0	+4.77	Miss P Robson	2-2
A Dobbin	61-172	35.5	+8.49	L Lungo	28-70
T J Murphy	5-24	20.8	-2.00	M Pipe	4-11
R Johnson	7-35	20.0	-5.92	P Hobbs	5-12
R Thornton	3-17	17.6	-5.25	A King	3-13
N Hannity	3-17	17.6	+30.00	A Whillans	1-1
G Lee	22-125	17.6	-15.60	J Howard Johnson	10-34
R Walsh	5-29	17.2	-15.71	P Nicholls	5-28
L McGrath	5-30	16.7	-5.60	R C Guest	2-6
V T Keane	3-19	15.8	+19.50	J Jefferson	2-4
D N Russell	5-33	15.2	-9.50	F Murphy	4-22
I Jardine	3-21	14.3	+13.00	A Whillans	3-16
K Renwick	18-138	13.0	-15.40	P Monteith	7-41

Bangor-on-Dee, Nr Wrexham,
Clwyd. Tel 01948 860438

BANGOR

Chases

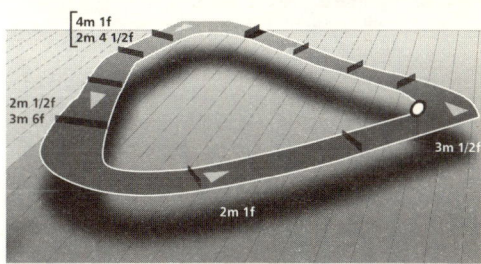

How to get there – Road: A525.
Rail: Wrexham

Features: 1m4f LH, quite sharp.
Last fence gets plenty of fallers

2006-07 Fixtures: Oct 7, Nov 8,
Dec 13, Feb 9, Mar 4, 24, Apr 21

Winning Pointers: Back all Paul
Nicholls' chasers and Alan
King's hurdlers is the most
pertinent advice here. Tony
McCoy and Richard Johnson
get far more rides than any
other jockeys and do pretty well
with them despite returning
small losses.

Hurdles

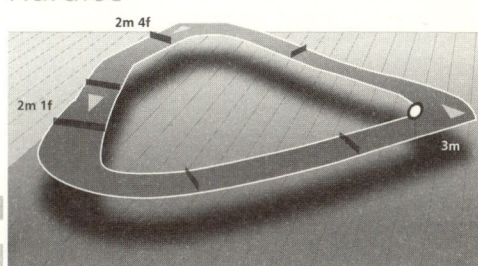

Favourites

Chase	32.1%	-£24.10
Hurdle	36.2%	-£17.23
Overall	34.4%	-£41.34

Trainers	Wins-Runs	%	Hurdles	Chases	£1 level stks
J J Quinn	3-5	60.0	3-4	0-1	+9.50
Mrs K Walton	3-6	50.0	2-4	1-2	+7.63
P Nicholls	14-41	34.1	4-17	9-23	+28.46
N Richards	5-15	33.3	3-9	1-2	+6.00
C Tinkler	3-10	30.0	3-6	0-2	+7.38
M Pipe	29-101	28.7	21-63	8-35	-20.92
Mrs E Crow	3-11	27.3	0-0	3-11	+1.30
A King	12-45	26.7	9-29	2-14	+33.13
P R Wobber	10-40	25.0	4-14	5-18	+37.67
M Sheppard	3-13	23.1	2-8	1-5	+4.50
E Williams	4-18	22.2	2-8	2-9	+16.25
T George	6-27	22.2	2-9	4-17	+9.33
N Twiston-Davies	13-60	21.7	5-29	3-19	-4.33

Jockeys	Wins-Rides	%	£1 level stks	Best Trainer	W-R
R Walsh	3-9	33.3	-1.75	P Nicholls	3-7
A McCoy	33-112	29.5	-32.11	M Pipe	15-27
P Robson	3-12	25.0	+15.00	R Phillips	1-1
P C O'Neill	3-13	23.1	+6.00	Miss V Williams	3-10
R Biddlecombe	3-13	23.1	+1.75	N Twiston-Davies	2-3
R Johnson	21-97	21.6	-7.94	P Hobbs	5-22
T J Murphy	7-34	20.6	-14.23	M Pipe	7-16
B J Crowley	7-34	20.6	-14.22	Miss V Williams	6-24
T Siddall	5-25	20.0	+1.35	Jonjo O'Neill	5-15
R McGrath	5-25	20.0	+1.04	Mrs K Walton	2-3
L Cooper	7-35	20.0	-8.90	Jonjo O'Neill	7-35
T Scudamore	9-45	20.0	+39.88	C Tinkler	2-2
Christian Williams	8-43	18.6	+32.46	P Nicholls	3-9

CARLISLE

Blackwell, Carlisle, Cumbria, CA2 4TS. Tel: 01228 522973.

How to get there – Road: M6 Jctn 42. Rail: 2m from Citadel Station, Carlisle

Features: Pear-shaped, 1m5f circuit, RH, undulating, tough uphill home stretch

2006-07 Fixtures: Oct 6, 15, 29, Nov 6, 12, 23, Jan 14, Feb 7, 19, Mar 8, 18, Apr 7

Winning Pointers: Nicky Richards is the star at England's northernmost racecourse. Howard Johnson and Graham Lee were also a potent combination prior to their split – will Johnson enjoy the same success with Paddy Brennan taking over riding duties?

Chases

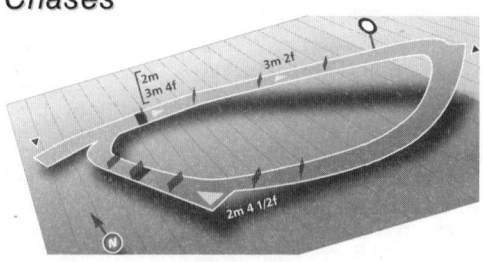

Hurdles

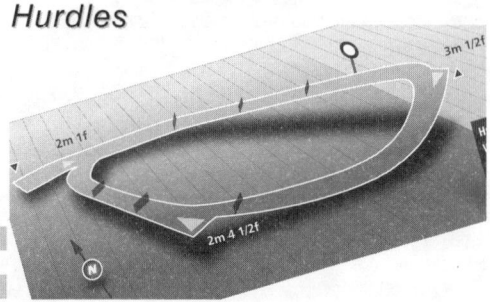

Favourites

Chase	31.0%	-£25.67
Hurdle	33.8%	-£25.10
Overall	32.5%	-£50.78

Trainers

Trainers	Wins-Runs	%	Hurdles	Chases	£1 level stks
N Richards	15-51	29.4	9-32	4-12	+8.05
J Howard Johnson	19-68	27.9	9-37	9-23	-8.41
Jonjo O'Neill	13-47	27.7	8-27	2-13	+18.38
Mrs A Hamilton	3-12	25.0	1-7	1-3	+9.00
Miss V Williams	4-19	21.1	1-5	3-12	+0.16
Mrs S J Smith	21-105	20.0	10-51	10-44	-1.05
L Lungo	22-111	19.8	13-69	7-27	+2.65
R C Guest	14-72	19.4	3-24	10-41	+3.96
M W Easterby	7-37	18.9	5-15	1-9	+14.63
P Niven	3-16	18.8	1-11	2-4	+47.00
W Coltherd	3-17	17.6	0-6	3-9	+1.75
Mrs M Reveley	8-46	17.4	6-28	2-15	-7.32
M Todhunter	6-43	14.0	2-25	4-17	-5.27

Jockeys

Jockeys	Wins-Rides	%	£1 level stks	Best Trainer	W-R
P C O'Neill	4-12	33.3	+8.00	R C Guest	2-7
P Robson	3-11	27.3	-3.02	Dave Parker	1-1
A Dobbin	34-129	26.4	-3.25	N Richards	12-27
T Greenall	6-24	25.0	+31.13	M W Easterby	5-16
L Cooper	6-24	25.0	+2.58	Jonjo O'Neill	6-24
A O'Keeffe	3-13	23.1	+1.16	Miss V Williams	2-6
A McCoy	4-18	22.2	+1.50	Jonjo O'Neill	3-10
B Orde-Powlett	3-15	20.0	+1.50	J Walton	2-7
H Oliver	5-26	19.2	+8.75	R C Guest	4-24
G Lee	25-132	18.9	+11.57	J Howard Johnson	13-44
D Elsworth	12-67	17.9	-10.25	Mrs S J Smith	11-48
D N Russell	4-28	14.3	0.00	F Murphy	4-23
W Marston	4-28	14.3	-17.70	Mrs S J Smith	4-17

Cartmel, Grange-over-Sands,
Penrith, Cumbria, CA10 2HG.
Tel 015935 36340

CARTMEL

How to get there – Road: M6
Jctn 36, A591. Rail: Cark-in-Cart-
mel or Grange-over-Sands

Features: Tight LH, only 1m
round, undulating, half-mile run-
in from last (longest in country)

2006-07 Fixtures: Only hosts
summer jumps racing

Winning Pointers: Not surprisingly, the big stables don't really
feature in these stats, preferring
to keep their powder dry for the
season proper. Charlie Mann is
one of the exceptions and his
rare visits rarely go unrewarded.

Chases

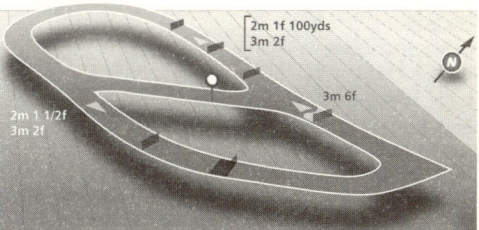

Hurdles

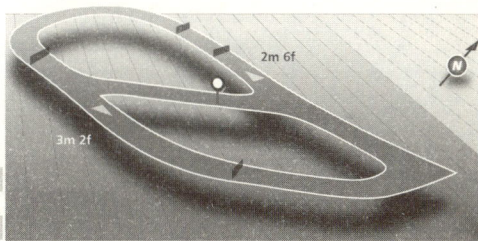

Favourites

Chase	29.5%	-£7.16
Hurdle	30.2%	-£10.85
Overall	29.9%	-£18.01

Trainers	Wins-Runs	%	Hurdles	Chases	£1 level stks
A Whillans	3-4	75.0	2-3	1-1	+30.00
A Sadik	4-9	44.4	0-4	4-5	+6.50
C Mann	3-8	37.5	3-6	0-2	-1.55
Miss S Forster	4-12	33.3	1-8	3-4	+13.67
A Berry	5-16	31.3	5-15	0-1	+16.00
M D Hammond	4-14	28.6	2-8	2-6	+1.25
D Burchell	6-21	28.6	1-11	5-10	+12.50
N Wilson	3-12	25.0	2-9	1-3	+16.00
Mrs S J Smith	7-38	18.4	1-17	6-21	-6.50
M Todhunter	6-34	17.6	6-26	0-8	-6.42
R C Guest	9-57	15.8	6-40	3-17	-16.93
F Murphy	3-21	14.3	2-12	1-9	+3.17
R Ford	3-23	13.0	1-11	2-12	-10.25

Jockeys	Wins-Rides	%	£1 level stks	Best Trainer	W-R
C Storey	4-10	40.0	+15.67	Miss S Forster	4-10
N Fehily	3-9	33.3	-2.55	C Mann	3-8
J M Maguire	4-15	26.7	+0.50	A Sadik	4-9
W Marston	5-19	26.3	-2.16	Mrs S J Smith	2-7
N Mulholland	3-13	23.1	+5.50	I A Duncan	1-1
J Crowley	9-43	20.9	+33.75	M D Hammond	2-4
K J Mercer	3-17	17.6	+19.00	A Berry	1-1
L McGrath	4-23	17.4	+1.42	R C Guest	4-16
H Oliver	4-25	16.0	-11.60	R C Guest	4-24
L Vickers	3-22	13.6	+3.00	M Chapman	3-20
K Renwick	3-22	13.6	-5.00	P Monteith	2-6
G Lee	7-59	11.9	-23.67	M Todhunter	2-6
R Garritty	3-26	11.5	-16.75	J J Quinn	1-6

CATTERICK

Catterick Bridge, Richmond,
N.Yorkshire, DL10 7PE.
Tel: 01748 811478

How to get there – Road: A1.
Rail: Darlington

Features: LH 1m2f oval,
undulating, sharp turns,
favouring small, handy horses

2006-07 Fixtures: Nov 29, Dec
14, 28, Jan 1, 11, 24, Feb 2, 27,
Mar 7

Winning Pointers: Once again
Nicky Richards and Howard
Johnson are the kings up north,
with Len Lungo not too far
behind. Sue Smith doesn't fare
quite as well though.

Chases

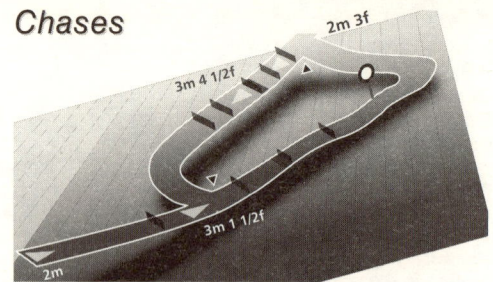

Hurdles

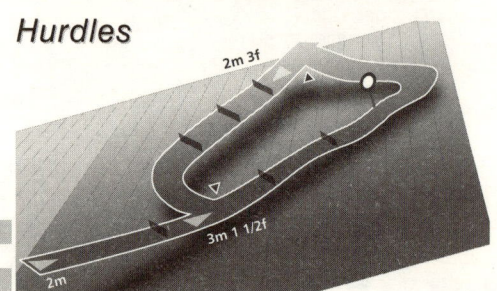

Favourites

Chase	18.1%	-£34.00
Hurdle	31.6%	-£11.46
Overall	26.5%	-£45.47

Trainers	Wins-Runs	%	Hurdles	Chases	£1 level stks
N Richards	3-10	30.0	2-7	0-2	+3.17
J Howard Johnson	15-62	24.2	11-46	3-13	-17.13
J J Quinn	3-15	20.0	2-9	1-4	-0.92
L Lungo	5-25	20.0	0-14	1-5	+3.66
T Easterby	9-48	18.8	7-29	2-15	-5.57
R Fahey	6-33	18.2	1-21	4-8	+26.50
K G Reveley	8-51	15.7	4-29	3-15	-2.99
R C Guest	10-66	15.2	4-38	5-21	+70.50
J Moffatt	3-21	14.3	3-17	0-2	+3.50
F Kirby	4-28	14.3	1-13	3-15	+56.00
M D Hammond	5-35	14.3	1-17	4-15	+8.50
Mrs S J Smith	12-88	13.6	8-50	2-23	-24.62
J Jefferson	5-50	10.0	2-29	2-15	-20.75

Jockeys	Wins-Rides	%	£1 level stks	Best Trainer	W-R
D Elsworth	10-45	22.2	+4.25	Mrs S J Smith	8-34
G Lee	14-76	18.4	-15.02	J Howard Johnson	8-27
G Berridge	3-19	15.8	+4.50	L Lungo	2-7
P Whelan	9-57	15.8	+60.37	R Fahey	5-22
R McGrath	11-80	13.8	-21.65	K G Reveley	5-30
D O'Meara	7-51	13.7	+32.18	T Easterby	5-14
G Carenza	5-38	13.2	-4.83	M W Easterby	2-16
C McCormack	3-23	13.0	+20.50	J Goldie	1-1
A Dobbin	8-62	12.9	-28.50	J Moffatt	1-1
R Garritty	7-67	10.4	-33.42	T Easterby	4-27
N Mulholland	3-38	7.9	-15.50	M D Hammond	2-4
D C Costello	4-51	7.8	-21.50	G A Swinbank	2-10
P Robson	3-40	7.5	+16.00	R Barr	1-2

Prestbury Park, Cheltenham,
Glos GL50 4SH.
Tel. 01242 513014.

CHELTENHAM

How to get there - Road: A435, 5 miles north of M5 Jcts 9, 10, 11.
Rail: Cheltenham

Features: There are two LH courses; the Old Course is 1m4f around, the slightly longer New Course is similar. Both end with a testing uphill finish, making Cheltenham a stiff track.

2006-07 Fixtures: Oct 24, 25, Nov 10, 11, 12, Dec 8, 9, Jan 1, 27, Mar 13, 14, 15, 16, Apr 18, 19.

Winning Pointers: Astonishingly, despite hosting the most competitive racing in the country, punters have got one over the bookmakers at Cheltenham over the last five years with favourites returning a £1 level-stakes profit of £38.01. The stats would be even better if punters learned to pass over any favourites ridden by Tony McCoy. While McCoy's record here is excellent, his mounts are often sent off way too short, whereas Ruby Walsh is in profit with his rides, particularly for Paul Nicholls.

Favourites: Chase 30.8% -£5.97   Hurdle 37.4% +£43.98   All 34% +£38.01

New Course

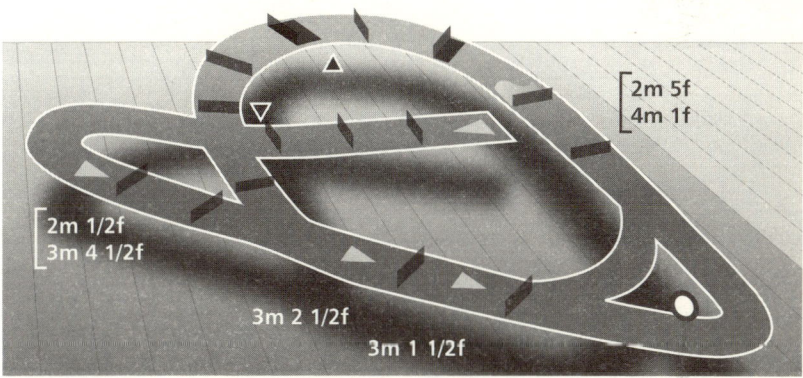

Hurdles

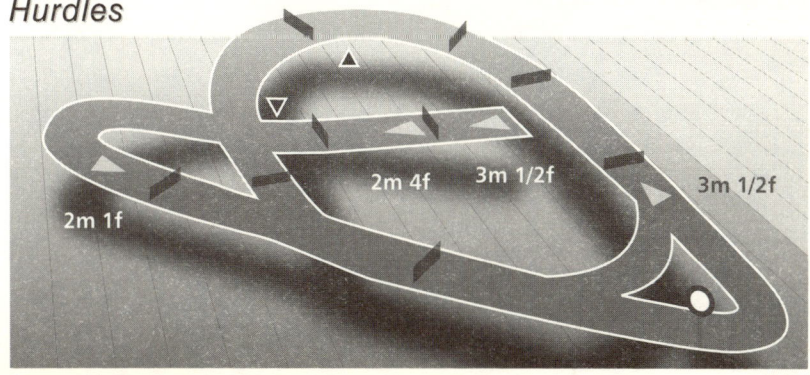

CHELTENHAM ctd

Trainers	Wins-Runs	%	Hurdles	Chases	£1 level stks
P Nolan	3-8	37.5	2-4	1-4	+20.83
E Bolger	5-17	29.4	0-0	5-17	+10.63
D Hughes	4-19	21.1	4-13	0-6	+37.50
P Haslam	3-15	20.0	2-11	1-4	-1.42
P Nicholls	51-316	16.1	22-107	29-203	-12.84
J Fanshawe	3-20	15.0	2-17	1-3	-7.88
P Bowen	4-29	13.8	4-16	0-12	-18.10
E O'Grady	3-22	13.6	3-11	0-11	-2.50
Mrs J Harrington	3-22	13.6	1-10	2-11	-5.75
Jonjo O'Neill	24-183	13.1	13-105	9-64	+8.09
M Harris	3-23	13.0	2-14	1-8	+24.50
R Phillips	3-24	12.5	0-10	2-11	+9.75
H Daly	7-57	12.3	1-12	6-43	-0.75
M Pipe	61-519	11.8	28-290	32-216	-13.01
C Egerton	3-26	11.5	2-17	1-5	+21.12
R Alner	4-36	11.1	0-13	4-23	-22.20
A King	12-109	11.0	8-75	4-28	-31.17
F Doumen	4-37	10.8	2-21	2-15	-4.75
N Henderson	19-177	10.7	3-72	14-96	-7.97

Old Course

Chases

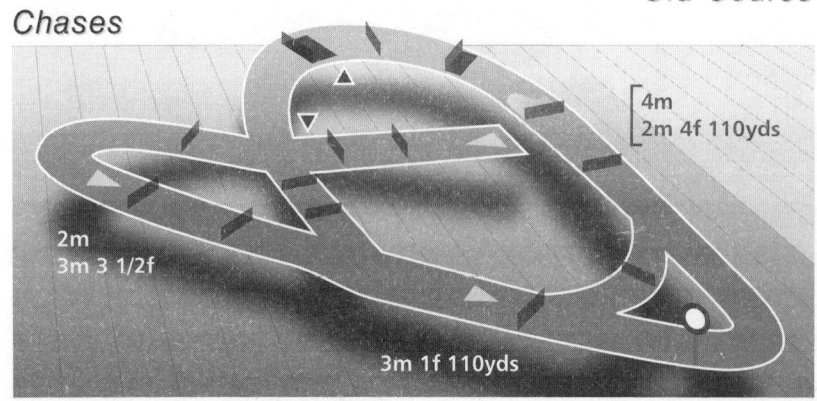

4m
2m 4f 110yds

2m
3m 3 1/2f

3m 1f 110yds

Hurdles

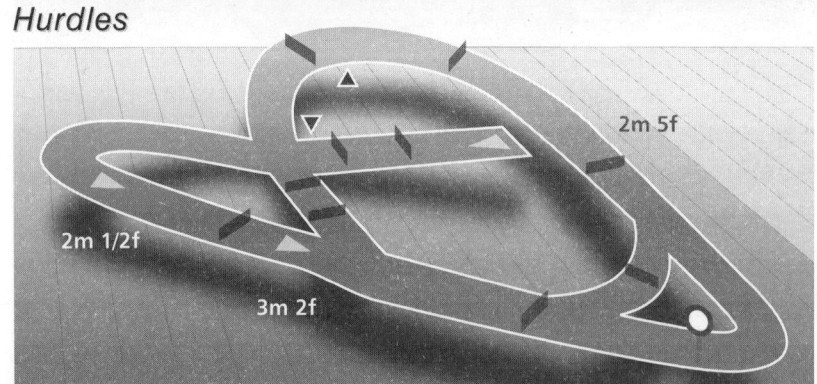

2m 5f

2m 1/2f

3m 2f

Jockeys	Wins-Rides	%	£1 level stks	Best Trainer	W-R
A Goschen	3-9	33.3	+9.33	P Nicholls	3-7
J T McNamara	5-22	22.7	+5.63	E Bolger	5-11
R Walsh	41-214	19.2	+4.77	P Nicholls	36-148
A McCoy	50-267	18.7	-63.71	M Pipe	23-133
N Williams	3-18	16.7	-5.62	R Barber	2-3
T J Murphy	35-222	15.8	+65.58	M Pipe	24-115
D N Russell	6-39	15.4	-4.50	F Murphy	4-12
O McPhail	3-20	15.0	+54.50	M Harris	2-11
D R Dennis	4-28	14.3	+2.50	I Williams	3-21
B J Geraghty	14-99	14.1	+39.75	Mrs J Harrington	3-11
A O'Keeffe	3-24	12.5	+31.33	P Haslam	1-1
R Johnson	27-216	12.5	-31.07	P Hobbs	18-128
R Thornton	16-143	11.2	+21.83	A King	10-81
L Cooper	4-36	11.1	-21.75	Jonjo O'Neill	4-33
N Williamson	3-28	10.7	-19.32	C Egerton	1-1
M Fitzgerald	17-159	10.7	-66.22	N Henderson	13-98
A Thornton	5-54	9.3	-30.20	R Alner	4-21
Paul Carberry	7-76	9.2	+9.16	N Meade	3-33
Christian Williams	7-80	8.8	-23.09	P Nicholls	3-46
T J Malone	3-36	8.3	+27.50	M Pipe	2-27

SPOT THEDIFFERENCE: largely responsible for JT McNamara's record here

CHEPSTOW

Chepstow, Gwent, NP6 5YH.
Tel: 01291 622260.

How to get there – Road: three mins west of Severn Bridge (M4). Rail: Chepstow

Features: LH undulating oval, nearly 2m round, suits long-striding front-runners

2006-07 Fixtures: Oct 7, 21, Nov 1, 22, Dec 2, 27, Jan 6, 19, Feb 2, 15, 24, Mar 10, 21, Apr 10, 14, 27

Winning Pointers: Paul Nicholls regularly sends his horses to the Welsh track but, despite a respectable strike-rate, they turn over a small loss. Nigel Twiston-Davies is more profitable to follow.

Chases

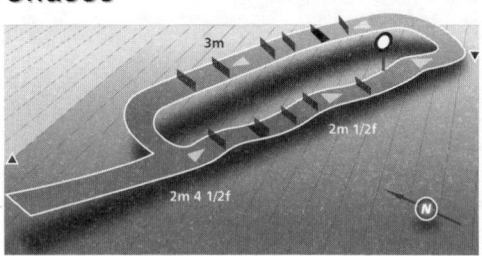

Hurdles

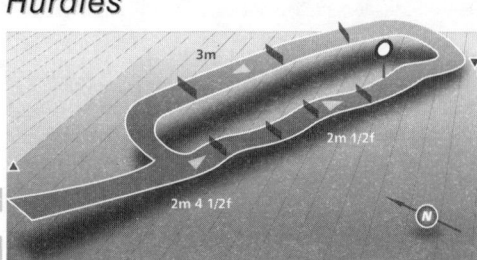

Favourites

Chase	37.3%	-£2.39
Hurdle	35.9%	-£14.36
Overall	36.5%	-£16.75

Trainers	Wins-Runs	%	Hurdles	Chases	£1 level stks
C Tinkler	3-8	37.5	2-6	0-0	+21.25
S Gollings	3-10	30.0	2-7	0-0	+18.20
P Nicholls	52-203	25.6	22-102	24-78	-27.18
A King	6-27	22.2	5-17	1-5	+2.45
N Twiston-Davies	21-97	21.6	9-52	8-32	+12.66
Miss G Browne	3-14	21.4	2-7	1-6	+12.50
P Hobbs	22-108	20.4	10-72	9-28	-3.38
J Portman	4-20	20.0	2-11	2-8	+6.00
N Henderson	4-21	19.0	2-14	1-6	+1.50
M J Evans	3-16	18.8	0-2	3-14	+5.33
P Bowen	6-32	18.8	4-17	2-13	-1.92
M Pipe	27-165	16.4	14-107	11-53	-65.80
Jonjo O'Neill	16-98	16.3	10-63	4-24	-17.60

Jockeys	Wins-Rides	%	£1 level stks	Best Trainer	W-R
E Williams	3-4	75.0	+5.42	E Williams	2-2
S Crawford	3-8	37.5	+3.38	N Twiston-Davies	3-6
R Walsh	26-84	31.0	-5.22	P Nicholls	25-80
A McCoy	27-106	25.5	-8.14	M Pipe	12-53
R Johnson	27-131	20.6	-13.08	P Hobbs	14-58
D Jacob	5-26	19.2	+21.75	D Keane	2-7
N Williams	3-16	18.8	+3.00	P Nicholls	2-4
L Cooper	5-27	18.5	-0.08	Jonjo O'Neill	5-27
M Fitzgerald	5-27	18.5	-0.12	N Henderson	3-8
P Flynn	7-39	17.9	-4.34	P Hobbs	6-20
P C O'Neill	3-17	17.6	+15.00	Miss V Williams	2-7
C Llewellyn	17-97	17.5	+59.78	N Twiston-Davies	15-64
T J Murphy	14-84	16.7	-7.30	M Pipe	6-29

Grand Stand, Leger Way,
Doncaster, DN2 6BB.
Tel: 01302 320066/7.

How to get there – Road: M18
Jctn 3, A638, A18 to Hull. Rail:
Doncaster Central

Features: LH, flat, 2m, run-in of
just over a furlong, rarely heavy,
speed horses are generally
favoured.

2006-07 Fixtures: Dec 8, 9, 23

Winning Pointers: Paul Nicholls
and Martin Pipe have long
played second fiddle at
Doncaster to the likes of Noel
Chance, Philip Hobbs, Jonjo
O'Neill and Venetia Williams.

Chases

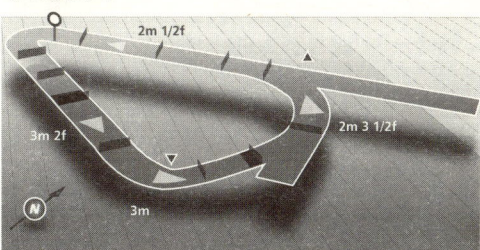

Hurdles

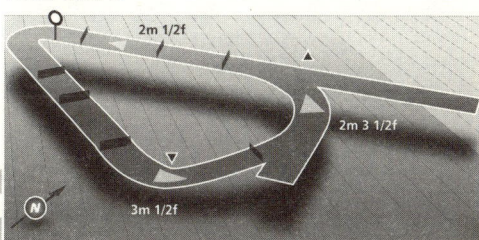

Favourites

Chase	24.4%	-£26.71
Hurdle	38.2%	+£17.80
Overall	32.3%	-£8.92

Trainers	Wins-Runs	%	Hurdles	Chases	£1 level stks
N Chance	3-7	42.9	3-5	0-1	+3.33
P Hobbs	6-15	40.0	1-5	5-10	+13.13
R Phillips	3-9	33.3	1-7	1-1	+4.38
M Pitman	3-10	30.0	1-3	2-7	+16.50
Jonjo O'Neill	8-27	29.6	7-17	1-7	+5.31
T Tate	3-11	27.3	0-2	2-4	+2.38
C Mann	4-16	25.0	3-12	1-4	+21.25
T George	4-16	25.0	3-7	1-9	+23.50
Miss V Williams	10-40	25.0	3-16	7-24	+27.00
N Henderson	7-30	23.3	3-15	3-12	-7.81
H Daly	4-19	21.1	2-11	2-8	+1.75
P Nicholls	4-20	20.0	1-3	3-17	+2.33
M Pipe	5-25	20.0	1-10	3-14	-6.55

Jockeys	Wins-Rides	%	£1 level stks	Best Trainer	W-R
L Cooper	5-10	50.0	+13.18	Jonjo O'Neill	5-10
R P McNally	3-7	42.9	+7.83	P Nicholls	2-3
T J Malone	4-10	40.0	+11.08	M Pipe	3-6
S Thomas	9-28	32.1	+32.75	Miss V Williams	7-22
M Fitzgerald	3-10	30.0	-4.54	N Henderson	2-8
P J Brennan	7-24	29.2	+11.98	P Hobbs	4-6
B J Crowley	5-18	27.8	+40.33	M Francis	2-4
R Johnson	4-17	23.5	-4.12	P Hobbs	1-2
N Fehily	7-30	23.3	+17.63	C Mann	4-11
R Thornton	6-26	23.1	+4.31	J Fanshawe	2-2
J Culloty	5-22	22.7	+30.25	Miss H Knight	2-13
M Foley	4-19	21.1	+0.86	N Henderson	3-9
J M Maguire	4-21	19.0	+13.38	T Tate	3-6

EXETER

How to get there – Road: 5m south of M5, A38. Rail: Exeter

Features: RH, 2m, hilly, the half-mile home straight is all uphill, with a 300yds run-in

2006-07 Fixtures: Oct 4, 17, 31, Nov 7, 17, Dec 1, 14, 21, Jan 1, Feb 11, 25, Mar 6, 20, Apr 11, 17

Winning Pointers: Paul Nicholls may get plenty of winners here, but the prices are nothing to write home about, and he shows a level-stakes loss. Philip Hobbs does better from an even bigger sample, particularly when teaming up with Richard Johnson.

Chases

Hurdles

Favourites

Chase	33.5%	-£12.32
Hurdle	35.1%	-£27.13
Overall	34.5%	-£39.45

Trainers	Wins-Runs	%	Hurdles	Chases	£1 level stks
C G Cox	4-12	33.3	3-6	1-5	+35.25
Mrs L Taylor	5-18	27.8	2-5	3-12	+31.00
H Daly	6-25	24.0	4-9	0-13	+2.74
P Hobbs	54-242	22.3	29-145	25-88	-21.53
Mrs A Thorpe	5-23	21.7	5-21	0-2	+44.00
D Gandolfo	3-14	21.4	3-11	0-3	-0.25
N Henderson	7-36	19.4	3-19	3-11	+12.62
Miss H Knight	14-73	19.2	6-34	7-34	+30.71
T George	7-37	18.9	2-20	5-17	+15.91
P Bowen	4-22	18.2	3-16	1-5	+16.75
P Nicholls	29-162	17.9	16-80	11-67	-59.90
E Williams	4-24	16.7	3-16	1-8	+32.00
K Bishop	12-76	15.8	10-43	2-27	+26.02

Jockeys	Wins-Rides	%	£1 level stks	Best Trainer	W-R
W A Worthington	3-7	42.9	-2.73	I Williams	3-6
N Williams	5-17	29.4	+18.63	P Nicholls	2-6
R Johnson	52-199	26.1	-3.89	P Hobbs	43-145
R Walsh	15-69	21.7	-23.66	P Nicholls	14-62
A McCoy	34-160	21.3	-4.30	M Pipe	21-88
M Bradburne	9-48	18.8	-2.67	C G Cox	3-6
J P McNamara	5-31	16.1	+20.00	K Bailey	2-9
J Culloty	9-57	15.8	+12.80	Miss H Knight	9-37
R Thornton	13-89	14.6	-31.00	A King	7-41
C Llewellyn	8-55	14.5	+67.75	N Twiston-Davies	4-33
T J Murphy	16-110	14.5	+5.86	M Pipe	8-44
M Foley	5-35	14.3	-9.75	J Auvray	1-1
M Fitzgerald	6-44	13.6	-10.39	N Henderson	4-17

The Racecourse, Fakenham, Norfolk,
NR21 7NY. Tel 01328 862 388

FAKENHAM

How to get there – Road:
A1065 from Swaffham, A148
Kings Lynn, A1067 from
Norwich. Rail: Kings Lynn,
Norwich

Features: LH, 1m round,
undulating, a run-in of little more
than a furlong, unsuitable for
long-striding horses

2006-07 Fixtures: Oct 20, Nov
14, Dec 4, 20, Jan 15, Feb 16,
Mar 16, Apr 9

Winning Pointers: Some outstanding strike-rates on show
here, not least from James
Fanshawe. Timmy Murphy rides
the track well on his rare visits.

Chases

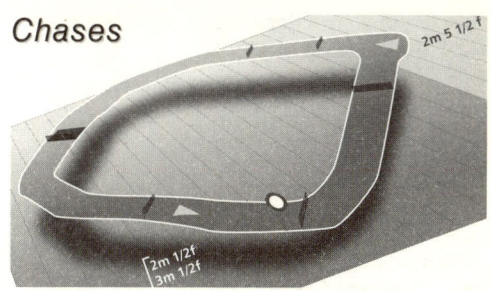

Hurdles

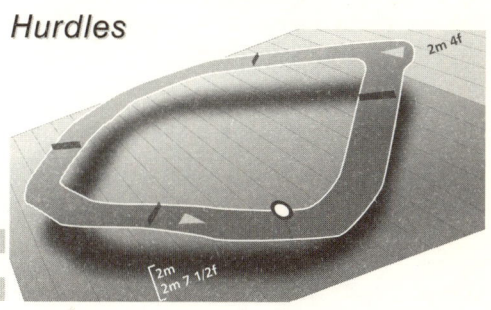

Favourites

Chase	37.2%	-£0.49
Hurdle	32.6%	-£6.34
Overall	34.6%	-£6.83

Trainers	Wins-Runs	%	Hurdles	Chases	£1 level stks
J Fanshawe	3-4	75.0	3-4	0-0	+22.01
M Bradstock	3-6	50.0	1-2	2-4	+9.88
A Blackmore	6-13	46.2	6-12	0-1	+20.25
P Nicholls	6-15	40.0	1-6	5-9	-1.30
C Mann	8-23	34.8	3-10	5-12	+9.00
Mrs J Buckley	3-10	30.0	0-1	3-8	+17.17
J S Smith	3-10	30.0	1-4	2-6	+6.50
J Jefferson	3-11	27.3	2-4	1-5	+2.00
N Chance	3-11	27.3	2-8	0-0	-1.24
A King	3-12	25.0	1-3	1-5	-2.07
Mrs H Dalton	4-17	23.5	0-7	4-9	+18.38
N Twiston-Davies	3-13	23.1	1-5	1-6	-7.62
Jonjo O'Neill	3-15	20.0	1-9	2-5	-8.57

Jockeys	Wins-Rides	%	£1 level stks	Best Trainer	W-R
C Honour	13-39	33.3	+39.00	A Blackmore	6-13
T J Murphy	5-16	31.3	+35.25	J S Smith	2-2
R Flavin	3-10	30.0	+17.00	G Brown	2-3
A McCoy	9-30	30.0	-8.29	J Fanshawe	2-2
G Lee	3-11	27.3	-0.50	J Jefferson	2-5
N Fehily	11-45	24.4	+19.26	C Mann	5-12
M Bradburne	4-18	22.2	+1.25	H Daly	2-3
A Tinkler	3-14	21.4	+18.00	J A Harris	1-1
S Durack	3-14	21.4	-5.02	S Kirk	1-1
B J Crowley	3-14	21.4	+0.62	Miss V Williams	3-10
H Oliver	3-14	21.4	+0.33	R C Guest	3-12
J E Moore	4-19	21.1	-1.02	O Brennan	3-7
W Marston	7-36	19.4	+8.83	Mrs P Sly	5-21

FOLKESTONE

Westenhanger, Hythe, Kent.
Tel: 01303 266407.

How to get there – Road: M20 Jctn 11, A20 nr Westenhanger. Rail: Westenhanger

Features: RH, easy-turning, undulating, about 1m3f round

2006-07 Fixtures: Nov 14, 27, Dec 12, Jan 2, 16, 30, Feb 13, 28

Winning Pointers: Nicky Henderson's record of 11 winners from 23 runners is brilliant, even if the main man Mick Fitzgerald isn't normally on board – Marcus Foley and Andrew Tinkler have both done well on Henderson inmates.

Chases

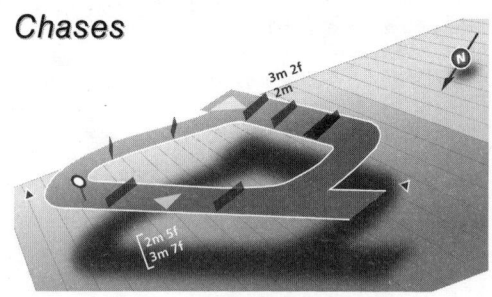

Hurdles

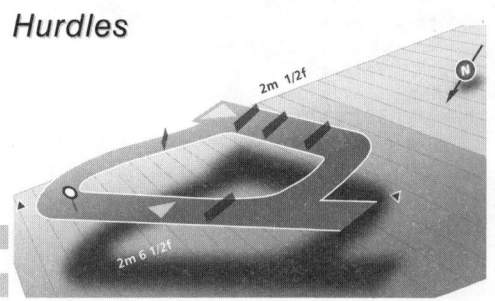

Favourites

Chase	40.6%	+£21.43
Hurdle	36.3%	-£2.56
Overall	38.4%	+£18.87

Trainers

	Wins-Runs	%	Hurdles	Chases	£1 level stks
G Landau	3-4	75.0	0-0	3-4	+16.20
P Bowen	3-6	50.0	1-2	2-3	+13.00
N Henderson	11-23	47.8	5-13	2-5	+16.47
J King	4-9	44.4	0-1	4-8	+6.58
M Hogan	4-11	36.4	4-7	0-4	+9.75
Mrs S Alner	3-9	33.3	0-0	3-9	+5.95
P Nicholls	13-39	33.3	6-19	6-16	-6.37
H Morrison	3-10	30.0	2-8	0-1	+2.61
M Pipe	8-31	25.8	7-26	0-4	-4.80
M Pitman	11-46	23.9	8-27	2-11	+2.28
N Chance	4-18	22.2	3-11	0-0	0.00
O Sherwood	6-27	22.2	2-8	1-13	+8.38
Miss E Lavelle	3-14	21.4	1-7	2-5	-4.75

Jockeys

	Wins-Rides	%	£1 level stks	Best Trainer	W-R
R Burton	3-4	75.0	+16.20	G Landau	3-3
D Jacob	3-5	60.0	+7.40	R Alner	1-1
A Hickman	3-9	33.3	+11.00	Mrs S Hickman	2-5
M Foley	6-19	31.6	+5.45	N Henderson	2-3
R Walsh	8-26	30.8	-3.74	P Nicholls	8-25
A McCoy	15-51	29.4	-5.80	M Pipe	4-11
A Tinkler	6-22	27.3	+3.42	N Henderson	4-7
S Thomas	7-28	25.0	-3.10	Miss V Williams	6-20
Christian Williams	4-17	23.5	-8.43	D L Williams	2-3
S Durack	5-23	21.7	-0.50	M Pitman	2-8
T J Murphy	11-55	20.0	-7.60	M Pitman	6-16
J Morgan	3-16	18.8	+58.75	L Wells	3-14
B J Crowley	6-34	17.6	-5.25	Miss V Williams	3-14

Sponsored by Stan James

Fontwell Park, Nr Arundel,
W Sussex BN18 0SX
Tel 01243 543 335

How to get there – Road: A29
to Bognor Regis. Rail: Barnham

Features: 1m4f LH, quite sharp.
Last fence gets plenty of fallers

2006-07 Fixtures: Nov 3, 12, 26,
Dec 5, 23, Jan 4, 25, Feb 4, 18,
Mar 7, 18, Apr 10, 26

Winning Pointers: Gary Moore
only sneaks in at the bottom of
our top trainer list, but given the
size of the sample his stats hold
up incredibly well with a 21 per
cent strike-rate and a level-
stakes profit. In keeping with
Moore's record, son Jamie rides
the track as well as anyone.

FONTWELL

Chases

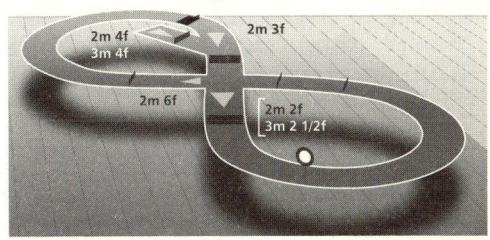

Hurdles

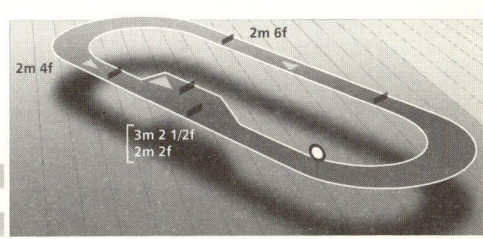

Favourites

Chase	30.2%	-£56.79
Hurdle	30.1%	-£71.06
Overall	30.2%	-£127.85

Trainers	Wins-Runs	%	Hurdles	Chases	£1 level stks
G Wareham	5-12	41.7	2-5	3-7	+16.10
S Dow	8-20	40.0	6-17	2-3	+9.98
I Williams	8-25	32.0	6-19	2-6	-5.60
V Dartnall	5-17	29.4	3-12	1-4	+11.95
M Pipe	36-138	26.1	25-104	6-27	-13.92
P Bowen	9-36	25.0	3-20	6-14	+16.33
N Chance	4-17	23.5	4-16	0-1	-4.12
Mrs L Taylor	3-13	23.1	0-3	3-10	+20.00
P Nicholls	24-104	23.1	9-44	12-49	-45.75
J Auvray	4-18	22.2	4-14	0-3	+20.25
Miss S West	6-27	22.2	6-25	0-1	+62.75
Miss H Knight	7-32	21.9	5-22	2-10	+11.73
G L Moore	50-230	21.7	37-155	12-68	+16.00

Jockeys	Wins-Rides	%	£1 level stks	Best Trainer	W-R
N Harris	3-6	50.0	+38.50	J Scott	1-2
R Stephens	4-10	40.0	+13.25	A Ennis	1-1
W McCarthy	3-9	33.3	+8.00	T George	2-4
R Walsh	8-25	32.0	-5.48	P Nicholls	8-23
A McCoy	47-151	31.1	-19.11	M Pipe	17-46
E J Jones	4-14	28.6	+9.33	B J Llewellyn	3-7
M Fitzgerald	15-59	25.4	+48.51	N Henderson	7-24
J Culloty	5-21	23.8	+3.33	Miss H Knight	2-9
D R Dennis	4-17	23.5	-2.90	I Williams	3-7
W Kennedy	4-18	22.2	+6.82	A Ennis	2-3
T J Malone	5-23	21.7	+2.94	M Pipe	4-10
J E Moore	31-144	21.5	+45.14	G L Moore	19-96
R P McNally	5-24	20.8	-8.00	P Nicholls	5-14

HAYDOCK

Newton-Le-Willows, Lancashire, WA12 0HQ. Tel: 01942 725963.

How to get there – Road: M6 Jctn 23 on A49 to Wigan. Rail: Wigan or Warrington Bank Quay (main line)

Features: 1m5f round, flat, with a quarter-mile run-in, chase course suits galloping-types, hurdles track is sharper

2006-07 Fixtures: Oct 19, Nov 2, 18, Dec 16, 30, Jan 6, 20, Feb 17, 22, Apr 7

Winning Pointers: Never underestimate anything trained by Sue Smith here. Clearly many punters have fallen into that trap, though, as her horses yield a colossal £84.82 profit to £1 level stakes having been sent off at some huge prices.

Chases

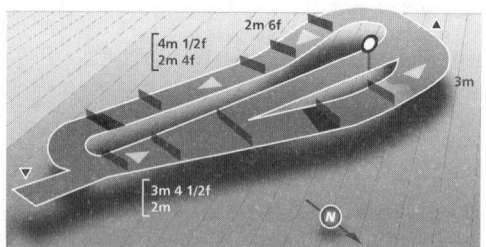

Hurdles

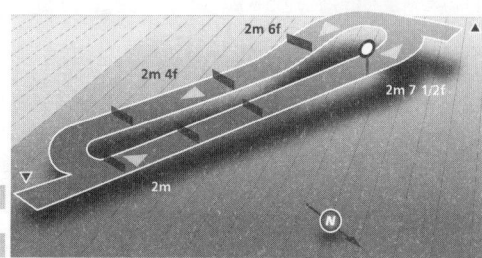

Favourites

Chase	29.7%	-£16.99
Hurdle	39.9%	+£28.33
Overall	35.9%	+£11.35

Trainers

Trainers	Wins-Runs	%	Hurdles	Chases	£1 level stks
D M Forster	3-5	60.0	0-0	3-4	+34.50
J Howard Johnson	10-30	33.3	8-22	2-8	+15.02
C Mann	3-12	25.0	0-4	3-7	+35.00
C Grant	3-12	25.0	2-8	1-4	+16.50
Jonjo O'Neill	24-108	22.2	17-78	2-18	-15.71
P R Webber	3-14	21.4	1-5	2-6	+7.50
A King	7-34	20.6	5-22	1-6	-0.75
Mrs S J Smith	28-136	20.6	13-73	15-54	+84.82
P Haslam	3-15	20.0	2-9	0-4	+5.20
D Keane	3-15	20.0	0-10	3-5	+2.50
N Henderson	6-30	20.0	2-12	2-10	-11.71
P Hobbs	10-51	19.6	5-31	5-15	-5.67
Miss V Williams	11-63	17.5	4-27	7-35	-9.96

Jockeys

Jockeys	Wins-Rides	%	£1 level stks	Best Trainer	W-R
J Kavanagh	3-8	37.5	+5.75	D M Forster	1-2
B J Geraghty	5-16	31.3	-3.75	Jonjo O'Neill	4-7
P J Brennan	4-14	28.6	+16.00	P Hobbs	2-8
T J Murphy	10-37	27.0	-1.32	M Pipe	3-10
J E Moore	6-23	26.1	+33.91	M Pipe	5-18
S Thomas	5-21	23.8	+1.05	Miss V Williams	5-18
F King	8-36	22.2	+12.00	J Jefferson	4-10
J Crowley	5-23	21.7	-2.13	M Barnes	1-1
R Walford	3-14	21.4	+25.00	T Walford	2-3
L Cooper	6-28	21.4	-3.50	Jonjo O'Neill	6-28
N Fehily	8-40	20.0	+38.25	C Mann	3-9
D Elsworth	18-90	20.0	+20.77	Mrs S J Smith	16-75
R Johnson	8-45	17.8	-15.00	P Hobbs	5-21

Roman Road, Holmer, Hereford
HR4 9QU. Tel 01981 250 436

HEREFORD

Chases

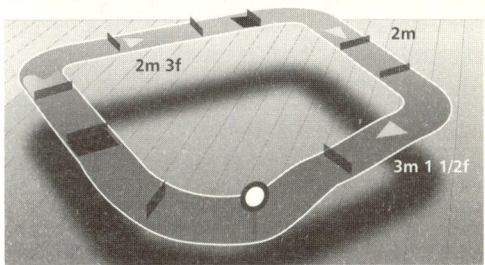

How to get there – Road: A49 1m north of Hereford. Rail: Hereford

Features: RH, 1m4f round, fences trickier than those at most minor tracks

2006-07 Fixtures: Oct 15, Nov 5, 16, 28, Dec 22, 23, Jan 11, 26, Feb 11, 26, Mar 5, 29, Apr 11

Winning Pointers: Alan King is the man to follow here, with his 16 winners helping him to a significant level-stakes profit. Ruby Walsh and Paul Nicholls win with 40 per cent of their runners, yet still show a small loss.

Hurdles

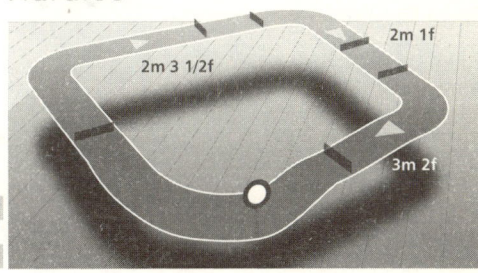

Favourites

Chase	32.1%	-£20.78
Hurdle	34.8%	-£25.38
Overall	33.7%	-£46.16

Trainers	Wins-Runs	%	Hurdles	Chases	£1 level stks
C Tinkler	4-8	50.0	4-6	0-0	+12.50
C Egerton	5-17	29.4	2-7	1-5	+5.66
M Pipe	24-91	26.4	17-67	7-20	-8.81
J Needham	3-12	25.0	1-7	2-3	+28.50
O Sherwood	6-24	25.0	4-13	1-8	-4.06
A King	16-64	25.0	11-43	5-14	+43.00
P Hobbs	21-89	23.6	12-45	9-41	-12.97
N Chance	4-17	23.5	3-12	1-3	-3.67
N Henderson	9-40	22.5	6-21	2-13	+19.00
P Nicholls	11-49	22.4	7-28	4-15	-18.87
J Mackie	4-18	22.2	4-17	0-1	-0.42
B Eckley	3-14	21.4	3-7	0-2	+52.00
B Ryall	4-19	21.1	0-2	4-17	+39.00

Jockeys	Wins-Rides	%	£1 level stks	Best Trainer	W-R
L Cummins	3-6	50.0	+12.50	Miss E Lavelle	2-2
R Walsh	6-15	40.0	-1.74	P Nicholls	6-15
Marc Barber	3-8	37.5	+4.90	H Daly	3-3
A McCoy	33-104	31.7	-20.29	M Pipe	15-35
K J Mercer	3-10	30.0	+1.00	F Murphy	3-9
R Stephens	3-11	27.3	+23.50	J Flint	1-1
L Stephens	9-40	22.5	+98.08	D Burchell	5-14
R Johnson	24-110	21.8	+26.01	P Hobbs	11-47
A Tinkler	5-25	20.0	-3.50	C Tinkler	2-6
R Thornton	20-100	20.0	+29.24	A King	12-41
J Culloty	9-48	18.8	+32.41	Miss H Knight	4-23
J M Maguire	11-64	17.2	+49.25	T George	7-30
R Biddlecombe	4-24	16.7	+9.75	Miss H Knight	2-6

HEXHAM

High Yarridge, Hexham,
Northumberland NE46 2JP.
Tel 01434 606 881

How to get there – Road: A69.
Rail: Hexham

Features: LH, 1m4f round, very
stiff, back straight runs downhill
most of the way and is followed
by a steep uphill run from the
bottom turn

2006-07 Fixtures: Oct 7, Nov 3,
15, Dec 6, Feb 5, Mar 15, Apr 1,
23

Winning Pointers: One of the
few tracks to have escaped the
clutches of Paul Nicholls and
Martin Pipe down the years, with
Len Lungo the most regular
figure in the winner's enclosure.
Tony Dobbin fits the bill for the
jockeys, but beware his enormous level-stakes loss.

Chases

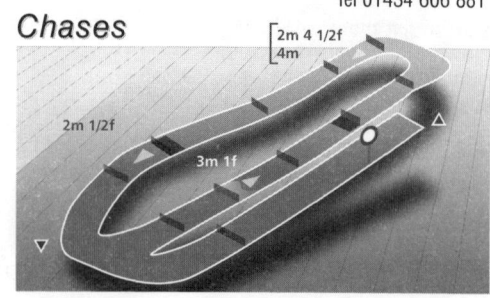

Hurdles

Favourites

Chase	28.4%	-£29.10
Hurdle	40.9%	-£13.48
Overall	35.8%	-£42.57

Trainers	Wins-Runs	%	Hurdles	Chases	£1 level stks
P R Webber	3-4	75.0	3-4	0-0	+0.57
Miss V Scott	4-10	40.0	2-7	2-2	+36.75
J J Quinn	5-15	33.3	3-13	1-1	+13.63
P Haslam	5-16	31.3	3-13	2-3	-0.75
H Hogarth	3-10	30.0	0-1	3-9	+13.50
N Richards	12-45	26.7	5-27	6-12	+12.42
G A Swinbank	7-31	22.6	2-20	0-1	-13.86
L Lungo	22-100	22.0	15-70	6-22	-10.66
R Fahey	4-19	21.1	2-13	1-3	-9.50
G Harker	4-19	21.1	0-5	0-5	+4.50
M Todhunter	11-60	18.3	8-34	3-21	+51.77
M D Hammond	7-39	17.9	4-18	3-18	-15.58
Mrs S J Smith	15-84	17.9	8-43	6-32	+20.10

Jockeys	Wins-Rides	%	£1 level stks	Best Trainer	W-R
J M Maguire	3-9	33.3	+26.00	T Tate	2-2
T Doyle	3-9	33.3	-4.81	P R Webber	2-2
P Robson	3-9	33.3	+10.25	Miss P Robson	1-1
A McCoy	4-12	33.3	-3.43	C Egerton	2-2
A Thornton	8-25	32.0	+17.29	P Haslam	2-3
M J McAlister	4-13	30.8	+54.00	M Smith	1-1
A Tinkler	3-12	25.0	+11.75	N Henderson	1-1
T Scudamore	3-12	25.0	-0.50	M Scudamore	2-9
D N Russell	6-31	19.4	-7.76	F Murphy	6-24
A Dobbin	30-157	19.1	-61.63	L Lungo	11-34
P Whelan	11-59	18.6	+29.50	R Fahey	3-15
K J Mercer	8-44	18.2	+17.25	F Murphy	5-21
L McGrath	8-44	18.2	+43.85	R C Guest	6-28

Brampton, Huntingdon, Cambs
PE18 8NN. Tel 01480 453373

HUNTINGDON

Chases

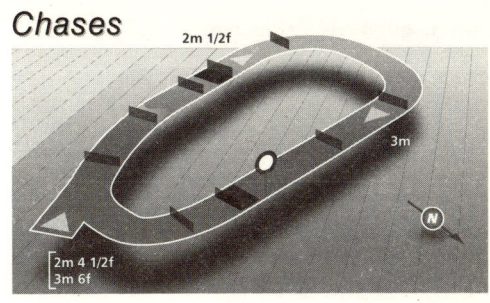

How to get there – Road: Off A14 Cambridge to Kettering road. Rail: Huntingdon

Features: RH, flat track, short 200yds run-in gets plenty horses beaten for toe

2006-07 Fixtures: Oct 3, Nov 1, 18, Dec 7, 26, Jan 12, 24, Feb 8, 22, Mar 4, 14, Apr 9

Winning Pointers: Charlie Egerton has done terrifically well with seven out of 14 hitting the target. From a bigger sample, Nicky Henderson and Venetia Williams have done well. Richard Johnson has an awesome level-stakes profit in the saddle.

Hurdles

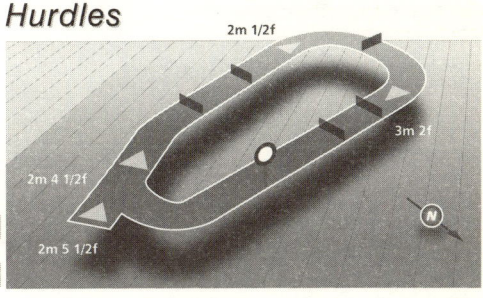

Favourites

Chase	33.6%	-£34.30
Hurdle	31.9%	-£29.87
Overall	32.7%	-£64.17

Trainers

Trainers	Wins-Runs	%	Hurdles	Chases	£1 level stks
C Egerton	7-14	50.0	6-12	1-2	+30.00
J Fanshawe	3-7	42.9	2-6	1-1	+5.80
Mrs P Dutfield	4-10	40.0	4-9	0-0	+23.83
D Cantillon	7-20	35.0	7-15	0-3	+2.92
R Ford	4-12	33.3	4-7	0-5	+19.50
Miss S West	3-10	30.0	3-10	0-0	+27.75
K G Reveley	11-38	28.9	6-18	2-13	+17.94
E Williams	4-14	28.6	1-8	3-6	+5.75
P Hobbs	12-44	27.3	6-19	6-23	-8.37
N Henderson	15-59	25.4	11-36	2-15	+1.43
Miss V Williams	13-52	25.0	5-21	8-29	+27.91
R Lee	9-37	24.3	0-13	9-24	+28.08
T George	12-55	21.8	5-21	6-30	+52.76

Jockeys

Jockeys	Wins-Rides	%	£1 level stks	Best Trainer	W-R
R Burton	3-7	42.9	+12.88	G Landau	1-1
P Gundry	3-5	60.0	+8.00	Mrs O Bush	1-1
S Curling	4-8	50.0	+37.58	N Henderson	3-4
P Kinsella	3-7	42.9	+7.00	K G Reveley	2-5
D Gallagher	3-7	42.9	+8.50	P R Webber	2-3
R Walsh	5-13	38.5	+1.48	P Nicholls	5-10
J Crowley	5-14	35.7	+3.55	K G Reveley	4-5
R McGrath	6-19	31.6	+22.76	K G Reveley	4-11
R Johnson	28-89	31.5	+52.14	H Daly	9-16
J Culloty	17-63	27.0	+28.98	Miss H Knight	7-31
S Morris	4-15	26.7	+61.80	W Warner	2-4
A McCoy	22-91	24.2	-22.36	Jonjo O'Neill	5-34
L Cooper	4-20	20.0	+9.60	Jonjo O'Neill	4-20

KELSO

Kelso, Roxburghshire.
Tel 01668 281 611

How to get there – Road: 1m north of Kelso on B6461 to Ednam. Rail: Berwick on Tweed

Features: Tight, LH, hurdles course is 1m2f round, chase course 1m3f, quarter-mile run-in

2006-07 Fixtures: Oct 1, 21, Nov 4, 17, Dec 3, Jan 12, 28, Feb 15, Mar 3, Apr 2, 15

Winning Pointers: It's a massive trek from Lambourn to Kelso, so little wonder Noel Chance likes to make it pay – he's won with four out of five runners. The Richards-Dobbin partnership has done well without making punters rich.

Chases

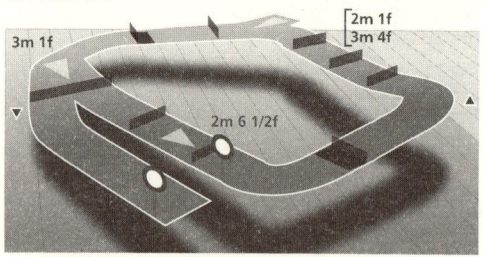

Hurdles

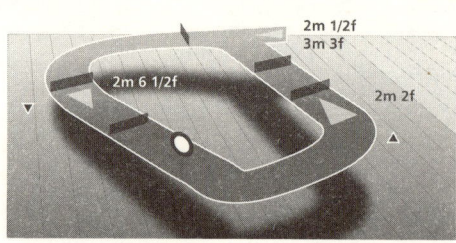

Favourites

Chase	29.6%	-£37.25
Hurdle	38.7%	-£15.20
Overall	34.5%	-£52.45

Trainers	Wins-Runs	%	Hurdles	Chases	£1 level stks
N Chance	4-5	80.0	3-4	1-1	+3.53
R Ford	4-10	40.0	1-4	3-6	-0.25
N Twiston-Davies	3-8	37.5	1-4	2-3	+2.88
P Nicholls	3-8	37.5	0-4	3-4	-3.17
G Bewley	3-8	37.5	0-0	3-8	+9.10
Mrs S J Smith	10-29	34.5	5-11	5-18	+10.34
S Marshall	7-22	31.8	1-6	6-16	+74.00
P Bowen	3-10	30.0	2-7	1-3	-3.23
N Richards	25-89	28.1	21-73	4-14	-3.27
J O'Keeffe	3-12	25.0	3-9	0-2	+8.08
P Haslam	5-20	25.0	4-15	1-5	+7.70
T Easterby	6-25	24.0	2-12	4-13	-0.75
J R Turner	3-14	21.4	0-8	3-6	+5.50

Jockeys	Wins-Rides	%	£1 level stks	Best Trainer	W-R
W Marston	4-13	30.8	+8.43	R Phillips	2-2
D Elsworth	10-36	27.8	+7.84	Mrs S J Smith	9-21
A Dobbin	49-179	27.4	-1.57	N Richards	19-36
M J McAlister	6-23	26.1	+52.61	S Marshall	4-7
A McCoy	4-16	25.0	-8.98	P Bowen	2-5
D Jewett	4-17	23.5	+12.13	R Kyle	1-1
T J Dreaper	3-13	23.1	-3.25	F Murphy	2-5
J P McNamara	3-15	20.0	-7.17	G A Swinbank	2-2
B Storey	6-33	18.2	+9.50	A Parker	3-8
R Davidson	4-23	17.4	+10.00	Mrs H Graham	2-6
R Garritty	6-44	13.6	-14.25	T Easterby	3-15
M Bradburne	9-69	13.0	-16.75	Mrs S Bradburne	6-36
N Hannity	3-24	12.5	-6.00	G Harker	3-14

KEMPTON

How to get there – Road: M3
Jctn 1, A308 towards Kingston-
on-Thames
Rail: Kempton Park from Waterloo

Features: A sharp RH track with
the emphasis very much on
speed

2006-07 Fixtures: Oct 14, Nov
7, 21, Dec 26, 27, Jan 13, Feb 9,
24, Mar 3, 28

Winning Pointers: One of the
few tracks at which Tony McCoy
turns over a profit – despite his
former employer Martin Pipe not
having the best of records.
Philip Hobbs is the track's most
regular supporter.

Chases

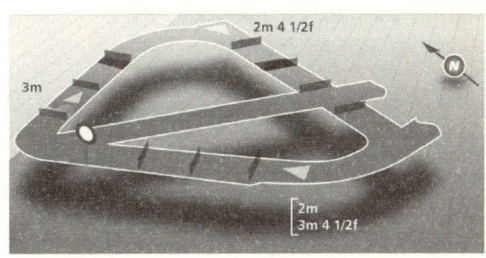

Hurdles

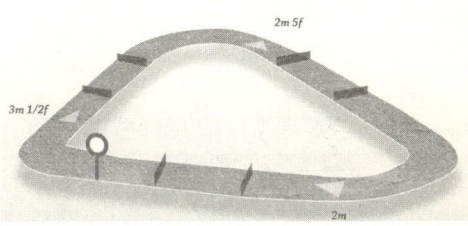

Favourites

Chase	41.7%	+£19.86
Hurdle	33.0%	-£30.79
Overall	37.1%	-£10.94

Trainers	Wins-Runs	%	Hurdles	Chases	£1 level stks
C L Tizzard	3-10	30.0	1-5	1-4	+48.00
V Dartnall	3-10	30.0	2-7	1-2	-4.34
P Bowen	4-14	28.6	3-10	1-4	+7.83
P Nicholls	13-57	22.8	5-26	8-31	-8.52
R Phillips	3-14	21.4	0-7	2-6	+1.50
I Williams	4-20	20.0	2-12	2-7	+30.50
P Hobbs	19-95	20.0	10-50	9-41	-9.42
Jonjo O'Neill	8-42	19.0	6-26	1-13	-21.25
J R Dest	3 16	18.8	0-3	3-11	-4.50
G Balding	3-16	18.8	2-10	1-6	-0.50
N Henderson	18-97	18.6	8-46	9-44	-16.86
N Twiston-Davies	7-38	18.4	6-22	1-11	-9.13
Miss V Williams	8-52	15.4	4-23	4-28	+16.13

Jockeys	Wins-Rides	%	£1 level stks	Best Trainer	W-R
T Doumen	3-9	33.3	+15.00	F Doumen	2-7
A McCoy	22-68	32.4	+6.20	M Pipe	8-30
R Biddlecombe	3-10	30.0	+8.50	N Twiston-Davies	3-6
B J Geraghty	3-15	20.0	-2.50	T Taaffe	1-2
R Walsh	10-52	19.2	-4.81	P Nicholls	8-40
M Fitzgerald	15-81	18.5	-26.24	N Henderson	9-55
P Flynn	4-22	18.2	-7.50	P Hobbs	4-15
W Marston	4-22	18.2	+9.25	R Phillips	2-4
C Llewellyn	5-33	15.2	-5.63	N Twiston-Davies	4-21
R Johnson	13-86	15.1	-41.09	P Hobbs	9-53
J Culloty	8-54	14.8	+8.37	Miss H Knight	6-37
S Durack	6-41	14.6	+10.00	A Balding	1-1
S Thomas	4-28	14.3	+22.00	Miss V Williams	4-24

LEICESTER

How to get there – Road: On A6, 2m south of city centre, 5m from M1 Jctn 21. Rail: Leicester

Features: RH, 1m6f round, stiffish uphill run-in

2006-07 Fixtures: Nov 13, 26, 30, Dec 6, 28, Jan 9, 23, 31, Feb 14, 27, Mar 9

Winning Pointers: Kevin Bishop has an astonishing level-stakes profit, but that will always happen with small samples. Robert Alner's impressive record is more significant, as is the more than respectable strike-rate of Venetia Williams.

Chases

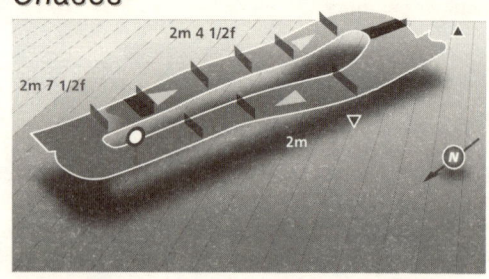

Hurdles

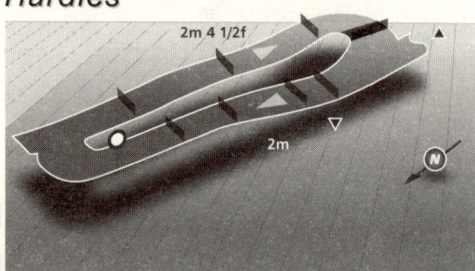

Favourites

Chase	35.2%	-£24.82
Hurdle	31.5%	-£18.49
Overall	33.7%	-£43.31

Trainers

Trainers	Wins-Runs	%	Hurdles	Chases	£1 level stks
K Bishop	3-6	50.0	0-1	3-5	+95.50
P Nicholls	4-9	44.4	1-3	3-6	+2.02
R Alner	9-31	29.0	2-10	7-21	+17.13
N Twiston-Davies	7-25	28.0	3-10	4-15	+2.51
A King	8-29	27.6	6-15	2-14	+3.08
Miss V Williams	14-54	25.9	4-21	10-33	-8.48
S T Lewis	4-16	25.0	2-13	2-3	+40.25
O Sherwood	4-17	23.5	4-9	0-8	+6.83
B J Llewellyn	3-13	23.1	3-12	0-1	+5.50
I Williams	6-29	20.7	4-11	2-18	+47.50
M Pipe	10-49	20.4	8-40	2-9	+6.50
N Henderson	4-20	20.0	0-2	4-18	-13.52
J Old	4-21	19.0	2-8	2-13	-1.73

Jockeys

Jockeys	Wins-Rides	%	£1 level stks	Best Trainer	W-R
D Jacob	3-4	75.0	+22.83	R Alner	2-2
L Stephens	3-5	60.0	+18.50	Miss V Williams	2-2
A McCoy	16-42	38.1	+22.54	M Pipe	3-9
P C O'Neill	4-13	30.8	+6.75	Miss V Williams	2-4
B Fenton	4-13	30.8	+19.69	B De Haan	1-1
T J Dreaper	3-11	27.3	+28.50	J Jefferson	2-3
J Tizzard	5-19	26.3	+17.29	S Sherwood	2-5
T J Murphy	9-38	23.7	+2.20	M Pipe	3-16
M Foley	6-26	23.1	+52.91	S T Lewis	3-7
P Flynn	5-25	20.0	-3.22	P R Webber	2-2
S Thomas	8-40	20.0	-18.72	Miss V Williams	8-33
A Thornton	9-49	18.4	-25.42	R Alner	6-19
R Thornton	9-50	18.0	+0.33	A King	6-20

Lingfield, Surrey, RH7 6PQ.
Tel: 01342 834800

LINGFIELD

How to get there – Road: M25 Jctn 6, south on A22.

Rail: Lingfield (from London Bridge and Victoria)

Features: LH, hilly, 1m4f round

2006-07 Fixtures: Nov 8, 22, Dec 9, Jan 4, 26, Feb 21, Mar 8, 21

Winning Pointers: A fairly limited sample of stats for the Surrey track given the scarcity of jumps meetings in recent years, but Paul Nicholls is in profit, as was Martin Pipe prior to his retirement. Andrew Thornton rides well around here, particularly for Robert Alner.

Chases

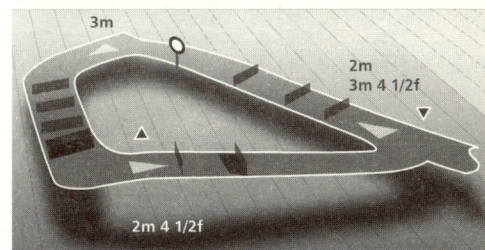

Hurdles

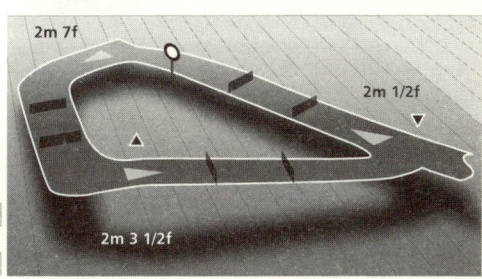

Favourites

Chase	31.0%	-£13.95
Hurdle	30.5%	-£10.21
Overall	30.7%	-£24.17

Trainers	Wins-Runs	%	Hurdles	Chases	£1 level stks
Nick Williams	2-4	50.0	2-2	0-1	+4.50
C Tinkler	2-4	50.0	1-3	1-1	+7.75
K Bishop	2-5	40.0	0-1	2-4	+7.40
M Pipe	5-17	29.4	1-7	4-9	+17.50
P Nicholls	6-22	27.3	2-7	4-14	+8.62
T George	4-15	26.7	1-4	3-10	+3.19
N Henderson	4-17	23.5	1-7	3-9	-3.92
J Mullins	3-13	23.1	1-7	1-1	+4.00
A King	3-14	21.4	1-4	0-3	+2.10
R Alner	6-30	20.0	4-11	2-19	+3.00
G L Moore	7-45	15.6	3-26	3-14	+27.16
Jonjo O'Neill	3-20	15.0	2-9	1-11	+1.50

Jockeys	Wins-Rides	%	£1 level stks	Best Trainer	W-R
L Stephens	3-5	60.0	+18.50	Miss V Williams	2-2
Christian Williams	4-8	50.0	+9.62	P Nicholls	4-6
M Foley	3-7	42.9	+9.33	N Henderson	2-4
A Thornton	10-37	27.0	+22.12	R Alner	6-21
A McCoy	5-19	26.3	-6.13	T Doumen	1-1
A Tinkler	2-8	25.0	+£2.38	C Tinkler	1-1
M Fitzgerald	4-18	22.2	-7.50	N Henderson	2-10
P Hide	7-34	20.6	+75.83	G L Moore	5-16
J A McCarthy	3-18	16.7	+0.50	Mrs Jeremy Young	1-1
T Doyle	3-20	15.0	-6.50	D Gandolfo	1-2
R Johnson	3-20	15.0	-3.75	M Pipe	1-1
J E Moore	3-28	10.7	-3.17	P S McEntee	1-2

LUDLOW

Bromfield, Ludlow, Shrewsbury, Shropshire. Tel 01981 250 052

How to get there – Road: 2m north of Ludlow on A49. Rail: Ludlow

Features: Flat, RH, sharp corners and a testing run-in of 450yds.

2006-07 Fixtures: Oct 12, 19, Nov 9, 20, Dec 7, 21, Jan 8, 18, 29, Feb 7, 21, Mar 1, 22

Winning Pointers: Nicky Henderson does very well here, and this is another track where Ian Williams, another underrated handler, has had the odd long-priced winner. Charlotte Stucley has been successful in a few hunter chases around here.

Chases

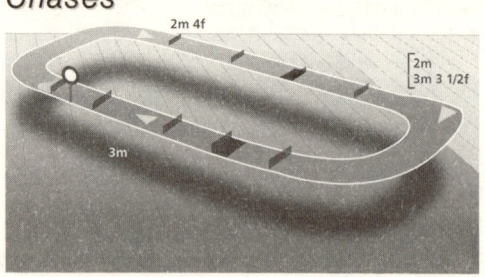

Hurdles

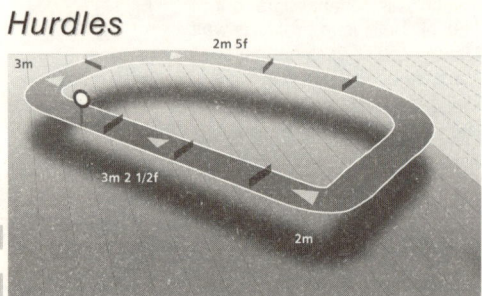

Favourites

Chase	32.5%	-£35.94
Hurdle	28.7%	-£63.56
Overall	30.2%	-£99.49

Trainers	Wins-Runs	%	Hurdles	Chases	£1 level stks
C Tinkler	6-17	35.3	2-11	0-1	+11.75
N Henderson	18-65	27.7	10-41	3-13	+29.61
Mrs H Dalton	6-24	25.0	5-13	1-7	+52.66
P Nicholls	14-60	23.3	3-23	10-31	+11.45
Miss E Lavelle	3-13	23.1	2-8	1-5	+3.00
G Balding	4-18	22.2	3-8	1-5	+6.13
P Hobbs	21-95	22.1	8-50	11-35	-32.14
E Williams	11-52	21.2	7-20	3-27	+6.57
I Williams	15-74	20.3	9-36	5-34	+110.24
Mrs L Williamson	4-20	20.0	0-8	4-10	+3.25
O Sherwood	10-55	18.2	4-28	4-18	-10.50
C Mann	5-28	17.9	5-20	0-6	-2.75
M Pipe	18-106	17.0	13-75	5-28	-42.56

Jockeys	Wins-Rides	%	£1 level stks	Best Trainer	W-R
Jim Crowley	3-5	60.0	+10.25	T G Dascombe	2-2
P Stringer	3-6	50.0	+76.00	S T Lewis	2-3
C Stucley	3-6	50.0	+26.00	Miss B Lewis	1-1
T Best	3-7	42.9	+14.88	G Balding	3-6
W A Worthington	4-12	33.3	+8.58	I Williams	3-6
A Tinkler	10-34	29.4	+14.62	C Tinkler	6-11
R Johnson	29-122	23.8	-2.58	P Hobbs	13-47
B Fenton	7-30	23.3	+32.00	C Hemsley	2-2
A McCoy	30-129	23.3	-40.61	M Pipe	7-29
J Culloty	14-66	21.2	+36.64	Miss H Knight	11-42
Christian Williams	13-64	20.3	+24.01	P Nicholls	6-22
D Mansell	3-15	20.0	+18.00	S Flook	3-5
T J Murphy	18-98	18.4	+7.98	Miss H Knight	6-22

Legsby Rd, Mkt Rasen,
Lincolnshire LN8 3EA. Tel
01673 843434

MARKET RASEN

Chases

How to get there – Road: A46 to Market Rasen, course on A631. Rail: Market Rasen (1m)

Features: RH, easy fences, run-in of 250yds

2006-07 Fixtures: Oct 1, Nov 5, 16, 30, Dec 26, Feb 6, 19, Mar 11, 19, Apr 15, 28

Winning Pointers: Peter Bowen sends his runners here fairly regularly and has a very good strike rate. Charlie Mann and Nigel Twiston-Davies have more modest strike rates but they are often bigger value.

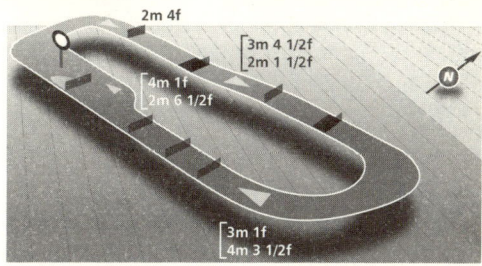

Hurdles

Favourites

Chase	34.4%	-£6.76
Hurdle	33.1%	-£26.51
Overall	33.6%	-£33.27

Trainers	Wins-Runs	%	Hurdles	Chases	£1 level stks
P Bowen	19-47	40.4	10-26	9-19	+35.29
A King	6-17	35.3	4-10	2-4	+1.38
N Chance	4-12	33.3	3-8	0-1	+1.90
C Egerton	5-15	33.3	3-11	2-3	-4.65
D Burchell	3-10	30.0	2-8	1-2	+15.50
P Haslam	4-14	28.6	4-13	0-1	+4.00
C Mann	11-41	26.8	6-26	5-15	+27.85
N Twiston-Davies	7-27	25.9	3-17	3-7	+36.00
L Dace	3-12	25.0	2-11	1-1	+28.00
H Daly	5-20	25.0	2-9	3-10	+16.48
R Gray	3-13	23.1	2-12	1-1	+9.50
G Harker	3-13	23.1	2-6	0-2	-3.76
G A Swinbank	4-18	22.2	1-8	1-4	+9.98

Jockeys	Wins-Rides	%	£1 level stks	Best Trainer	W-R
V Slattery	3-8	37.5	+55.00	P Hiatt	1-1
J Culloty	3-11	27.3	-0.80	Miss H Knight	2-7
B J Crowley	6-23	26.1	+10.29	Miss V Williams	5-17
A McCoy	32-129	24.8	-27.44	Jonjo O'Neill	13-65
G Carenza	8-34	23.5	+3.13	M W Easterby	4-10
P Merrigan	3-13	23.1	+4.50	Mrs H Dalton	2-5
Antony Evans	3-13	23.1	+34.00	N Twiston-Davies	2-5
R Flavin	3-13	23.1	+6.75	S Kirk	2-2
D Elsworth	15-69	21.7	+34.33	Mrs S J Smith	14-59
T J Murphy	10-50	20.0	+6.29	M Pipe	5-23
N Fehily	18-90	20.0	+53.40	C Mann	9-30
W Marston	13-67	19.4	-9.08	P Bowen	4-5
W Kennedy	8-42	19.0	-5.86	S Gollings	3-25

MUSSELBURGH

Musselburgh Racecourse, East Lothian. Tel: 01316 652859.

How to get there – Road: A1 east out of Edinburgh.

Rail: Musselburgh from Edinburgh

Features: RH, 1m2f round, almost perfectly flat, sharp bends favour handily-placed runners and pace-setters

2006-07 Fixtures: Nov 24, Dec 10, 20, 30, Jan 5, 19, Feb 4, 14

Winning Pointers: Richard Fahey is much better known for his exploits on the Flat but he does very well with his jumpers at the Edinburgh track. Graham Lee has ridden well, but may lack opportunities without the support of Howard Johnson.

Chases

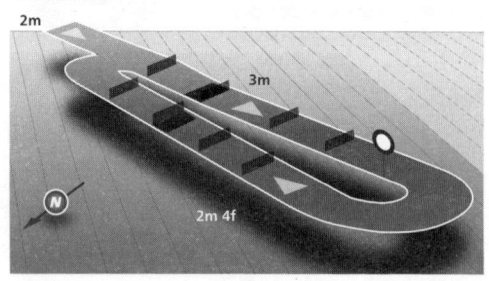

Hurdles

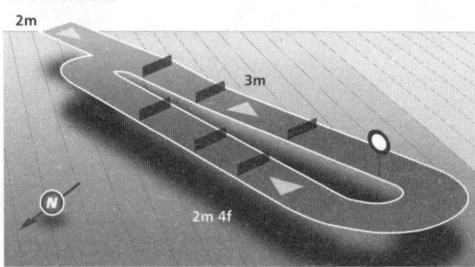

Favourites

Chase	30.3%	-£14.25
Hurdle	41.0%	-£9.28
Overall	37.2%	-£23.54

Trainers	Wins-Runs	%	Hurdles	Chases	£1 level stks
K Ryan	3-6	50.0	0-3	1-1	+3.87
D McCain	4-11	36.4	1-5	3-6	+14.00
S Donohoe	5-17	29.4	3-8	1-3	+9.25
L Lungo	16-59	27.1	9-31	6-19	+0.51
R Fahey	7-26	26.9	4-17	0-2	+14.50
T Easterby	3-12	25.0	1-4	1-6	+7.00
J Howard Johnson	22-90	24.4	17-73	3-7	-0.73
K G Reveley	8-38	21.1	4-21	3-11	+30.40
G A Swinbank	4-21	19.0	3-11	0-2	+6.55
Mrs M Reveley	5-29	17.2	2-14	2-6	-4.35
N Richards	5-31	16.1	3-20	2-7	-13.60
J Charlton	3-20	15.0	0-6	3-10	+24.75
A Parker	3-23	13.0	0-4	3-16	-11.85

Jockeys	Wins-Rides	%	£1 level stks	Best Trainer	W-R
A J McNamara	5-8	62.5	+18.25	S Donohoe	5-8
S J Craine	4-8	50.0	+31.50	D McCain	3-4
R Davidson	3-7	42.9	+5.30	N Richards	3-4
C F Swan	3-9	33.3	+2.20	C Swan	2-6
B Gibson	6-20	30.0	+0.90	L Lungo	6-11
G Lee	26-103	25.2	+13.31	J Howard Johnson	16-52
T Greenall	3-13	23.1	+6.25	M W Easterby	2-6
A McCoy	3-13	23.1	-8.44	M Pipe	2-5
J Crowley	7-33	21.2	+25.18	G A Swinbank	4-8
G Berridge	5-32	15.6	-3.12	L Lungo	4-16
A Dobbin	14-90	15.6	-49.96	J Howard Johnson	4-14
F King	5-34	14.7	-18.48	Mrs M Reveley	3-10
P Whelan	6-42	14.3	-4.50	R Fahey	6-21

Sponsored by Stan James

Newbury, Berkshire, RG14 7NZ.
Tel: 01635 40015 or 41485.

NEWBURY

How to get there – Road: Signposted from M4 and A34.

Rail: Newbury racecourse

Features: LH, flat, 1m6f round, suits galloping sorts with stamina, tough fences

2006-07 Fixtures: Nov 24, 25, 26, Dec 13, 29, Jan 17, Feb 10, Mar 2, 3, 23, 24

Winning Pointers: A happy hunting ground for Paul Nicholls, who hits the mark with more than one in four of his runners, and they often go off a fair price to boot. Philip Hobbs also has good memories of Newbury.

Chases

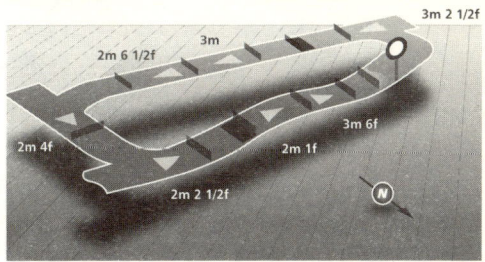

Hurdles

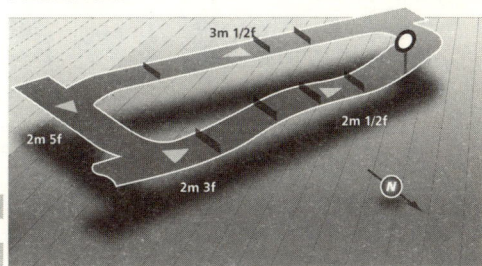

Favourites

Chase	35.1%	+£16.63
Hurdle	34.1%	+£1.38
Overall	34.5%	+£18.01

Trainers	Wins-Runs	%	Hurdles	Chases	£1 level stks
P Nicholls	34-134	25.4	12-50	20-75	+27.12
F Doumen	3-12	25.0	3-7	0-4	+5.88
A Balding	4-18	22.2	3-7	1-10	-5.45
C Egerton	5-26	19.2	1-13	4-9	+5.03
N Henderson	33-192	17.2	22-121	9-50	-4.67
H Morrison	4-24	16.7	2-17	0-3	+4.50
P Hobbs	19-142	13.4	11-70	8-59	+21.75
H Daly	4-30	13.3	2-11	2-18	-0.50
Jonjo O'Neill	15-117	12.8	7-67	4-41	-41.91
N Chance	5-44	11.4	3-29	0-5	+18.50
M Pipe	22-193	11.4	8-103	11-72	-68.47
Miss E Lavelle	6-53	11.3	4-25	2-19	+7.17
N Twiston-Davies	9-81	11.1	3-38	6-32	0.00

Jockeys	Wins-Rides	%	£1 level stks	Best Trainer	W-R
B J Geraghty	6-22	27.3	+8.63	M J O'Brien	1-1
R Walsh	23-94	24.5	+15.36	P Nicholls	23-80
M Foley	7-39	17.9	+34.50	N Henderson	6-22
M Fitzgerald	25-145	17.2	-53.18	N Henderson	24-118
A McCoy	25-150	16.7	-60.70	M Pipe	11-61
Christian Williams	5-32	15.6	+13.12	P Nicholls	4-14
C Llewellyn	13-97	13.4	+43.50	N Twiston-Davies	9-57
R Johnson	18-136	13.2	+32.38	P Hobbs	11-87
L Cooper	3-24	12.5	-10.75	Jonjo O'Neill	3-24
S Thomas	7-59	11.9	-11.38	Miss V Williams	5-44
T J Murphy	16-152	10.5	-49.72	M Pipe	7-42
P J Brennan	5-50	10.0	+8.00	P Hobbs	2-14
S Durack	5-54	9.3	-0.50	N Chance	2-14

NEWCASTLE

High Gosforth Park, Newcastle-Upon-Tyne, NE3 5HP. Tel: 01912 362020.

How to get there – Road: Signposted from A1.

Rail: Newcastle Central (4m)

Features: LH, 1m6f round, half-mile straight is all uphill, fences are stiff

2006-07 Fixtures: Nov 10, 25, Dec 16, Jan 5, 17, 31, Feb 13, 24, Mar 6, 17

Winning Pointers: Several trainers are in profit here, but Nicky Richards deserves a special mention as he is the only one to have managed it from a sample of more than 20 runners.

Chases

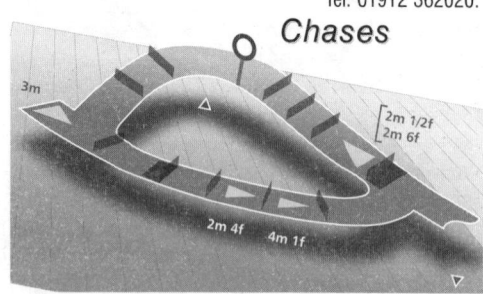

Hurdles

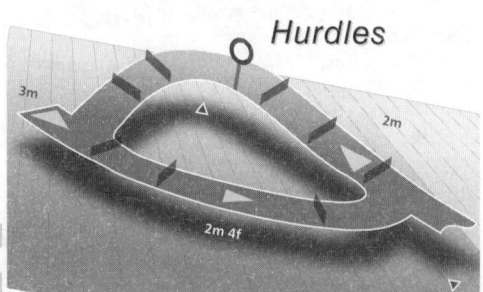

Favourites

Chase	34.4%	-£9.94
Hurdle	31.9%	-£22.62
Overall	33.0%	-£32.55

Trainers	Wins-Runs	%	Hurdles	Chases	£1 level stks
T Tate	6-8	75.0	2-3	2-3	+14.69
Mrs J Candlish	3-5	60.0	0-2	3-3	+14.75
H Hogarth	7-13	53.8	0-3	7-10	+38.62
A Scott	3-7	42.9	3-7	0-0	+6.38
N Twiston-Davies	4-10	40.0	4-5	0-5	+8.74
Mrs A Hamilton	4-12	33.3	3-7	1-4	+21.26
R Phillips	6-20	30.0	3-12	2-5	-3.97
R Ford	3-11	27.3	1-5	2-6	+10.00
N Richards	14-53	26.4	8-40	3-8	+23.12
P Haslam	4-16	25.0	3-12	1-4	+17.50
N Mason	5-20	25.0	1-7	4-11	+18.00
M Barnes	4-17	23.5	4-14	0-3	+51.00
M Todhunter	7-31	22.6	2-18	5-11	+26.63

Jockeys	Wins-Rides	%	£1 level stks	Best Trainer	W-R
R Johnson	5-10	50.0	+8.65	R Phillips	3-4
R Guest	5-11	45.5	+14.12	N Mason	3-6
T J Murphy	4-10	40.0	+3.19	P Monteith	2-4
P McDonald	3-9	33.3	+3.25	F Murphy	2-5
J M Maguire	4-14	28.6	+5.24	T Tate	2-2
R Davidson	3-12	25.0	+21.00	A Whillans	1-1
A Dobbin	18-90	20.0	-34.42	N Richards	8-18
L McGrath	7-40	17.5	+8.50	R C Guest	5-21
T Greenall	5-30	16.7	+5.50	M W Easterby	4-20
D O'Meara	9-59	15.3	+1.12	H Hogarth	6-12
D Elsworth	5-36	13.9	-15.34	Mrs S J Smith	5-22
G Lee	16-127	12.6	-58.25	J Howard Johnson	5-27
G Berridge	5-40	12.5	-18.85	L Lungo	3-15

Newton Abbot, Devon
TQ12 3AF.
Tel 01626 53235

NEWTON ABBOT

How to get there – Road: On A380 Newton Abbot to Torquay road. Rail: Newton Abbot

Features: LH, tight, 1m1f round

2006-07 Fixtures: Apr 1,7, 27

Winning Pointers: Martin Pipe used to love sending his horses to Newton Abbot, running an unbelievable 373 in the last five years, but despite a decent proportion of them winning the sheer volume of runners and the paucity of the winning SP made them easy to ignore. Philip Hobbs and Richard Johnson are a fine combination here.

Chases

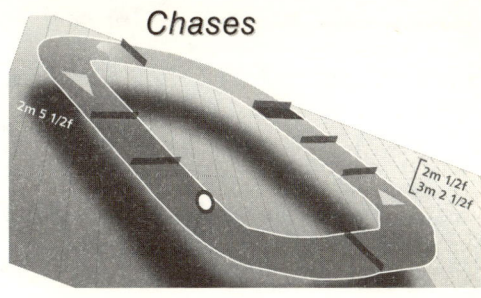

Hurdles

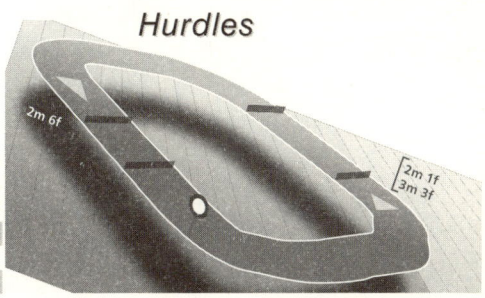

Favourites

Chase	35.1%	-£34.08
Hurdle	33.6%	-£47.93
Overall	34.2%	-£82.01

Trainers

Trainers	Wins-Runs	%	Hurdles	Chases	£1 level stks
L Wells	3-5	60.0	2-4	1-1	+36.00
N Chance	5-10	50.0	3-4	2-2	+9.45
Mrs K Sanderson	3-7	42.9	0-1	3-6	+0.88
G Balding	3-10	30.0	2-6	0-1	+5.75
P Bowen	11-40	27.5	3-22	8-15	+17.00
R Lee	5-19	26.3	3-7	2-12	+3.00
P Nicholls	28-107	26.2	8-35	18-56	+1.53
N Henderson	3-12	25.0	2-8	0-2	+2.50
Jonjo O'Neill	17-73	23.3	11-42	3-22	-17.99
P Hobbs	42-191	22.0	13-101	26-81	+5.58
Mrs H Dalton	3-15	20.0	0-3	3-10	+0.25
Nick Williams	8-40	20.0	5-21	3-19	+32.75
M Pipe	68-373	18.2	42-247	21-113	-135.40

Jockeys

Jockeys	Wins-Rides	%	£1 level stks	Best Trainer	W-R
R Walsh	14-35	40.0	+0.50	P Nicholls	14-34
T Best	3-9	33.3	+6.75	G Balding	3-7
S Gaisford	5-17	29.4	+24.38	J Frost	3-8
A McCoy	58-203	28.6	-27.24	M Pipe	33-109
G Richards	4-15	26.7	+0.80	J G O'Shea	3-7
R Johnson	52-198	26.3	+54.15	P Hobbs	28-106
R P McNally	5-21	23.8	+1.61	P Nicholls	5-11
W Kennedy	3-13	23.1	-2.83	N Chance	2-2
T J Murphy	17-84	20.2	-16.34	M Pipe	16-57
A O'Keeffe	4-20	20.0	+1.00	Miss V Williams	2-11
J E Moore	12-63	19.0	-14.01	M Pipe	6-32
R Thornton	16-87	18.4	+20.38	A King	4-23
S Durack	12-78	15.4	+70.96	P Bowen	3-8

PERTH

How to get there – Road: Off A93. Rail: Perth, free bus service

Features: RH, flat, 1m2f round

2006-07 Fixtures: Apr 25, 26, 27

Winning Pointers: Once again the remarkable Nicky Richards does brilliantly at a northern track, with 29 winners and a healthy level-stakes profit since 2001. Paul Nicholls does well on his occasional visits, and Keith Mercer, a massive emerging talent, rides the track excellently.

Chases

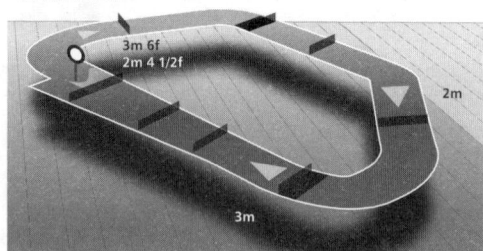

Hurdles

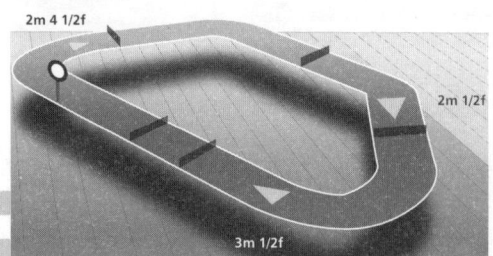

Favourites

Chase	31.7%	-£25.89
Hurdle	39.5%	+£1.81
Overall	36.5%	-£24.07

Trainers

Trainers	Wins-Runs	%	Hurdles	Chases	£1 level stks
P Bowen	7-11	63.6	3-6	4-4	+11.20
G Harker	8-19	42.1	5-13	1-3	+38.58
T George	18-53	34.0	8-27	9-24	+46.53
N Twiston-Davies	18-60	30.0	13-39	3-18	+27.25
M Todhunter	11-37	29.7	10-26	1-9	-0.49
P Nicholls	8-27	29.6	2-7	5-19	-2.26
N Richards	29-108	26.9	19-78	9-26	+20.38
J Goldie	15-58	25.9	9-40	6-16	+19.36
G M Moore	5-22	22.7	3-12	2-9	+1.25
R Fahey	4-18	22.2	2-10	0-3	-5.68
P Hobbs	10-45	22.2	6-25	4-20	-16.74
Jonjo O'Neill	8-42	19.0	5-24	2-14	-12.97
Mrs S J Smith	3-16	18.8	0-7	3-8	+18.00

Jockeys

Jockeys	Wins-Rides	%	£1 level stks	Best Trainer	W-R
B Hughes	3-5	60.0	+25.50	J Howard Johnson	3-4
T Greenway	3-9	33.3	-0.14	N Twiston-Davies	3-4
M Fitzgerald	4-13	30.8	-2.55	N Henderson	2-5
A McCoy	16-53	30.2	-5.46	Jonjo O'Neill	6-17
D R Dennis	3-10	30.0	+8.00	Mrs S Bradburne	1-1
J M Maguire	13-46	28.3	+13.02	T George	11-37
A Dobbin	49-182	26.9	-27.30	N Richards	19-58
C Llewellyn	13-50	26.0	+28.38	N Twiston-Davies	12-43
S Thomas	4-16	25.0	+14.17	Miss V Williams	4-15
R Walsh	4-17	23.5	-7.56	P Nicholls	4-11
A Thornton	3-13	23.1	+5.50	P Nicholls	1-1
Philip Carberry	3-14	21.4	-3.12	J G Carr	2-13
K J Mercer	9-44	20.5	+36.75	F Murphy	4-15

Sponsored by Stan James

PLUMPTON

How to get there – Road: A274 or A275, off B2116.

Rail: Plumpton

Features: LH, 1m1f round, emphatic undulations, straight is uphill, track is so quirky that it has many course specialists who are quick, handy jumpers

2006-07 Fixtures: Oct 16, 30, Nov 19, 29, Dec 11, Jan 7, 15, Feb 12, 26, Mar 12, 26, Apr 8, 9, 23

Winning Pointers: Emma Lavelle is always worth a second look, and for more reasons than one at Plumpton where she has racked up a £45 profit to £1 level stakes.

Chases

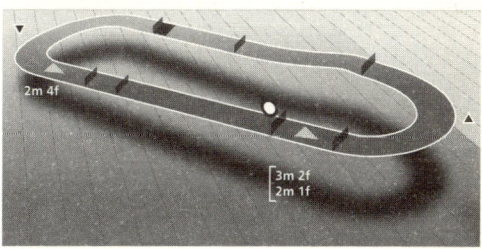

Hurdles

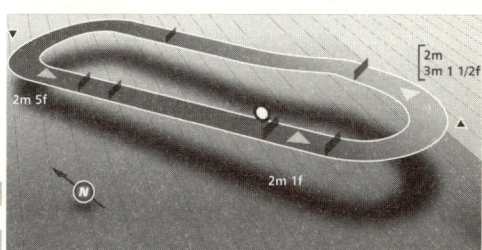

Favourites

Chase	33.3%	-£20.02
Hurdle	30.8%	-£53.43
Overall	31.8%	-£73.44

Trainers	Wins-Runs	%	Hurdles	Chases	£1 level stks
J J Best	3-5	60.0	3-4	0-1	+19.00
G Wareham	3-7	42.9	0-1	3-6	+17.00
Mrs A Perrett	4-10	40.0	3-8	1-2	-3.62
C Egerton	5-14	35.7	4-8	0-3	-1.67
N Henderson	14-43	32.6	9-26	4-15	-7.48
Miss E Lavelle	9-28	32.1	7-14	2-10	+45.83
E Williams	3-10	30.0	2-7	1-3	+6.75
Mrs A Thorpe	7-25	28.0	5-15	2-9	+10.75
P Nicholls	17-62	27.4	5-21	11-33	-5.00
P Hobbs	8-30	26.7	5-20	3-9	+0.93
B J Llewellyn	5-20	25.0	5-17	0-2	+21.00
D Keane	6-26	23.1	1-14	5-11	+13.93
M Pipe	26-114	22.8	19-86	3-21	-16.95

Jockeys	Wins-Rides	%	£1 level stks	Best Trainer	W-R
C Tizzard	3-4	75.0	+9.25	P Nicholls	2-2
R Walsh	7-14	50.0	+10.08	P Nicholls	7-13
R Wakley	4-11	36.4	+26.50	A Hales	2-6
A McCoy	35-125	28.0	+37.27	M Pipe	14-47
M Nicolls	5-18	27.8	+20.50	M Appleby	1-1
M Fitzgerald	15-56	26.8	-3.76	N Henderson	11-27
T J Malone	5-19	26.3	+19.50	A Whiting	1-1
P J Brennan	10-38	26.3	+20.43	P Nicholls	2-4
R P McNally	3-12	25.0	-0.64	P Nicholls	2-6
D Jacob	3-13	23.1	+16.00	N Mitchell	1-2
R Walford	4-18	22.2	+23.00	R Alner	4-13
T J Murphy	16-74	21.6	+1.39	M Pipe	6-23
A Honeyball	4-19	21.1	+5.38	R Buckler	2-7

SANDOWN

How to get there – Road: From north and south-west M25 Jctn 10 and A3, from south-east M25 Jctn 9 and A224. Rail: Esher (from Waterloo)

Features: RH, 1m5f round, tough fences of which three are close together down the back, steep uphill finish puts a premium on stamina

2006-07 Fixtures: Nov 4, Dec 1, 2, Jan 6, Feb 3, 16, 23, Mar 9, 10

Winning Pointers: Another track at which Tony McCoy really excels, with a huge level-stakes profit despite old employer Martin Pipe not figuring on the trainer stats.

Chases

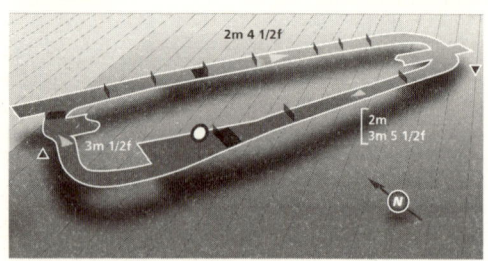

Hurdles

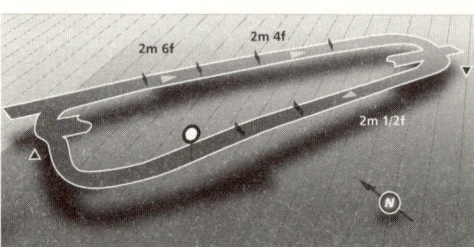

Favourites

Chase	28.5%	-£35.62
Hurdle	33.1%	-£7.63
Overall	30.8%	-£43.25

Trainers	Wins-Runs	%	Hurdles	Chases	£1 level stks
A Balding	4-7	57.1	2-5	2-2	+19.70
Mrs J Harrington	3-8	37.5	1-3	2-5	+3.00
N Chance	3-8	37.5	1-4	1-2	+13.50
P Chamings	5-14	35.7	1-5	4-8	+17.00
V Dartnall	4-15	26.7	2-9	0-2	+10.25
F Doumen	5-22	22.7	2-13	2-8	-0.22
P Nicholls	32-159	20.1	6-53	26-105	-32.74
N Gifford	3-15	20.0	2-9	1-6	+9.50
Miss H Knight	11-55	20.0	2-20	9-28	+5.25
C Egerton	3-16	18.8	0-9	3-7	-0.38
N Henderson	22-122	18.0	10-66	10-47	-13.63
J Howard Johnson	6-34	17.6	3-19	3-14	+6.00
P R Webber	6-37	16.2	1-12	3-21	+3.25

Jockeys	Wins-Rides	%	£1 level stks	Best Trainer	W-R
J Snowden	7-8	87.5	+12.20	P Nicholls	3-3
B J Geraghty	12-42	28.6	+16.73	P Nicholls	5-17
A McCoy	34-119	28.6	+84.33	M Pipe	15-47
R Walsh	16-82	19.5	-2.24	P Nicholls	14-72
R Johnson	18-107	16.8	+0.60	P Hobbs	11-68
T Doyle	8-49	16.3	+7.75	P R Webber	3-23
A Dobbin	5-32	15.6	-1.50	D McCain	1-1
M Fitzgerald	18-119	15.1	-26.30	N Henderson	15-72
J P McNamara	3-20	15.0	-2.25	B Powell	2-3
B Fenton	7-49	14.3	+23.50	R Rowe	3-12
G Lee	6-45	13.3	-8.25	J Howard Johnson	4-24
T J Murphy	12-94	12.8	-23.17	Miss H Knight	6-10
J Culloty	7-55	12.7	-13.50	Miss H Knight	5-31

Sedgefield, Cleveland TS21 2HW.
Tel 01740 621 925

SEDGEFIELD

Chases

How to get there – Road: A689, 2 mins from A1. Rail: Stockton, Darlington

Features: LH, 1m2f round, no water jump, undulating and sharp, suits handy types

2006-07 Fixtures: Oct 25, Nov 7, 21, Dec 5, 12, 26, Jan 9, 23, Feb 6, 20, Mar 13, 27, Apr 9, 23

Winning Pointers: Grant Tuer has won with an amazing five of his seven runners, and five out of six when he rides them himself. Of the big guns, Howard Johnson is a big fan of the track and has regularly clocked up the winners down the years.

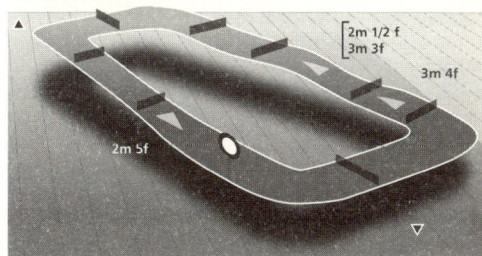

Hurdles

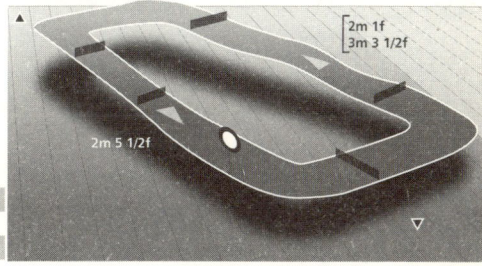

Favourites

Chase	33.0%	-£34.00
Hurdle	32.2%	-£20.80
Overall	32.5%	-£54.80

Trainers	Wins-Runs	%	Hurdles	Chases	£1 level stks
J G Carr	3-4	75.0	2-2	1-2	+15.00
G Tuer	5-7	71.4	0-0	5-7	+2.48
R Bastiman	3-9	33.3	3-8	0-0	+28.25
R Phillips	5-17	29.4	3-8	2-9	-2.87
Mrs A Hamilton	5-19	26.3	2-12	3-6	+3.25
Mrs S Watt	3-12	25.0	1-6	2-6	+4.75
G A Swinbank	9-36	25.0	4-24	4-5	+24.05
J Howard Johnson	39-163	23.9	25-109	14-48	+5.00
E Williams	5-22	22.7	1-14	3-7	+25.51
N Richards	13-58	22.4	6-44	6-13	-11.80
C Pogson	5-23	21.7	4-12	1-10	+20.25
P Haslam	6-28	21.4	5-23	1-5	+10.66
M D Hammond	11-52	21.2	7-25	4-27	+41.31

Jockeys	Wins-Rides	%	£1 level stks	Best Trainer	W-R
G Tuer	5-6	83.3	+3.48	G Tuer	5-6
C Mulhall	3-5	60.0	+10.25	P Maddison	1-1
C Ford	3-10	30.0	+4.50	R Ford	3-10
R Thornton	3-12	25.0	+20.00	P Haslam	1-1
D Elsworth	16-65	24.6	+29.75	Mrs S J Smith	14-50
S J Craine	3-13	23.1	+7.33	D McCain	3-12
M Foley	3-13	23.1	+5.50	R Wood	2-5
G Lee	52-258	20.2	+15.93	J Howard Johnson	28-86
D N Russell	9-47	19.1	+24.41	F Murphy	8-41
R Garritty	20-108	18.5	+28.39	G M Moore	10-48
J Crowley	23-124	18.5	+33.61	Mrs K Walton	3-5
A Thornton	5-29	17.2	-10.32	P Haslam	2-5
A Dobbin	31-182	17.0	-37.55	L Lungo	7-22

SOUTHWELL

Rolleston, Nr. Newark, Notts, NG25 0TS. Tel: 01636 814481.

How to get there – Road: A1 to Newark, A617 to Southwell or M1 to A52 to Nottingham then A612 to Southwell.

Rail: Rolleston

Features: LH, 1m2f round, flat

2006-07 Fixtures: Jan 27, Mar 3

Winning Pointers: Not many jump meetings at this track these days, but Jonjo O'Neill likes to send one here whenever possible, as does Venetia Williams, and the pair have similarly decent records.

Chases

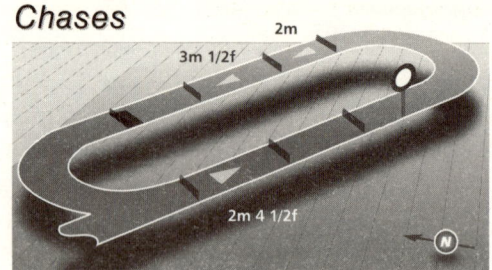

Hurdles

Favourites

Chase	32.0%	-£14.60
Hurdle	37.0%	-£8.72
Overall	34.8%	-£23.33

Trainers

Trainers	Wins-Runs	%	Hurdles	Chases	£1 level stks
C Dore	3-4	75.0	3-4	0-0	+7.45
Miss E Lavelle	3-6	50.0	2-2	1-4	+11.38
C Egerton	6-14	42.9	4-8	2-5	+21.99
J Mullins	5-13	38.5	1-2	4-11	+9.41
E Williams	9-26	34.6	5-13	4-13	+13.34
H Daly	3-9	33.3	1-2	2-6	+0.08
R Alner	3-10	30.0	1-3	2-7	+3.50
Mrs L Wadham	3-10	30.0	3-9	0-1	-2.62
Miss V Williams	10-37	27.0	6-23	3-12	-5.34
Jonjo O'Neill	16-61	26.2	7-33	8-25	+4.77
P Blockley	3-12	25.0	2-8	1-4	+13.00
J Spearing	3-12	25.0	1-8	2-3	-1.27
J G O'Shea	3-12	25.0	2-9	1-3	+11.00

Jockeys

Jockeys	Wins-Rides	%	£1 level stks	Best Trainer	W-R
Christian Williams	7-26	26.9	+4.21	E Williams	7-21
A McCoy	20-75	26.7	-19.67	Jonjo O'Neill	7-29
R Johnson	14-55	25.5	+15.18	Miss K Milligan	4-8
S Thomas	5-21	23.8	+20.75	Miss V Williams	3-13
A Thornton	13-55	23.6	+28.17	E Williams	2-2
N Fehily	8-36	22.2	+19.75	C Mann	2-8
T Doyle	5-23	21.7	+4.04	P R Webber	2-6
A O'Keeffe	6-29	20.7	-7.59	R Lee	2-4
L McGrath	4-20	20.0	+1.00	R C Guest	3-10
B J Crowley	3-17	17.6	-10.07	Miss V Williams	3-12
C Llewellyn	4-23	17.4	+33.75	N Twiston-Davies	2-10
D Elsworth	8-47	17.0	-13.00	Mrs S J Smith	8-46
L Aspell	4-25	16.0	+18.62	A Streeter	1-1

Luddington Road, Stratford,
Warwickshire CV37 9SE.
Tel 01789 267 949

STRATFORD

Chases

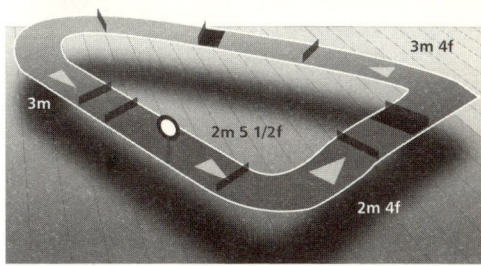

3m 4f

3m

2m 5 1/2f

2m 4f

How to get there – Road: M40 Jctn 15, A3400, B439, A46.

Rail: Stratford-upon-Avon

Features: Sharp, LH, 1m2f round

2006-07 Fixtures: Oct 14, 26, Feb 3, 12, 26, Apr 22

Winning Pointers: In terms of winners, Philip Hobbs is out on his own, and roughly one in three of his horses that come here wins. He is well in front of Jonjo O'Neill from a similar sample. This is clearly a track that rewards great horsemanship with Tony McCoy, Ruby Walsh and Richard Johnson topping the stats.

Hurdles

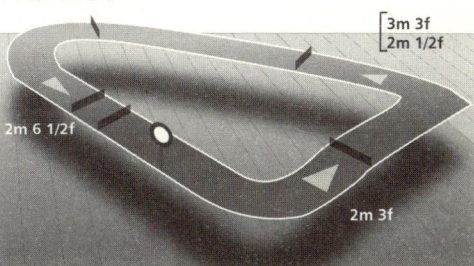

3m 3f
2m 1/2f

2m 6 1/2f

2m 3f

Favourites

Chase	33.3%	-£13.64
Hurdle	30.9%	-£46.29
Overall	32.0%	-£59.93

Trainers	Wins-Runs	%	Hurdles	Chases	£1 level stks
D Elsworth	3-7	42.9	1-4	2-3	+8.30
C Tinkler	5-13	38.5	2-9	2-3	+25.75
P Hobbs	34-113	30.1	18-56	16-54	+33.40
S Sherwood	3-11	27.3	0-5	2-5	+19.50
Mrs L Taylor	4-16	25.0	0-4	4-12	+0.38
P Nicholls	14-57	24.6	4-21	10-36	-1.71
P R Webber	6-25	24.0	2-12	3-12	+50.24
Miss E Lavelle	6-26	23.1	3-12	3-14	+25.00
M Pitman	5-23	21.7	4-14	1-9	+19.00
Jonjo O'Neill	23-106	21.7	11-64	11-39	-14.15
Mrs S J Smith	3-14	21.4	1-6	2-8	-0.50
D L Williams	3-15	20.0	2-8	1-7	+6.29
J Jefferson	4-20	20.0	3-14	1-6	+16.00

Jockeys	Wins-Rides	%	£1 level stks	Best Trainer	W-R
A McCoy	41-134	30.6	+3.26	M Pipe	16-42
R Walsh	6-23	26.1	-6.54	P Nicholls	4-18
J P McNamara	5-20	25.0	+23.00	K Bailey	2-4
R Johnson	39-156	25.0	+22.94	P Hobbs	22-70
B Fenton	4-17	23.5	+14.50	Miss E Lavelle	2-6
T Doyle	12-52	23.1	+68.24	P R Webber	6-20
L Cooper	5-25	20.0	-14.99	Jonjo O'Neill	5-23
Christian Williams	13-66	19.7	+2.99	P Nicholls	5-15
P Flynn	8-44	18.2	-0.60	P Hobbs	4-14
J Tizzard	5-30	16.7	+12.75	B Powell	1-2
M Foley	5-30	16.7	+5.00	J Adam	2-3
S Walsh	3-21	14.3	+5.00	Miss E Lavelle	1-1
A O'Keeffe	5-36	13.9	+1.00	Miss V Williams	2-13

TAUNTON

Orchard Portman, Taunton, Somerset TA3 7BL.
Tel 01823 337 172

How to get there – Road: M5 Jctn 25. Rail: Taunton

Features: RH, 1m2f round

2006-07 Fixtures: Oct 26, Nov 9, 23, Dec 7, 18, 29, Jan 8, 18, 30, Feb 8, 20, Mar 1, 12, 25, Apr 12, 20

Winning Pointers: Another of Martin Pipe's favourite old haunts, but his strike-rate was so poor he doesn't even make our list. Paul Nicholls and Philip Hobbs are usually fairly reliable, particularly Hobbs.

Chases

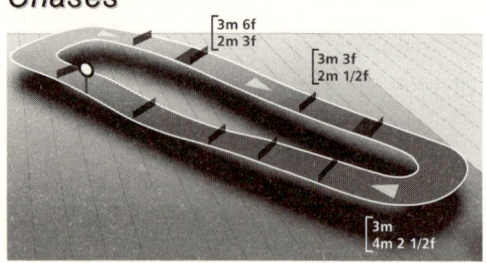

Hurdles

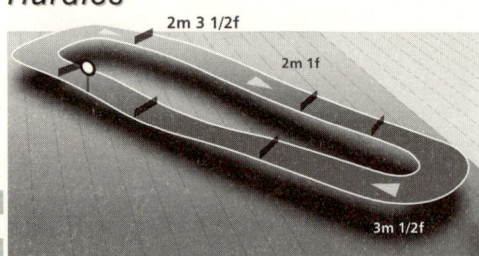

Favourites

Chase	30.9%	-£21.28
Hurdle	35.9%	-£30.57
Overall	34.2%	-£51.85

Trainers	Wins-Runs	%	Hurdles	Chases	£1 level stks
V Dartnall	3-8	37.5	2-6	1-2	+11.25
Mrs K Sanderson	3-9	33.3	0-1	3-8	-1.83
Mrs K Waldron	3-10	30.0	2-9	1-1	+11.83
M Bradstock	3-12	25.0	2-9	0-2	+2.25
P Nicholls	36-152	23.7	18-79	14-58	-27.09
Miss E Lavelle	6-27	22.2	2-17	4-7	+6.25
P Hobbs	34-156	21.8	23-99	10-49	+5.74
G L Moore	8-37	21.6	5-30	3-7	+9.13
N Henderson	8-37	21.6	4-25	2-7	-6.46
J Spearing	3-15	20.0	2-12	1-3	+19.25
R Phillips	5-25	20.0	2-17	3-8	+3.25
A King	5-25	20.0	4-18	0-4	+2.60
C Roberts	3-16	18.8	3-15	0-1	+39.50

Jockeys	Wins-Rides	%	£1 level stks	Best Trainer	W-R
R Walsh	13-44	29.5	-2.76	P Nicholls	12-41
R Thornton	11-39	28.2	+17.85	A King	4-16
A McCoy	21-77	27.3	-12.61	M Pipe	15-38
M Fitzgerald	9-38	23.7	-0.67	N Henderson	5-16
T Best	3-13	23.1	+7.25	Mrs K Waldron	1-1
R Johnson	22-98	22.4	+1.35	P Hobbs	14-63
J E Moore	16-75	21.3	+13.53	M Pipe	8-31
L Heard	4-19	21.1	-1.50	V Dartnall	2-3
D Jacob	3-15	20.0	+19.75	R Alner	3-9
M Foley	4-20	20.0	-2.63	A E Jones	2-6
T J Murphy	14-78	17.9	-26.29	M Pipe	7-27
B Fenton	5-29	17.2	-1.92	Miss E Lavelle	4-16
A Tinkler	5-30	16.7	+27.00	A E Jones	2-6

Easton Newston, Towcester, Northants
NN12 7HS. Tel 01327 353 414

TOWCESTER

How to get there – Road: M1
Jctn 15a, A43 west, south from
Towcester. Rail: Northampton
(8m) and bus service

Features: RH, 1m6f round,
demanding uphill run from back
straight

2006-07 Fixtures: Oct 4, 22,
Nov 2, 19, 25, Dec 26, Jan 21,
Feb 1, 18, Mar 28, 29, Apr 8, 24,
30

Winning Pointers: The track
suits strong National Hunt types
with its huge stamina demands,
so traditional hunting yards
often do well, such as Caroline
Bailey. Of the professionals
Venetia Williams is £48 in profit
to £1 level stakes.

Chases

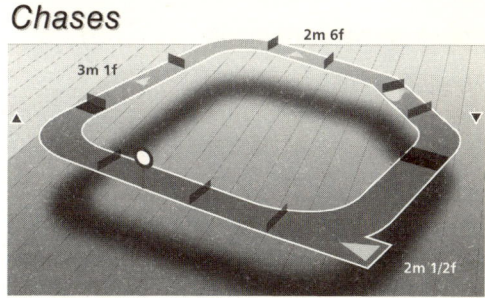

Hurdles

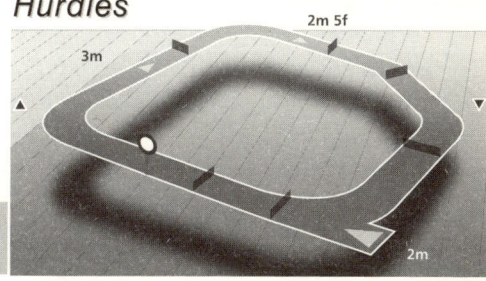

Favourites

Chase	27.8%	-£34.70
Hurdle	28.2%	-£56.55
Overall	28.0%	-£91.25

Trainers	Wins-Runs	%	Hurdles	Chases	£1 level stks
Mrs C Bailey	3-4	75.0	0-0	3-4	+10.75
T Easterby	3-6	50.0	2-3	1-2	+11.50
C Egerton	3-7	42.9	2-4	0-1	+2.32
P Haslam	4-10	40.0	2-5	1-3	+9.63
N Gaselee	3-8	37.5	1-3	2-5	+10.25
R Hodges	3-9	33.3	3-7	0-1	+14.25
Miss V Williams	26-87	29.9	10-32	15-48	+48.96
M Pipe	8-32	25.0	5-21	2-9	-6.13
Jonjo O'Neill	9-38	23.7	7-25	2-11	-13.84
A King	4-17	23.5	4-12	0-3	+13.75
O Sherwood	4-18	22.2	1-8	3-8	-3.25
N Henderson	3-14	21.4	1-6	1-5	-1.63
R C Guest	6-28	21.4	3-14	3-13	-5.62

Jockeys	Wins-Rides	%	£1 level stks	Best Trainer	W-R
N Williams	4-8	50.0	+17.00	E Williams	2-3
A McCoy	19-49	38.8	-1.57	Jonjo O'Neill	4-6
L Cooper	4-12	33.3	-2.72	Jonjo O'Neill	4-10
R Garritty	3-10	30.0	+13.25	T Easterby	2-5
S Morris	3-10	30.0	+21.50	Miss S Loggin	1-1
B J Crowley	7-24	29.2	+15.44	Miss V Williams	7-11
S Thomas	16-55	29.1	+0.59	Miss V Williams	14-42
O Nelmes	5-18	27.8	+3.75	P A Pritchard	3-9
R Walford	4-16	25.0	+5.23	Mrs S Williams	1-1
R Hobson	7-28	25.0	+36.50	J Cornwall	5-16
T J Malone	3-13	23.1	+19.38	N Berry	1-1
Antony Evans	4-18	22.2	+5.30	N Twiston-Davies	4-9
A Pogson	3-16	18.8	+0.50	J Cornwall	2-7

UTTOXETER

Wood Lane, Uttoxeter, Staffs ST14 8BD.
Tel 01889 562 561

How to get there – Road: M6 Jctn 14, M1 Jctns 22-25, A38, A5151. Rail: Uttoxeter

Features: LH, 1m2f round, undulating, sweeping curves, suitable for gallopers

2006-07 Fixtures: Oct 1, 11, 27, Nov 11, 23, Dec 15, Jan 27, Feb 17, Mar 17, 31

Winning Pointers: Once again, from a decent sample, Philip Hobbs turns over a sizeable profit, further testament to his skills. Tony McCoy shows up well, but that was largely due to a one-in-three association with Martin Pipe and can largely be discounted.

Chases

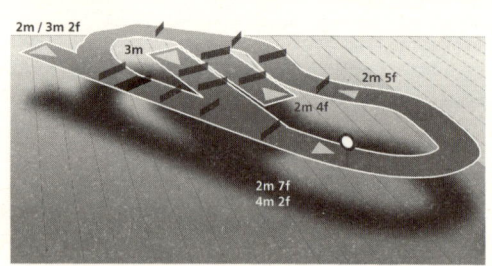

Hurdles

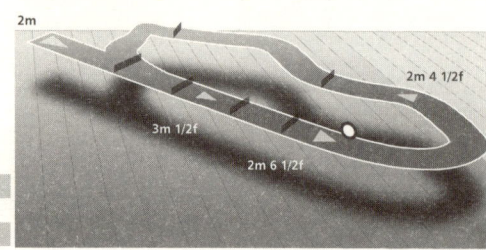

Favourites

Chase	30.0%	-£35.27
Hurdle	29.9%	-£71.72
Overall	29.9%	-£106.99

Trainers	Wins-Runs	%	Hurdles	Chases	£1 level stks
J Portman	3-5	60.0	2-3	1-2	+15.25
Mrs P Robeson	4-11	36.4	2-5	2-4	+39.33
V Dartnall	6-17	35.3	3-8	2-5	-1.88
Nick Williams	4-12	33.3	2-6	2-6	+25.00
P Hobbs	19-67	28.4	11-37	8-29	+27.11
R Buckler	4-15	26.7	1-5	3-10	+1.95
J Hetherton	3-12	25.0	2-9	1-2	+29.00
N Richards	3-12	25.0	3-9	0-3	+20.25
C Mann	8-33	24.2	4-21	4-11	+31.96
N Twiston-Davies	14-58	24.1	8-26	5-24	-4.91
C Tinkler	4-17	23.5	2-9	0-2	+1.63
Mrs D Hamer	4-17	23.5	4-15	0-2	+11.50
Jonjo O'Neill	28-128	21.9	16-75	11-42	-23.05

Jockeys	Wins-Rides	%	£1 level stks	Best Trainer	W-R
L Cooper	6-16	37.5	+1.44	Jonjo O'Neill	6-16
R Biddlecombe	4-12	33.3	-2.71	N Twiston-Davies	1-1
F King	5-15	33.3	+24.25	J Jefferson	3-8
A McCoy	36-132	27.3	-23.99	M Pipe	11-33
P Robson	3-12	25.0	+63.50	J O'Keeffe	1-1
D Elsworth	9-36	25.0	+36.13	Mrs S J Smith	9-34
B J Geraghty	3-13	23.1	-4.92	Jonjo O'Neill	2-7
R Walsh	5-22	22.7	-0.75	P Nicholls	3-18
R McGrath	5-22	22.7	+16.75	C Grant	2-3
C Llewellyn	16-71	22.5	+22.83	N Twiston-Davies	11-37
R Johnson	29-141	20.6	-12.02	P Hobbs	12-41
T Doyle	12-59	20.3	+34.13	P R Webber	4-18
B Fenton	3-15	20.0	+3.75	J Ryan	1-1

Hampton Street, Warwick CV34 6HN.
Tel 01926 491 553

WARWICK

How to get there – Road: M40 Jctn 15, A429, follow signs to town centre. Rail: Warwick

Features: LH, 1m6f round, full of undulations

2006-07 Fixtures: Oct 30, Nov 15, Dec 3, Jan 13, 25, Feb 10, 23, Mar 11, 20

Winning Pointers: Nothing spectacular in terms of stats, with the now retired Mark Pitman returning the best level-stakes profit at £20.38. Will Carl Llewellyn be able to keep his record going?

Chases

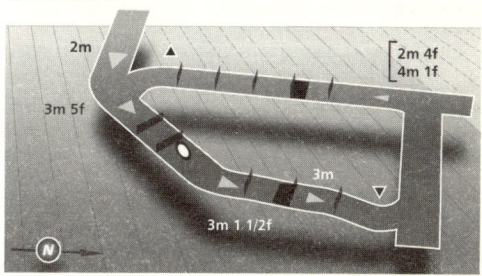

Hurdles

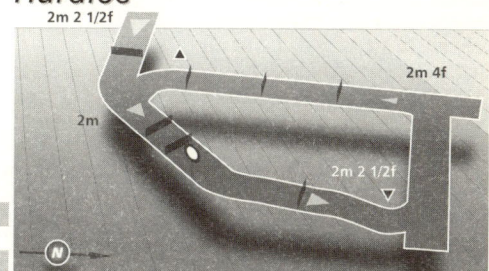

Favourites

Chase	41.5%	+£1.79
Hurdle	36.9%	+£9.07
Overall	38.9%	+£10.86

Trainers

Trainers	Wins-Runs	%	Hurdles	Chases	£1 level stks
J Howard Johnson	3-6	50.0	2-3	1 2	+0.49
P Nicholls	17-55	30.9	4-18	13-35	-0.62
M Pitman	4-13	30.8	2 5	1-4	+20.38
Mrs L Williamson	3-11	27.3	0-3	3-7	+4.00
N Chance	4-15	26.7	3-8	0-2	+1.36
N Henderson	8-31	25.8	1-15	5-8	+3.36
H Daly	10-40	25.0	6-18	4-17	+7.55
A King	14-60	23.3	8-36	6-14	-0.85
P Winkworth	4-19	21.1	2-11	2-6	+1.60
R Alner	6-29	20.7	5-19	1-10	-2.25
J Upson	3-15	20.0	1-6	2-8	+4.33
Miss V Williams	8-42	19.0	4-22	3-16	-7.00
Jonjo O'Neill	11-62	17.7	4-32	3-22	-13.31

Jockeys

Jockeys	Wins-Rides	%	£1 level stks	Best Trainer	W-R
R Walsh	11-26	42.3	+14.63	P Nicholls	10-24
M Fitzgerald	12-46	26.1	+1.29	N Henderson	7-21
G Lee	6-24	25.0	-0.76	J Howard Johnson	3-5
A McCoy	17-69	24.6	-9.52	Jonjo O'Neill	4-16
S Thomas	7-29	24.1	+2.50	Miss V Williams	6-21
Antony Evans	6-29	20.7	+75.03	N Twiston-Davies	3-12
T J Murphy	8-39	20.5	-1.01	M Pipe	4-18
R Thornton	18-89	20.2	+10.07	A King	11-42
W Kennedy	3-15	20.0	0.00	N Chance	3-5
R Walford	3-15	20.0	+5.00	D Elsworth	1-1
J E Moore	4-20	20.0	-11.42	M Pipe	2-5
J Tizzard	5-25	20.0	-14.15	C L Tizzard	2-6
Christian Williams	5-29	17.2	+9.75	P A Pritchard	1-1

WETHERBY

York Road, Wetherby, West Yorks L22 5EJ.
Tel 01937 582 035

How to get there – Road: A1, from Leeds A58, from York B1224. Rail: Leeds, Harrogate, York

Features: Long, LH, chases 1m4f round, hurdles 1m2f, long-striding gallopers do well

2006-07 Fixtures: Oct 11, 27, 28, Nov 11, 22, Dec 2, 26, 27, Jan 13, Feb 3, 12, 28, Mar 17, Apr 3, 16, 29

Winning Pointers: Howard Johnson has an awesome record here, with 18 winners and a £76.16 level-stakes profit in the last five years. Nigel Twiston-Davies also does well.

Chases

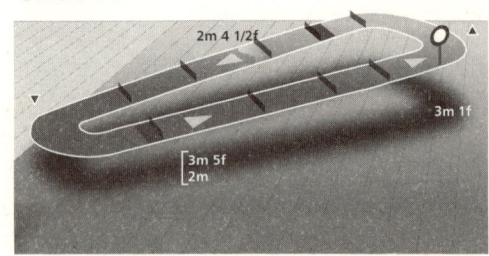

Hurdles

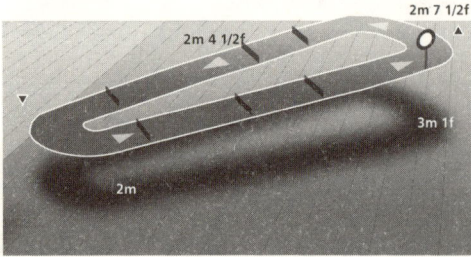

Favourites

Chase	34.8%	-£32.50
Hurdle	34.5%	-£13.33
Overall	34.6%	-£45.83

Trainers	Wins-Runs	%	Hurdles	Chases	£1 level stks
Mrs P Robeson	3-7	42.9	2-6	1-1	+7.50
C Mann	3-8	37.5	1-5	2-3	-0.50
N Henderson	6-18	33.3	4-10	2-8	-0.93
K Ryan	5-18	27.8	3-12	1-5	+28.50
A Carroll	6-22	27.3	5-16	1-5	+17.58
P Nicholls	9-37	24.3	2-13	7-24	-22.90
P Hobbs	3-13	23.1	3-7	0-6	-2.40
N Twiston-Davies	7-31	22.6	3-17	2-10	-2.09
J J Quinn	4-18	22.2	4-17	0-1	+4.25
J Howard Johnson	18-82	22.0	14-54	4-22	+76.16
Jonjo O'Neill	16-73	21.9	10-41	5-29	-9.10
M Scudamore	3-14	21.4	2-11	1-1	+6.13
R Phillips	3-15	20.0	3-12	0-2	-6.00

Jockeys	Wins-Rides	%	£1 level stks	Best Trainer	W-R
R Johnson	5-15	33.3	+4.52	A King	2-2
A Tinkler	5-16	31.3	+16.95	V Dartnall	1-1
Christian Williams	3-10	30.0	-4.27	P Nicholls	2-4
D Crosse	3-10	30.0	+47.00	C Mann	2-4
J Tizzard	8-29	27.6	-8.25	P Nicholls	4-14
P Merrigan	3-11	27.3	+6.70	P Haslam	2-5
W Dowling	3-12	25.0	-2.00	L Lungo	3-10
T J Murphy	4-16	25.0	+4.40	A Carroll	2-4
M Foley	4-17	23.5	-2.64	Mrs P Robeson	2-2
A McCoy	9-40	22.5	-9.82	Jonjo O'Neill	5-13
D Elsworth	25-113	22.1	+0.32	Mrs S J Smith	24-100
B Hughes	3-14	21.4	+32.00	J Howard Johnson	3-10
A Dobbin	29-136	21.3	+28.35	L Lungo	7-24

Wincanton, Somerset BA9 8BJ.
Tel 01963 323 44

WINCANTON

Chases

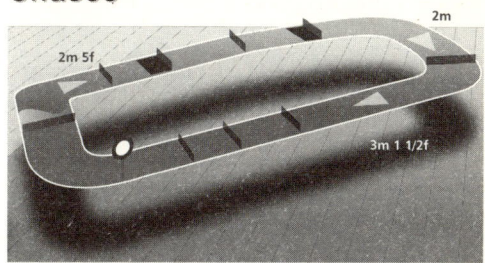

How to get there – Road: A303 to Wincanton, track on B3081, 1m from town centre.

Rail: Gillingham

Features: RH, fast-drying, 1m4f round

2006-07 Fixtures: Oct 5, 22, Nov 4, 16, 30, Dec 26, Jan 10, 20, Feb 1, 17, Mar 8, 19, Apr 5, 22

Winning Pointers: Paul Nicholls is the regular punters' pal at his local track. A Wincanton card never goes by without a few fancied Nicholls runners, and generally they oblige. Christian Williams partners most of them, but pay even closer attention when Ruby Walsh takes over.

Hurdles

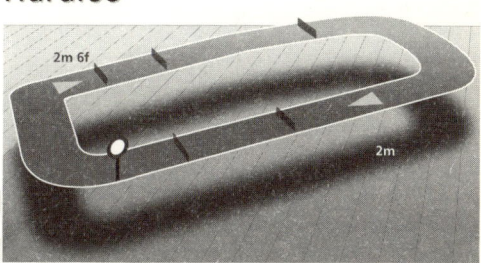

Favourites

Chase	38.7%	+£7.62
Hurdle	35.2%	-£26.88
Overall	36.8%	-£19.26

Trainers	Wins-Runs	%	Hurdles	Chases	£1 level stks
C St V Fox	3-4	75.0	0-0	3-4	+4.69
G Brown	3-7	42.9	1-3	2-4	+5.33
B De Haan	3-10	30.0	0-3	3-6	+3.75
P Nicholls	87-300	29.0	42-158	38-120	+12.89
N Henderson	14-49	28.6	5-30	6-15	+9.65
J Spearing	3-11	27.3	2-6	1-3	+12.00
A E Jones	3-11	27.3	0-4	3-6	+15.50
J Portman	4-17	23.5	1-5	3-12	+0.50
Dr J Naylor	5-22	22.7	0-10	5-11	+18.00
T George	10-48	20.8	5-21	5-25	+16.75
Miss H Knight	14-80	17.5	4-41	10-31	-10.57
A King	20-117	17.1	11-70	9-32	-17.93
P Hobbs	30-181	16.6	18-90	9-81	-43.09

Jockeys	Wins-Rides	%	£1 level stks	Best Trainer	W-R
C Tizzard	4-8	50.0	+19.25	C St V Fox	2-2
B J Geraghty	4-8	50.0	+15.00	P Nicholls	2-3
R Walsh	31-84	36.9	+31.67	P Nicholls	30-82
T Best	3-9	33.3	+4.50	G Balding	3-7
A McCoy	23-74	31.1	-2.36	P Nicholls	6-18
G Lee	3-10	30.0	+5.50	M G Rimell	1-1
J Culloty	16-70	22.9	+16.02	Miss H Knight	13-46
M Fitzgerald	13-58	22.4	-4.59	N Henderson	7-23
T J Murphy	15-70	21.4	+11.37	P Nicholls	5-14
Christian Williams	21-99	21.2	-7.68	P Nicholls	14-62
P Flynn	8-39	20.5	-6.52	P Hobbs	5-19
L Heard	5-25	20.0	-7.91	P Nicholls	5-21
R Stephens	4-21	19.0	+9.08	P Hobbs	2-10

After a triumphant two-year return, which included a victory for the mighty Baracouda in 2004, National Hunt racing at Windsor is no more with Ascot's return to the scene

Pitchcroft, Worcester WR1 3EJ.
Tel 01905 253 64

WORCESTER

How to get there – Road: From north M5 Jctn 6, from south Jctn 7 or A38. Rail: Worcester (Forgate St)

Features: LH, 1m5f round, subject to flooding from the nearby Severn

2006-07 Fixtures: Oct 5, 18, Mar 25, Apr 14, 25

Winning Pointers: David Pipe has much to live up to here given Martin's great record. This is also a favourite haunt of Philip Hobbs and Peter Bowen, while Ruby Walsh and Graham Lee ride the track extremely well.

Chases

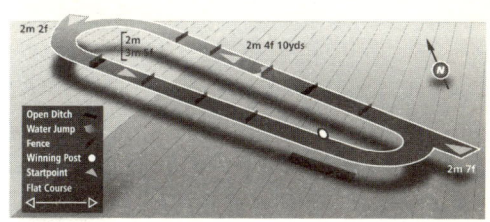

Hurdles

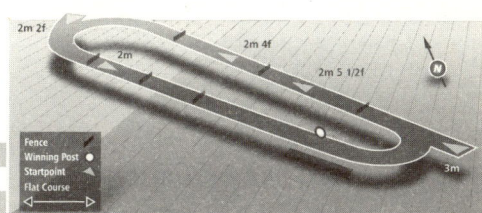

Favourites

Chase	27.0%	-£39.98
Hurdle	36.6%	-£3.82
Overall	33.3%	-£43.79

Trainers

	Wins-Runs	%	Hurdles	Chases	£1 level stks
Nick Williams	4-13	30.8	3-9	1-3	+10.75
P Nicholls	15-53	28.3	5-18	6-22	+32.15
O Brennan	3-11	27.3	1-4	2-4	+38.00
Mrs L Wadham	4-15	26.7	4-12	0-3	+55.65
M Pipe	33-144	22.9	21-103	9-33	+25.03
Miss V Williams	10-44	22.7	7-27	3-15	-3.37
N Henderson	7-33	21.2	1-14	2-6	-10.82
L Dace	5-25	20.0	5-22	0-1	+11.25
P R Webber	6-31	19.4	3-16	2-9	-3.37
J Old	5-27	18.5	4-18	1-8	+14.50
P Hobbs	26-144	18.1	14-84	11-53	-71.22
P Bowen	16-90	17.8	9-47	7-28	-17.65
Karen Georgo	3-17	17.6	3-16	0-1	+4.50

Jockeys

	Wins-Rides	%	£1 level stks	Best Trainer	W-R
P Robson	3-4	75.0	-0.75	M D Hammond	1-1
R Walsh	5-17	29.4	+0.02	P Nicholls	5-17
T J O'Brien	3-11	27.3	+3.50	Miss V Williams	1-1
G Lee	7-26	26.9	+24.50	J Jefferson	2-6
A McCoy	52-200	26.0	-17.75	M Pipe	18-44
G Carenza	3-15	20.0	-4.27	Mrs S J Smith	2-9
R Johnson	50-253	19.8	-8.51	P Hobbs	24-101
T J Malone	3-16	18.8	+20.00	H Manners	1-1
T J Murphy	12-73	16.4	-8.76	M Pipe	6-23
D Elsworth	7-43	16.3	-11.60	Mrs S J Smith	7-43
G Supple	3-19	15.8	+14.00	B Johnson	1-1
N Fehily	12-77	15.6	+3.86	C Mann	5-26
M Foley	7-47	14.9	+17.92	K Bishop	2-6

Record times, standard times

Course

Distance (number of obstacles)	Record holder (date set)	record time	standard time
Aintree, Mildmay course			
2m Ch (12)	Nohalmdun (7 Apr 1990)	3m45.30s	3m48s
2m110yds Hdl (9)	Spinning (3 Apr 1993)	3m44.80s	3m50s
2m1f110yds Ch (14)	Pats Minstrel (17 Nov 1995)	4m21.90s	/
2m4f Ch (16)	Wind Force (2 Apr 1993)	4m46.60s	4m48s
2m4f Hdl (11)	Gallateen (2 Apr 1993)	4m37.10s	4m40s
3m110yds Hdl (13)	Andrew's First (1 Apr 1993)	5m50.70s	5m51s
3m1f Ch (19)	Cab On Target (2 Apr 1993)	6m3.40s	6m6s
Aintree, Grand National course			
2m5f110yds Ch (18)	Its Time For A Win (5 Apr 2002)	5m25.60s	5m21s
2m6f Ch (18)	Sirrah Jay (1 Apr 1993)	5m26.50s	5m29s
3m3f Ch (22)	Young Hustler (18 Nov 1995)	6m54.50s	6m49s
4m4f Ch (30)	Mr Frisk (7 Apr 1990)	8m47.80s	9m5s
Ascot			
2m Ch (12)	With Gods Help (1 May 1990)	3m45.80s	3m48s
2m110yds Hdl (9)	Fred The Tread (13 Apr 1988)	3m43.40s	3m46s
2m3f110yds Ch (16)	Wise King (7 Apr 1999)	4m38.20s	4m41s
2m4f Hdl (11)	Babil (31 Mar 1990)	4m38.50s	4m40s
3m Hdl (13)	Shah's Choice (13 Apr 1988)	5m25.20s	5m39s
3m110yds Ch (20)	Lord Seamus (3 Apr 2002)	6m2.10s	6m3s
3m1f110yds Hdl (14)	Floyd (15 Dec 1990)	6m6.40s	6m0s
3m5f Ch (22)	Kilburn (17 Feb 1966)	7m54.50s	7m15s
Ayr			
2m Ch (12)	Clay County (12 Oct 1991)	3m38.60s	3m43s
2m Hdl (9)	Secret Ballot (19 Apr 1980)	3m27.40s	3m37s
2m4f Ch (17)	Chandigar (15 May 1972)	4m44.10s	4m44s
2m4f Hdl (11)	Moss Royal (19 Apr 1974)	4m35.00s	4m36s
2m5f110yds Ch (18)	Star To The North (9 May 2001)	5m10.20s	5m6s
2m6f Hdl (12)	Any Second (19 Apr 1980)	5m6.80s	5m7s
3m110yds Hdl (12)	Nautical Lad (6 Apr 1964)	5m42.00s	5m43s
3m1f Ch (19)	Top 'N' Tale (12 May 1982)	5m57.70s	5m59s
3m2f110yds Hdl (14)	Meditator (18 Apr 1997)	6m26.90s	6m14s
3m3f110yds Ch (21)	Joacci (15 Apr 2005)	6m50.20s	6m39s
3m5f Ch (24)	Prime Example (7 Dec 1998)	8m24.30s	7ms2s
4m1f Ch (27)	Young Ash Leaf (17 Apr 1971)	8m0.40s	8m4s
Bangor			
2m1f Hdl (9)	Andy Rew (24 Apr 1982)	3m44.50s	3m50s
2m1f110yds Ch (12)	Bunrannoch House (16 Aug 1986)	4m7.70s	4m9s
2m4f Hdl (11)	Smithy's Choice (25 Apr 1987)	4m34.10s	4m34s
2m4f110yds Ch (15)	Midnight Gold (25 Jul 2006)	4m54.60s	4m57s
2m7f110yds Hdl (12)	Desperate (12 Apr 1993)	5m41.00s	5m25s
3m Hdl (12)	General Pershing (20 Apr 1991)	5m34.00s	5m32s

Sponsored by Stan James

3m110yds Ch (18)	Hehasalife (8 Sep 2006)	5m54.60s	5m58s
3m6f Ch (21)	Kaki Crazy (23 May 2001)	7m34.10s	7m24s
4m1f Ch (24)	Nazzaro (13 Dec 1995)	8m50.60s	8m14s

Carlisle

2m Ch (12)	Cape Felix (20 Apr 1981)	3m55.80s	3m58s
2m1f Hdl (9)	Supertop (25 Oct 1997)	4m2.60s	4m5s
2m4f Ch (16)	Flying Dancer (29 Sep 1990)	5m3.90s	4m58s
2m4f Hdl (11)	Gods Law (29 Sep 1990)	4m50.60s	4m47s
2m4f110yds Ch (16)	Pentlands Flyer (25 Oct 1997)	5m1.80s	/
2m4f110yds Hdl (11)	Sujud (21 Sep 1996)	4m45.40s	/
3m Ch (18)	The Blue Boy (21 Sep 1996)	5m59.90s	6m33s
3m110yds Hdl (12)	Kinda Groovy (25 Oct 1997)	5m46.50s	5m53s
3m2f Ch (19)	Lady Of Gortmerron (6 Oct 2000)	6m40.40s	/
3m4f Ch (21)	Cedar Green (15 Jan 2002)	7m55.20s	7m4s

Cartmel

2m1f110yds Ch (12)	Clever Folly (27 May 1992)	4m7.50s	4m10s
2m1f110yds Hdl (8)	Sayeh (28 Aug 1999)	3m57.90s	3m59s
	Indian Jockey (24 May 1997)	3m57.90s	
	Kalshan (26 May 1990)	3m57.90s	
2m5f110yds Ch (14)	Corrarder (30 May 1994)	5m6.50s	5m9s
2m6f Hdl (11)	Woodstock Wanderer (23 May 1998)	5m14.50s	5m6s
3m2f Ch (18)	Better Times Ahead (28 Aug 1999)	6m13.40s	6m16s
3m2f Hdl (12)	Portonia (30 May 1994)	5m58.00s	6m4s
3m6f Ch (20)	I'm The Man (27 May 2000)	7m29.30s	7m16s

Catterick

2m Ch (12)	Preston Deal (18 Dec 1971)	3m44.60s	3m47s
2m Hdl (8)	Lunar Wind (22 Apr 1982)	3m36.50s	3m39s
2m3f Ch (15)	Fear Siuil (24 Nov 2001)	4m41.90s	4m37s
2m3f Hdl (10)	Sovereign State (1 Dec 2004)	4m34.00s	4m23s
3m1f110yds Ch (19)	Clever General (7 Nov 1981)	6m14.00s	6m15s
3m1f110yds Hdl (12)	Seamus O'Flynn (8 Nov 1986)	6m3.80s	6m4s
3m4f110yds Ch (21)	The Wilk (19 Jan 1990)	7m15.30s	7m3s
3m6f Ch (23)	Harlov (24 Jan 2004)	7m48.40s	7m26s

Cheltenham, New course

2m110yds Ch (14)	Samakaan (16 Mar 2000)	3m52.40s	3m55s
2m1f Hdl (8)	Detroit City (17 Mar 2006)	3m51.20s	3m55s
2m4f110yds Hdl (9)	Sir Dante (15 Apr 1997)	4m45.00s	4m40s
2m5f Ch (17)	Barnbrook Again (18 Apr 1990)	5m1.60s	5m4s
2m5f110yds Hdl (10)	Fashion House (19 Sep 1968)	4m53.60s	5m1s
3m Hdl (12)	Bacchanal (16 Mar 2000)	5m36.60s	5m39s
3m1f110yds Ch (21)	Bigsun (15 Mar 1990)	6m13.40s	6m18s
3m2f110yds Ch (22)	Looks Like Trouble (16 Mar 2000)	6m30.30s	6m34s
3m4f110yds Ch (24)	*not known*		7m4s
4m1f Ch (27)	Hot Weld (16 Mar 2006)	8m33.20s	8m17s

Cheltenham, Old course

2m Ch (12)	Edredon Bleu (15 Mar 2000)	3m44.70s	3m50s
2m110yds Hdl (8)	Istabraq (14 Mar 2000)	3m48.10s	3m51s

2m4f110yds Ch (15)	Dark Stranger (15 Mar 2000)	4m49.60s	5m0s
2m5f Hdl (10)	Monsignor (15 Mar 2000)	4m52.00s	4m59s
3m110yds Ch (19)	Marlborough (14 Mar 2000)	5m59.70s	6m6s
3m1f110yds Hdl (13)	Rubhahunish (14 Mar 2000)	6m3.40s	6m10s
3m2f Ch (19)	The Pooka (26 Sep 1973)	6m20.60s	6m30s
3m3f110yds Ch (21)	Shardam (15 Nov 2003)	7m1.00s	6m54s
4m Ch (24)	Relaxation (15 Mar 2000)	8m0.60s	8m4s

Cheltenham, Park course

2m110yds Ch (13)	Clever Folly (3 Oct 1991)	3m56.00s	3m59s
2m110yds Hdl (8)	Cloghans Bay (29 Sep 1993)	3m54.40s	3m55s
2m4f110yds Hdl (9)	Gospel (20 Apr 1994)	4m45.00s	/
2m5f Ch (16)	Tri Folene (29 Sep 1993)	5m5.90s	5m8s
	Lusty Light (29 Sep 1994)	5m5.90s	
2m5f110yds Hdl (10)	Fuzzy Logic (20 Oct 1993)	5m11.20s	5m8s
2m7f110yds Hdl (12)	Bankroll (29 Sep 1993)	5m29.90s	5m37s
3m1f110yds Ch (19)	Whatagale (29 Sep 1994)	6m15.80s	6m18s

Cheltenham, cross-country course

3m1f Ch (25)	Linden's Lotto (1 Jan 1999)	6m59.30s	/
3m7f Ch (32)	Linden's Lotto (13 Nov 1998)	8m22.70s	/

Chepstow

2m110yds Ch (12)	Panto Prince (9 Apr 1989)	3m54.10s	3m58s
2m110yds Hdl (8)	Tingle Bell (4 Oct 1986)	3m43.20s	3m45s
2m3f110yds Ch (16)	Armala (14 May 1996)	4m45.00s	4m47s
2m4f Hdl (11)	Court Appeal (8 May 1990)	4m38.80s	4m32s
2m4f110yds Hdl (11)	Aileen's Cacador (23 Apr 1957)	4m36.20s	/
3m Ch (18)	Broadheath (4 Oct 1986)	5m47.90s	5m51s
3m Hdl (12)	Chucklestone (11 May 1993)	5m33.60s	5m35s
3m2f110yds Ch (22)	Jaunty Jane (26 May 1975)	6m39.40s	6m33s
3m5f110yds Ch (22)	Creeola (27 Apr 1957)	7m24.00s	7m25s

Doncaster

2m110yds Ch (12)	Itsgottabealright (28 Jan 1989)	3m51.90s	3m57s
2m110yds Hdl (8)	Good For A Loan (24 Feb 1993)	3m46.60s	3m49s
2m3f Ch (15)	Kalca Mome (11 Dec 2004)	4m48.70s	4m38s
2m3f110yds Ch (15)	Powder Horn (25 Feb 1985)	4m45.40s	/
2m3f110yds Hdl (10)	Down's Folly (19 Dec 2005)	4m36.20s	4m32s
2m4f Hdl (10)	Magic Court (21 Nov 1964)	4m34.60s	/
3m Ch (18)	Dalkey Sound (26 Jan 1991)	5m52.40s	5m54s
3m110yds Hdl (11)	Pondolfi (4 Nov 1972)	5m45.30s	5m47s
3m2f Ch (19)	Saggarts Choice (25 Mar 1970)	6m18.40s	6m24s
3m4f Ch (21)	Shraden Leader (5 Mar 1994)	7m4.80s	6m56s
4m Ch (24)	Drops O'Brandy (10 Mar 1994)	8m11.70s	8m2s

Exeter

2m1f Ch (12)	Niknaks Nephew (28 Aug 1998)	4m6.80s	/
2m1f Hdl (8)	Made In France (28 Sep 2004)	3m52.20s	3m54s
2m1f110yds Ch (12)	Some Jinks (23 Aug 1984)	4m6.80s	4m7s
2m1f110yds Hdl (8)	Athar (4 Aug 1993)	3m57.20s	/
2m2f Ch (12)	Travado (2 Nov 1993)	4m13.80s	/

Sponsored by Stan James

2m2f Hdl (8)	Major Dundee (15 Apr 1997)	4m03.10s	/
2m3f Ch (15)	James Pigg (25 Aug 1995)	4m31.50s	/
2m3f Hdl (9)	Il Capitano (9 Oct 2002)	4m16.50s	4m20s
2m3f110yds Ch (15)	Gay Edition (2 Oct 1990)	4m34.80s	4m36s
2m3f110yds Hdl (9)	Northern Starlight (15 Apr 1997)	4m23.70s	/
2m6f Hdl (11)	Owenius (21 Aug 1980)	4m59.90s	/
2m6f110yds Ch (17)	James Pigg (6 Sep 1995)	5m22.70s	5m23s
2m6f110yds Hdl (11)	Glacial Delight (5 Oct 2005)	5m18.90s	5m13s
2m7f Hdl (11)	Fly-Away Gunner (21 Mar 2000)	5m29.00s	/
2m7f110yds Ch (17)	Noyan (23 Apr 2002)	5m31.80s	5m36s
3m110yds Hdl (12)	Il Capitano (1 Oct 2002)	5m42.30s	5m42s
3m1f Ch (19)	Hand Woven (17 May 2000)	6m07.30s	/
3m1f110yds Ch (19)	Saffron Sun (5 Oct 2005)	6m08.30s	6m8s
3m2f Ch (19)	The Leggett (24 Mar 1993)	6m30.70s	6m7s
3m6f Ch (21)	Samlee (7 Mar 2000)	8m9.40s	7m19s
3m6f110yds Ch (21)	Mister One (5 Mar 2002)	7m48.60s	7m27s
4m Ch (21)	Lancastrian Jet (7 Dec 2001)	8m17.90s	7m52s

Fakenham

2m Hdl (9)	Cobbet (CZE) (9 May 2001)	3m45.70s	3m42s
2m110yds Ch (12)	Cheekie Ora (23 Apr 1984)	3m44.90s	3m56s
2m110yds Hdl (9)	Tom Clapton (25 May 1992)	3m47.80s	3m50s
2m4f Hdl (11)	Ayem (16 May 1999)	4m41.20s	4m42s
2m5f Hdl (11)	Lobric (21 Apr 1992)	4m51.80s	4m57s
2m5f110yds Ch (16)	Skipping Tim (25 May 1992)	5m10.30s	5m12s
2m7f110yds Hdl (13)	Laughing Gas (20 May 1995)	5m37.10s	5m34s
3m Ch (18)	Saldatore (23 Apr 1984)	5m55.70s	5m50s
3m110yds Ch (18)	Specialize (16 May 1999)	5m56.90s	5m58s
3m5f110yds Ch (22)	Ibin St James (24 Nov 2002)	8m11.30s	7m18s

Folkestone

2m Ch (12)	High Gale (30 Apr 1999)	3m48.80s	3m50s
2m1f110yds Hdl (9)	Super Tek (14 Nov 1983)	3m56.20s	4m5s
2m4f110yds Hdl (10)	Circus Colours (2 Apr 1996)	4m57.00s	4m50s
2m5f Ch (15)	Silver Buck (14 Nov 1983)	5m6.40s	5m7s
2m6f110yds Hdl (11)	Royalty Miss (30 Apr 1985)	5m18.20s	5m20s
3m1f Ch (18)	Highland (23 May 2001)	6m11.40s	6m10s
3m2f Ch (19)	Bolt Hole (26 Apr 1988)	6m23.00s	6m26s
3m4f Hdl (13)	North West (25 Nov 1985)	6m43.20s	6m46s

Fontwell

2m2f Ch (13)	A Thousand Dreams (3 Jun 2002)	4m14.50s	4m18s
2m2f Hdl (9)	Fighting Days (14 Aug 1990)	4m5.90s	/
2m2f110yds Hdl (9)	Hyperion Du Moulin II (3 Jun 2002)	4m6.80s	4m11s
2m3f Ch (14)	Connaught Cracker (3 May 1999)	4m32.00s	4m33s
2m4f Ch (15)	Chalcedony (3 Jun 2002)	4m38.10s	4m46s
2m4f Hdl (10)	Hillswick (27 Aug 1999)	4m30.50s	4m33s
2m6f Ch (16)	Contes (3 Jun 2002)	5m13.90s	5m17s
2m6f Hdl (11)	Doualago (29 May 1995)	5m3.00s	/
2m6f110yds Hdl (11)	Mister Pickwick (3 Jun 2002)	5m6.70s	5m9s
3m2f110yds Ch (19)	Il Capitano (6 May 2002)	6m24.30s	6m25s
3m2f110yds Hdl (13)	Punch's Hotel (27 Apr 1995)	6m14.80s	/

3m3f Hdl (13)	Lord of The Track (18 Aug 2003)	6m21.60s	6m19s
3m4f Ch (21)	General Tantrum (20 Mar 2005)	7m14.10s	6m48s

Haydock

2m Ch (12)	Another Joker (23 Oct 2003)	3m53.20s	3m55s
2m Hdl (8)	She's Our Mare (1 May 1999)	3m32.30s	3m40s
2m4f Ch (15)	Hallo Dandy (12 Dec 1984)	4m56.50s	4m57s
2m4f Hdl (10)	Moving Out (6 May 1995)	4m35.30s	4m41s
2m6f Ch (17)	Arlequin de Sou (24 Oct 2002)	5m27.70s	5m29s
2m6f Hdl (12)	Peter the Butchers (3 May 1982)	5m12.70s	5m13s
2m7f110yds Hdl (12)	Boscean Chieftain (3 May 1993)	5m32.30s	5m37s
3m Ch (18)	Eau de Cologne (29 Mar 2003)	6m1.60s	6m3s
3m4f110yds Ch (22)	Jurancon II (28 Feb 2004)	7m0.40s	7m19s
4m110yds Ch (25)	Jer (29 Nov 1979)	8m37.40s	8m23s

Hereford

2m Ch (12)	Smolensk (21 Mar 1998)	3m46.10s	3m48s
2m1f Hdl (8)	Tasty Son (11 Sep 1973)	3m42.20s	3m45s
2m3f Ch (14)	Kings Wild (28 Sep 1990)	4m30.00s	4m31s
2m3f110yds Hdl (10)	Polden Pride (6 May 1995)	4m22.20s	4m23s
3m1f110yds Ch (19)	Gilston Lass (8 Apr 1995)	6m10.60s	6m11s
3m2f Hdl (13)	Wee Danny (10 Sep 2003)	6m2.80s	6m6s

Hexham

2m Hdl (8)	In Good Faith (17 Jun 2000)	3m46.20s	/
2m110yds Ch (12)	Adamatic (17 Jun 2000)	3m53.60s	3m56s
2m110yds Hdl (8)	Francies Fancy (19 June 2005)	3m57.80s	3m53s
2m4f110yds Ch (15)	Mr Laggan (14 Sep 2003)	4m55.40s	4m57s
2m4f110yds Hdl (10)	Pappa Charlie (27 May 1997)	4m31.50s	4m50s
3m Hdl (12)	Fingers Crossed (29 Apr 1991)	5m45.50s	5m46s
3m1f Ch (19)	Silent Snipe (1 Jun 2002)	6m7.60s	6m6s
4m Ch (25)	Rubika (15 Mar 1990)	8m37.60s	8m0s

Huntingdon

2m110yds Ch (12)	Who's To Say (19 Sep 1998)	3m54.40s	3m55s
2m110yds Hdl (8)	Wakeel (19 Sep 1998)	3m35.00s	3m38s
2m4f110yds Ch (16)	Peccadillo (26 Dec 2004)	4m46.40s	4m52s
2m4f110yds Hdl (10)	Richies Delight (30 Aug 1999)	4m32.90s	4m36s
2m5f110yds Hdl (10)	Sound of Laughter (14 Apr 1984)	4m45.80s	4m50s
3m Ch (19)	Ozzie Jones (18 Sep 1998)	5m44.40s	5m48s
3m2f Hdl (12)	Weather Wise (18 Sep 1998)	5m54.60s	5m59s
3m6f110yds Ch (25)	Kinnahalla (24 Nov 2001)	8m2.70s	7m33s

Kelso

2m110yds Hdl (8)	The Premier Expres (2 May 1995)	3m39.60s	3m42s
2m1f Ch (12)	Mr Coggy (2 May 1984)	4m2.40s	4m4s
2m2f Hdl (10)	All Welcome (15 Oct 1994)	4m11.40s	4m7s
2m6f110yds Ch (17)	Bas De Laine (13 Nov 1996)	5m29.60s	5m26s
2m6f110yds Hdl (11)	Hit The Canvas (30 Sep 1995)	5m12.20s	5m13s
3m1f Ch (19)	McGregor The Third (19 Sep 1999)	6m1.20s	6m3s
3m3f Hdl (13)	Dook's Delight (19 May 1995)	6m10.10s	6m15s
3m4f Ch (21)	Seven Towers (2 Dec 1996)	7m2.30s	6m53s

4m Ch (24)	Seven Towers (17 Jan 1997)	8m7.50s	7m58s

Kempton

2m Ch (13)	Young Pokey (27 Dec 1991)	3m42.90s	3m47s
2m Hdl (8)	Freight Forwarder (20 Oct 1979)	3m37.00s	3m40s
2m4f110yds Ch (17)	Mr Entertainer (27 Dec 1991)	4m55.80s	4m56s
2m5f Hdl (10)	Grand Canyon (15 Oct 1977)	4m51.60s	4m53s
3m Ch (19)	One Man (26 Dec 1996)	5m45.30s	5m50s
3m110yds Hdl (12)	Esmenella (17 Oct 1964)	5m45.60s	5m47s
3m4f110yds Ch (23)	Master Oats (26 Feb 1994)	7m52.70s	7m0s

Leicester

2m Ch (12)	Got One Too (30 Nov 2002)	3m55.40s	3m57s
2m Hdl (9)	Ryde Again (20 Nov 1989)	3m39.60s	3m41s
2m1f Ch (12)	Noon (2 Nov 1971)	4m10.20s	4m12s
2m4f110yds Ch (15)	Prairie Minstrel (4 Dec 2003)	5m0.50s	5m6s
2m4f110yds Hdl (12)	Prince of Rheims (5 Dec 1989)	4m45.50s	4m47s
2m7f110yds Ch (18)	MacGeorge (17 Feb 1998)	5m51.10s	5m51s
3m Ch (18)	Sorbus (24 Apr 1967)	5m55.40s	/
3m Hdl (13)	King Tarquin (1 Apr 1967)	5m48.00s	5m44s

Lingfield

2m Ch (12)	Cotapaxi (19 Jan 1992)	3m51.90s	3m54s
2m110yds Hdl (8)	Va Utu (19 Mar 1993)	3m48.00s	3m51s
2m3f110yds Hdl (10)	Bellezza (20 Mar 1993)	4m37.30s	4m39s
2m4f110yds Ch (14)	Copsale Lad (29 Oct 2005)	5m04.00s	5m3s
2m7f Hdl (12)	His Nibs (11 Nov 2003)	5m38.80s	5m30s
3m Ch (18)	Mighty Frolic (19 Mar 1993)	5m58.40s	5m57s
3m4f110yds Ch (21)	Tylo Steamer (16 Mar 2001)	8m37.50s	7m6s

Ludlow

2m Ch (13)	Mark Man (25 Apr 2004)	3m48.60s	3m52s
2m Hdl (9)	Desert Fighter (11 Oct 2001)	3m36.40s	3m36s
2m4f Ch (17)	Cosmocrat (24 Apr 2005)	4m51.30s	4m49s
2m5f Hdl (11)	Willy Willy (11 Oct 2001)	4m54.70s	4m49s
3m Ch (19)	Hodalko (4 March 2004)	5m50.50s	5m49s
3m Hdl (12)	Rift Valley (12 May 2005)	5m36.60s	5m34s
3m2f110y Hdl (13)	Gysart (9 Oct 1997)	6m7.50s	6m10s
3m3f110y Ch (22)	Act In Time (13 Dec 2001)	6m58.50s	6m40s
3m7f Ch (26)	Storm Of Gold (28 Feb 2002)	8m51.80s	7m3/s

Market Rasen

2m1f110yds Ch (12)	Cape Felix (14 Aug 1982)	4m11.90s	4m14s
2m1f110yds Hdl (8)	Border River (30 Jul 1977)	3m54.40s	4m0s
2m3f110yds Hdl (10)	Coble Lane (29 May 1999)	4m30.70s	4m32s
2m4f Ch (15)	Fleeting Mandate (24 Jul 1999)	4m42.80s	4m51s
2m5f110yds Hdl (10)	Pandolfi (3 Oct 1970)	5m3.80s	5m3s
2m6f110yds Ch (15)	Annas Prince (19 Oct 1979)	5m24.20s	5m27s
3m Hdl (12)	Trustful (21 May 1977)	5m38.80s	5m40s
3m1f Ch (19)	Allerlea (1 May 1985)	6m1.00s	6m6s
3m4f110yds Ch (21)	Cromwell (5 Oct 2003)	7m17.50s	7m1s
4m1f Ch (23)	Barkin (23 Nov 1991)	8m51.20s	8m12s

Musselburgh

2m Ch (12)	Sonsie Mo (6 Dec 1993)	3m48.10s	3m49s
2m Hdl (9)	Joe Bumpas (11 Dec 1989)	3m35.90s	3m38s
2m1f Hdl (9)	Bodfari Signet (3 Apr 2001)	4m4.60s	3m54s
2m4f Ch (16)	Bohemian Spirit (18 Dec 2005)	4m44.50s	4m53s
2m4f Hdl (12)	Old Feathers (3 Apr 2001)	4m40.70s	4m41s
3m Ch (18)	Snowy (18 Dec 2005)	5m47.70s	5m52s
3m Hdl (13)	Supertop (17 Dec 1996)	5m39.10s	5m42s

Newbury

2m110yds Hdl (8)	Dhofar (25 Oct 1985)	3m45.20s	3m49s
2m1f Ch (13)	Barnbrook Again (25 Nov 1989)	3m58.20s	4m1s
2m2f110yds Ch (15)	Rubberdubber (4 Mar 2006)	4m31.90s	4m24s
2m3f Hdl (11)	Schapiro (2 Apr 2005)	4m30.50s	4m27s
2m4f Ch (16)	Espy (25 Oct 1991)	4m47.90s	4m49s
2m5f Hdl (12)	Penneyrose Bay (2 Apr 2005)	4m51.20s	4m57s
2m6f110yds Ch (17)	Von Origny (3 Mar 2006)	5m35.50s	5m27s
3m Ch (18)	Red Devil Robert (2 Apr 2005)	5m43.50s	5m49s
3m110yds Hdl (13)	Landsdowne (25 Oct 1996)	5m45.40s	5m48s
3m2f110yds Ch (21)	Topsham Bay (26 Mar 1993)	6m27.10s	6m29s

Newcastle

2m Hdl (9)	Padre Mio (25 Nov 1995)	3m40.70s	3m42s
2m110yds Ch (14)	Greenheart (7 May 1990)	3m56.70s	3m58s
2m110yds Hdl (8)	Mr Woodcock (23 Oct 1991)	3m49.40s	/
2m4f Ch (17)	Snow Blessed (19 May 1984)	4m46.70s	4m51s
2m4f Hdl (11)	Mils Mij (13 May 1989)	4m42.00s	4m42s
3m Ch (20)	Even Swell (30 Oct 1975)	5m48.10s	5m51s
3m Hdl (13)	Withy Bank (29 Nov 1986)	5m40.10s	5m42s
3m6f Ch (25)	Charlie Potheen (28 Apr 1973)	7m30.00s	7m30s
4m1f Ch (27)	Domaine Du Pron (21 Feb 1998)	8m30.40s	8m20s

Newton Abbot

2m110yds Ch (13)	Noble Comic (24 Jun 2000)	3m53.20s	3m51s
2m1f Hdl (8)	Windbound Lass (1 Aug 1988)	3m45.00s	3m48s
2m3f Hdl	Decisive (20 Aug 2005)	4m22.40s	4m18s
2m5f Ch (15)	Rahiib (13 Aug 1987)	4m56.40s	/
2m5f110yds Ch (16)	Karadin (13 Aug 2002)	5m6.30s	5m4s
2m6f Hdl (10)	Virbian (30 Jun 1983)	4m55.40s	4m58s
3m2f110yds Ch (20)	Just In Business (14 May 2001)	6m21.50s	6m19s
3m3f Hdl (12)	La Carotte (31 Jul 1989)	6m17.60s	6m18s

Perth

2m Ch (12)	Beldine (22 Aug 1992)	3m47.50s	3m50s
2m110yds Hdl (8)	Molly Fay (23 Sep 1971)	3m40.40s	3m44s
2m4f110yds Ch (15)	Ball O Malt (6 Jul 2006)	4m53.50s	4m57s
2m4f110yds Hdl (10)	Valiant Dash (19 May 1994)	4m41.20s	4m43s
3m Ch (18)	Montreal (6 Jun 2004)	5m52.00s	5m56s
3m110yds Hdl (12)	Mystic Memory (20 Aug 1994)	5m43.10s	5m45s
3m2f110yds Ch (20)	Creon (25 Apr 2002)	6m46.50s	6m37s

Sponsored by Stan James

3m3f Hdl (14)	Pontius (25 Apr 2003)	6m48.50s	6m24s
3m7f Ch (23)	General Wolfe (25 Apr 2002)	7m58.90s	7m48s

Plumpton

2m Ch (13)	Brinkwater (10 Aug 1991)	3m47.10s	3m49s
2m Hdl (9)	Royal Derbi (19 Sep 1988)	3m31.00s	3m40s
2m1f Ch (12)	Janiture (19 Apr 2003)	4m5.90s	4m4s
2m1f Hdl (10)	Striding Edge (7 Aug 1992)	3m58.60s	3m54s
2m2f Ch (14)	Pats Minstrel (15 Apr 1995)	4m24.10s	4m19s
2m4f Ch (14)	Blakeney Coast (8 May 2005)	4m48.20s	4m49s
2m4f Hdl (12)	Director's Choice (30 Apr 1994)	4m37.60s	4m38s
2m5f Ch (16)	Preenka Girl (4 Aug 1995)	5m4.20s	/
2m5f Hdl (12)	Majestic (18 Oct 1999)	4m50.10s	4m52s
3m1f110yds Ch (20)	Betton Gorse (29 Apr 1982)	6m9.20s	6m14s
3m1f110yds Hdl (14)	Bali Strong (18 Oct 1999)	6m0.10s	6m1s
3m2f Ch (18)	Sunday Habits (19 Apr 2003)	6m23.50s	6m21s
3m5f Ch (21)	Ecuyer Du Roi (15 Apr 02)	7m19.80s	7m8s

Sandown

2m Ch (13)	News King (23 Apr 1982)	3m44.30s	3m49s
2m110yds Hdl (8)	Olympian (13 Mar 1993)	3m42.00s	3m47s
2m4f110yds Ch (17)	Coulton (29 Apr 1995)	4m57.10s	4m58s
2m4f110yds Hdl (9)	Yes Sir (23 Apr 2005)	4m43.80s	4m46s
2m6f Hdl (11)	Kintbury (5 Nov 1983)	5m5.60s	5m8s
3m Hdl (12)	Rostropovich (27 Apr 2002)	5m39.10s	5m38s
3m110yds Ch (22)	Arkle (6 Nov 1965)	5m59.00s	6m0s
3m5f110yds Ch (24)	Cache Fleur (29 Apr 1995)	7m9.10s	7m15s

Sedgefield

2m110yds Ch (13)	Suas Leat (16 Sep 1997)	3m53.60s	3m54s
2m1f Ch (13)	Stay Awake (18 May 1994)	4m0.40s	/
2m1f Hdl (8)	Country Orchid (5 Sep 1997)	3m45.70s	3m48s
2m1f110yds Hdl (8)	Byzantine (4 Sep 1992)	3m51.50s	/
2m5f Ch (16)	Pennybridge (30 Sep 1997)	4m59.20s	5m0s
2m5f110yds Hdl (10)	Palm House (4 Sep 1992)	4m46.30s	4m50s
3m3f Ch (21)	The Gallopin' Major (14 Sep 1996)	6m29.30s	6m31s
3m3f110yds Hdl (13)	Pikestaff (25 Jul 2005)	6m19.70s	6m21s
3m4f Ch (22)	Mister Muddypaws (5 May 2000)	6m46.50s	6m46s

Southwell

2m Ch (13)	Stay Awake (11 May 1994)	3m51.30s	3m52s
2m Hdl (9)	Merlins Wish (2 May 1994)	3m36.60s	3m40s
2m1f Ch (14)	Versicium (19 Jul 2002)	4m4.80s	4m6s
2m1f Hdl (10)	Jack Dawson (13 Sep 2002)	3m52.10s	3m54s
2m2f Hdl (10)	Here's The Deal (8 May 1995)	4m19.60s	4m12s
2m4f110yds Ch (16)	Bally Parson (8 May 1995)	5m2.90s	5m4s
2m4f110yds Hdl (11)	Man of The Grange (2 May 1994)	4m47.90s	4m49s
2m5f110yds Ch (17)	Castle Folly (13 Sep 2002)	5m16.60s	5m18s
2m5f110yds Hdl (12)	Glacial Missile (12 Aug 2002)	5m3.70s	5m3s
3m110yds Ch (19)	Soloman Springs (6 May 1999)	6m1.90s	6m6s
3m110yds Hdl (13)	Soloman Springs (8 May 1995)	5m47.10s	5m48s
3m2f Ch (21)	Son Of Light (12 Aug 2002)	6m25.90s	6m28s

| 3m2f Hdl (15) | Navarre Samson (12 Aug 2002) | 6m15.10s | 6m10s |

Stratford

2m110yds Hdl (9)	Chusan (7 May 1956)	3m40.40s	3m44s
2m1f110yds Ch (13)	Money In (5 Sep 1981)	4m0.20s	4m2s
2m3f Hdl (10)	Mister Ermyn (29 Jul 2000)	4m19.70s	4m20s
2m4f Ch (15)	Stately Home (11 Jul 1999)	4m42.00s	4m42s
2m5f110yds Ch (16)	Keltic Lord (10 Jul 2005)	5m3.00s	5m3s
2m6f110yds Hdl (12)	Numitas (29 Jul 2004)	4m40.40s	5m11s
3m Ch (18)	Horus (28 Jun 2002)	5m43.60s	5m44s
3m3f Hdl (14)	Burren Moonshine (11 Jun 2006)	6m13.10s	6m19s
3m4f Ch (21)	Gold Castle (1 Jun 1985)	6m44.80s	6m47s
4m Ch (24)	Stewarts Pride (1 Jul 2001)	7m53.90s	7m50s

Taunton

2m110yds Ch (12)	I Have Him (28 Apr 1995)	3m49.50s	3m51s
2m1f Hdl (9)	Indian Jockey (3 Oct 1996)	3m39.40s	3m44s
2m3f Ch (14)	Harik (24 Mar 2003)	4m30.70s	4m31s
2m3f110yds Hdl (10)	Nova Run (14 Nov 1996)	4m21.70s	4m23s
2m7f110yds Ch (17)	Glacial Delight (24 Apr 2006)	5m39.80s	5m46s
3m110yds Hdl (12)	On My Toes (15 Oct 1998)	5m30.20s	5m33s
3m3f Ch (19)	Even More (25 Nov 2004)	6m52.90s	6m30s
3m6f Ch (21)	Torside (26 Mar 1987)	7m50.50s	7m20s
4m2f110yds Ch (24)	Woodlands Genhire (16 Jan 1997)	9m1.50s	8m33s

Towcester

2m Hdl (8)	Nascracker (22 May 1987)	3m39.50s	3m45s
2m110yds Ch (12)	Silver Knight (25 May 1974)	3m59.00s	4m1s
2m3f110yds Ch (13)	Caveman (2 Jun 2006)	5m06.90s	4m53s
2m3f110yds Hdl (10)	Keswick (2 Jun 2006)	4m54.70s	/
2m5f Hdl (11)	Mailcom (3 May 1993)	5m0.90s	5m1s
2m6f Ch (16)	Whiskey Eyes (10 May 1988)	5m30.00s	5m24s
3m Hdl (12)	Dropshot (25 May 1984)	5m44.00s	5m46s
3m110yds	Sir Cumference (27 May 2005)	6m12.30s	6m13s

Uttoxeter

2m Ch (12)	Tapageur (8 Aug 1991)	3m41.50s	3m49s
2m Hdl (10)	Mill De Lease (21 Sep 1989)	3m28.20s	3m38s
2m4f Ch (15)	Bertone (5 Oct 1996)	4m42.60s	4m47s
2m4f110yds Hdl (12)	Chicago's Best (11 Jun 1995)	4m39.10s	4m43s
2m5f Ch (16)	McKenzie (27 Apr 1974)	4m54.20s	5m2s
2m6f110yds Hdl (12)	Springfield Scally (18 Mar 2000)	5m14.90s	5m12s
2m7f Ch (16)	Certain Angle (9 Jun 1996)	5m26.80s	5m34s
3m Ch (18)	Terramarique (31 Jul 2006))	5m49.80s	5m49s
3m110yds Hdl (14)	Volcanic Dancer (19 Sep 1991)	5m35.30s	5m40s
3m2f Ch (20)	McGregor The Third (5 Oct 1996)	6m23.60s	6m20s
3m4f Ch (21)	Ottowa (7 Feb 1998)	7m33.90s	6m52s
4m110yds (24)	Stormez (30 Jun 2002)	8m8.10s	8m10s
4m2f Ch (24)	Seven Towers (15 Mar 1997)	8m33.70s	8m34s

Warwick

| 2m Ch (12) | Super Sharp (2 Nov 1996) | 3m49.10s | / |

2m Hdl (8)	High Knowl (17 Sep 1988)	3m30.80s	3m37s
2m110yds Ch (12)	Bambi De L'orme (7 May 2005)	3m46.30s	3m51s
2m2f110yds Hdl (9)	Itsonlyme (2 Nov 1999)	4m22.60s	/
2m3f Hdl (10)	Runaway Pete (2 Nov 1996)	4m15.00s	4m20s
2m4f Ch (17)	Dictum (2 Nov 1999)	4m56.20s	/
2m4f110yds Ch (17)	Dudie (16 May 1987)	4m53.30s	4m54s
2m4f110yds Hdl (11)	Carrymore (19 Sep 1970)	4m43.00s	/
2m5f Hdl (11)	Three Eagles (11 May 2002)	4m43.60s	4m48s
3m110yds Ch (18)	Shephards Rest (2 Apr 2002)	6m3.90s	5m56s
3m1f Hdl (11)	City Poser (2 Apr 2002)	5m53.50s	5m50s
3m1f110yds Ch (20)	Brush With Fame (2 Nov 1999)	6m30.00s	/
3m2f Ch (20)	Castle Warden (6 May 1989)	6m16.10s	6m19s
3m5f Ch (22)	Purple Haze (18 Sep 1982)	7m13.20s	7m9s
4m1f110yds Ch (27)	Jolly's Clump (24 Jan 1976)	8m36.40s	8m20s

Wetherby

2m Ch (12)	Cumbrian Challenge (22 Oct 1995)	3m47.20s	3m48s
2m Hdl (9)	Gimmick (15 Oct 2003)	3m38.00s	3m41s
2m4f110yds Ch (15)	Toogood To Be True (11 Oct 1995)	4m52.00s	4m55s
2m4f110yds Hdl (10)	Master Sandy (8 May 1996)	4m45.30s	4m46s
2m5f Ch (14)	Don't Forget (9 May 1984)	5m1.40s	5m3s
2m7f Hdl (12)	Canada Street (30 Apr 2006)	5m39.40s	5m24s
2m7f110yds Ch (18)	Joint Account (23 Apr 2002)	5m43.70s	5m40s
3m110yds Ch (16)	Barton Bank (28 Oct 1995)	6m0.60s	/
3m1f Ch (18)	See More Business (30 Oct 1999)	6m3.50s	6m5s
3m1f Hdl (12)	Gralmano (1 Nov 2003)	5m56.50s	5m53s

Wincanton

2m Ch (13)	Kescast (11 May 1988)	3m44.40s	3m46s
2m Hdl (8)	Well Chief (8 Nov 2003)	3m28.10s	3m34s
2m5f Ch (17)	Edredon Bleu (26 Oct 2003)	4m59.20s	5m2s
2m6f Hdl (11)	St Mellion Green (9 May 1995)	5m1.80s	5m4s
3m1f110yds Ch (21)	Swansea Bay (8 Nov 2003)	6m9.70s	6m14s

Windsor

2m Ch	Guiburns Nephew (20 Nov 1989)	3m54.00s	3m56s
2m Hdl	Skylander (21 Nov 1983)	3m41.80s	3m43s
2m5f Ch	Fight To Win (8 Mar 1993)	5m13.10s	5m13s
2m6f110yds Hdl	Qannaas (20 Nov 1989)	5m19.10s	5m20s
3m Ch	Acarine (18 Nov 1985)	5m56.20s	5m57s
3m4f110yds Ch	Farm Week (8 Mar 1993, dd-ht)	7m7.80s	7m9s
3m4f110yds Ch	Brave Defender (8 Mar 1993, dd-ht)	7m7.80s	7m9s

Worcester

2m Ch (12)	Rooster's Reunion (22 Aug 2006)	3m44.00s	3m49s
2m Hdl (8)	Santopadre (11 May 1988)	3m35.30s	3m40s
2m2f Hdl (9)	Lady For Life (5 Aug 2000)	4m2.50s	4m6s
2m4f Hdl (10)	Dancing Hill (19 Jul 2006)	4m32.10s	4m35s
2m4f110yds Ch (15)	Ross Comm (5 Sep 2004)	4m54.30s	4m57s
2m5f110yds Hdl (10)	Elite Reg (19 May 1993)	4m48.50s	4m56s
2m7f Ch (18)	Tanora (2 May 1981)	5m37.60s	/
2m7f110yds Ch (18)	Arlas (22 Jul 1998)	5m43.00s	5m43s
3m Hdl (12)	Polar Champ (5 Aug 2000)	5m29.80s	5m32s

Evan Williams
Two years on!

EVAN WILLIAMS (standing): sharing a joke on returning from exercise

Profile by Nick Watts

"IF it ain't broke, then why bother fixing it?" An expression that can be applied to Evan Williams, who has provided readers of this annual with a steady stream of winners over the past two seasons.

For that reason, it seems silly to leave him out this time around, especially as 2006/2007 could be the most exciting campaign yet.

"I think he wants a fence." You wouldn't find this in any book of proverbs, but it's a particular favourite of Williams' and is uttered with huge regularity on any visit of Aberogwrn Farm when discussing the latest batch of inmates ready to do battle this winter.

Included in that batch are three horses recently sent to South Wales by one of the most prominent figures in National Hunt racing – Sir Robert Ogden.

Backpage, **Robin De La Gard** and **Royal Arms** (the latter from the family of Squire Silk – Tote Gold Trophy winner, second in an Arkle) have all made the journey over the Severn Bridge, and their arrival represents

a ringing endorsement of Williams' flourishing training establishment that is still very much in its infancy.

They might represent the future, but the present is dominated by a horse called **State Of Play** (pictured opposite), who made a stunning transition to fences last season, and of whom big things are expected this season.

He first appeared in the 2004/2005 annual when trained by Paul Webber, for whom he won a bumper at Ludlow in March 2004 and a novice hurdle at Hereford in June 2005.

Modest gains you might think, but it's fair to say that Webber always thought a bit about State Of Play, and last season, his first for Williams, has certainly proved that original assessment to be true.

Novice chases at Chepstow (fencing debut) and Plumpton were routinely dispatched, and while a crack at the Feltham on King George day didn't yield much, a medium-term plan was hatched that day for a handicap at Aintree on the Friday of the Grand National meeting.

An 18-runner race over the stiff Mildmay fences is a daunting enough prospect, but State Of Play made light of it, giving Betfred winner Lacdoudal a 16l beating.

It was a committed display of running and sound jumping, and provided Williams with his first success at a major Festival – a big step forward.

Things will inevitably be tougher this season, running off a mark of 145. However, being only six years of age and with only four chases under his belt, there must be a good chance he can progress further.

The Hennessy has been mooted as a possible early-season target, with the Welsh National a viable alternative if he isn't ready in time for Newbury.

In other developments since last year, on the same day that Lacdoudal was advertising Aintree form at Sandown, the name 'E Williams' appeared against the name of **Corran Ard** in a mile Flat handicap.

A printing error? Another trainer with the same initials? No, it was the Glamorgan E Williams winning his first ever Flat race with the ex-Irish import.

To prove it wasn't a fluke, Corran Ard then followed up on his next start, again at Sandown, over 1m2f, and then he went and won at Pontefract! Everything will now be geared towards a hurdling campaign over the winter, where he ought to do well granted a bit of give in the ground.

Big Business is another interesting type, a six-year-old who has come over from the Tom Taaffe stable.

His dam was the great race mare Absalom's Lady, who has already produced two winners in War General and the very useful Bob Bob Bobbin'.

However, that can be made three winners now, as Big Business won on his British debut in a 2m6f novice hurdle at Fontwell in August, looking a thorough stayer in the process (maybe he wants a fence!).

Other names to note are **Piran**, who had a cracking season over hurdles last term, culminating in a great effort at the Punchestown Festival when he finished fifth of 25 in an ultra-competitive handicap, and **High Chimes**.

The latter was an extremely useful pointer for Sheila Crow two seasons ago, winning a restricted and a confined in eye-catching style.

With a bit of luck, the above-named horses will be enough to keep the stable going through the winter and add to the growing reputation in the game of Evan Williams and his team.

STATE OF PLAY: put up a dominant display when winning at Aintree last April

234

Sponsored by Stan James

WIN!

. . . . a free subscription to Chaseform!

WE'RE OFFERING a free subscription to Chaseform, the BHB's official form book – every week from November to April, you could be getting the previous week's results in full, with note-book comments highlighting future winners, adjusted Official Ratings and Raceform's *Performance* ratings.

All you have to do is identify the **two horses** on the following pages. We'll give you a clue – both are potential future superstars who managed the rare feat of a Cheltenham and Aintree double. That's enough clues from us for now, so get your thinking caps on!

Send your answers along with your details on the entry form below, to:

**Jumps Annual Competition, Racing & Football Outlook,
Floor 23, 1 Canada Square, London, E14 5AP.**

Entries must reach us no later than first post on Friday November 10. The winner and the right answers will be printed in the RFO's November 14 edition. Six runners-up will receive a copy of last year's complete form book.

1	
2	

Name

Address

Town

Postcode

In the event of more than one correct entry, the winner will be drawn at random from the correct entries. The Editor's decision is final and no correspondence will be entered into.

Sponsored by Stan James

Horse index

All horses discussed, with page numbers, except for references in the 'Big Race Results' section, for which there is a seperate index following that section

A Glass In Thyne 24
Accordion Etoile............................40, 49
According To John...........................61
Afistfullofdollars 13
Afsoun 53
Air Force One...............................55
Aitmatov 13
Amorini 8
Andreas 41
Apollo LAdy 54
Arcalis.....................................38
Arturius....................................8
Ashley Brook 39
Asian Maze................................37, 41
Aux Le Bahnn..............................32
Azalea.....................................13
Back In Front 47
Back To Bid 13
Bajan Sunshine 59
Ballyagran 13
Ballytrim 17
Barbers Shop..............................53
Beau Torero 24
Beauchamp Oracle 75
Beef Or Salmon 47
Bewley's Berry 61
Billy Bonnie 13
Black Apalachi 8
Black Jack Ketchum 38, 41, 59, 82
Blairgowrie 55
Bleak House...............................61
Blue Shark.................................32
Blue Sovereign.............................30
Bosham Mill 73
Boss Mak 72
Bouncing Back.............................26
Bradley Boy 55
Brave Inca 36
Bronson F'Sure 69
Capitalise 72
Casey Jones 13
Cathedral World 66
Celestial Gold..............................46
Chaim.....................................70
Cheveley Flyer 72
Christy Beamish 74
Church Island..............................47
Cleni Boy 13
Cloone River 41
Cloudy Lane...............................32, 63
Cold Turkey 66

Commercial Flyer...........................46
Conna Castle 17
Contraband 41
Cool Blues 8
Copsale Lad...............................53
Cornish Rebel 47
Corrigeenroe 13
Crownfield 24
Crozan 53
Cuan Na Grai 38
Curraheen Chief...........................30
Cyrlight....................................47
Dance World 72
Dark Bolero 9
Darkness 46
De Soto 68
Dempsey 41, 55
Denman 47, 56, 80
Desert Quest 38
Detroit City.......................37, 42, 58, 83
Dickensbury Lad 30
Dino's Dandy 24
Don Castille 68
Don't Be Shy 45
Dusky Warbler 66
Duly Noted 55
Emmasflora...............................69
Esprit De Saint............................54
Failte Arais 13
Feathard Lady 37
Felix Rex...................................72
Fenix 70
Fire Dragon 41
Firth Of Forth 17
Flash Cummins 80
Fondmort 53
Foreman 40
Forget The Past 45
Fota Island 41
Four Chimneys.............................9
Freddie Foster 14
French Saulaie............................58, 76
Game On 25
General Striker............................74
Glencove Marina 18
Goblin......................................72
Gold Medallist 33
Golden Bay 66
Golden Cross..............................42, 50
Good Step 18
Gotcha Covered............................9

Grande Jete 53
Grangehill Dancer 9
Granit Jack.......................................33, 76
Green Tango 67
Gungadu 43
Hakim 30
Halcon Genelardais 33, 54
Harchibald 14, 36
Hard Act To Follow................................61
Hardy Eustace 38, 42
Harmony Brig..61
Heathcote...66
Hedgehunter 44
Hi Cloy 47
Hoh Viss 55
Honest Abe 25
Hop Fair 30
Hotel Hilamar 14
Howle Hill 54
Idle Talk 47
Iktitaf...14, 37
Il Duce 54
In Compliance 45, 48
Inglis Drever...42
Is It Me 59
Its A Dream 53
Jack Dawson 72
Jacks Craic 31
Jagoes Mills 18
Jak Dream 9
Jamaaron 31
Jazz Messenger 14
Jean Le Poisson.....................................53
Joes Edge 62
Joyryder 55
Justified 40, 46
Kauto Star 39, 46, 56
Kadount 63
Kalderon...51
Karello Bay 53
Katchit 54
Kayf Aramis 31
Keltic Bard 55
Ken's Dream 71
Kerryhead Windfarm 18
Khetaam...14
Kicking King 44
Kicks For Free 57
Killaghy Castle 65
Kimi 55
King Of Confusion 62
Kingscliff..47
King's Mill...71
L'Antartique 33, 62
La Marette 69
Lacdoudal 47
Launde 25

Leading Run..14
Le Volfoni 34
Lennon 61
Little Bit Of Hush 55
Little Rocker..55
Little Shilling...26
Lord Baskerville......................................69
Lord Lumey 14
Loughanelteen 9
Macs Joy 36
Made In Montot 57
Major Catch 68
Major Stampi 14
Mam Ratagan..53
Material World 66
Mattock Ranger 14
Maurice 63, 77
Mid Dancer...47
Mighty Man 42, 67, 80
Missed That 45
Mission Possible 9
Mollies Dolly...9
Moncada 55
Monet's Garden 40, 45, 60
Money Trix 60
Monkerhostin 47
Monoceros 9
Moon Over Miami 55
Moorlands Again 69
Moscow Leader 25
Mossbank 19
Mounthenry 43
Mr Blacktie 9
Mr Boo 66
Mr Nick...65
Mr Nosie 14
Mughas 54
Murphy's Cardinal 54
My Obsession 72
My Petra 54
My Way De Solzen 34, 42, 47, 54,76
Nadover 55
Natal...57
Native Jack..10
Neptune Collonges 43, 47
Never Awol...25
New Alco 62
New Little Bric 76
Newmill...39, 82
Nicanor...15, 43
Nickname...47
Nightfly..55
Nine De Sivola 62
Noble Request...................................38, 58
No Refuge 42
No Telling 26
No Half Session 15

Noland 34, 57
Nycteos 57
Ofarel D'Airy....................................76
O'Muircheartaigh 19
Opera De Coeur....................................68
Orcadian 71
Orinocovsky 25
Oscardeal....................................69
Ostrogoth 53
Oulart 19
Oumeyade 34
Our Ben 47
Over The Creek 35, 80
Pangbourne 54
Patriarch Express 62
Penalty Clause 72
Penzance 54
Pirate Flagship 57
Pouvoir....................................54
Power Elite 15
Pressgang 68
Pretty Star 54
Publican....................................50
Push The Port 66
Racing Demon 45
Ransboro 61
Rapallo 55
Rathgar Beau 41
Ravenscar 69
Rebel Raider 25
Reel Missile 68
Refinement....................................43
Regal Heights 63
Reveillez....................................70
River City 41
Roll Along....................................55
Rosaker 15
Royaldou 19
Royals Darling 53
Rule Supreme 43
Russian Around 65
Samakin 26
Sashenka....................................31
Scotland Yard....................................58
Senorita Rumbalita 54
Shaka's Pearl 65
Sharaab 72
Shearbolt 10
Ship's Hill 53
Sigma Digital 15
Silver Adonis 10
Simon....................................31
Simplified 72
Sir Jimmy Shand 53
Sir Oj 15
Skippers Brig 80
Sky's The Limit....................................42

Slim Pickings 20
Snakebite....................................55
Snow Tern 16
Soulard....................................31
Southern Tide 72
Spear Thistle 66
Star De Mohaison 46
Stoway....................................54
Straw Bear 35, 37, 64
Southern Vic 47
Supreme Builder 62
Sweet Serenade....................................71
Sweet Wake 16
Swing Bill 77
Take The Stand 47
Taranis 47, 76
Tarlac 53
Teamgeist....................................55
Temoin 43, 53, 77
The Black Mouse 10
The Bonus King 72
The Dark Lord 70
The Listener 46
The Market Man....................................43
The Pious Prince 35, 63
Thief 54
Tidal Bay 35, 61
Toofarback....................................16
Trabolgan....................................44, 53
Trackattack....................................72
Travino 20
Turpin Green 46, 61
United....................................70
Urban Tiger 54, 77
Useyourimagination....................................10
Verasi 66
Victoria's Gem 70
Voy Por Ustedes 40, 54, 83
Wantage Road 53
War Of Attrition....................................44
Watch My Back 61
Watson Lake 16, 41
Wee Robbie 65
Well Chief....................................40, 58, 82
Wellbeing....................................38
Westmere 31
Whitehills 20
Whyso Mayo 73
Wild Passion 16, 40
Witness Run....................................65
Wogan 53
Wolf Creek 20
Wyldello....................................54
Yes Sir 59
Zum See....................................16

Sponsored by Stan James